CUDA Fortran for Scientists and Engineers

CUDA Fortran for Scientists and Engineers
Best Practices for Efficient CUDA Fortran Programming

Second Edition

Gregory Ruetsch
Massimiliano Fatica

MK

MORGAN KAUFMANN PUBLISHERS

ELSEVIER AN IMPRINT OF ELSEVIER

For information on all Morgan Kaufmann publications
visit our website at https://www.elsevier.com/books-and-journals

Publisher: Mara Conner
Acquisitions Editor: Craig Smith
Editorial Project Manager: Soumya Yadav
Production Project Manager: Neena S. Maheen
Cover Designer: Matthew Limbert

Typeset by VTeX

Working together
to grow libraries in
developing countries

www.elsevier.com • www.bookaid.org

To Fortran programmers, who know a good thing when they see it.

Contents

PART 3   Appendices

Preface to the Second Edition

While quite a bit has changed in CUDA Fortran since the first edition of this book was published, almost nothing *requires* change as far as the programming practices described in the first edition. The code in the first edition compiles with the latest CUDA Fortran releases and runs on the latest NVIDIA GPUs.

In a nutshell, what has changed since the first edition of this book is the addition of programming features and tools to make the CUDA Fortran programmer's life easier. For example, in addition to explicit data management between the host and device memory spaces, managed memory is now available, which relieves the programmer from having to explicitly move data between memory spaces. Using texture memory for read-only data required setting up and using texture references at the time the first edition was published. Now read-only caches can be used simply by declaring arguments in device code with the intent(in) attribute. In addition to language features, new programming tools are available for checking correctness and profiling performance. The CUDA Fortran compiler is now distributed with the NVIDIA HPC SDK, and there are new compiler options. The operating systems supported have also changed, as now only Linux is fully supported and the Windows Linux Subsystem is required to run on Windows. Although all of these new aspects of CUDA Fortran do not invalidate the approaches used in the first edition of this book, they have become so numerous that we felt a second edition is needed.

Although much in CUDA Fortran has changed, the goal of this book remains the same, which we state verbatim from the first edition:

> This document is intended for scientists and engineers who develop or maintain computer simulations and applications in Fortran, and who would like to harness parallel processing power of graphics processing units (GPUs) to accelerate their code. The goal here is to provide the reader with the fundamentals of GPU programming using CUDA Fortran as well as some typical examples, without having the task of developing CUDA Fortran code become an end in itself.

Since the first edition of this book, we have assisted in porting many Fortran codes to CUDA Fortran and have developed some stylistic approaches that can greatly reduce the amount of code that needs changing. We describe these approaches in the relevant sections of this text, in hope that their adoption can greatly facilitate the goal quoted above.

This edition is organized in the same way as the first edition. The first part is a tutorial on CUDA Fortran programming, and the second part is an expanded collection of case studies where concepts in the first part are put to use. This second edition is based on the 23.9 version of the NVIDIA HPC SDK, and features introduced in subsequent compiler releases are not discussed in this edition. The prerequisites for this second edition are the same as the first: the reader should be familiar with Fortran, but no prior experience in parallel programming is required.

Preface to the First Edition

This document is intended for scientists and engineers who develop or maintain computer simulations and applications in Fortran, and who would like to harness parallel processing power of graphics processing units (GPUs) to accelerate their code. The goal here is to provide the reader with the fundamentals of GPU programming using CUDA Fortran as well as some typical examples, without having the task of developing CUDA Fortran code become an end in itself.

The CUDA architecture was developed by NVIDIA to allow use of the GPU for general purpose computing without requiring the programmer to have a background in graphics. There are many ways to access the CUDA architecture from a programmer's perspective, including through C/C++ from CUDA C, or through Fortran using PGI's CUDA Fortran. This document pertains to the latter approach. PGI's CUDA Fortran should be distinguished from the PGI Accelerator and OpenACC Fortran interfaces to the CUDA architecture, which are directive-based approaches to using the GPU. CUDA Fortran is simply the Fortran analog to CUDA C.

The reader of this book should be familiar with Fortran 90 concepts, such as modules, derived types, and array operations. For those familiar with earlier versions of Fortran but looking to upgrade to a more recent version of Fortran, there are several excellent books that cover this material (e.g., Metcalf et al., 2011). Some features introduced in Fortran 2003 will be used in this book, but these concepts will be explained in detail. Although this book does assume some familiarity with Fortran 90, no experience with parallel programming (on the GPU or otherwise) is required. Part of the appeal of parallel programming on GPUs using CUDA is that the programming model is simple and novices can get parallel code up and running very quickly.

One often comes to CUDA Fortran with the goal of porting existing, sometimes rather lengthy, Fortran code to code that leverages the GPU. Because CUDA is a hybrid programming model, where both GPU and CPU are utilized, CPU code can be incrementally ported to the GPU. CUDA Fortran is also used by those porting applications to GPUs mainly using the directive-based OpenACC approach, but who want to improve the performance of a few critical sections of code by hand-coding CUDA Fortran. Both OpenACC and CUDA Fortran can coexist in the same code.

This document is divided into two main parts. The first part is a tutorial on CUDA Fortran programming, from the basics of writing CUDA Fortran code to some tips on optimization. The second part of this document is a collection of case studies that demonstrate how the principles in the first part are applied to real-world examples.

This document makes use of the PGI 13.x compilers, which can be obtained from http://pgroup.com. Although the examples can be compiled and run on any supported operating system in a variety of development environments, the examples in this document are compiled from the command line as one would do under Linux or Mac OS X.

Acknowledgments

Writing this book has been an enjoyable and rewarding experience for us, largely due to the interactions with the people who helped shape the book into the form you have before you. There are many people who have helped with this book, both directly and indirectly, and at the risk of leaving someone out, we would like to thank the following people for their assistance.

We would first like to thank Peter Shirley for allowing us to adapt material in his ray tracing tutorials *Ray Tracing in One Weekend* and *Ray Tracing: The Next Week* to CUDA Fortran, which resulted in Chapter 12.

At the time of printing the first edition of this book, CUDA Fortran was developed as a joint effort between Nvidia and PGI. Since then, Nvidia was fortunate to have acquired PGI, further enabling our interaction with a great team. While we thank the entire team, we would specifically like to thank Brent Leback, Zhen Wang, and Michael Wolfe.

The authors often reflect on how computations used in their theses, which required many, many hours on large vector machines of the day, can now run on an NVIDIA GPU in less time than it takes to get a cup of coffee. We would like to thank those at NVIDIA who help to enable this technological breakthrough. We would like to thank past and present members of the CUDA software team for answering the many questions we have asked them, especially Philip Cuadra, Mark Hairgrove, Michael Houston, Stephen Jones, Tim Murray, and Joel Sherpelz.

Much of the material in this book grew out of collaborative efforts in performance tuning applications. We would like to thank our collaborators on such efforts, including Mauro Bisson, Pedro Costa, Norbert Juffa, Patrick Legresley, Paulius Micikevicius, Everett Phillips, and Josh Romero.

As with the first edition of this book, we would like to thank Ian Buck for allowing us to spend time at work on this endeavor, and we would like to thank our families for understanding while we also worked at home.

Finally, we would again like to thank all of our teachers. They enabled us to write this book, and we hope in some way we have continued the chain of helping others.

CUDA Fortran programming

1

CUDA Fortran programming

Introduction

1

1.1 A brief history of GPU computing

Parallel computing has been around in one form or another for many decades. In the early stages, it was generally confined to practitioners who had access to large and expensive machines. Today, things are very different. Almost all consumer desktop and laptop computers have central processing units, or CPUs, with multiple cores. Even processors in cell phones and tablets have multiple cores. The principal reason for the nearly ubiquitous presence of multiple cores in CPUs is the difficulty encountered in increasing performance in single-core designs by boosting the clock speed. As a result, since about 2005, CPU designs have "scaled out" to multiple cores rather than "scaled up" to higher clock rates. While CPUs are available with a few to tens of cores, this amount of parallelism pales in comparison to the number of cores in a graphics processing unit, or GPU. For example, the NVIDIA A100 contains 6,912 cores. GPUs were highly parallel architectures from their beginning in the mid 1990s, as graphics processing is an inherently parallel task.

The use of GPUs for general purpose computing, often referred to as GPGPU, was initially a challenging endeavor. One had to program to the graphics application programming interface, or graphics API, which proved to be very restrictive in the types of algorithms that could be mapped to the GPU. Even when such a mapping was possible, the programming required to make this happen was difficult and not intuitive for scientists and engineers outside of the computer graphics vocation. As such, adoption of the GPU for scientific and engineering computations was slow.

Things changed for GPU computing with the advent of the CUDA architecture from NVIDIA in 2007. The CUDA architecture included both hardware components on NVIDIA's GPUs and a software programming environment, which eliminated the barriers to adoption that plagued GPGPU. Since its first appearance in 2007, the adoption of CUDA has been tremendous, to the point where currently a large percentage of supercomputers in the Top 500 list use GPUs. One of the reasons for this very fast adoption of CUDA is that the programming model was very simple. CUDA C, the first interface to the CUDA architecture, is essentially C with a few extensions that can offload portions of an algorithm to run on the GPU. It is a hybrid approach where both CPU and GPU are used, so porting computations to the GPU can be performed incrementally.

In the late 2009, a joint effort between the Portland Group (PGI, which was later acquired by NVIDIA in 2013) and NVIDIA led to the CUDA Fortran compiler. Just as CUDA C is C with extensions, CUDA Fortran is essentially Fortran with a few extensions that allow the user to leverage the power of GPUs in their computations. Although much of the material for writing efficient CUDA C translates easily to CUDA Fortran, as the underlying architecture is the same, there is still a need for material that addresses how to write efficient code in CUDA Fortran. There are a couple of reasons for this. First, although CUDA C and CUDA Fortran are similar, there are some differences that affect how

CUDA Fortran for Scientists and Engineers. https://doi.org/10.1016/B978-0-44-321977-1.00010-3

3

code is written. This is not surprising as CPU code written in C and Fortran typically take on a different character as projects grow. Also, there are some features in CUDA C that are not present in CUDA Fortran. Conversely, there are some features in CUDA Fortran, such as the `device` variable attribute used to denote data that resides on the GPU, that are not present in CUDA C.

This book is written for those who want to use parallel computation as a tool in getting other work done rather than as an end in itself. The aim is to give the reader a basic set of skills necessary for them to write reasonably optimized CUDA Fortran code that takes advantage of the NVIDIA computing hardware. The reason for taking this approach rather than attempting to teach how to extract every last ounce of performance from the hardware is the assumption that those using CUDA Fortran do so as a means rather than an end. Such users typically value clear and maintainable code that is simple to write and performs reasonably well across many generations of CUDA-enabled hardware and CUDA Fortran software.

But where is the line drawn in terms of the effort-performance tradeoff? In the end, it is up to the developer to decide how much effort to put into optimizing code. In making this decision, we need to know what type of payoff we can expect when eliminating various bottlenecks, and what effort is involved in doing so. One goal of this book is to help the reader develop an intuition needed to make such a return-on-investment assessment. To achieve this end, bottlenecks encountered when writing common algorithms in science and engineering applications in CUDA Fortran are discussed. Multiple workarounds are presented when possible, along with the performance impact of each optimization effort.

1.2 Parallel computation

Before jumping into writing CUDA Fortran code, we should say a few words about where CUDA fits in with other types of parallel programming models. Familiarity with and an understanding of other parallel programming models in not a prerequisite for this book, but for those that do have some parallel programming experience, this section might be helpful in categorizing CUDA.

We have already mentioned that CUDA is a hybrid computing model, where both the CPU and GPU are used in an application. This is advantageous for development as sections of an existing CPU code can be ported to the GPU incrementally. It is possible to overlap computation on the CPU with computation on the GPU, so this is one aspect of parallelism.

A far greater degree of parallelism occurs within the GPU itself. Subroutines that run on the GPU are executed by many threads in parallel. Although all threads execute the same code, these threads typically operate on different data. This *data parallelism* is a fine-grained parallelism, where it is most efficient to have adjacent threads operate on adjacent data, such as elements of an array. This model of parallelism is very different from a model like Message Passing Interface, commonly known as MPI, which is a coarse-grained model. In MPI, data are typically divided into large segments or partitions, and each MPI process performs calculations on an entire data partition.

There are a few characteristics of the CUDA programming model that are very different from CPU-based parallel programming models. One difference is that there is very little overhead associated with creating GPU threads. In addition to fast thread creation, context switches – where threads change from active to inactive and vice versa – are very fast for GPU threads compared to CPU threads. The reason context switching is essentially instantaneous on the GPU is because the GPU does not have to store state as the CPU does when switching threads between being active and inactive. As a result of this fast context switching, it is advantageous to heavily oversubscribe GPU cores, that is, have many more resident threads than GPU cores, so that memory latencies can be hidden. It is not uncommon to have the number of resident threads on a GPU an order of magnitude larger than the number of cores on the GPU. In the CUDA programming model, we essentially write a serial code that is executed by many GPU threads in parallel. Each thread executing this code has a means of identifying itself to operate on different data, but the code that CUDA threads execute is very similar to what we would write for serial CPU code. On the other hand, the code of many parallel CPU programming models differs greatly from serial CPU code. We will revisit each of these aspects of the CUDA programming model and architecture as they arise in the following discussion.

1.3 Basic concepts

This section contains a progression of simple CUDA Fortran code examples used to demonstrate various basic concepts of programming in CUDA Fortran.

Before we start, we need to define a few terms. CUDA Fortran is a hybrid programming model, meaning that code sections can execute either on the CPU or GPU, or more precisely, on the *host* or *device*. The term *host* is used to refer to the CPU and its memory, and the term *device* is used to refer to GPU and its memory, both in the context of a CUDA Fortran program. Going forward, we use the term CPU code to refer to a CPU-only implementation. A subroutine that executes on the device but is called from the host is called a *kernel*.

1.3.1 A first CUDA Fortran program

As a reference, we start with a Fortran 90 code that increments an array. The code is arranged so that the incrementing is performed in a subroutine, which itself is in a Fortran 90 module. The subroutine loops over and increments each element of an array by the value of the parameter b that is passed into the subroutine.

```
1   module m
2   contains
3     subroutine increment(a, b)
4       implicit none
5       integer, intent(inout) :: a(:)
6       integer, intent(in) :: b
7       integer :: i, n
8
9       n = size(a)
10      do i = 1, n
11         a(i) = a(i)+b
12      enddo
13
14    end subroutine increment
15  end module m
16
17
```

```
18  program incrementCPU
19    use m
20    implicit none
21    integer, parameter :: n = 256
22    integer :: a(n), b
23
24    a = 1
25    b = 3
26    call increment(a, b)
27
28    if (any(a /= 4)) then
29       print *, '**** Program Failed ****'
30    else
31       print *, 'Program Passed'
32    endif
33  end program incrementCPU
```

In practice, we would not accomplish such an operation in this fashion. We would use Fortran 90's array syntax within the main program to accomplish the same operation in a single line. However, for comparison to the CUDA Fortran version and to highlight the sequential nature of the operations in CPU code, we use the above format.

The equivalent CUDA Fortran code is the following:

```
1   module m
2   contains
3     attributes(global) subroutine increment(a, b)
4       implicit none
5       integer, intent(inout) :: a(*)
6       integer, value :: b
7       integer :: i
8
9       i = threadIdx%x
10      a(i) = a(i)+b
11
12    end subroutine increment
13  end module m
14
15
16  program incrementGPU
17    use cudafor
18    use m
19    implicit none
20    integer, parameter :: n = 256
21    integer :: a(n), b
22    integer, device :: a_d(n)
23
24    a = 1
25    b = 3
26
27    a_d = a
28    call increment <<<1,n>>>(a_d, b)
29    a = a_d
```

```
30
31      if (any(a /= 4)) then
32          print *, '**** Program Failed ****'
33      else
34          print *, 'Program Passed'
35      endif
36   end program incrementGPU
```

The first difference between the Fortran 90 and CUDA Fortran code we run across is the `attributes(global)` prefix to the subroutine on line 3 of the CUDA Fortran implementation. The attribute `global` indicates that the code is to run on the device but is called from the host. (The term `global`, as with all subroutine attributes, describes the scope – the subroutine is seen from both the host and device.)

The second major difference we notice is that the do loop on lines 10–12 of the Fortran 90 example has been replaced in the CUDA Fortran code by the statement initializing the index i on line 9 and the content of the loop on line 10. This difference arises out of the serial versus parallel execution of these two codes. In the CPU code, incrementing elements of the array "a" is performed sequentially in the do loop by a single CPU thread. In the CUDA Fortran version, the subroutine is executed by many GPU threads concurrently. Each thread identifies itself via the built-in `threadIdx` variable that is available in all device code and uses this variable as an index of the array. Note that this parallelism, where sequential threads modify adjacent elements of an array, is termed a *fine-grained* parallelism. For those familiar with CUDA C, note that the `threadIdx` components in CUDA Fortran are unit-based, as opposed to zero-based in CUDA C.

The main program in the CUDA Fortran code is executed on host. The CUDA Fortran definitions and derived types are contained in the `cudafor` module, which is used on line 17 along with the m module on line 18. As was alluded to earlier, CUDA Fortran deals with two separate memory spaces, one on the host and one on the device. Both these spaces are visible from host code, and the `device` attribute is used when declaring variables to indicate they reside in device memory, for example, when declaring the device variable `a_d` on line 22 of the CUDA Fortran code. The "_d" variable suffix is not required but is a useful convention for differentiating device from host variables in host code. Because CUDA Fortran is strongly typed in this regard, data transfers between host and device can be performed by assignment statements. This occurs on line 27, where after the array a is initialized on the host, the data are transferred to the device memory in DRAM.

Once the data have been transferred to device memory in DRAM, the kernel, or subroutine that executes on the device, can be launched, as is done on line 28. The group of parameters specified within the triple chevrons between the subroutine name and the argument list on line 28 is called the *execution configuration* and determines the number of GPU threads used to execute the kernel. We will go into the execution configuration in depth a bit later, but for now, it is sufficient to say that an execution configuration of <<<1,n>>> specifies that the kernel is executed by n GPU threads.

Although kernel array arguments such as `a_d` must reside in device memory, this is not the case with scalar arguments such as the second kernel argument b, which resides in host memory. The CUDA runtime will take care of the transfer of host scalar arguments, but it expects the argument to be passed by value. By default Fortran passes arguments by reference, but arguments can be passed by value using the `value` variable attribute, as shown on line 6 of the CUDA Fortran code. The `value` attribute was introduced in Fortran 2003 as part of a mechanism for interoperating with C code.

One issue that we must contend with in a hybrid programming model such as CUDA is that of *synchronization* between the host and device. For this program to execute correctly, we need to know that the host-to-device data transfer on line 27 completes before the kernel begins execution and that the kernel completes before the device-to-host transfer on line 29 commences. We are assured of such behavior because the data transfers via assignment statements on lines 27 and 29 are blocking or synchronous transfers. Such transfers do not initiate until all previous operations on the GPU are complete, and subsequent operations on the GPU will not begin until the data transfer is complete. The blocking nature of these data transfers are helpful in implicitly synchronizing the CPU and GPU.

Whereas the data transfers via assignment statements are blocking or synchronous operations, kernel launches are nonblocking or asynchronous. Once the kernel on line 28 is launched, control returns to the host immediately. However, we are assured of the desired behavior because the data transfer on line 29 does not initiate due the blocking nature of the transfer.

There are routines that perform asynchronous transfers so that computation on the device can overlap communication between host and device, as well as a means to synchronize the host and device, which will be discussed in Section 4.1.3.

1.3.1.1 *CUDA Fortran compilation*

CUDA Fortran codes are compiled using the nvfortran Fortran compiler distributed with the NVIDIA HPC SDK. Files with the .cuf or .CUF extensions have CUDA Fortran enabled by default; otherwise, the compiler option -cuda can be used to explicitly specify compilation for execution on the device when files with other extensions (such as .f90) are used. Compiling and executing the above code is done with

```
$ nvfortran increment.cuf
$ ./a.out
 Program Passed
```

We will discuss the use of nvfortran in greater detail in Section 1.6.

1.3.2 **Extending to larger arrays**

The above example has the limitation that with the execution configuration <<<1,n>>>, the parameter n and hence the array size must be small. For currently supported cards, the limit is n=1024, but for earlier generations of devices, this limit was n=512. The way to accommodate larger arrays is to modify the first execution configuration parameter, as essentially the product of these two execution configuration parameters gives the number of GPU threads that execute the code. So, why is this done? Why are GPU threads grouped in this manner? This grouping of threads in the programming model mimics the grouping of processing elements in hardware on the GPU.

The basic computational unit on the GPU is a thread processor, also referred to simply as a core. In essence, a thread processor or core is a floating-point unit. Thread processors are grouped into multiprocessors, which contain a limited amount of resources used by resident threads, namely registers and shared memory. This is illustrated in Fig. 1.1, which shows a CUDA-capable device containing a GPU with four multiprocessors, and each multiprocessor contains 32 thread processors.

The analog to a multiprocessor in the programming model is a *thread block*. Thread blocks are groups of threads that are assigned to a multiprocessor and do not migrate once assigned. Multiple

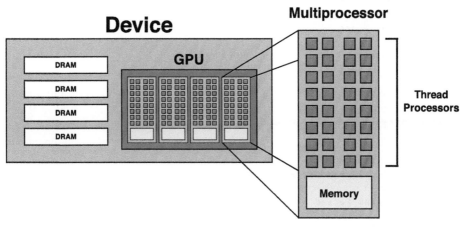

FIGURE 1.1

Hierarchy of computational units in a GPU, where thread processors are grouped together in multiprocessors.

thread blocks can reside on a single multiprocessor, but the number of thread blocks that can simultaneously reside on a multiprocessor is limited by the resources available on a multiprocessor and by the resources required by each thread block.

Turning back to our example code, when the kernel is invoked, it launches a *grid* of thread blocks. The number of thread blocks launched is specified by the first parameter of the execution configuration, and the number of threads in a thread block is specified by the second parameter. So our first CUDA Fortran program launched a grid consisting of a single thread block of 256 threads. We can accommodate larger arrays by launching multiple thread blocks, as in the following code:

```
 1  module m
 2  contains
 3    attributes(global) subroutine increment(a, n, b)
 4      implicit none
 5      integer, intent(inout) :: a(*)
 6      integer, value :: n, b
 7      integer :: i
 8
 9      i = blockDim%x*(blockIdx%x-1) + threadIdx%x
10      if (i <= n) a(i) = a(i)+b
11
12    end subroutine increment
13  end module m
14
15
16  program multiblock
17    use cudafor
18    use m
19    implicit none
20    integer, parameter :: n = 1024*1024
21    integer, allocatable :: a(:)
```

```
22   integer, device, allocatable :: a_d(:)
23   integer :: b, tPB = 256
24
25   allocate(a(n), a_d(n))
26   a = 1
27   b = 3
28
29   a_d = a
30   call increment<<<(n-1)/tPB+1,tPB>>>(a_d, n, b)
31   a = a_d
32
33   if (any(a /= 4)) then
34      print *, '**** Program Failed ****'
35   else
36      print *, 'Program Passed'
37   endif
38   deallocate(a, a_d)
39 end program multiblock
```

In the host code, we declare both host and device arrays to be allocatable. This is not needed for using a larger array; we do this just to demonstrate that device arrays can be allocated and deallocated just as host arrays. In fact, both host and device arrays can be used in the same allocate() and deallocate() statements, as on lines 25 and 38.

Aside from using allocatable arrays, the program above contains only a few modifications to the CUDA Fortran code in Section 1.3.1. In the host code, the parameter tPB representing the number of threads per block is defined on line 23. When launching a kernel with multiple thread blocks, all thread blocks in a single kernel launch must be the same size, which is specified by the second execution configuration parameter. In our example, when the number of elements in the array is not evenly divisible by the number of threads per block, we need to make sure enough threads are launched to process each element of the array, but also make sure we do not access the array out-of-bounds. The expression (n-1)/tPB+1 on line 30 is used to determine the number of thread blocks required to process all array elements. In device code, the if condition of line 10 makes sure the kernel does not read or write off the end of the array.

In addition to checking for out-of-bounds memory accesses, the device code also differs from the single-block example in Section 1.3.1 in the calculation of the array index i on line 9. The predefined variable threadIdx is the index of a thread within its thread block. When using multiple thread blocks, as is the case here, this value needs to be offset by the number of threads in previous thread blocks to obtain unique integers used to access elements of an array. This offset is determined using the predefined variables blockDim and blockIdx, which contain the number of threads in a block and the index of the block within the grid, respectively. As with the threadIdx variable, the blockIdx variable is unit-based in CUDA Fortran (in contrast to CUDA C's zero-based convention). An illustration of how the predefined variables in device code are used to calculate the global array indices is shown in Fig. 1.2. The expression (blockIdx%x-1)*blockDim%x+threadIdx%x is very common in CUDA Fortran and used when mapping threads in a kernel to indices of a global array.

In both of the CUDA Fortran examples we have discussed, the kernel code accesses the x fields of the predefined variables, and as you might expect, these data types can accommodate multidimensional arrays, which we explore next.

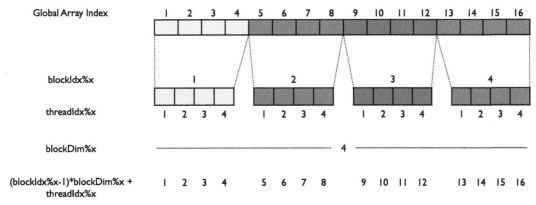

FIGURE 1.2

Calculation of the global array index in terms of predefined variables `blockDim`, `blockIdx`, and `threadIdx`. Four thread blocks with four threads each are used for simplicity. In actual CUDA Fortran code, thread blocks with much higher thread counts are used.

1.3.3 Multidimensional arrays

We can extend our example to work on a multidimensional array relatively easily. This is facilitated since the predefined variables in device code are of a derived type dim3, which contains x, y, and z fields. In terms of the host code, thus far we have specified the blocks per grid and threads per block execution configuration parameters as integers, but these parameters can also be of type dim3. Using other fields of the dim3 type, the multidimensional version of our code becomes

```fortran
 1  module m
 2  contains
 3    attributes(global) subroutine increment(a, n1, n2, b)
 4      implicit none
 5      integer :: a(n1,n2)
 6      integer, value :: n1, n2, b
 7      integer :: i, j
 8
 9      i = (blockIdx%x-1)*blockDim%x + threadIdx%x
10      j = (blockIdx%y-1)*blockDim%y + threadIdx%y
11      if (i<=n1 .and. j<=n2) a(i,j) = a(i,j) + b
12    end subroutine increment
13  end module m
14
15
16
17  program multidim
18    use cudafor
19    use m
20    implicit none
21    integer, parameter :: nx=1024, ny=512
22    integer :: a(nx,ny), b
23    integer, device :: a_d(nx,ny)
```

```
24      type(dim3) :: grid, tBlock
25
26      a = 1
27      b = 3
28
29      tBlock = dim3(32,8,1)
30      grid = dim3((nx-1)/tBlock%x+1, &
31                    (ny-1)/tBlock%y+1, 1)
32      a_d = a
33      call increment<<<grid,tBlock>>>(a_d, nx, ny, b)
34      a = a_d
35
36      if (any(a /= 4)) then
37          print *, '**** Program Failed ****'
38      else
39          print *, 'Program Passed'
40      endif
41  end program multidim
```

After declaring the parameters nx and ny along with the host and device arrays for this two-dimensional example, we declare two variables of type dim3 used in the execution configuration on line 24. On line 29 the three components of the dim3 type specifying the number of threads per block are set, in the case each block has a 32 × 8 arrangement of threads. In the following two lines, the number of blocks in the x and y dimensions required to increment all the elements of the array is determined. The kernel is then launched with these variables as the execution configuration parameters on line 33. In the kernel code, the dummy argument a is declared as a two-dimensional array. An additional index j is assigned a value on line 10 in an analogous manner to i on line 9, and both i and j are checked for in-bounds access before a(i,j) is incremented.

1.3.4 Interfaces for device code

One requirement in writing CUDA Fortran is that an interface to device code must be provided. In the previous examples, declaring kernels within a Fortran module provides an interface implicitly; however, we can also write device code outside a module and provide an explicit interface, as in the following modified multidimensional array increment example:

```
1   attributes(global) subroutine increment(a, n1, n2, b)
2      implicit none
3      integer :: a(n1, n2)
4      integer, value :: n1, n2, b
5      integer :: i, j
6
7      i = (blockIdx%x-1)*blockDim%x + threadIdx%x
8      j = (blockIdx%y-1)*blockDim%y + threadIdx%y
9      if (i<=n1 .and. j<=n2) a(i,j) = a(i,j) + b
10  end subroutine increment
11
12  program explicitInterface
13      use cudafor
14      implicit none
```

```
15   integer, parameter :: nx=1024, ny=512
16   integer :: a(nx,ny), b
17   integer, device :: a_d(nx,ny)
18   type(dim3) :: grid, tBlock
19   interface
20      attributes(global) subroutine increment(a, n1, n2, b)
21         integer :: a(n1, n2)
22         integer, value :: n1, n2, b
23      end subroutine increment
24   end interface
25
26   a = 1
27   b = 3
28
29   tBlock = dim3(32,8,1)
30   grid = dim3(ceiling(real(nx)/tBlock%x), &
31                ceiling(real(ny)/tBlock%y), 1)
32   a_d = a
33   call increment<<<grid,tBlock>>>(a_d, nx, ny, b)
34   a = a_d
35
36   if (any(a /= 4)) then
37      print *, '**** Program Failed ****'
38   else
39      print *, 'Program Passed'
40   endif
41 end program explicitInterface
```

where the increment kernel is now an external subroutine, and the interface block on lines 19–24 is required for correct program execution.

    Although providing explicit interfaces for user-written device code is a valid approach, code maintenance becomes an issue since changing the formal arguments requires the added step of changing the interface. With Fortran modules, the implicit interfaces will be updated automatically when recompiling, and as such is the recommended approach for writing CUDA Fortran code. This is not to say interface blocks do not have their role in CUDA Fortran programming, as they are used heavily when interfacing with CUDA C code and libraries.

1.3.5 Managed data

A new feature in CUDA Fortran, since the previous edition of this book, is *managed* memory. In the above example, the programmer is responsible for declaring arrays on the host and on the device, as well as explicitly managing the data transfers between the host and device arrays. We can do away with maintaining separate host and device copies of the data by declaring a single array with the managed variable attribute, as seen in the managed memory version of our multidimensional increment example:

```
1 module m
2 contains
3    attributes(global) subroutine increment(a, n1, n2, b)
4       implicit none
5       integer :: a(n1,n2)
```

```
 6        integer, value :: n1, n2, b
 7        integer :: i, j
 8
 9        i = (blockIdx%x-1)*blockDim%x + threadIdx%x
10        j = (blockIdx%y-1)*blockDim%y + threadIdx%y
11        if (i<=n1 .and. j<=n2) a(i,j) = a(i,j) + b
12      end subroutine increment
13   end module m
14
15
16
17   program main
18     use cudafor
19     use m
20     implicit none
21     integer, parameter :: nx=1024, ny=512
22     integer, managed :: a(nx,ny)
23     integer :: b, istat
24     type(dim3) :: grid, tBlock
25
26     a = 1
27     b = 3
28
29     tBlock = dim3(32,8,1)
30     grid = dim3(ceiling(real(nx)/tBlock%x), &
31                 ceiling(real(ny)/tBlock%y), 1)
32
33     call increment<<<grid,tBlock>>>(a, nx, ny, b)
34     istat = cudaDeviceSynchronize()
35
36     if (any(a /= 4)) then
37        print *, '**** Program Failed ****'
38     else
39        print *, 'Program Passed'
40     endif
41   end program main
```

Aside from the introduction of the managed variable attribute in declaration of the variable a in host code, there are other changes, as well as code that has not changed, that we should point out. Note that the kernel has not changed at all, so device code developed in conjunction with host code where kernel arguments are declared with the device attribute work, unmodified, in code where the kernel arguments are declared with the managed attribute. As far as what has changed in the managed code, several things are different that make the code shorter and simpler. There is only one array, a, declared with the managed attribute. The host-to-device transfer a_d=a used prior to the kernel invocation and the device-to-host transfer a=a_d used after the kernel launch are gone. The data transfers are now taken care of implicitly. The explicit device-to-host transfer after the kernel launch in earlier versions of this code served as a synchronization barrier between the host and device: the data transfer did not begin until the kernel completed execution (the kernel launch is asynchronous, so control returns to the host code before the kernel is finished). The cudaDeviceSynchronize() routine called after the kernel launch on line 34 blocks the host execution until the kernel has finished. The data are then safely transferred to the host for the correctness check on line 36.

We can specify that all allocatable variables in a code implicitly have the managed attribute by compiling with the -gpu=managed option. We modify the code above so that the array is allocatable rather than managed:

```
1   module m
2   contains
3     attributes(global) subroutine increment(a, n1, n2, b)
4       implicit none
5       integer :: a(n1,n2)
6       integer, value :: n1, n2, b
7       integer :: i, j
8
9       i = (blockIdx%x-1)*blockDim%x + threadIdx%x
10      j = (blockIdx%y-1)*blockDim%y + threadIdx%y
11      if (i<=n1 .and. j<=n2) a(i,j) = a(i,j) + b
12    end subroutine increment
13  end module m
14
15
16
17  program main
18    use cudafor
19    use m
20    implicit none
21    integer, parameter :: nx=1024, ny=512
22    integer, allocatable :: a(:,:)
23    integer :: b, istat
24    type(dim3) :: grid, tBlock
25
26    allocate(a(nx,ny))
27
28    a = 1
29    b = 3
30
31    tBlock = dim3(32,8,1)
32    grid = dim3(ceiling(real(nx)/tBlock%x), &
33                ceiling(real(ny)/tBlock%y), 1)
34
35    call increment<<<grid,tBlock>>>(a, nx, ny, b)
36    istat = cudaDeviceSynchronize()
37
38    if (any(a /= 4)) then
39       print *, '**** Program Failed ****'
40    else
41       print *, 'Program Passed'
42    endif
43
44    deallocate(a)
45  end program main
```

We can compile and run the code as follows:

```
$ nvfortran -gpu=managed managedImplicit.cuf
$ ./a.out
 Program Passed
```

The implicit managed attribution via the -gpu=managed compilation flag will not propagate into subroutines when such arrays are passed as arguments. Therefore, it is preferable to explicitly specify the managed attribute when declaring such variables.

1.3.6 Kernel loop directives and CUF kernels

Just as managed memory automatically handles data transfer between the host and device so the programmer does not have to write explicit data transfers, kernel loop directives automatically generate and invoke CUF kernels, so the programmer does not have to write explicit kernels.

The CUF kernel version of our multidimensional increment code is

```
1  program multidimCUF
2    use cudafor
3    implicit none
4    integer, parameter :: nx=1024, ny=512
5    integer :: a(nx,ny), b, i, j
6    integer, device :: a_d(nx,ny)
7
8    a = 1
9    b = 3
10
11   a_d = a
12   !$cuf kernel do (2) <<<*,*>>>
13   do j = 1, ny
14      do i = 1, nx
15         a_d(i,j) = a_d(i,j) + b
16      enddo
17   enddo
18   a = a_d
19
20   if (any(a /= 4)) then
21      print *, '**** Program Failed ****'
22   else
23      print *, 'Program Passed'
24   endif
25 end program multidimCUF
```

where the module with the explicit kernel is gone, replaced by a nested loop on lines 13–17. The nested loops are preceded by a kernel loop directive on line 12 instructing the compiler to generate a kernel by mapping the two loops, specified by the (2) in the directive, to grid and block values used to launch the kernel. We can specify the grid and block in the execution configuration at the end of the directive, but here we use wildcards "*" and allow the compiler and runtime to choose the grid and block parameters for us.

Note that arrays in the CUF kernel loops are device arrays, where scalars can be host variables. The scalars are passed by value to the generated kernel, as we have done when explicitly writing kernels for this code.

The ease of having the compiler automatically write and launch CUF kernels with kernel loop directives can be combined with the ease of letting the runtime handle data transfers between host and device with managed variables. Here is our increment code with both these features:

```
1   program managedCUF
2     use cudafor
3     implicit none
4     integer, parameter :: nx=1024, ny=512
5     integer, managed :: a(nx,ny)
6     integer :: b, i, j
7
8     a = 1
9     b = 3
10
11    !$cuf kernel do (2) <<<*,*>>>
12    do j = 1, ny
13       do i = 1, nx
14          a(i,j) = a(i,j) + b
15       enddo
16    enddo
17    i = cudaDeviceSynchronize()
18
19    if (any(a /= 4)) then
20       print *, '**** Program Failed ****'
21    else
22       print *, 'Program Passed'
23    endif
24  end program managedCUF
```

which aside from the use cudafor statement, managed attribute, kernel loop directive, and cudaDeviceSynchronize() call looks like CPU code. In fact, if we were to remove or comment out the kernel loop directive, then the code would run on the host.

We can write a single source code that can be compiled for execution on either the host or device by using the sentinel !@cuf in addition to the !$cuf directive as follows:

```
1   program managedCUF
2     !@cuf use cudafor
3     implicit none
4     integer, parameter :: nx=1024, ny=512
5     integer :: a(nx,ny)
6     !@cuf attributes(managed):: a
7     integer :: b, i ,j
8
9     a = 1
10    b = 3
11    !$cuf kernel do (2) <<<*,*>>>
12    do j=1,ny
13       do i=1,nx
```

```
14            a(i,j)=a(i,j)+b
15         end do
16      end do
17      !@cuf i=cudaDeviceSynchronize()
18
19      !@cuf print *, "Running CUDA version ..."
20      if(any(a /= 4)) then
21         print *, "**** Program Failed ****"
22      else
23         print *, "Program Passed"
24      end if
25   end program managedCUF
```

The text on the line following the !@cuf sentinel is only included when the code is compiled for CUDA Fortran; otherwise, it appears as a comment. The use of the sentinel on lines 2, 6, 17, along with the !$cuf directive on line 11, allow the code above to be compiled with any Fortran compiler and will therefore run on the host (assuming that a filename extension such as .f90 is used). The nvfortran compiler can also be used here:

```
$ nvfortran managedCUF2.f90
$ ./a.out
 Program Passed
```

When compiled with nvfortran -cuda, the same exact code will be compiled for execution on the device:

```
$ nvfortran -cuda managedCUF2.f90
$ ./a.out
 Running CUDA version ...
 Program Passed
```

where the !@cuf sentinel is again used on line 19 to indicate that the code was compiled for execution on the device.

There are limits to what loops can be offloaded to the GPU using CUF kernels, and in some cases, writing explicit kernels can achieve better performance, which is why we introduce this concept here rather than at the start. But for cases where CUF kernels can be used and are performant, they can be a great asset in writing CUDA Fortran codes. We will explore CUF kernels in detail in the Performance Optimization chapter in Section 5.3.2.2 and in the Porting Techniques and Tips chapter in Section 6.1.

1.4 Determining CUDA hardware features and limits

There are many different CUDA-capable devices available, spanning different product lines (GeForce, professional GPUs, as well as Data Center GPUs) in addition to different generations of architecture. We have already discussed the limitation of the number of threads per block, which is 1024 on currently supported hardware, and there are many other features and limits that vary between different devices. In this section, we cover the device management API, which contains routines for determining the number and types of CUDA-capable cards available on a particular system and what features and limits such cards have.

Before we go into the device management API, we should briefly discuss the notion of *compute capability*. The compute capability of CUDA-enabled device indicates the architecture and is given in *Major.Minor* format. The *Major* component of the compute capability reflects the generation of the architecture, and the *Minor* component reflects the revision within that generation. Pascal-, Volta-, Ampere-, and Hopper-generation cards have compute capabilities of 6.x, 7.x, 8.x, and 9.x, respectively. The one exception to this naming convention is the Turing generation of cards, which has a compute capability of 7.5. Some CUDA features correlate with the compute capability, and other features do not correlate with compute capability but can be determined through the device management API.

The device management API has routines for getting information on the number of cards available on a system, as well as for selecting a card amongst available cards. This API makes use of the cudaDeviceProp derived type for inquiring about the features of individual cards, which is demonstrated in the following program:

```fortran
program deviceQuery
  use cudafor
  implicit none

  type (cudaDeviceProp) :: prop
  integer :: nDevices=0, i, ierr

  ! Number of CUDA-capable devices

  ierr = cudaGetDeviceCount(nDevices)

  if (nDevices == 0) then
     print "(/,'No CUDA devices found',/)"
     stop
  else if (nDevices == 1) then
     print "(/,'One CUDA device found',/)"
  else
     print "(/,i0,' CUDA devices found',/)", nDevices
  end if

  ! Loop over devices (N.B. 0-based enumeration)

  do i = 0, nDevices-1

     print "('Device Number: ',i0)", i

     ierr = cudaGetDeviceProperties(prop, i)

     ! General device info

     print "('  Device Name: ', a)", trim(prop%name)
     print "('  Compute Capability: ',i0,'.',i0)", &
          prop%major, prop%minor
     print "('  Number of Multiprocessors: ',i0)", &
          prop%multiProcessorCount
```

```
36    print "('  Single- to Double-Precision Perf Ratio: &
37          &', i0)", &
38          prop%singleToDoublePrecisionPerfRatio
39    print "('  Max Threads per Multiprocessor: ',i0)", &
40          prop%maxThreadsPerMultiprocessor
41    if (prop%cooperativeLaunch == 0) then
42       print "('  Supports Cooperative Kernels: No',/)"
43    else
44       print "('  Supports Cooperative Kernels: Yes',/)"
45    end if
46    print "('  Global Memory (GB): ',f9.3,/)", &
47          prop%totalGlobalMem/1024.0**3
48
49
50    ! Execution Configuration
51
52    print "('  Execution Configuration Limits')"
53    print "('    Max Grid Dims: ',2(i0,' x '),i0)", &
54          prop%maxGridSize
55    print "('    Max Block Dims: ',2(i0,' x '),i0)", &
56          prop%maxThreadsDim
57    print "('    Max Threads per Block: ',i0,/)", &
58          prop%maxThreadsPerBlock
59
60    ! Has managed memory
61
62    print "('  Managed Memory')"
63    if (prop%managedMemory == 0) then
64       print "('    Can Allocate Managed Memory: No')"
65    else
66       print "('    Can Allocate Managed Memory: Yes')"
67    endif
68    if (prop%concurrentManagedAccess == 0) then
69       print "('    Device/CPU Concurrent Access &
70             &to Managed Memory: No',/)"
71    else
72       print "('    Device/CPU Concurrent Access &
73             &to Managed Memory: Yes',/)"
74    endif
75
76   enddo
77
78 end program deviceQuery
```

This code determines the number of CUDA-capable devices attached to the system from the cudaGetDeviceCount() routine on line 10 and then loops over each device, retrieving the device properties from the cudaGetDeviceProperties() routine. This code lists only a small portion of the fields available in the cudaDeviceProp type. A full list of the members of the cudaDeviceProp derived type is provided in the *CUDA Runtime API* document available online from NVIDIA.

We list the output of this code on a variety of devices with different compute capabilities. We start with the Pascal generation of GPU's:

```
One CUDA device found

Device Number: 0
  Device Name: Tesla P100-PCIE-16GB
  Compute Capability: 6.0
  Number of Multiprocessors: 56
  Single- to Double-Precision Perf Ratio: 2
  Max Threads per Multiprocessor: 2048
  Supports Cooperative Kernels: Yes

  Global Memory (GB):    15.899

  Execution Configuration Limits
    Max Grid Dims: 2147483647 x 65535 x 65535
    Max Block Dims: 1024 x 1024 x 64
    Max Threads per Block: 1024

  Managed Memory
    Can Allocate Managed Memory: Yes
    Device/CPU Concurrent Access to Managed Memory: Yes
```

Note that *the enumeration of devices is zero-based rather than unit-based.* The P100 is a device of compute capability 6.0 and contains 56 multiprocessors. Multiprocessors of different compute capabilities can have different ratios of single- to double-precision performance. The ratio reported by the singleToDoublePrecisionPerfRatio is the throughput of single- to double-precision add, multiply, and multiply-add operations per core clock cycle. A multiprocessor's single-precision throughput of add, multiply, and multiply-add operations per clock cycle is commonly referred to as the number of "cores" of the multiprocessor. All devices with the same compute capability have multiprocessors with the same single- and double precision throughput per clock cycle, whereas the clock rate and number of multiprocessors per device can differ. The next line of output is the Max Threads per Multiprocessor that refers to the maximum number of *concurrent* threads that can reside on a multiprocessor. The Global Memory indicated in the following line of output is the amount of available memory in device DRAM.

The next block of output text refers to limits of the Execution Configuration parameters specified when launching kernels. The first two lines denote the limits in each dimension of the first two execution configuration parameters: the number and configuration of thread blocks in a kernel launch and the number and configuration of threads in a thread block. The product of the three thread-block components specified in the execution configuration must be less than or equal to the Max Threads per Block limit of 1024 for this device. You may have noticed that the limit of the first grid dimension is quite large compared to the limit in the other two grid dimensions, 2147483647 versus 65535. This is to accommodate very large arrays in a one-dimensional fashion in kernels, such as our one-dimensional multi-block example, which could have n = 2147483647 * 1024 elements in the array (assuming that enough global memory is available). All of the values for these execution configuration limits are the same for devices of the same compute capability, and we will also see that these have remained unchanged for currently supported devices. The final block of statements indicates whether managed memory is supported on the device, and if so, whether simultaneous access to managed memory from the CPU an GPU is allowed.

The Volta generation of cards, which includes the NVIDIA V100, produces

```
One CUDA device found

Device Number: 0
  Device Name: Tesla V100-PCIE-32GB
  Compute Capability: 7.0
  Number of Multiprocessors: 80
  Single- to Double-Precision Perf Ratio: 2
  Max Threads per Multiprocessor: 2048
  Supports Cooperative Kernels: Yes

  Global Memory (GB):    31.749

  Execution Configuration Limits
    Max Grid Dims: 2147483647 x 65535 x 65535
    Max Block Dims: 1024 x 1024 x 64
    Max Threads per Block: 1024

  Managed Memory
    Can Allocate Managed Memory: Yes
    Device/CPU Concurrent Access to Managed Memory: Yes
```

and a machine with two Ampere GPUs generates

```
2 CUDA devices found

Device Number: 0
  Device Name: NVIDIA A100-PCIE-40GB
  Compute Capability: 8.0
  Number of Multiprocessors: 108
  Single- to Double-Precision Perf Ratio: 2
  Max Threads per Multiprocessor: 2048
  Supports Cooperative Kernels: Yes

  Global Memory (GB):    39.586

  Execution Configuration Limits
    Max Grid Dims: 2147483647 x 65535 x 65535
    Max Block Dims: 1024 x 1024 x 64
    Max Threads per Block: 1024

  Managed Memory
    Can Allocate Managed Memory: Yes
    Device/CPU Concurrent Access to Managed Memory: Yes

Device Number: 1
  Device Name: NVIDIA A100-PCIE-40GB
  Compute Capability: 8.0
```

```
Number of Multiprocessors: 108
Single- to Double-Precision Perf Ratio: 2
Max Threads per Multiprocessor: 2048
Supports Cooperative Kernels: Yes

Global Memory (GB):    39.586

Execution Configuration Limits
   Max Grid Dims: 2147483647 x 65535 x 65535
   Max Block Dims: 1024 x 1024 x 64
   Max Threads per Block: 1024

Managed Memory
   Can Allocate Managed Memory: Yes
   Device/CPU Concurrent Access to Managed Memory: Yes
```

Table 1.1 summarizes some of the data from our deviceQuery code. With the exception of the maximum number of thread blocks that can simultaneously reside on a multiprocessor, all of the data in Table 1.1 were obtained from members of the cudaDeviceProp derived type.

Taking the product of the number of multiprocessors on these devices and the maximum number of threads per multiprocessor, we see that in all cases the number of concurrent threads on each device can be in the tens of thousands of threads.

All NVIDIA Data Center GPUs have the error correcting code (ECC) feature, which can be turned on or off. On the latest generations of NVIDIA GPUs utilizing HBM memory, the use of ECC does not affect the amount of global memory available or the memory bandwidth (HBM memory has additional storage specifically for ECC already built in the memory chips). On non-HBM-based GPU, enabling ECC will result in slightly lower memory capacity and bandwidth (some of the existing memory is used to store parity data for ECC). Whether ECC is enabled or disabled can be queried from the ECCEnabled field of the cudaDeviceProp derived type.

Although the data in Table 1.1 were obtained from particular NVIDIA Data Center devices, much of the data applies to other devices with the same compute capability. The only data from the Table 1.1 that will vary between devices of the same compute capability are the amount of global memory and the number of multiprocessors on the device. While the maximum threads per multiprocessor and maximum thread blocks per multiprocessor are uniform for all devices depicted in Table 1.1, historically this has not been the case.

Table 1.1 Characteristics of different NVIDIA Data Center GPUs.

GPU	P100	P40	V100	T4	A100	A40	H100
Compute Capability	6.0	6.1	7.0	7.5	8.0	8.6	9.0
Number of multiprocessors	56	30	80	40	108	84	114/132[*]
Max threads per multiprocessor				2048			
Max thread blocks per multiprocessor	32	32	32	32	32	16	32
Max threads per thread block				1024			
Global memory (GB)	12/16	24	16/32	16	40/80	48	80

[*] *Numbers are for the PCIe and SXM H100 devices, respectively.*

By varying the multiprocessor count, a wide range of devices can be made using the same multiprocessor architecture. A laptop computer with a GeForce RTX3050 GPU has 20 multiprocessors, in contrast to the 108 multiprocessors on an NVIDIA A100. Despite this difference in processing power, the codes in the previous sections can run on each of these devices without any alteration. This is one benefit of grouping threads into thread blocks in the programming model. The thread blocks are distributed to the multiprocessors by the scheduler as resources become available. Thread blocks are independent, so the order in which they execute does not affect the outcome. This independence of thread blocks in the programming model allows the scheduling to be done behind the scenes, so that the programmer need only worry about programming for threads within a thread block.

Regardless of the number of multiprocessors on a device, the number of thread blocks launched by a kernel can be quite large. One could launch a kernel using a one-dimensional grid of one-dimensional thread blocks with 2147483647 × 1024 threads on the laptop GPU! Once again the independence of thread blocks allows the scheduler to assign thread blocks to multiprocessors as space becomes available, all of which is done without intervention by the programmer.

Before spending the time to implement a full-blown version of the deviceQuery code, note that the nvaccelinfo utility included with the NVIDIA HPC SDK provides this information. Sample output from nvaccelinfo on a system with a single NVIDIA A100 is below:

```
$ nvaccelinfo
CUDA Driver Version:            12020
NVRM version:                   NVIDIA UNIX x86_64 Kernel Module   535.54.03
                                Tue Jun  6 22:20:39 UTC 2023

Device Number:                  0
Device Name:                    NVIDIA A100-PCIE-40GB
Device Revision Number:         8.0
Global Memory Size:             42298834944
Number of Multiprocessors:      108
Concurrent Copy and Execution:  Yes
Total Constant Memory:          65536
Total Shared Memory per Block:  49152
Registers per Block:            65536
Warp Size:                      32
Maximum Threads per Block:      1024
Maximum Block Dimensions:       1024, 1024, 64
Maximum Grid Dimensions:        2147483647 x 65535 x 65535
Maximum Memory Pitch:           2147483647B
Texture Alignment:              512B
Clock Rate:                     1410 MHz
Execution Timeout:              No
Integrated Device:              No
Can Map Host Memory:            Yes
Compute Mode:                   default
Concurrent Kernels:             Yes
ECC Enabled:                    Yes
Memory Clock Rate:              1215 MHz
Memory Bus Width:               5120 bits
L2 Cache Size:                  41943040 bytes
Max Threads Per SMP:            2048
Async Engines:                  3
```

```
Unified Addressing:              Yes
Managed Memory:                  Yes
Concurrent Managed Memory:       Yes
Preemption Supported:            Yes
Cooperative Launch:              Yes
Default Target:                  cc80
```

Another useful utility for determining what devices are available on a system, and their configuration, is the nvidia-smi utility. The nvidia-smi utility has many options that can display, and in some cases modify, the devices and their configurations. We will discuss nvidia-smi in greater detail in the appendix and in other chapters where its use is relevant to the topic, but here we simply show the output of nvidia-smi without any options, as seen in Fig. 1.3.

```
+-----------------------------------------------------------------------------+
| NVIDIA-SMI 530.30.02    Driver Version: 530.30.02    CUDA Version: 12.1     |
|-------------------------------+----------------------+----------------------+
| GPU  Name            Persistence-M| Bus-Id        Disp.A | Volatile Uncorr. ECC |
| Fan  Temp  Perf      Pwr:Usage/Cap|          Memory-Usage | GPU-Util  Compute M. |
|                               |                      |               MIG M. |
|===============================+======================+======================|
|   0  NVIDIA A100-PCIE-40GB       On | 00000000:3B:00.0 Off |                   0 |
| N/A   46C    P0          36W / 250W|      34MiB / 40960MiB |      0%      Default |
|                               |                      |              Disabled |
+-------------------------------+----------------------+----------------------+
|   1  NVIDIA A100-PCIE-40GB       On | 00000000:5E:00.0 Off |                   0 |
| N/A   33C    P0          32W / 250W|      58MiB / 40960MiB |      0%      Default |
|                               |                      |              Disabled |
+-------------------------------+----------------------+----------------------+
|   2  NVIDIA A100-PCIE-40GB       On | 00000000:86:00.0 Off |                   0 |
| N/A   36C    P0          33W / 250W|     106MiB / 40960MiB |      0%      Default |
|                               |                      |              Disabled |
+-------------------------------+----------------------+----------------------+
|   3  NVIDIA A100-PCIE-40GB       On | 00000000:AF:00.0 Off |                   0 |
| N/A   34C    P0          32W / 250W|      36MiB / 40960MiB |      0%      Default |
|                               |                      |              Disabled |
+-------------------------------+----------------------+----------------------+

+-----------------------------------------------------------------------------+
| Processes:                                                                  |
|  GPU   GI   CI        PID   Type   Process name                  GPU Memory |
|        ID   ID                                                   Usage      |
|=============================================================================|
|  No running processes found                                                 |
+-----------------------------------------------------------------------------+
```

FIGURE 1.3

Snapshot of nvidia-smi default output on a machine with four GPUs.

1.4.1 Choosing a device to run on

At this point, you are able to determine what CUDA-capable GPUs are in your system and what features they have. On a system with multiple CUDA-capable devices, we will likely want to know which device is used for data transfers and kernel executions and how to target specific GPUs for running CUDA Fortran codes. By default, the GPU used for data transfers and kernel executions is device 0. We can target a specific GPU by either selecting the device from within the CUDA Fortran program or by changing how the devices are enumerated prior to running the code.

The device management API function cudaSetDevice() takes an integer argument, which specifies on which device all subsequent data transfers and kernels takes place. Use of this function is discussed in detail in Chapter 8 on multi-GPU programming.

How the devices are enumerated can be changed using several environment variables. The environment variable CUDA_DEVICE_ORDER can be set to either FASTEST_FIRST, which results in the default enumeration where a heuristic is used to determine the fastest device, or PCI_BUS_ID, where the PCI bus enumeration is used. The cudaDeviceProp derived type has a pciBusID, which we can use to check the device enumeration, as in the following code:

```fortran
program pciBusID
  use cudafor
  implicit none

  type (cudaDeviceProp) :: prop
  integer :: nDevices=0, i, ierr

  ! Number of CUDA-capable devices

  ierr = cudaGetDeviceCount(nDevices)

  if (nDevices == 0) then
     print "(/,'No CUDA devices found',/)"
     stop
  else if (nDevices == 1) then
     print "(/,'One CUDA device found',/)"
  else
     print "(/,i0,' CUDA devices found',/)", nDevices
  end if

  ! Loop over devices

  do i = 0, nDevices-1

     print "('Device Number: ',i0)", i

     ierr = cudaGetDeviceProperties(prop, i)

     ! General device info

     print "('   Device Name: ', a)", trim(prop%name)
     print "('   Compute Capability: ',i0,'.',i0)", &
           prop%major, prop%minor
     print "('   PCI Bus ID: ',i0)", prop%pciBusID

  enddo

end program pciBusID
```

Running this code on a system with four A100 GPUs, we obtain

```
4 CUDA devices found

Device Number: 0
  Device Name: NVIDIA A100-PCIE-40GB
  Compute Capability: 8.0
  PCI Bus ID: 2
Device Number: 1
  Device Name: NVIDIA A100-PCIE-40GB
  Compute Capability: 8.0
  PCI Bus ID: 3
Device Number: 2
  Device Name: NVIDIA A100-PCIE-40GB
  Compute Capability: 8.0
  PCI Bus ID: 130
Device Number: 3
  Device Name: NVIDIA A100-PCIE-40GB
  Compute Capability: 8.0
  PCI Bus ID: 131
```

The CUDA_VISIBLE_DEVICES environment variable takes a comma-separated list, which can be used to make GPUs invisible on the system (from a CUDA perspective) or to change the enumeration of the devices. For example, issuing the command

```
$ export CUDA_VISIBLE_DEVICES=3,2,1,0
```

reverses the order of the GPUs, which we can check by running the pciBusID.cuf code again:

```
4 CUDA devices found

Device Number: 0
  Device Name: NVIDIA A100-PCIE-40GB
  Compute Capability: 8.0
  PCI Bus ID: 131
Device Number: 1
  Device Name: NVIDIA A100-PCIE-40GB
  Compute Capability: 8.0
  PCI Bus ID: 130
Device Number: 2
  Device Name: NVIDIA A100-PCIE-40GB
  Compute Capability: 8.0
  PCI Bus ID: 3
Device Number: 3
  Device Name: NVIDIA A100-PCIE-40GB
  Compute Capability: 8.0
  PCI Bus ID: 2
```

Note that the values specified in the comma-separated list to CUDA_VISIBLE_DEVICES are the values of the default enumeration, meaning that repeated execution of

```
$ export CUDA_VISIBLE_DEVICES=3,2,1,0
```

will result in the same reverse enumeration. Devices not present in the comma-separated list are invisible from a CUDA perspective. We can select an individual GPU with

```
$ export CUDA_VISIBLE_DEVICES=3
```

The output of the pciBusID.cuf code after issuing the above command is

```
One CUDA device found

Device Number: 0
  Device Name: NVIDIA A100-PCIE-40GB
  Compute Capability: 8.0
  PCI Bus ID: 131
```

Using CUDA_VISIBLE_DEVICES to select a subset of available GPUs is often helpful in avoiding performance degradation on inhomogeneous systems (systems with GPUs of different compute capabilities). Even if a particular GPU is not used when executing the code, the fact that it is "visible" to the CUDA application can result in performance degradation.

1.4.2 Floating point precision

The thread processors in a multiprocessor are capable of performing single-precision floating-point arithmetic, whereas double-precision floating-point arithmetic is performed in separate double-precision cores contained within the multiprocessor. In addition, as of compute capability 7.0, multiprocessors contain tensor cores, which are programmable matrix multiply and accumulate units. The floating-point resources on various cards are summarized in Table 1.2.

The tensor core data in Table 1.2 are shown for completeness, but for now, we focus on the single- and double-precision cores. In general, both single- and double-precision resources have significantly

Table 1.2 Floating-point resources on various NVIDIA Data Center GPUs.

GPU	P100	P40	V100	T4	A100	A40	H100
Compute Capability	6.0	6.1	7.0	7.5	8.0	8.6	9.0
Number of multiprocessors	56	30	80	40	108	84	114/132[*]
Single-precision cores per multiprocessor	64	128	64	64	64	128	128
Total single-precision cores	3584	3840	5120	2560	6912	10,752	14,592/16,896[*]
Double-precision cores per multiprocessor	32	4	32	2	32	4	64
Total double-precision cores	1792	120	2560	80	3456	168	7296/8448[*]
Single- to double-precision per ratio	2	32	2	32	2	64	2
Tensor cores per multiprocessor	–	–	8	8	4	4	4
Half-precision FMA per cycle per tensor core	–	–	64	64	256	256	512
Total half-precision tensor-core FMA per cycle	–	–	40,960	20,480	110,592	86,016	270,336/233,472[*]
Double-precision FMA per cycle per tensor core	–	–	–	–	16	16	32
Total double-precision tensor-core FMA per cycle	–	–	–	–	6912	5376	14,592/16,896[*]
Max threads per multiprocessor	2048	2048	2048	2048	2048	2048	2048

[*] *Numbers are for the PCIe and SXM H100 devices, respectively.*

increased with each generation of cards. We included the maximum number of threads per multiprocessor in the last row of Table 1.2 to illustrate that the number of resident threads can far exceed the computational resources on a multiprocessor, in every case by more than a factor of 10. This is by design. Because context switching between GPU threads is so efficient and latencies to global memory are large, we want to oversubscribe a multiprocessor with threads to hide the large latencies to global memory.

1.4.2.1 *Accommodating variable precision*

It is often desirable to develop code using single-precision variables on a small problem size and then deploy the code on a larger problem size using double precision, or to be able to easily toggle between the two precisions to see if and when the greater precision is needed.

Fortran 2008 includes the intrinsic module iso_fortran_env that defines the kind type parameters real32 and real64, which can be used to specify a floating-point variable with storage of 32 and 64 bits, respectively. We can define a module with an integer parameter set to one of the kind type parameter constants in iso_fortran_env:

```
module precision_m
  use, intrinsic :: iso_fortran_env
  integer, parameter :: fp_kind = real64
end module precision_m
```

and then use this module and the parameter fp_kind when declaring floating point variables in code:

```
use precision_m
real(fp_kind), device :: a_d(n)
```

This allows us to toggle between the two precisions simply by changing the fp_kind definition in the precision module.

Another option for toggling between single and double precision that does not involve modifying source code is through use of the preprocessor, where the precision module can be modified as

```
module precision_m
  use, intrinsic :: iso_fortran_env

#ifdef DOUBLE
  integer, parameter :: fp_kind = real64
#else
  integer, parameter :: fp_kind = real32
#endif
end module precision_m
```

Here we can compile for double precision by compiling the precision module with the compiler options -Mpreprocess -DDOUBLE, or if the .F90 or .CUF file extensions are used, then compiling with just -DDOUBLE.

We make extensive use of the precision module throughout this book for several reasons: it allows us to easily assess the performance characteristics of the two precisions on various codes, and it is a good practice in terms of code reuse.

This technique can be extended to facilitate mixed-precision code. For example, in a code simulating reacting flow, we may want to experiment with different precisions for the flow variables and chemical species. To do so, we can declare variables in the code as follows:

```
real(flow_kind), device :: u(nx,ny,nz), v(nx,ny,nz), &
                           w(nx,ny,nz)
real(chemistry_kind), device :: q(nx,ny,nz,nspecies)
```

where flow_kind and chemistry_kind are declared as either single or double precision in the precision_m module. When using this programming style, we should also define floating-point literals using a specified kind, for example:

```
real(fp_kind), parameter :: factorOfTwo = 2.0_fp_kind
```

1.5 Error handling

The return values for the host CUDA functions in the device query example, as well as all host CUDA API functions, can be used to check for errors that occurred during their execution. To illustrate such error handling, the successful execution of cudaGetDeviceCount() of line 10 in the deviceQuery example in Section 1.4 can be checked as follows:

```
ierr = cudaGetDeviceCount(nDevices)
if (ierr /= cudaSuccess) print *, cudaGetErrorString(ierr)
```

The variable cudaSuccess is defined in the cudafor module that is used in this code. If there is an error, then the function cudaGetErrorString() is used to return a character string describing the error, as opposed to just listing the numeric error code. One error that can occur in the above case is when the code is run on a machine without any CUDA-capable devices. Without a device to run on, the command cannot execute, and an error is returned without modifying the contents of nDevices. It is for this reason that nDevices is initialized to 0 when it is declared on line 6.

Error handling of kernels is a bit more complicated since kernels are subroutines and therefore do not have a return value. In addition, kernels execute asynchronously with respect to the host. To aid in error checking kernel execution, as well as other asynchronous operations, the CUDA runtime maintains an error variable that is overwritten each time an error occurs. The function cudaPeekAtLastError() returns the value of this variable, and the function cudaGetLastError() returns the value of the variable and also resets it to cudaSuccess. Error checking for kernel execution can be done using the following approach:

```
call increment<<<1,n>>>(a_d, b)
ierrSync = cudaGetLastError()
ierrAsync = cudaDeviceSynchronize()
if (ierrSync /= cudaSuccess) &
    print *, 'Sync kernel error: ', &
    trim(cudaGetErrorString(ierrSync))
if (ierrAsync /= cudaSuccess) &
    print *, 'Async kernel error: ', &
    trim(cudaGetErrorString(ierrAsync))
```

which checks for both synchronous and asynchronous errors. Invalid execution configuration parameters would be reflected in the value of `ierrSync` returned by `cudaGetLastError()`. Asynchronous errors, which occur on the device after control is returned to the host, require a synchronization mechanism such as `cudaDeviceSynchronize()` that blocks the host thread until all previously issued commands on the device, such as the kernel launch, have completed. Any such errors will be reflected by the return value of `cudaDeviceSynchronize()`. We could also check for asynchronous errors and reset the variable that the runtime maintains by modifying the last line as follows:

```
call increment<<<1,n>>>(a_d, b)
ierrSync = cudaGetLastError()
ierrAsync = cudaDeviceSynchronize()
if (ierrSync /= cudaSuccess) &
  print *, 'Sync kernel error:', &
  trim(cudaGetErrorString(ierrSync))
if (ierrAsync /= cudaSuccess) &
  print *, 'Async kernel error:', &
  trim(cudaGetErrorString(cudaGetLastError()))
```

If in our increment code, we attempt to launch the kernel with 5000 threads per block:

```
integer, parameter :: n = 5000
integer :: a(n), b
integer, device :: a_d(n)
integer :: ierrSync, ierrAsync
a = 1
b = 3
a_d = a
call increment<<<1,n>>>(a_d, b)
ierrSync = cudaGetLastError()
ierrAsync = cudaDeviceSynchronize()
```

then the code compiles correctly, but we get a runtime synchronous error:

```
$ nvfortran syncError.cuf
$ ./a.out
 Sync kernel error: invalid configuration argument
**** Program Failed ****
```

If we launch the kernel with a valid execution configuration but change the device array to an uninitialized device pointer:

```
integer, parameter :: n = 256
integer :: a(n), b
integer, device, pointer :: a_d(:)
integer :: ierrSync, ierrAsync
a = 1
b = 3
call increment<<<1,n>>>(a_d, b)
ierrSync = cudaGetLastError()
ierrAsync = cudaDeviceSynchronize()
```

then the kernel launches fine, but we get an asynchronous error:

```
$ nvfortran asyncError.cuf
$ ./a.out
 Async kernel error: an illegal memory access was encountered
 **** Program Failed ****
```

1.6 Compiling CUDA Fortran code

CUDA Fortran codes are compiled using the nvfortran Fortran compiler distributed with the NVIDIA HPC SDK. Files with the .cuf or .CUF extensions have CUDA Fortran enabled automatically, and the compiler option −cuda can be used when compiling files with other extensions (e.g. .f90) to enable CUDA Fortran. In addition, all of the features used in CPU code, such as OpenMP and SSE vectorizing features, are available for host code. Compilation of CUDA Fortran code can be as simple as issuing the command

```
nvfortran increment.cuf
```

Behind the scenes, a multistep process takes place. The device source code is compiled into a intermediate representation called PTX (Parallel Thread eXecution). This forward-compatible PTX representation is then further compiled to executable code for different compute capabilities. The host code is compiled by the host compiler.

We can view or specify which compute capabilities are being targeted via the −gpu option. Compiling our increment example with −gpu=ptxinfo generates the following output:

```
% nvfortran -gpu=ptxinfo increment.cuf
ptxas info    : 0 bytes gmem
ptxas info    : Compiling entry function 'm_increment_' for 'sm_80'
ptxas info    : Function properties for m_increment_
    0 bytes stack frame, 0 bytes spill stores, 0 bytes spill loads
ptxas info    : Used 14 registers, 376 bytes cmem[0]
```

The output from compilation with −gpu=ptxinfo contains useful information about the compilation of binary code from PTX, such as the number of registers and the amount of different types of memory utilized by the kernel, but for now, let us focus on the compute capabilities that are targeted. This output indicates that binary code is generated for a compute capability of 8.0 (denoted here by sm_80), which is the compute capability of all the devices on this system. By default, binary code is generated for the compute capabilities of all cards on the system.

We can generate code that targets all compute capabilities supported by the particular platform and CUDA Toolkit version by specifying −gpu=ccall, and for the first revision of each generation of GPUs supported by the platform and CUDA Toolkit version (recall that the first number in the compute capability refers to the generation of the device architecture, and the second number refers to the revision within that generation) by specifying −gpu=ccall-major:

```
$ nvfortran -gpu=ccall-major,ptxinfo increment.cuf
ptxas info    : 0 bytes gmem
ptxas info    : Compiling entry function 'm_increment_' for 'sm_50'
```

```
ptxas info    : Function properties for m_increment_
    0 bytes stack frame, 0 bytes spill stores, 0 bytes spill loads
ptxas info    : Used 12 registers, 344 bytes cmem[0]
ptxas info    : 0 bytes gmem
ptxas info    : Compiling entry function 'm_increment_' for 'sm_60'
ptxas info    : Function properties for m_increment_
    0 bytes stack frame, 0 bytes spill stores, 0 bytes spill loads
ptxas info    : Used 12 registers, 344 bytes cmem[0]
ptxas info    : 0 bytes gmem
ptxas info    : Compiling entry function 'm_increment_' for 'sm_70'
ptxas info    : Function properties for m_increment_
    0 bytes stack frame, 0 bytes spill stores, 0 bytes spill loads
ptxas info    : Used 14 registers, 376 bytes cmem[0]
ptxas info    : 0 bytes gmem
ptxas info    : Compiling entry function 'm_increment_' for 'sm_80'
ptxas info    : Function properties for m_increment_
    0 bytes stack frame, 0 bytes spill stores, 0 bytes spill loads
ptxas info    : Used 14 registers, 376 bytes cmem[0]
ptxas info    : 16 bytes gmem
ptxas info    : Compiling entry function 'm_increment_' for 'sm_90'
ptxas info    : Function properties for m_increment_
    0 bytes stack frame, 0 bytes spill stores, 0 bytes spill loads
ptxas info    : Used 14 registers
```

Binary device code is compatible with any device of the same generation that has an equal or greater revision than the revision targeted by compilation. As such, this binary will run on all GPUs of generation 5 (Maxwell), 6 (Pascal), 7 (Volta and Turing), 8 (Ampere), and 9 (Hopper). At runtime, the most appropriate device code to load and execute is selected.

A specific CUDA Toolkit version can be specified with -gpu=cudaX.Y, which used in conjunction with -gpu=ccall (or -gpu=ccall-major) will indicate all the supported compute capabilities (or architecture generations) supported by the specified CUDA Toolkit:

```
$ nvfortran -gpu=ccall-major,cuda11.0,ptxinfo increment.cuf
ptxas info    : 4 bytes gmem
ptxas info    : Compiling entry function 'm_increment_' for 'sm_35'
ptxas info    : Function properties for m_increment_
    0 bytes stack frame, 0 bytes spill stores, 0 bytes spill loads
ptxas info    : Used 6 registers, 344 bytes cmem[0]
ptxas info    : 4 bytes gmem
ptxas info    : Compiling entry function 'm_increment_' for 'sm_50'
ptxas info    : Function properties for m_increment_
    0 bytes stack frame, 0 bytes spill stores, 0 bytes spill loads
ptxas info    : Used 12 registers, 344 bytes cmem[0]
ptxas info    : 4 bytes gmem
ptxas info    : Compiling entry function 'm_increment_' for 'sm_60'
ptxas info    : Function properties for m_increment_
    0 bytes stack frame, 0 bytes spill stores, 0 bytes spill loads
ptxas info    : Used 12 registers, 344 bytes cmem[0]
ptxas info    : 4 bytes gmem
ptxas info    : Compiling entry function 'm_increment_' for 'sm_70'
ptxas info    : Function properties for m_increment_
    0 bytes stack frame, 0 bytes spill stores, 0 bytes spill loads
```

```
ptxas info     : Used 14 registers, 376 bytes cmem[0]
ptxas info     : 4 bytes gmem
ptxas info     : Compiling entry function 'm_increment_' for 'sm_80'
ptxas info     : Function properties for m_increment_
    0 bytes stack frame, 0 bytes spill stores, 0 bytes spill loads
ptxas info     : Used 14 registers, 376 bytes cmem[0]

$ nvfortran -gpu=ccall-major,cuda12.2,ptxinfo increment.cuf
ptxas info     : 0 bytes gmem
ptxas info     : Compiling entry function 'm_increment_' for 'sm_50'
ptxas info     : Function properties for m_increment_
    0 bytes stack frame, 0 bytes spill stores, 0 bytes spill loads
ptxas info     : Used 12 registers, 344 bytes cmem[0]
ptxas info     : 0 bytes gmem
ptxas info     : Compiling entry function 'm_increment_' for 'sm_60'
ptxas info     : Function properties for m_increment_
    0 bytes stack frame, 0 bytes spill stores, 0 bytes spill loads
ptxas info     : Used 12 registers, 344 bytes cmem[0]
ptxas info     : 0 bytes gmem
ptxas info     : Compiling entry function 'm_increment_' for 'sm_70'
ptxas info     : Function properties for m_increment_
    0 bytes stack frame, 0 bytes spill stores, 0 bytes spill loads
ptxas info     : Used 14 registers, 376 bytes cmem[0]
ptxas info     : 0 bytes gmem
ptxas info     : Compiling entry function 'm_increment_' for 'sm_80'
ptxas info     : Function properties for m_increment_
    0 bytes stack frame, 0 bytes spill stores, 0 bytes spill loads
ptxas info     : Used 14 registers, 376 bytes cmem[0]
ptxas info     : 16 bytes gmem
ptxas info     : Compiling entry function 'm_increment_' for 'sm_90'
ptxas info     : Function properties for m_increment_
    0 bytes stack frame, 0 bytes spill stores, 0 bytes spill loads
ptxas info     : Used 14 registers
```

Although -gpu=ccall-major generates device binary code that guarantees compatibility of CUDA Fortran applications on a wide range of devices, there are occasions where we would like to target a particular compute capability. The size of the resulting fat binary may be an issue. We can target a compute capability, or several compute capabilities, explicitly using -gpu=ccXY, as in

```
$ nvfortran -gpu=cc61,ptxinfo increment.cuf
ptxas info     : 0 bytes gmem
ptxas info     : Compiling entry function 'm_increment_' for 'sm_61'
ptxas info     : Function properties for m_increment_
    0 bytes stack frame, 0 bytes spill stores, 0 bytes spill loads
ptxas info     : Used 12 registers, 344 bytes cmem[0]
```

If we specify code generation for a specific compute capability, then the version of the CUDA Toolkit used will be adjusted if need be to a version that supports that generation of architecture.

If we attempt to run an application on a device that does not have a compatible target in the fat binary, then the PTX code that is embedded in the fat binary is used to just-in-time (JIT) compile the device code for device's compute capability. JIT compilation from PTX can be controlled with the environment variables CUDA_DISABLE_JIT and CUDA_CACHE_DISABLE. The first of these environment variables disables JIT compilation, and the second disables fetching of code from the JIT cache. As an example, if on a machine with a device of compute capability 8.0, we compile for a compute capability of 6.0 and execute the code, then we have

```
$ nvfortran -gpu=ptxinfo,cc60 increment.cuf
ptxas info    : 0 bytes gmem
ptxas info    : Compiling entry function 'm_increment_' for 'sm_60'
ptxas info    : Function properties for m_increment_
    0 bytes stack frame, 0 bytes spill stores, 0 bytes spill loads
ptxas info    : Used 12 registers, 344 bytes cmem[0]
$ ./a.out
 Program Passed
```

However, after disabling JIT compilation and the JIT cache, we have

```
$ export CUDA_DISABLE_PTX_JIT=1
$ export CUDA_CACHE_DISABLE=1
$ env | grep CUDA
CUDA_CACHE_DISABLE=1
CUDA_DISABLE_PTX_JIT=1
$ ./a.out
 **** Program Failed ****
```

If we add error checking to the kernel launch in the increment code:

```
1   module m
2   contains
3     attributes(global) subroutine increment(a, b)
4       implicit none
5       integer, intent(inout) :: a(*)
6       integer, value :: b
7       integer :: i
8
9       i = threadIdx%x
10      a(i) = a(i)+b
11
12    end subroutine increment
13  end module m
14
15
16  program asyncError
17    use cudafor
18    use m
19    implicit none
20    integer, parameter :: n = 256
21    integer :: a(n), b
22    integer, device :: a_d(n)
23    integer :: ierrSync, ierrAsync
24
25    a = 1
26    b = 3
```

```
27
28    a_d = a
29    call increment<<<1,n>>>(a_d, b)
30    ierrSync = cudaGetLastError()
31    ierrAsync = cudaDeviceSynchronize()
32    a = a_d
33
34    if (ierrSync /= cudaSuccess) &
35        print *, 'Sync kernel error: ', &
36        trim(cudaGetErrorString(ierrSync))
37    if (ierrAsync /= cudaSuccess) &
38        print *, 'Async kernel error: ', &
39        trim(cudaGetErrorString(ierrAsync))
40
41    if (any(a /= 4)) then
42        print *, '**** Program Failed ****'
43    else
44        print *, 'Program Passed'
45    endif
46 end program asyncError
```

then we see the cause of the failure:

```
$ nvfortran -gpu=ptxinfo,cc60 errorHandling.cuf
ptxas info    : 0 bytes gmem
ptxas info    : Compiling entry function 'm_increment_' for 'sm_60'
ptxas info    : Function properties for m_increment_
    0 bytes stack frame, 0 bytes spill stores, 0 bytes spill loads
ptxas info    : Used 12 registers, 344 bytes cmem[0]
$ env | grep CUDA
CUDA_CACHE_DISABLE=1
CUDA_DISABLE_PTX_JIT=1
$ ./a.out
 Sync kernel error: PTX JIT compilation was disabled
 **** Program Failed ****
```

Aside from generating PTX information and targeting specific device architectures, there are many other arguments to the -gpu compiler option. A list of such arguments can be generated with nvfortran -gpu -help. The output of this command includes

```
$ nvfortran -gpu -help
-gpu=ccnative|ccXY|sm_XY|ccall|ccall-major|cudaX.Y|[no]debug|fastmath|
[no]flushz|nvlamath|[no]fma|keep|[no]lineinfo|[no]lto|nolto|zeroinit|
[no]autocollapse|deepcopy|loadcache:{L1|L2}|maxregcount:<n>|pinned|
[no]rdc|safecache|stacklimit:<1>|nostacklimit|ptxinfo|[no]unroll|
[no]managed|beta|autocompare|redundant|[no]implicitsections
                    Select specific options for GPU code generation
      ccnative      Detects the visible GPUs on the system and generates
                    codes for them. If no device is available,
                    the compute capability matching NVCC default will be used.
      ccXY          Compile for compute capability X.Y;
                    supported values: 35 50 60 61 70 75 80 86 89 90
```

```
sm_XY               Compile for compute capability X.Y;
                    supported values: 35 50 60 61 70 75 80 86 89 90
ccall               Compile for all supported compute capabilities
ccall-major         Compile for all major supported compute capabilities.
cudaX.Y             Use CUDA X.Y Toolkit compatibility, where installed
[no]debug           Generate GPU debug information
fastmath            Use fast math library
[no]flushz          Enable flush-to-zero mode on the GPU
nvlamath            Use nvlamath module in program units
[no]fma             Generate fused mul-add instructions (default at -O3)
keep                Keep kernel files
[no]lineinfo        Generate GPU line information
[no]lto             Perform link-time optimization of device code.
                    Must be specified at both compile and link time
zeroinit            Initialize allocated device memory with zero
[no]autocollapse
                    Automatically collapse tightly nested OpenACC parallel loops
deepcopy            Enable Full Deepcopy support in OpenACC Fortran
loadcache           Choose what hardware level cache to use for global memory loads
  L1                Use L1 cache
  L2                Use L2 cache
maxregcount:<n>     Set maximum number of registers to use on the GPU
pinned              Use CUDA Pinned Memory
[no]rdc             Generate relocatable device code
safecache           Allows variable-sized array sections in OpenACC cache
                    directives and assumes they fit into CUDA shared memory
stacklimit:<l>|nostacklimit
                    Sets the limit of stack variables in a procedure or kernel,
                    in KB
ptxinfo             Print ptxas information
[no]unroll          Enable automatic inner loop unrolling (default at -O3)
[no]managed         Use CUDA Managed Memory
beta                Enable beta code generation features
autocompare         Automatically compare OpenACC CPU/GPU results: implies
                    redundant
redundant           Redundant OpenACC CPU/GPU execution
[no]implicitsections
                    Implicitly convert array element to array section
                    in OpenMP or OpenACC data clauses
```

We have already discussed targeting specific architectures and using different CUDA Toolkits. We will go over many of these options in detail later in the text, but for now, we present a summary of some of these options. Note that many of the -gpu options are relevant to OpenACC rather than CUDA Fortran.

CUDA has a set of fast, but less accurate, intrinsics for single-precision functions like sin() and cos(), which can be enabled by -gpu=fastmath. The option -gpu=maxregcount:N can be used to limit the number of registers used per thread to N. The -gpu=keep option dumps kernel files, including the PTX.

In addition to -gpu flag, the -cuda flag contains several options that affect CUDA Fortran. Array descriptors for allocatable device data declared at module scope are placed in global memory by default.

In code that allocates device memory only from host code, we can store the module array descriptors in constant memory using the -cuda=madconst option, which may improve performance.

Though not CUDA specific, other compiler options are the -v and -V options. Compiling with the -v option provides verbose output of the compilation and linking steps. The -V option can be used to verify the version of the CUDA Fortran compiler and to select the compiler version amongst those installed on the machine given the appropriate argument.

By default, CUDA Fortran compiles with relocatable device code, or -gpu=rdc, which allows device functions in one module to be used with device functions in a different module. This differs from earlier versions of the compiler (used in the previous edition of this book), where the default was -gpu=nordc. In previous versions of the compiler, PTX code was embedded in the fat binary only when compiled with -gpu=nordc. This is no longer the case, and PTX is embedded in the fat binary regardless of whether compiled for relocatable device code or not.

1.7 CUDA Driver, Toolkit, and compatibility

In Section 1.4, we discussed hardware features, many of which are related to the compute capability, and how this information can be obtained from the device management API. In this short section, we discuss the software equivalent of this, namely the CUDA Driver and the CUDA Toolkit.

To build a CUDA Fortran application, the development system must have a CUDA Toolkit installed, which consists of the CUDA runtime, libraries, and tools. To run a CUDA Fortran application, the system must have a CUDA Driver that is compatible with the CUDA Toolkit used to build the application, along with any dynamic libraries from the CUDA Toolkit needed by the application. The versions of the CUDA Driver and Toolkit determine this compatibility.

The CUDA Driver on a system can be determined from the first line of output from nvaccelinfo, as well as from the output of nvidia-smi under CUDA Version. The CUDA Toolkits available on a system can be obtained from looking in the cuda directory in the HPC SDK. The CUDA Driver and Toolkit versions can be queried at runtime using the routines cudaDriverGetVersion() and cudaRuntimeGetVersion(), as in the following code:

```
1  program version
2    use cudafor
3    implicit none
4    integer :: istat, ver
5    istat = cudaDriverGetVersion(ver)
6    print *, 'Driver version:  ', ver
7    istat = cudaRuntimeGetVersion(ver)
8    print *, 'Runtime version: ', ver
9  end program version
```

whose output will be something like

```
Driver version:       11080
Runtime version:      11070
```

Just like the hardware's compute capability, the CUDA Driver and Toolkit versions have major and minor components. The major and minor components are expressed in the single numbers above using the relation *1000*Major* + *10*Minor*. In the above case the CUDA Driver and Toolkit versions are 11.8 and 11.7, respectively. Backward compatibility guarantees that an application built with a CUDA Toolkit version will run on a newer CUDA Driver version, so the above system's CUDA Driver and Toolkit are compatible.

As of CUDA 11, there is also a Minor Version Compatibility, where applications compiled with a CUDA Toolkit release can run, with limited feature-set, on an older CUDA Driver as long as the CUDA Driver is from the same major release family and is at least the minimum required version. This minimum required CUDA Driver is listed in the release notes of the CUDA Toolkit documentation. Some new features may require both a new CUDA Driver and a new CUDA Toolkit; in this case, running an application with a driver older than the toolkit used to build the application may return the error code cudaErrorCallRequiresNewDriver.

There can be multiple CUDA Toolkits installed on a system. The compiler option -gpu=cudaX.Y can be used to specify a particular CUDA Toolkit to use when building an application. If none is specified, then the compiler will look for a CUDA Toolkit version that matches the version of the CUDA Driver installed on the system. As of CUDA 11.2, if an exact match is not found, then the compiler will search for the closest version newer than the CUDA Driver version but within the same major release. Prior to CUDA 11.2, the compiler searches for the newest CUDA Toolkit version that is not newer than the CUDA Driver version.

Correctness, accuracy, and debugging

2

Before we can address performance optimization on the GPU, there are several preliminary steps that need to be performed. The first is verifying correctness of the results obtained from the GPU. We discuss two aspects of correctness in this chapter. The first aspect concerns numerical accuracy issues inherent in any floating-point computation performed in parallel, as well as some compiler flags that affect numerical accuracy on the GPU. The second aspect concerns programming errors and tools, such as cuda-memcheck and cuda-gdb, that can aid in correcting such errors.

2.1 Assessing correctness of results

Floating-point computation has inherent inaccuracies, as it is not possible to represent an infinite number of values using a finite-length floating-point representation. CUDA Fortran follows the IEEE 754-2008 standard for floating-point arithmetic with a few minor exceptions. These exceptions are discussed in the Floating-Point Standard section in the Compute Capability chapter of the CUDA C Programming Guide; briefly, the differences are the use of directed rounding intrinsics for math operations rather than rounding modes and the handling of floating-point exceptions and NaNs in some operations. When comparing results from a CUDA Fortran computation to a serial computation performed on the CPU, numerical differences are likely due to the non-associativity of floating-point operations, the use of the fused multiply–add instruction on the GPU, and some compilation flags used to trade accuracy for speed of computation. We explore these in detail in the following subsections.

2.1.1 Non-associativity of floating point arithmetic

A common cause for the disparity between floating point results from serial and parallel computation is that floating point arithmetic is not associative, meaning that the order in which arithmetic operations occur affects the result. As an example, consider the following code, which calculates the sum of integers from 1 to 1,000,000 using several different techniques:

```
1   program main
2     use cudafor
3     implicit none
4     integer, parameter :: n=1000000
5     integer(8), parameter :: n8 = n
6
7     real :: suminc = 0.0, sumdec = 0.0, a(n)
8     real, device :: a_d(n)
9     integer :: i
10
11     do i = 1, n
```

```
12        a(i) = i
13        suminc = suminc + i
14     enddo
15
16     do i = n, 1, -1
17        sumdec = sumdec + i
18     end do
19
20     print *, 'n: ', n
21     print *,'n*(n+1)/2: ', n8/2*(n8+1)
22
23     print *, 'from sum(a):           ', sum(a)
24     print *, 'incr accumulation:     ', suminc
25     print *, 'decr accumulation:     ', sumdec
26     a_d = a
27     print *, 'from sum(a_d):         ', sum(a_d)
28  end program main
```

The actual result is obtained from the relation $\sum_{i=1}^{n} i = n(n+1)/2$, which for $n = 1,000,000$ is $500,000,500,000$ as displayed on the second line of output:

```
n:          1000000
n*(n+1)/2:              500000500000
from sum(a):            4.9994138E+11
incr accumulation:      4.9994138E+11
decr accumulation:      4.9987368E+11
from sum(a_d):          5.0000003E+11
```

The other methods of calculating the sum use single-precision floating point arithmetic. The array of integers is stored in the single-precision host array a, which is used as an argument to the sum intrinsic. Manual accumulations are also performed in loops with increasing (line 13) and decreasing (line 17) values. All three of these floating-point calculations are in error, and the result in the third, where the sum is accumulated in decreasing values, differs from the first two. This is an expected result, as the summation of values is most accurate when the values are sorted in increasing order. In the last line of output, the summation occurs on the device using the overloaded sum() intrinsic operating on the device array a_d. The result from this differs from the host results as the order of accumulation is different. The sum() intrinsic on the device is implemented using two kernels: the first kernel calculates block-wise partial sums and stores these values to a global array, which is summed by the second kernel. Note that using multiple accumulators as is done with the partial sums in the device implementation is more accurate than using a single accumulator as in the host version without any compiler optimization. The host versions are not immune from the non-associativity of floating-point arithmetic as compiling with different optimization levels can result in a different order of execution, as seen when running the code after compiling with the -fast compiler option:

```
n:          1000000
n*(n+1)/2:              500000500000
from sum(a):            5.0000000E+11
incr accumulation:      4.9999987E+11
decr accumulation:      5.0000095E+11
from sum(a_d):          5.0000003E+11
```

The issue of the accuracy of floating-point accumulation is presented in more detail in the Monte Carlo Method case study in Section 9.4.

2.1.2 **Fused-multiply add**

By default CUDA Fortran uses the FMA or fused multiply–add instruction, which combines multiply and add operations into a single instruction whenever possible. The FMA instruction uses only a single rounding operation, as opposed to two rounding operations when separate multiply and add instructions are performed, and as a result generally produces a more accurate result compared to separate multiply and add instructions.

We can easily determine if FMA is responsible for observed differences by suppressing its use with the –gpu=nofma option. The presence or absence of the FMA instruction can be verified by examining the PTX intermediate code dumped when using the –gpu=keep option or by using the tool cuobjdump or nvdisasm to disassemble CUDA binary. The cuobjdump utility accepts both *.o object files and the *.bin file generated from the –gpu=keep compiler option, whereas nvdisasm only accepts the latter. Both these utilities are available in the cuda/bin directory in the HPC SDK. To illustrate this, we investigate the PTX and SASS generated from the code

```
1  module m
2  contains
3    attributes(global) subroutine s(a, b, c)
4      real :: a, b, c
5      a = a+b*c
6    end subroutine s
7  end module m
```

Compiling with the –gpu=keep instruction generates several files including those with the .ptx and .bin extensions. Searching this PTX file for fma shows the presence and absence of the FMA instruction:

```
$ nvfortran -c -gpu=keep fma.cuf
$ grep fma fma.n001.ptx
      fma.rn.ftz.f32   %f4, %f2, %f3, %f1;
$ nvfortran -c -gpu=keep,nofma fma.cuf
$ grep fma fma.n001.ptx
$
```

Likewise, searching for FMA in the output from cuobjdump -sass indicates the presence or absence of the FMA instruction:

```
$ nvfortran -c -gpu=keep fma.cuf
$ cuobjdump -sass fma.o | grep FMA
      /*0070*/                    FFMA.FTZ R0, R3, R2, R0 ;
$ nvfortran -c -gpu=keep,nofma fma.cuf
$ cuobjdump -sass fma.o | grep FMA
$
```

The generation of FMAs is suppressed when specifying -gpu=nofma because the multiplication in device code typically written using $*$ is instead written using the intrinsic __nv_fmul_rn(), which is never converted to an FMA instruction. We can verify this from the NVVM intermediate representation (based on LLVM IR) in the .gpu file generated when using -gpu=keep:

```
$ nvfortran -c -gpu=keep fma.cuf
$ grep fmul_rn fma.n001.gpu
$
$ nvfortran -c -gpu=keep,nofma fma.cuf
$ grep fmul_rn fma.n001.gpu
   %li10 = call float @__nv_fmul_rn(float %li5, float %li7), !dbg !18
declare float @__nv_fmul_rn(float, float) nounwind
```

2.1.3 Flags affecting floating-point accuracy

In the previous section, we discussed in detail how the -gpu=nofma compiler option can be used to control the generation of the FMA instruction. In this section, we discuss other compiler options that can affect floating-point accuracy.

The option -gpu=[no]flushz controls single-precision denormals support. Code compiled with -gpu=flushz flushes denormals to zero; otherwise, denormals are used.

CUDA has a set of fast but less accurate intrinsics for 32-bit floating-point data that can be enabled per compilation unit via the -gpu=fastmath compiler option or selectively in device code using the cudadevice module and explicitly calling the routines __fdividef(x,y), __sinf(x), __cosf(x), __tanf(x), __sincosf(x, s, c), __logf(x), __log2f(x), __log10f(x), __expf(x), __exp10f(x), and __powf(x,y).

2.2 Debugging

There are several options available for debugging device code. These range from using write or print statements in device code to using CUDA-aware debuggers that allow one to step through device code while examining program state. After a short discussion on printing from device code, the remainder of this chapter focuses on using the cuda-gdb debugger and the compute-sanitizer suite of tools available with the CUDA C Toolkit.

2.2.1 Printing from device code

In some cases, it is desirable to print from within device code, which is possible in CUDA Fortran using print *, or write(*,*), but in placing such statements in device code, realize that device code is typically being executed by many threads and that, in general, their order of execution is not deterministic. For example, adding a print statement to the array increment example in the previous chapter we have

```
1   module simpleOps_m
2   contains
3     attributes(global) subroutine increment(a, b, n)
4       implicit none
5       integer, intent(inout) :: a(*)
6       integer, value :: b, n
7       integer :: i
8
9       i = blockDim%x*(blockIdx%x-1) + threadIdx%x
10      if (i <= n) a(i) = a(i)+b
11      if (i > 30 .and. i < 34) print *, 'i, a(i):', i, a(i)
12    end subroutine increment
13  end module simpleOps_m
14
15
16  program main
17    use cudafor
18    use simpleOps_m
19    implicit none
20    integer, parameter :: n = 1024*1024
21    integer, allocatable :: a(:)
22    integer, device, allocatable :: a_d(:)
23    integer :: b, tPB = 256
24
25    allocate(a(n), a_d(n))
26    a = 1
27    b = 3
28
29    a_d = a
30    call increment<<<(n-1)/tPB+1,tPB>>>(a_d, b, n)
31    a = a_d
32
33    if (any(a /= 4)) then
34        print *, '**** Program Failed ****'
35    else
36        print *, 'Program Passed'
37    endif
38    deallocate(a, a_d)
39  end program main
```

which when compiled and executed gives

```
$ nvfortran print.cuf
$ ./a.out
 i, a(i):            33            4
 i, a(i):            31            4
 i, a(i):            32            4
 Program Passed
```

Note that here the output is not in numerical order – the order of execution of the threads in general can not be determined.

2.2.2 Debugging with cuda-gdb

The cuda-gdb debugger distributed with the CUDA Toolkit supports debugging CUDA Fortran programs. In this section, we describe the basic use of cuda-gdb with features of CUDA Fortran that have been covered up to this point. The use of cuda-gdb with language features in later chapters is covered in those sections. For detailed information regarding cuda-gdb, consult the CUDA-GDB CUDA Debugger manual distributed with the CUDA C Toolkit.

2.2.2.1 *System requirements*

CUDA Fortran is supported in cuda-gdb on 64-bit Linux systems. On devices with a compute capability of 6.0 and higher, cuda-gdb can be used to debug applications on the same GPU that is running the desktop graphical user interface. On a system with multiple devices of compute capability less than 6.0, use the CUDA_VISIBLE_DEVICES environment variable to select devices that are not driving the desktop manager. On systems where all GPUs are required to run the code, we can either stop the desktop manager or alternately set the environment variable CUDA_DEBUGGER_SOFTWARE_PREEMPTION=1.

2.2.2.2 *Compilation*

To compile CUDA Fortran codes with the debugging information necessary for CUDA-GDB to work properly, the -g or -gopt compiler option must be used, and it is recommended to use the -gpu=nordc option if possible.

To illustrate the use of cuda-gdb, we will step through a simple example code, essentially the increment example used in Chapter 1 with a few changes such as different array sizes and initial values:

```
1   module simpleOps_m
2   contains
3     attributes(global) subroutine increment(a, n, b)
4       implicit none
5       integer, intent(inout) :: a(*)
6       integer, value :: n, b
7       integer :: i
8
9       i = blockDim%x*(blockIdx%x-1) + threadIdx%x
10      if (i <= n) then
11         a(i) = a(i)+b
12      endif
13    end subroutine increment
14  end module simpleOps_m
15
16
17  program main
18    use cudafor
19    use simpleOps_m
20    implicit none
21    integer, parameter :: tPB=32*5, n=tPB*5+1, b = 3
22    integer :: a(n), r(n), i
23    integer, device :: a_d(n)
24
25    do i = 1, n
26       a(i) = i
27    end do
```

```
28
29    a_d = a
30    call increment<<<(n-1)/tPB+1,tPB>>>(a_d, n, b)
31    r = a_d
32
33    if (any(r /= a+b)) then
34        print *, '**** Program Failed ****'
35    else
36        print *, 'Program Passed'
37    endif
38  end program main
```

Compiling the code and running cuda-gdb is performed simply by

```
$ nvfortran -g -gpu=nordc debug.cuf
$ cuda-gdb a.out
```

2.2.2.3 *Setting breakpoints*

There are several methods of setting breakpoints in device code.

Symbolic breakpoints can also be set to break upon entry into a function. In our example, to set a breakpoint upon entry into the increment kernel, which is contained in the simpleOps_m module, we use

```
(cuda-gdb) break simpleops_m_increment_
Breakpoint 1 at 0x401392: file debug.cuf, line 3.
```

Note the trailing underscore as well as lower case letters when specifying the symbolic name. We can also set a breakpoint at the first instruction of every kernel as follows:

```
(cuda-gdb) set cuda break_on_launch application
```

where the argument application here refers to a kernel launched by the user application. The argument system can be used, which sets breakpoints at all kernels launched by the driver, and all will set breakpoints for both application and system kernel launches.

2.2.2.4 *Focus — software and hardware coordinates*

Having set a breakpoint using one of the methods above, we can now run the code

```
(cuda-gdb) run
Starting program: a.out
[Thread debugging using libthread_db enabled]
Using host libthread_db library "/lib/x86_64-linux-gnu/libthread_db.so.1".
[New Thread 0x7fffebdff000 (LWP 8052)]
[Detaching after fork from child process 8053]
[New Thread 0x7fffeb39d000 (LWP 8063)]
[New Thread 0x7fffeab9c000 (LWP 8064)]
[New Thread 0x7fffea13a000 (LWP 8065)]
[Switching focus to CUDA kernel 0, grid 1, block (0,0,0), thread (0,0,0),
```

```
   device 0, sm 0, warp 0, lane 0]

Thread 1 "a.out" hit Breakpoint 1, simpleops_m_increment_<<<(6,1,1),(160,1,1)>>> ()
   at debug.cuf:9
9              i = blockDim%x*(blockIdx%x-1) + threadIdx%x
```

Here the last two lines indicate that we have stopped in our kernel at the breakpoint, along with the execution configuration used to launch the kernel: six blocks of 160 threads per block. The previous line shows that the cuda-gdb focus has switched from the host thread to the device. The focus is specified in both software and hardware coordinates. The software coordinates are specified by the kernel, block, and thread. Note that here the block and thread use the zero-offset values associated with CUDA C. The hardware coordinates for the focus are specified by the device, sm (streaming multiprocessor), warp, and lane. Streaming multiprocessors execute instructions on groups of 32 threads at a time in current hardware, this group of threads is called a *warp* of threads. The position of a thread within a warp is called the *lane*. The specification of grid in the cuda-gdb output is somewhat redundant to kernel. The difference between is that the kernel enumeration is unique across all devices, whereas the grid enumeration is unique only within a device. Essentially, there is a one-to-one mapping between a kernel and the (grid, device) pair.

We can query and switch the current focus using the cuda command. Available subcommands are given by help cuda:

```
(cuda-gdb) help cuda
Print or select the CUDA focus.

List of cuda subcommands:

cuda block -- Print or select the current CUDA block
cuda device -- Print or select the current CUDA device
cuda grid -- Print or select the current CUDA grid
cuda kernel -- Print or select the current CUDA kernel
cuda lane -- Print or select the current CUDA lane
cuda sm -- Print or select the current CUDA SM
cuda thread -- Print or select the current CUDA thread
cuda warp -- Print or select the current CUDA warp

Type "help cuda" followed by cuda subcommand name for full documentation.
Type "apropos word" to search for commands related to "word".
Command name abbreviations are allowed if unambiguous.
```

We can query multiple coordinates at a time:

```
(cuda-gdb) cuda block thread warp lane
block (0,0,0), thread (0,0,0), warp 0, lane 0
```

When switching the current focus, provide values to be changed in either software or hardware coordinates:

```
(cuda-gdb) cuda block thread warp lane
block (0,0,0), thread (0,0,0), warp 0, lane 0
(cuda-gdb) cuda block 1
```

```
[Switching focus to CUDA kernel 0, grid 1, block (1,0,0), thread (0,0,0),
 device 0, sm 2, warp 0, lane 0]
9              i = blockDim%x*(blockIdx%x-1) + threadIdx%x
(cuda-gdb) cuda sm 2 lane 4
[Switching focus to CUDA kernel 0, grid 1, block (1,0,0), thread (4,0,0),
 device 0, sm 2, warp 0, lane 4]
9              i = blockDim%x*(blockIdx%x-1) + threadIdx%x
(cuda-gdb) cuda block 2 lane 0
Request cannot be satisfied. CUDA focus unchanged.
```

When switching focus, any unspecified coordinates are assumed unchanged. Also note that requests specifying mixed software and hardware coordinates, such as specifying the block and lane in the last command, will not be satisfied.

2.2.2.5 *CUDA activity status*

Information about current CUDA activities, as opposed to just the current focus, can be obtained from the info cuda command:

```
(cuda-gdb) help info cuda
Print informations about the current CUDA activities. Available options:
         devices : information about all the devices
            sms : information about all the SMs in the current device
          warps : information about all the warps in the current SM
          lanes : information about all the lanes in the current warp
        kernels : information about all the active kernels
       contexts : information about all the contexts
         blocks : information about all the active blocks in the
                  current kernel
        threads : information about all the active threads in the
                  current kernel
   launch trace : information about the parent kernels of the
                  kernel in focus
launch children : information about the kernels launched by the
                  kernels in focus
        managed : information about global managed variables
```

It is useful to discuss some of these options in more detail, as knowing the current state of all CUDA activity is helpful in determining how the hardware and software coordinates map, which can aid in stepping though device code. Using the devices option on this particular machine gives

```
(cuda-gdb) info cuda devices
  Dev PCI Bus/Dev ID              Name Description SM Type SMs Warps/SM
      Lanes/Warp Max Regs/Lane Active SMs Mask
*    0         02:00.0 NVIDIA A100-PCIE-40GB   GA100GL-B   sm_80 108   64
     32            256     0x0000000000000000000000000000000555
     1         03:00.0 NVIDIA A100-PCIE-40GB   GA100GL-B   sm_80 108   64
     32            256     0x0000000000000000000000000000000000
     2         82:00.0 NVIDIA A100-PCIE-40GB   GA100GL-B   sm_80 108   64
     32            256     0x0000000000000000000000000000000000
     3         83:00.0 NVIDIA A100-PCIE-40GB   GA100GL-B   sm_80 108   64
     32            256     0x0000000000000000000000000000000000
```

The "⋆" in the first row indicates that device 0 has the current focus. The Name (NVIDIA A100-PCIE-40GB) of the card is provided along with the Description or chip name (GA100GL-B) and the SM Type or compute capability (sm_80). The SMs or number of streaming multiprocessors on the device is also given (80), along with the maximum number of warps per SM (64). The Lanes/Warp refers to the warpsize (32), and the maximum number of registers per lane is also given (256). The Active SMs Mask indicates which SMs on the device are active. Each character in the mask represents four SMs, where values range from 0 to f indicating none to all four of these SMs are active. In this case, the mask of 0x0555 indicates that SMs 1,3,5,7,9, and 11 are active. This totals to 6 active SMs, which is also the number of blocks launched in our kernel, implying that the scheduler is distributing thread blocks to different multiprocessors. We can verify this using the info cuda sms command:

```
(cuda-gdb) info cuda sms
  SM  Active Warps Mask
Device 0
   0 0x000000000000001f
*  2 0x000000000000001f
   4 0x000000000000001f
   6 0x000000000000001f
   8 0x000000000000001f
  10 0x000000000000001f
(cuda-gdb)
```

which shows that SMs 0,2,4,6,8, and 10 are active. Once again the current focus is denoted by "⋆". Just as the output from info cuda devices lists the active streaming multiprocessors on each device, output from info cuda sms indicates the active warps on each streaming multiprocessor. Each block in our kernel has $160 = 5 * 32$ threads, or five warps, as indicated by the mask of 0x1f.

Going to the next level of hardware coordinate granularity, we have info cuda warps, which displays information on the warps in the current focus, in this case, block 1 on SM 2. We can reduce the output by applying a filter to info cuda warps:

```
(cuda-gdb) info cuda warps
  Wp Active Lanes Mask Divergent Lanes Mask Active Physical PC Kernel
     BlockIdx First Active ThreadIdx
Device 0 SM 2
*  0       0xffffffff            0x00000000 0x0000000000000400       0
     (1,0,0)                (0,0,0)
Device 0 SM 2
   1       0xffffffff            0x00000000 0x0000000000000400       0
     (1,0,0)                (32,0,0)
Device 0 SM 2
   2       0xffffffff            0x00000000 0x0000000000000400       0
     (1,0,0)                (64,0,0)
Device 0 SM 2
   3       0xffffffff            0x00000000 0x0000000000000400       0
     (1,0,0)                (96,0,0)
Device 0 SM 2
   4       0xffffffff            0x00000000 0x0000000000000400       0
     (1,0,0)                (128,0,0)
(cuda-gdb) info cuda warps sm current warp current
  Wp Active Lanes Mask Divergent Lanes Mask Active Physical PC Kernel
```

```
      BlockIdx First Active ThreadIdx
Device 0 SM 2
*   0             0xffffffff              0x00000000 0x0000000000000400        0
      (1,0,0)                    (0,0,0)
```

Issuing the command `info cuda warps sm all` would display info on all active warps. The data in the `Active Lanes Mask` column indicates that all 32 lanes are active, and the data in the `Kernel`, `BlockIDx` and `First Active ThreadIdx` columns indicate how these warps are mapped to the software coordinates. Continuing to the smaller hardware granularity, we can also get information on the lanes, used here with a filter to reduce the size of the output:

```
(cuda-gdb) info cuda lanes sm current warp current lane current
   Ln  State      Physical PC     ThreadIdx Exception
Device 0 SM 2 Warp 0
*   0  active 0x0000000000000400   (0,0,0)     None
```

We can also inquire about current CUDA activity from the software coordinate perspective:

```
(cuda-gdb) info cuda kernels
   Kernel Parent Dev Grid Status    SMs Mask GridDim   BlockDim
     Invocation
*      0       -   0    1 Active 0x00000555 (6,1,1)  (160,1,1)
     simpleops_m_increment_()
(cuda-gdb) info cuda blocks
   BlockIdx To BlockIdx Count    State
Kernel 0
*  (0,0,0)      (5,0,0)      6 running
(cuda-gdb) info cuda threads
   BlockIdx ThreadIdx To BlockIdx To ThreadIdx Count
     Virtual PC   Filename   Line
Kernel 0
*  (0,0,0)   (0,0,0)      (5,0,0)     (159,0,0)    960
     0x0000000000b94580 debug.cuf      9
```

Here the output is coalesced when possible. The output coalescing can be turned off, which yields more detailed information:

```
(cuda-gdb) set cuda coalescing off
Coalescing of the CUDA commands output is off.
(cuda-gdb) info cuda blocks
   BlockIdx    State Dev SM
Kernel 0
   (0,0,0) running   0  0
*  (1,0,0) running   0  2
   (2,0,0) running   0  4
   (3,0,0) running   0  6
   (4,0,0) running   0  8
   (5,0,0) running   0 10
```

where the mapping of thread blocks to SMs is clearly indicated.

2.2.2.6 *Single-stepping in device code*

The commands step and next can be used in device code to single step the warp that has current focus. The command info cuda threads, with output coalescing on, is helpful in determining the state of all threads:

```
(cuda-gdb) set cuda coalescing on
Coalescing of the CUDA commands output is on.
(cuda-gdb) info cuda threads
  BlockIdx ThreadIdx To BlockIdx To ThreadIdx Count
      Virtual PC  Filename  Line
Kernel 0
*  (0,0,0)    (0,0,0)      (5,0,0)     (159,0,0)    960
    0x0000000000b94580 debug.cuf     9
(cuda-gdb) step
10            if (i <= n) then
(cuda-gdb) info cuda threads
  BlockIdx ThreadIdx To BlockIdx To ThreadIdx Count
      Virtual PC  Filename  Line
Kernel 0
   (0,0,0)    (0,0,0)      (0,0,0)     (159,0,0)    160
       0x0000000000b94580 debug.cuf    9
*  (1,0,0)    (0,0,0)      (1,0,0)      (31,0,0)     32
       0x0000000000b94e00 debug.cuf    10
   (1,0,0)   (32,0,0)      (5,0,0)     (159,0,0)    768
       0x0000000000b94580 debug.cuf    9
```

which show the focus warp advancing to line 10 in the source. Setting a breakpoint at line 10 and issuing continue is one method of advancing the rest of the threads to this point:

```
(cuda-gdb) break
Breakpoint 1 at 0xb94e00: file debug.cuf, line 10.
(cuda-gdb) continue
Continuing.
[Switching focus to CUDA kernel 0, grid 1, block (0,0,0), thread (0,0,0),
   device 0, sm 0, warp 0, lane 0]

Thread 1 "a.out" hit Breakpoint 1,
   simpleops_m::increment <<<(6,1,1),(160,1,1)>>>
   (a=..., _V_b=3, _V_n=801) at debug.cuf:10
10            if (i <= n) then
```

2.2.2.7 *Examining program state*

Values of variables that are in scope can be displayed using the print command:

```
(cuda-gdb) print i
$1 = 1
(cuda-gdb) print n
$2 = 801
```

In this kernel, each CUDA thread processes a single element in the array a. Because array a contains 801 elements, and the kernel is launched with a thread block size of 160, only a single thread in the last thread block will increment the value of the array. By turning output coalescing off and setting the focus to the last block we can observe the divergent warp, where one thread is active inside the if block, and the others are divergent (i.e., do not participate):

```
(cuda-gdb) cuda block 5 thread 0
[Switching focus to CUDA kernel 0, grid 1, block (5,0,0), thread (0,0,0),
   device 0, sm 10, warp 0, lane 0]
11              a(i) = a(i)+b
(cuda-gdb) set cuda coalescing off
Coalescing of the CUDA commands output is off.
(cuda-gdb) info cuda lanes block current warp current
  Ln    State       Physical PC     ThreadIdx Exception
Device 0 SM 10 Warp 0
*  0    active   0x0000000000000cd0   (0,0,0)     None
Device 0 SM 10 Warp 0
   1 divergent 0x00000000000013d0   (1,0,0)     None
Device 0 SM 10 Warp 0
   2 divergent 0x00000000000013d0   (2,0,0)     None
Device 0 SM 10 Warp 0
   3 divergent 0x00000000000013d0   (3,0,0)     None
...
```

where we see that the first lane is active and others are divergent, indicating non-uniform evaluation of the condition on line 10 of the source code by threads of this warp.

We can step across line 11 and check that the addition was performed correctly:

```
(cuda-gdb) print a(i)
$3 = 801
(cuda-gdb) step
13          end subroutine increment
(cuda-gdb) print a(i)
$4 = 804
```

This section demonstrated the use of some of the CUDA extensions in cuda-gdb. There are other CUDA extensions that were not presented as they pertain to language features not yet discussed in the book. In sections of the book that cover such language features, we will present examples on how those features are accommodated in cuda-gdb. For detailed information on cuda-gdb, consult the *CUDA-GDB CUDA Debugger* manual distributed with the CUDA C toolkit.

2.2.3 `compute-sanitizer`

In addition to cuda-gdb, the compilers/bin directory in the HPC SDK comes with compute-sanitizer, a suite of tools used to check functional correctness of CUDA codes. The compute-sanitizer suite contains four tools: memcheck, which checks for various types of memory errors including out-of-bounds memory accesses and memory leaks; initcheck, which checks for use of uninitialized global memory variables; and racecheck and syncheck, which check for race conditions and synchronization errors. We will discuss the use of the memcheck and initcheck tools in this section. For more detail, consult the *Compute Sanitizer* manual distributed with the CUDA C Toolkit documents.

The memcheck component of compute-sanitizer can be used either as a standalone application or within cuda-gdb. When used with cuda-gdb, memcheck can be enabled by issuing the command

```
(cuda-gdb) set cuda memcheck on
```

before running the application. We illustrate the use of the memcheck tool by modifying the example code used in the cuda-gdb section:

```
1  module simpleOps_m
2  contains
3    attributes(global) subroutine increment(a, n, b)
4      implicit none
5      integer, intent(inout) :: a(*)
6      integer, value :: n, b
7      integer :: i
8
9      i = blockDim%x*(blockIdx%x-1) + threadIdx%x-1 ! *incorrect*
10     if (i <= n) then
11        a(i) = a(i)+b
12     end if
13   end subroutine increment
14 end module simpleOps_m
15
16
17 program main
18   use cudafor
19   use simpleOps_m
20   implicit none
21   integer, parameter :: tPB=32*5, n=tPB*5+1, b = 3
22   integer :: a(n), r(n), i
23   integer, device :: a_d(n)
24
25   do i = 1, n
26      a(i) = i
27   end do
28
29   a_d = a
30   call increment <<<ceiling(real(n)/tPB),tPB>>>(a_d, n, b)
31   r = a_d
32
33   if (any(r /= a+b)) then
34      print *, '**** Program Failed ****'
35   else
36      print *, 'Program Passed'
37   endif
38 end program main
```

Compiling and running this code will likely give the desired result, as all the elements of the array a() are incremented by the value b. However, there is a bug on line 9, where threadIdx%x-1 is used rather than threadIdx%x; as a result, the first thread has i=0 and accesses memory out of bounds. This is revealed from the first few lines of output when running the application under compute-sanitizer:

```
$ nvfortran memcheck.cuf
$ compute-sanitizer --language fortran a.out
========= COMPUTE-SANITIZER
========= Invalid __global__ read of size 4 bytes
=========     at 0x90 in /home/.../memcheck.cuf:11:simpleops_m_increment_
=========     by thread (1,1,1) in block (1,1,1)
=========     Address 0x7f461bdffffc is out of bounds
=========     and is 4 bytes before the nearest allocation
              at 0x7f461be00000 of size 3,204 bytes
```

Note that no special compilation flags are needed to use compute-sanitizer. By default, the memcheck tool is enabled, but we can also specify the option --tool memcheck explicitly. The option --language fortran causes the reported thread and block indices to be unit-based as opposed to zero-based. The output indicates an invalid read from global memory by thread (1,1,1) of thread block (1,1,1) on line 11 of the code. Specifically, it states that the attempted access occurs four bytes before the nearest allocation. In codes with many device arrays, the allocations can occur back-to-back in the virtual address space. As such, an out-of-bounds access for one array might map to a valid location in another array, and the access will not be flagged as out-of-bounds. The option --padding n can be used to specify that n bytes of padding be added to every allocation, where any access to that buffer will be reported as an error by memcheck, at the expense of using more device memory. In addition to out-of-bounds access errors, memcheck also reports misaligned memory accesses and memory leaks (via the --leak-check full option).

If we correct the indexing error but comment out the host-to-device data transfer on line 29, then the code will access uninitialized global memory. This can be revealed using the initcheck tool:

```
$ nvfortran initcheck.cuf
$ compute-sanitizer --tool initcheck --language fortran a.out | more
========= COMPUTE-SANITIZER
========= Uninitialized __global__ memory read of size 4 bytes
=========     at 0x90 in /home/.../initcheck.cuf:11:simpleops_m_increment_
=========     by thread (1,1,1) in block (1,1,1)
```

Here we only list the first few lines of output, as every thread issues a similar error message. Initcheck does not perform any memory access error checking, and therefore it is advisable to run memcheck prior to initcheck.

Performance measurement and metrics

3

After correctness of the results on the GPU has been verified, timing of code sections on the GPU can be performed using a variety of approaches, from instrumenting the code with CPU and GPU timers to using tools such as NVIDIA Nsight Systems and Compute. We then discuss how timing information can be used to determine the limiting factor of kernel execution. Finally, we discuss how to calculate performance metrics, especially related to bandwidth, and how such metrics should be interpreted.

3.1 Measuring execution time

Once correctness of the results generated on the GPU has been established, attention can focus on performance evaluation. The easiest way to obtain timing information is through nsys, the NVIDIA Nsight Systems performance analysis tool. We can also manually instrument their code to time specified code sections. Traditional CPU timers can be used, but in doing so, we must be careful to ensure correct synchronization between host and device for such measurements to be accurate. The CUDA event API routines, which are called from host code, can be used to calculate kernel execution time using the device clock. We discuss these approaches to timing GPU activity in the following sections.

3.1.1 Host–device synchronization and CPU timers

Care must be taken when timing GPU routines using traditional CPU timers. From the host perspective, kernel execution as well as many CUDA Fortran API functions are nonblocking or asynchronous: they return control back to the calling CPU thread prior to completing their work on the GPU. For example, in the code segment

```
1  a_d = a
2  call increment<<<1,n>>>(a_d, b)
3  a = a_d
```

although the host-to-device transfer, kernel execution, and device-to-host transfer will occur sequentially on the device, from the host perspective the picture is more complicated. Once the increment kernel is launched on line 2, control returns to the CPU. The host-to-device transfer on line 1 may return control to the CPU before the transfer completes depending on whether the host data is in pageable memory or not.[1] If we attempted to time kernel execution by inserting CPU timers before and after the kernel invocation,

```
1   a_d = a
2   t1 = myCPUTimer()
3   call increment<<<1,n>>>(a_d, b)
4   t2 = myCPUTimer()
5   a = a_d
```

then the elapsed time computed by t2-t1 would reflect only the launch time of the kernel and possibly part of the host-to-device data transfer. The correct way to time kernel execution using CPU timers is to place an explicit device synchronization before the timing calls:

```
1   a_d = a
2   istat = cudaDeviceSynchronize()
3   t1 = myCPUTimer()
4   call increment<<<1,n>>>(a_d, b)
5   istat = cudaDeviceSynchronize()
6   t2 = myCPUTimer()
7   a = a_d
```

The function cudaDeviceSynchronize() blocks the calling host thread until all CUDA calls previously issued by the host thread are completed, which is required for correct measurement of the increment kernel.

An alternative to using the second cudaDeviceSynchronize() call is to set the environment variable CUDA_LAUNCH_BLOCKING to 1, which turns kernel invocations into synchronous function calls. However, the first call to cudaDeviceSynchronize() is still needed for accurate kernel execution timing, and all kernel launches of a program would be affected and would therefore serialize any CPU code with kernel execution.

Another aspect of timing kernel execution using CPU timers is the granularity of the timer. The host timer might not have enough precision to accurately capture the kernel execution time. For this reason, along with the fact that code must be modified, we do not recommend using CPU timers to measure the kernel execution time. Profiling with the Nsight Systems command-line interface nsys, discussed in Section 3.1.3, provides accurate kernel execution times with no code modification or recompilation. This is not to say that CPU timers do not have a role in CUDA Fortran codes, as they are useful in timing large sections of code, but for timing single kernel invocations, there are far better options.

3.1.2 Timing via CUDA events

One problem with host–device synchronization points, such as those produced by the function cudaDeviceSynchronize() and the environment variable CUDA_LAUNCH_BLOCKING, is that they stall the GPU's processing pipeline. Unfortunately, such synchronization points are required using CPU timers. Luckily, CUDA offers a relatively light-weight alternative to using CPU timers via the CUDA event API. The CUDA event API provides calls that create and destroy events, record events (via a GPU timestamp), and convert timestamp differences into a floating-point value in units of milliseconds.

---

[1] See the Synchronization chapter for more detail.

CUDA events make use of the concept of CUDA streams, and before we discuss CUDA event code, we should say a few words about CUDA streams. A CUDA stream is simply a sequence of operations that are performed in order on the device. Operations in different streams can be interleaved and in some cases overlapped — a property that can be used to hide data transfers between the host and device, which we will discuss in detail later. Up to now, all operations on the GPU have occurred in the default stream, stream 0.

Typical use of the event API is as follows:

```
 1  module m
 2  contains
 3    attributes(global) subroutine increment(a, b)
 4      implicit none
 5      integer, intent(inout) :: a(*)
 6      integer, value :: b
 7      integer :: i
 8
 9      i = threadIdx%x
10      a(i) = a(i)+b
11
12    end subroutine increment
13  end module m
14
15
16  program events
17    use cudafor
18    use m
19    implicit none
20    integer, parameter :: n = 256
21    integer :: a(n), b
22    integer, device :: a_d(n)
23    type(cudaEvent) :: startEvent, stopEvent
24    real :: time
25    integer :: istat
26
27    a = 1
28    b = 3
29    a_d = a
30
31    istat = cudaEventCreate(startEvent)
32    istat = cudaEventCreate(stopEvent)
33
34    istat = cudaEventRecord(startEvent, 0)
35    call increment<<<1,n>>>(a_d, b)
36    istat = cudaEventRecord(stopEvent, 0)
37    istat = cudaEventSynchronize(stopEvent)
38    istat = cudaEventElapsedTime(time, startEvent, stopEvent)
39
40    a = a_d
41
42    if (any(a /= 4)) then
43       print *, '**** Program Failed ****'
44    else
```

```
45       print *, '  Time for kernel execution (ms): ', time
46    endif
47
48    istat = cudaEventDestroy(startEvent)
49    istat = cudaEventDestroy(stopEvent)
50
51  end program events
```

CUDA events are of type cudaEvent and are created and destroyed with cudaEventCreate() and cudaEventDestroy(). The cudaEventRecord() function is used to place the start and stop events into the default stream, stream 0. The device will record a timestamp for the event when it reaches that event in the stream. The cudaEventElapsedTime() function returns the time elapsed between the recording of the start and stop events on the GPU. This value is expressed in milliseconds and has a resolution of approximately half a microsecond. Because cudaEventRecord() is nonblocking, we require a synchronization before the call to cudaEventElapsedTime() to ensure that stopEvent has been recorded, which is the reason for the cudaEventSynchronize() call on line 37. cudaEventSynchronize() blocks CPU execution until the specified event has been recorded on the GPU.

For very simple kernels (such as out increment example), there can be some inaccuracy in timing using CUDA events resulting from CPU-side jitter. In such cases, more accurate results can be obtained from CUDA events by simple adding a no-op kernel just before the first CUDA event call, so that the cudaEventRecord() and subsequent kernel call will be queued up on the GPU.

3.1.3 Nsight Systems command-line interface nsys

The Nsight Systems command-line interface nsys provides a simple way to collect profile data from an application and then generate a report from the profile data. This two-step process allows us to collect performance data on a remote system using the command line and then transfer the resulting file to a different system to do performance analysis. This approach does not require any code modification or special compilation flags.

Before collecting profile data, we should check that the system will allow access to the system hooks needed for profiling. This can be checked using the nsys status -e command. Typical output is

```
$ nsys status -e
Timestamp counter supported: Yes

CPU Profiling Environment Check
Root privilege: disabled
Linux Kernel Paranoid Level = 0
Linux Distribution = Ubuntu
Linux Kernel Version = 6.2.0-26-generic: OK
Linux perf_event_open syscall available: OK
Sampling trigger event available: OK
Intel(c) Last Branch Record support: Available
CPU Profiling Environment (process-tree): OK
CPU Profiling Environment (system-wide): OK
```

If the output generates Fail instead of OK, then consult the NVIDIA Nsight Systems Installation Guide for steps to correct the issue(s).

In addition to checking that the system is set correctly for profiling, we should also check for code correctness. Specifically, memory access errors that might not terminate execution of the code under normal circumstances can cause problems when profiling. A simple way to check this is via the *mem-check* tool in the compute-sanitizer, as discussed in Section 2.2.3.

We will use the multidimensional increment code from the introduction to illustrate use of nsys profiling, included here for reference:

```
1   module m
2   contains
3     attributes(global) subroutine increment(a, n1, n2, b)
4       implicit none
5       integer :: a(n1,n2)
6       integer, value :: n1, n2, b
7       integer :: i, j
8
9       i = (blockIdx%x-1)*blockDim%x + threadIdx%x
10      j = (blockIdx%y-1)*blockDim%y + threadIdx%y
11      if (i<=n1 .and. j<=n2) a(i,j) = a(i,j) + b
12    end subroutine increment
13  end module m
14
15
16
17  program multidim
18    use cudafor
19    use m
20    implicit none
21    integer, parameter :: nx=1024, ny=512
22    integer :: a(nx,ny), b
23    integer, device :: a_d(nx,ny)
24    type(dim3) :: grid, tBlock
25
26    a = 1
27    b = 3
28
29    tBlock = dim3(32,8,1)
30    grid = dim3((nx-1)/tBlock%x+1, &
31                (ny-1)/tBlock%y+1, 1)
32    a_d = a
33    call increment<<<grid,tBlock>>>(a_d, nx, ny, b)
34    a = a_d
35
36    if (any(a /= 4)) then
37       print *, '**** Program Failed ****'
38    else
39       print *, 'Program Passed'
40    endif
41  end program multidim
```

At its simplest, to collect profile data the nsys command can be executed with the profile switch:

```
$ nsys profile -o multidim ./a.out
 Program Passed
Generating '/tmp/nsys-report-2053.qdstrm'
[1/1] [=========================100%] multidim.nsys-rep
Generated:
   /home/.../multidim.nsys-rep
```

which creates the file multidim.nsys-rep in the local directory. The nsys command can then be invoked with the stats switch to generate a series of summary or trace reports from that file. By default, the command nsys stats multidim.nsys-rep will generate a long list of reports. It is often convenient to specify individual reports, a list of which can be generated using the --help-reports option with the stats switch:

```
$ nsys stats --help-reports

The following built-in reports are available:

  cuda_api_gpu_sum[:base|:mangled] -- CUDA Summary (API/Kernels/MemOps)
  cuda_api_sum -- CUDA API Summary
  cuda_api_trace -- CUDA API Trace
  cuda_gpu_kern_gb_sum[:base|:mangled] -- CUDA GPU Kernel/Grid/Block Summary
  cuda_gpu_kern_sum[:base|:mangled] -- CUDA GPU Kernel Summary
  cuda_gpu_mem_size_sum -- CUDA GPU MemOps Summary (by Size)
  cuda_gpu_mem_time_sum -- CUDA GPU MemOps Summary (by Time)
  cuda_gpu_sum[:base|:mangled] -- CUDA GPU Summary (Kernels/MemOps)
  cuda_gpu_trace[:base|:mangled] -- CUDA GPU Trace
  cuda_kern_exec_sum[:base|:mangled] -- CUDA Kernel Launch & Exec Time Summary
  cuda_kern_exec_trace[:base|:mangled] -- CUDA Kernel Launch & Exec Time Trace
  dx11_pix_sum -- DX11 PIX Range Summary
  dx12_gpu_marker_sum -- DX12 GPU Command List PIX Ranges Summary
  dx12_pix_sum -- DX12 PIX Range Summary
  nvtx_gpu_proj_trace -- NVTX GPU Projection Trace
  nvtx_kern_sum[:base|:mangled] -- NVTX Range Kernel Summary
  nvtx_pushpop_sum -- NVTX Push/Pop Range Summary
  nvtx_pushpop_trace -- NVTX Push/Pop Range Trace
  nvtx_startend_sum -- NVTX Start/End Range Summary
  nvtx_sum -- NVTX Range Summary
  nvvideo_api_sum -- NvVideo API Summary
  openacc_sum -- OpenACC Summary
  opengl_khr_gpu_range_sum -- OpenGL KHR_debug GPU Range Summary
  opengl_khr_range_sum -- OpenGL KHR_debug Range Summary
  openmp_sum -- OpenMP Summary
  osrt_sum -- OS Runtime Summary
  um_cpu_page_faults_sum -- Unified Memory CPU Page Faults Summary
  um_sum[:rows=<limit>] -- Unified Memory Analysis Summary
  um_total_sum -- Unified Memory Totals Summary
  vulkan_api_sum -- Vulkan API Summary
  vulkan_api_trace -- Vulkan API Trace
  vulkan_gpu_marker_sum -- Vulkan GPU Range Summary
  vulkan_marker_sum -- Vulkan Range Summary
  wddm_queue_sum -- WDDM Queue Utilization Summary
```

```
For more information, use '--help-reports <report_name>'
```

The summary of activity on the GPU (kernels and memory operations) is given by the cuda_gpu_sum report:

```
$ nsys stats --report cuda_gpu_sum multidim.nsys-rep

** CUDA GPU Summary (Kernels/MemOps) (cuda_gpu_sum):

Time (%)  Total Time (ns)  Instances  Category      Operation
--------  ---------------  ---------  -----------   ------------------
    49.7          329,793          1  MEMORY_OPER   [CUDA memcpy HtoD]
    48.3          320,481          1  MEMORY_OPER   [CUDA memcpy DtoH]
     2.0           13,408          1  CUDA_KERNEL   m_increment_
```

This is an abbreviated output as the number of columns has been reduced to fit the page. In addition to the Total time column, the average, median, maximum, and minimum times are given in the actual output. Since we have only a single instance of each operation, the additional columns do not convey any new information. We can see from this report that the data copies between host and device memory account for the majority of time, whereas the increment kernel (denoted using the *module-name_kernel-name_* convention) accounts for 2% of time on the device. This is an important issue in performance tuning, as the bandwidth between the host and device memory is considerably less than the bandwidth between the device memory and GPU. The first section in the performance tuning chapter discusses ways to optimize data transfers between host and device.

The output of the cuda_gpu_sum report is ordered in terms of overtime spend for the operations. A timeline of GPU activity can be obtained using the --report cuda_gpu_trace option:

```
$ nsys stats --report cuda_gpu_trace multidim.nsys-rep

** CUDA GPU Trace (cuda_gpu_trace):

Start (ns)    Duration (ns)  Throughput (MBps)  Name
-----------   -------------  -----------------  ------------------
375,833,388         329,793          6,358.565  [CUDA memcpy HtoD]
376,174,253          13,408                     m_increment_
376,189,901         320,481          6,543.114  [CUDA memcpy DtoH]
```

Once again this is an abbreviated listing, which can fit the page. The actual output contains many more columns including the execution configuration for the kernel launch, on-chip memory use, size and kind of data transfers, amongst other fields. We will revisit the omitted output in later sections where they become relevant.

3.1.3.1 *Nsight Systems graphical user interface* nsys-ui

The graphical user interface nsys-ui can be used to obtain the same reports as the command-line interface. We can either use nsys-ui to both collect data and generate reports or can import data collected from the nsys profile command (by choosing Open from the File menu). Fig. 3.1 shows the nsys-ui window after loading the profile obtained with nsys profile, where the timeline at the

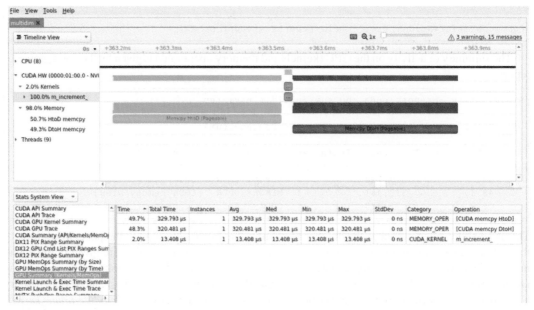

FIGURE 3.1

Snapshot of `nsys-ui` timeline and GPU summary report.

top has been zoomed in to show the GPU activity, and the `Stats System View` has been selected on the bottom to show all of the reports, of which GPU Summary is selected.

3.1.4 Customizing profiling with `nvtx`

The NVIDIA Tools Extension (NVTX) library lets developers annotate custom events and ranges within the profiling timelines generated using tools such as `nsys-ui`.

There are several versions of interfaces to NVTX: basic tooling interfaces, advanced tooling interfaces that target the NVTX v3 API, and automated instrumentation controlled by compilation flags that require no modification of source code. We cover each of these briefly in this section.

3.1.4.1 Basic NVTX tooling interfaces

The basic NVTX tooling interfaces are included in the `nvtx` module and consist of routines used to push and pop nested time ranges with user-defined labels and colors via the routines `nvtxStartRange()` and `nvtxEndRange()`. An example of the basic interface use is the following code:

```
1   program main
2     use nvtx
3     implicit none
4     character(len=4) :: nchar
5     integer :: n
6
7     call nvtxStartRange("Outer Label")
```

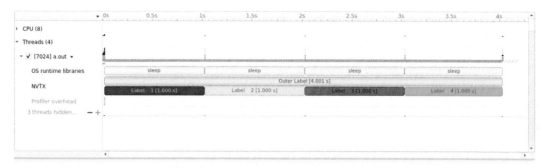

FIGURE 3.2

Timeline from **nsys-ui** showing NVTX labels from the basic NVTX interfaces.

```
8
9    do n = 1, 4
10       write(nchar, '(i4)') n
11       call nvtxStartRange('Label '//nchar,n)
12       call sleep(1)
13       call nvtxEndRange()
14    enddo
15
16    call nvtxEndRange()
17  end program main
```

The nvtxStartRange() routine takes a character string as the first argument and an optional integer as a second argument, which maps to a set of predefined colors. nvtxEndRange() takes no arguments. To compile this code link with the -cudalib=nvtx flag and, after profiling, with nsys:

```
$ nvfortran nvtxBasic.cuf -cudalib=nvtx
$ nsys profile -o nvtxBasic a.out
```

the timeline in nsys-ui shows the NVTX labels, as depicted in Fig. 3.2.

3.1.4.2 *Advanced NVTX tooling interfaces*

The advanced NVTX tooling interfaces target the NVTX v3 API. This API allows us to define multiple NVTX domains, which maintain separate stacks, markers for instances in time as well as ranges for time spans, and event attributes used to annotate markers and ranges. For these more advanced aspects of the NVTX API, see the *Fortran CUDA Library Interfaces Guide*. In this section, we show the advanced NVTX interface equivalent of the code used to demonstrate the basic NVTX interface:

```
1  program main
2    use nvtx
3    implicit none
4    type(nvtxRangeId) :: id1, id2
5    character(len=4) :: nchar
6    integer :: n
7
```

```
8    id1 = nvtxRangeStart("Outer label")
9
10   do n = 1, 4
11      write(nchar, '(i4)') n
12      id2 = nvtxRangeStart('Label '//nchar)
13      call sleep(1)
14      call nvtxRangeEnd(id2)
15   enddo
16
17   call nvtxRangeEnd(id1)
18 end program main
```

There are a few important differences between the advanced and basic NVTX routines. The first is the naming of the range start and end routines: the basic interface uses nvtxStartRange() and nvtxEndRange(), whereas the advanced interface uses nvtxRangeStart() and nvtxRangeEnd(). The second difference is the use of range IDs as defined by the nvtxRangeId derived type. Range IDs are returned by the function nvtxRangeStart() and provided as an argument to the subroutine nvtxRangeEnd(). This allows ranges that can be staggered as in the following code:

```
1  program main
2     use nvtx
3     implicit none
4     integer, parameter :: n=4
5     type(nvtxRangeId) :: id(n)
6     character(len=4) :: ichar
7     integer :: i
8
9     do i=1, n
10       write(ichar,'(i4)') i
11       id(i) = nvtxRangeStart('Label '//ichar)
12       call sleep(1)
13       if (i>1) call nvtxRangeEnd(id(i-1))
14    enddo
15
16    call nvtxRangeEnd(id(n))
17 end program main
```

rather than requiring ranges to be properly nested as with the basic interface. Graphical output of this code is shown in Fig. 3.3. The final difference is that the optional integer argument to nvtxStartRange() in the basic interface that maps to a label color is not available in the routine nvtxRangeStart() routine of the advanced interface. To add colors to the labels with the advanced interface, we need to call nvtxRangeStartEx(), which takes an nvtxEventAttribute instance as an argument. Both the label and color can be specified in the fields of the nvtxEventAttribute.

3.1.4.3 *Automated NVTX instrumentation*

Both the basic and advanced NVTX tooling interfaces require modification of source code. However, there is a facility for automatically adding NVTX ranges without modifying code. The first step to achieving this is to add the -Minstrument flag when compiling the files you want to add NVTX labels, which will cause the compiler to add calls at subprogram entry and exit. Next, when linking, add

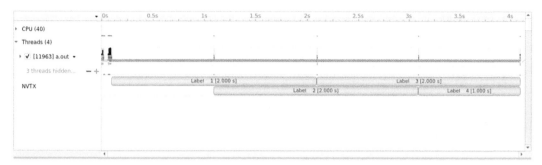

FIGURE 3.3

Timeline from `nsys-ui` showing staggered ranges from the NVTX advanced tooling interfaces.

the flags -traceback and -cudalib=nvtx. Without the -traceback flag, the label would contain the function address in hexadecimal rather than the function name.

3.2 Instruction, bandwidth, and latency bound kernels

Having the ability to time kernel execution, we can now talk about how to determine the limiting factor of a kernel's execution. There are several ways to do this; we can use analysis provided by tools such as Nsight Systems based on utilization of various subsystems (e.g., memory, arithmetic units). In this section, we describe a method where multiple versions of the kernel are created, which isolate the memory and math intensive aspects of the full kernel. Each kernel is timed, and a comparison of these times can reveal the limiting factor of kernel execution. This process is best understood by going through an example. The following code contains three kernels: (1) base(), a kernel that performs the desired overall operation; (2) memory(), a kernel that has the same device memory access patterns as the base() kernel but no math operations; and (3) math(), a kernel that performs the math operations of the base() kernel without accessing global memory:

```
module kernel_m
contains
  attributes(global) subroutine base(a, b)
    real :: a(*), b(*)
    integer :: i
    i = (blockIdx%x-1)*blockDim%x + threadIdx%x
    a(i) = sin(b(i)) + cos(b(i)) &
         + sin(2.0*b(i)) + cos(2.0*b(i)) &
         + sin(3.0*b(i)) + cos(3.0*b(i)) &
         + sin(4.0*b(i)) + cos(4.0*b(i))
  end subroutine base

  attributes(global) subroutine memory(a, b)
    real :: a(*), b(*)
    integer :: i
    i = (blockIdx%x-1)*blockDim%x + threadIdx%x
```

```
17        a(i) = b(i)
18      end subroutine memory
19
20      attributes(global) subroutine math(a, b, flag)
21        real :: a(*)
22        real, value :: b
23        integer, value :: flag
24        real :: v
25        integer :: i
26        i = (blockIdx%x-1)*blockDim%x + threadIdx%x
27        v = sin(b) + cos(b) &
28            + sin(2.0*b) + cos(2.0*b) &
29            + sin(3.0*b) + cos(3.0*b) &
30            + sin(4.0*b) + cos(4.0*b)
31        if (v*flag == 1) a(i) = v
32      end subroutine math
33    end module kernel_m
34
35    program limitingFactor
36      use cudafor
37      use kernel_m
38
39      implicit none
40
41      integer, parameter :: blockSize = 256
42      integer, parameter :: n = 64*1024*4*blockSize
43      real :: a(n)
44      real, device :: a_d(n), b_d(n)
45      b_d = 1.0
46      call base<<<n/blockSize,blockSize>>>(a_d, b_d)
47      call memory<<<n/blockSize,blockSize>>>(a_d, b_d)
48      call math<<<n/blockSize,blockSize>>>(a_d, 1.0, 0)
49      a = a_d
50      print *, a(1)
51    end program limitingFactor
```

For the math() kernel, care must be taken to trick the compiler as it can detect and eliminate operations that do not contribute to stores in device memory. So we need to put stores inside conditionals that always evaluate to false, as is done on line 31 in the code above. The conditional should be dependent not only on a flag passed into the subroutine but also an intermediate result; otherwise, the compiler could move the entire operation into the conditional.

If we compile this code without any optimization and run on an NVIDIA A100, then abridged output from the cuda_gpu_kern_sum report is

```
Time (%)  Total Time (ns)          Name
--------  ---------------   ----------------------
    43.1        1,553,195   kernel_m_base_
    35.7        1,285,637   kernel_m_math_
    15.1          545,252   kernel_m_memory_
     6.1          219,746   __pgi_dev_cumemset_16n
```

The base() kernel expectedly uses the most time, followed by the math() kernel and then the memory() kernel. We observe a fair amount of overlap of math and memory operations, as the sum of the time for the math() and memory() kernels is greater than the time for the base() kernel. However, because the math() kernel time is 83% of the base() kernel time and the memory() kernel time is 35% of the base() kernel time, the limiting factor based on execution time in this case is the math operations.

One method of speeding up the all of the kernels is to compile with a higher optimization level, such as –fast, which results in

```
Time (%)  Total Time (ns)           Name
--------  ---------------   ------------------------
    39.8        1,166,600   kernel_m_base_
    34.2        1,003,431   kernel_m_math_
    18.6          545,380   kernel_m_memory_
     7.5          219,393   __pgi_dev_cumemset_16n
```

Here the execution time for the base() and math() kernels has been reduced by 25% and 22%, respectively, whereas the memory() kernel execution time is roughly the same. The reason for the improved performance is that when compiling with –fast single call, the sincosf() routine is used to calculate both the sin() and cos(). This can be verified by inspecting the generated .gpu file obtained from compiling with –gpu=keep, which contains lines similar to

```
call void @__nv_sincosf(float %li20, float* %li21_sin, float* %li21_cos)
```

Another optimization that can be applied to this code is the use of the fast math intrinsics, __sinf() and __cosf(), contained in the cudadevice module. These fast versions for single-precision arguments sacrifice some accuracy for speed, so the user will need to check whether the reduction in accuracy is acceptable. To make use of this optimization, we can either modify the source code to explicitly use the __sinf() and __cosf() functions or compile with the –gpu=fastmath option. The use of the fast math functions can also be verified by inspecting the .gpu file generated from the –gpu=keep compiler option, which will contain lines similar to

```
%li35 = call float @__nv_fast_sinf(float %li33)
```

The profile when using the fast math functions is

```
Time (%)  Total Time (ns)           Name
--------  ---------------   ------------------------
    33.4          620,613   kernel_m_base_
    29.3          545,124   kernel_m_memory_
    25.5          473,860   kernel_m_math_
    11.8          218,657   __pgi_dev_cumemset_16n
```

Relative to results when compiled without any optimization, the math() kernel here runs in 37% of the time, and the base() kernel runs in 40% of the time. The math() kernel now takes less time than the memory kernel.

Combining both –fast and –gpu=fastmath options, which generates code that uses the fast version of sincos() in the .gpu file

```
call void @__nv_fast_sincosf(float %li20, float* %li21_sin,
                                          float* %li21_cos)
```

we get

```
Time (%)   Total Time (ns)              Name
--------   ---------------   -----------------------
    33.3           617,285   kernel_m_base_
    29.4           545,283   kernel_m_memory_
    25.5           471,811   kernel_m_math_
    11.7           217,185   __pgi_dev_cumemset_16n
```

which is basically the same performance as the version compiled with just -gpu=fastmath. At this point, further performance gains will come from optimizing device memory access, if possible.

Deciding whether or not we can improve memory accesses motivates the next section on memory bandwidth. However, before we jump into bandwidth metrics, we need to tie up some loose ends regarding this technique of modifying source code to determine the limiting factor of a kernel. When there is very little overlap of math and memory operations, a kernel is likely latency bound. This often occurs when the occupancy is low; there simply are not enough threads on the device at one time for any overlap of operations. The remedy for this can often be a modification to the execution configuration.

3.3 Memory bandwidth

Returning to the example code in Section 3.2, we are left with a memory bound kernel after using the fast math intrinsics to reduce time spent on evaluation of sin() and cos(). At this stage, we ask how well is the memory system used and whether there is room for improvement. To answer this question, we need to calculate the memory bandwidth.

Bandwidth – the rate at which data can be transferred – is one of the most important gating factors for performance. Almost all changes to code should be made in the context of how they affect bandwidth. Bandwidth can be dramatically affected by the choice of memory in which data is stored, how the data is laid out and the order in which it is accessed, as well as other factors.

When evaluating memory efficiency, both the theoretical peak memory bandwidth and the observed or effective memory bandwidth are used. When a code is memory bound and the effective bandwidth is much lower than the peak bandwidth, optimization efforts should focus on increasing the effective bandwidth.

3.3.1 Theoretical peak bandwidth

The theoretical peak memory bandwidth can be calculated from the memory clock and the memory bus width. Both these quantities can be queried through the device management API, as illustrated in the following code that calculates the theoretical peak bandwidth for all attached devices:

```
1  program peakBandwidth
2    use cudafor
3    implicit none
```

```
 4
 5     integer :: i, istat, nDevices=0
 6     type (cudaDeviceProp) :: prop
 7
 8     istat = cudaGetDeviceCount(nDevices)
 9     do i = 0, nDevices-1
10        istat = cudaGetDeviceProperties(prop, i)
11        print "(' Device Number: ',i0)", i
12        print "('    Device name: ',a)", trim(prop%name)
13        print "('    Memory Clock Rate (KHz): ', i0)", &
14              prop%memoryClockRate
15        print "('    Memory Bus Width (bits): ', i0)", &
16              prop%memoryBusWidth
17        print "('    Peak Memory Bandwidth (GB/s): ', f9.2)", &
18              2.0 * prop%memoryClockRate * &
19              (prop%memoryBusWidth / 8) * 1.e-6
20        print *
21     enddo
22  end program peakBandwidth
```

In the peak memory bandwidth calculation, the factor of `2.0` appears due to the double data rate of the RAM per memory clock cycle, the division by eight converts the bus width from bits to bytes, and the factor of `1.e-6` handles the kilohertz-to-hertz and byte-to-gigabyte conversions. (Note that some calculations use $1,024^3$ instead of $1,000^3$ for the byte-to-gigabyte conversion. Whichever factor you use, it is important to use the same factor when calculating theoretical and effective bandwidth so that the comparison is valid.)

Running this code on a variety of hardware we obtain

```
Device Number: 0
 Device name: H100 80GB HBM3
 Memory Clock Rate (KHz): 2619000
 Memory Bus Width (bits): 5120
 Peak Memory Bandwidth (GB/s):    3352.32
```

```
Device Number: 0
 Device name: NVIDIA A100 80GB PCIe
 Memory Clock Rate (KHz): 1512000
 Memory Bus Width (bits): 5120
 Peak Memory Bandwidth (GB/s):    1935.36
```

```
Device Number: 0
 Device name: NVIDIA A100-PCIE-40GB
 Memory Clock Rate (KHz): 1215000
 Memory Bus Width (bits): 5120
 Peak Memory Bandwidth (GB/s):    1555.20
```

```
Device Number: 0
 Device name: NVIDIA T4 32GB
 Memory Clock Rate (KHz): 6401000
```

```
Memory Bus Width (bits): 256
Peak Memory Bandwidth (GB/s):     409.66
```

```
Device Number: 0
 Device name: Tesla V100-PCIE-32GB
 Memory Clock Rate (KHz): 877000
 Memory Bus Width (bits): 4096
 Peak Memory Bandwidth (GB/s):     898.05
```

```
Device Number: 0
 Device name: Tesla V100-PCIE-16GB
 Memory Clock Rate (KHz): 877000
 Memory Bus Width (bits): 4096
 Peak Memory Bandwidth (GB/s):     898.05
```

```
Device Number: 0
 Device name: Tesla P100-PCIE-16GB
 Memory Clock Rate (KHz): 715000
 Memory Bus Width (bits): 4096
 Peak Memory Bandwidth (GB/s):     732.16
```

```
Device Number: 0
 Device name: Tesla M40
 Memory Clock Rate (KHz): 3004000
 Memory Bus Width (bits): 384
 Peak Memory Bandwidth (GB/s):     288.38
```

These calculations do not account for the effect of error-correcting code (ECC) on peak bandwidth. For devices with high bandwidth memory (HBM), such as the P100, V100, A100, and H100, there is native support for ECC without any reduction in bandwidth or memory capacity. Devices such as the M40 and T4 use GDDR memory, which does not have internal ECC protection, and, as a result, not only is the available amount of memory reduced due to storage of the ECC bits, but accessing these bits causes a reduction in memory bandwidth.

3.3.2 Effective bandwidth

Effective bandwidth is calculated by timing specific program activities and by knowing how data is accessed by the program. To do so, use the equation

$$BW_{\text{Effective}} = \frac{(R_B + W_B)/10^9}{t},$$

where $BW_{\text{Effective}}$ is the effective bandwidth in units of GB/s, R_B is the number of bytes read per kernel, W_B is the number of bytes written per kernel, and t is the elapsed time given in seconds.

It is helpful to obtain the effective bandwidth for a simple copy kernel on a variety of devices, as does the following code:

```fortran
module m
  use, intrinsic :: iso_fortran_env
  integer, parameter :: fpKind = real64
contains
  attributes(global) subroutine copy(lhs, rhs, n)
    implicit none
    real(fpKind) :: lhs(*)
    real(fpKind) :: rhs(*)
    integer, value :: n
    integer :: i
    i = blockDim%x * (blockIdx%x - 1) + threadIdx%x
    if (i <= n) lhs(i) = rhs(i)
  end subroutine copy
end module m


program stream
  use cudafor
  use m
  implicit none
  integer, parameter :: N = 32*1024*1024
  real(fpKind), device :: a_d(N), b_d(N)
  integer :: nBlocks, blockSize
  real :: time
  integer(8) :: nBytes
  type(cudaEvent) :: startEvent, stopEvent
  integer :: istat

  istat = cudaEventCreate(startEvent)
  istat = cudaEventCreate(stopEvent)

  blockSize = 256
  nBlocks = (N-1)/blockSize+1
  nBytes = 2 * sizeof(a_d)

  b_d = 1.0_fpKind
  istat = cudaDeviceSynchronize()
  istat = cudaEventRecord(startEvent, 0)
  call copy<<<nBlocks, blockSize>>>(a_d, b_d, N)
  istat = cudaEventRecord(stopEvent, 0)
  istat = cudaEventSynchronize(stopEvent)
  istat = cudaEventElapsedTime(time, startEvent, stopEvent)

  block
    type(cudaDeviceProp) :: prop
    istat = cudaGetDeviceProperties(prop, 0)
    print "(A)", trim(prop%name)
  end block
  if (fpKind == real64) print "('real64')"
  if (fpKind == real32) print "('real32')"
  print "('Array size (bytes): ', i0)", sizeof(a_d)
  print "('Copy effective bandwidth: ', f10.1)", &
```

```
53              nBytes/time/1.0E+6
54
55    end program stream
```

The number of bytes transferred is determined using the sizeof() function on the input array a_d and is multiplied by two because of the read and the write. The cudaEventElapsedTime() function returns in the first argument the elapsed time in milliseconds, and the conversion from milliseconds to seconds and bytes to gigabytes results in the factor of 10^6.

The measured effective bandwidth is dependent on many factors, such as the array size, precision or word size, and the execution configuration, just to name a few. We will go into how these factors affect performance later; for now, we just pick "reasonable" values. Here are some results for a variety of GPUs:

```
NVIDIA A100 80GB PCIe
real64
Array size (bytes): 268435456
Copy effective bandwidth:      1618.2
```

```
NVIDIA A100-PCIE-40GB
real64
Array size (bytes): 268435456
Copy effective bandwidth:      1310.7
```

```
Tesla V100-PCIE-32GB
real64
Array size (bytes): 268435456
Copy effective bandwidth:       793.0
```

```
Tesla P100-PCIE-16GB
real64
Array size (bytes): 268435456
Copy effective bandwidth:       536.2
```

3.3.3 Actual data throughput vs. effective bandwidth

It is possible to estimate the data throughput using the profiler counters. We must be cautious when comparing such calculated throughput to values obtained from the effective bandwidth calculation described above. One difference is that the profiler measures transactions using a subset of the GPU's multiprocessors and then extrapolates that number to the entire GPU, thus reporting an estimate of the data throughput.

Another distinction to be aware of is whether the counters used represent the actual data throughput or the requested data throughput. This distinction is important because the minimum memory transaction size is larger than most word sizes, and, as a result, the actual data transfer throughput will be equal to or larger than that of requested data throughput. The effective bandwidth is calculated based on the data relevant to the algorithm and therefore corresponds to the requested data throughput. Both actual and requested data throughput values are useful. The actual data throughput shows how close the code is to reaching the hardware limit, and the comparison of the effective bandwidth with the actual throughput indicates how much bandwidth is wasted by suboptimal memory access patterns.

The difference between actual data throughput and effective bandwidth is not an issue in the example codes used thus far, as all of the data accesses have been using contiguous data. However, when we access memory in a strided fashion, which we will explore in Chapter 5, the values for actual data throughput and effective bandwidth can diverge.

actual and requested data throughput values are useful. The actual data throughput shows how close the code is to reaching the hardware limit, and the comparison of the effective bandwidth with the actual throughput indicates how much bandwidth is wasted by suboptimal memory access patterns.

The difference between actual data throughput and effective bandwidth is not an issue in the example codes used thus far, as all of the data accesses have been using contiguous data. However, when we access memory in a strided fashion, which we will explore in Chapter 5, the values for actual data throughput and effective bandwidth can diverge.

Synchronization

4

In parallel programming, we want to have as many operations as possible executing simultaneously. The parallelism is built into the CUDA programming model by launching kernels with many independent threads. There are occasions, however, where operations are not completely independent: certain operations must complete before others can start, and sometimes it is advantageous to share data between otherwise independent operations. For such cases, we need to have mechanisms to synchronize between parallel efforts. This chapter covers CUDA Fortran language features related to synchronization in two main sections. The first main section is basically a macroscopic view, which deals with synchronization between the host thread, kernels, and data transfers between the host and device. We have already discussed some aspects of host–device synchronization, but in this section, we introduce the concept of *streams*, implicit synchronization that occurs with streams, and the various API calls that enforce synchronization. The second main section of this chapter covers synchronization between device threads running within a kernel, including barrier synchronizations, memory fences, and the cooperative groups feature introduced in the CUDA 9.0 Toolkit. This chapter focuses primarily on the language features and the related programming model concepts; how these features are used to optimize code will be discussed in Chapter 5.

4.1 Synchronization of kernel execution and data transfers

Before we delve into synchronization between the host thread and operations on the device, we need to discuss a few prerequisite topics such as pinned host memory and streams.

4.1.1 Pageable versus pinned host memory

Data transfers between the host and device can be a source of parallelism in CUDA Fortran. We can overlap such data transfers with computation on the host and execution of kernels on the device, and even with other host–device data transfers. We also need synchronization mechanisms to ensure that some or all of such data transfers have completed before other operations can commence, for example, launching a kernel that uses the data transferred. The ability to parallelize data transfers between the host and device with other operations, and the implicit synchronization of such operations, depends in part whether the host memory involved in the transfer is pageable or pinned memory.

When memory is allocated for variables that reside on the host, pageable memory is used by default. Pageable memory can be swapped out to disk to allow the program to use more memory in the code than is available in RAM on the host system. When data is transferred between the host and device, the direct memory access (DMA) engine on the GPU must target page-locked or *pinned* host memory.

CUDA Fortran for Scientists and Engineers. https://doi.org/10.1016/B978-0-44-321977-1.00013-9

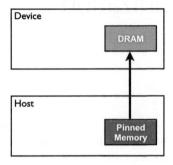

FIGURE 4.1

Depiction of host-to-device data transfer from pageable host memory (left) and pinned host memory (right). For pageable host memory, data is transferred to a temporary pinned memory buffer on the host before being transferred to the device. By using pinned memory from the outset, as on the right, the extra host data copy is eliminated.

Pinned memory cannot be swapped out and is therefore always available for such transfers. To accommodate data transfers from pageable host memory to the GPU, the host operating system first allocates a temporary pinned host buffer, copies the data to the pinned buffer, and then transfers the data to the device, as illustrated in Fig. 4.1. The pinned memory buffer may be smaller than the pageable memory holding the host data, in which case the transfer occurs in multiple stages. Pinned memory buffers are similarly used with transfers from the device to the host. The cost of the transfer between pageable memory and pinned host buffer can be avoided if we declare the host arrays to use pinned memory.

In CUDA Fortran, the use of pinned memory is denoted using the pinned variable qualifier, and such memory must be allocatable. It is possible for the allocate statement to fail to allocate pinned memory, in which case a pageable memory allocation will be attempted. The following code fragment demonstrates the declaration and allocation of pinned memory with error checking:

```
integer :: n, istat
logical :: pinnedFlag
real, allocatable, pinned :: a_h(:)
...
allocate(a_h(n), STAT = istat, PINNED = pinnedFlag)
if (istat /= 0) print *, 'Allocation of a_h failed'
if (.not. pinnedFlag) &
  print *, 'Pinned allocation of a_h failed'
```

We can verify whether pinned host memory was used in a transfer between host and device by profiling the application and generating a GPU trace report with nsys stats --report cuda_gpu_trace, which will list all data transfers and kernel executions. In the output of the report, the source and destination memory kind columns, SrcMemKnd and DstMemKnd, respectively, will display either Pageable or Pinned for the host memory, as in the abridged output below:

```
SrcMemKd   DstMemKd            Name
--------   --------    ------------------
Pageable   Device      [CUDA memcpy HtoD]
Device     Pageable    [CUDA memcpy DtoH]
Pinned     Device      [CUDA memcpy HtoD]
Device     Pinned      [CUDA memcpy DtoH]
```

Transfers between the host and device will not only differ in performance depending on whether the host memory involved is pinned or pageable (which will be discussed in detail in Section 5.1.1), but also will have different synchronization characteristics, as we will see further.

4.1.2 Streams

A stream is simply a sequence of operations that are performed in order on the device. Every operation that involves the device occurs in a stream, including kernels, data transfers between host and device, and Fortran intrinsics such as sum() and maxval(), which have been extended to operate on device data. Operations in different streams can be interleaved and in some cases overlapped.

Up to this point, all of the code we have discussed uses the null stream by default. For example, the sequence of commands

```
a_d = a_h
call kernel<<<gridSize,blockSize>>>(a_d)
a_h = a_d
```

where a_d and a_h are device and host variables, respectively, occurs sequentially in the null stream on the device. From the perspective of the device, the kernel on the second line will not commence until the host-to-device transfer on the first line is complete, and the device-to-host transfer on the third line will not start until the kernel completes. From the perspective of host, the situation is slightly more complicated depending on whether the host memory involved in the transfer is pageable or pinned. If the host data a_h are in pinned or page-locked memory, then the host-to-device data transfer on the first line will complete before control is returned to the CPU. If, on the other hand, the host data are in pageable memory, then control returns to the CPU after the copy from pageable memory to the pinned buffer completes. In that case the call statement for the kernel launch could be issued before the host-to-device transfer completes. In addition, kernel launches are asynchronous with respect to the host, so control returns to the CPU immediately after the kernel launch is issued. The device-to-host transfer on the following line will return control to the CPU only after the transfer completes, whether the host array is pinned or pageable. In any case, on the device, we are ensured of sequential execution since transfers and kernel execution occur in the same stream.

4.1.2.1 Creating streams

We can create different work queues by creating streams and issuing tasks to the streams. A stream can be created with the function cudaStreamCreate(), which takes a single argument, an integer of kind cuda_stream_kind, in which an identifier for the created stream is returned. A stream created with cudaStreamCreate() is a *blocking* stream. Blocking streams are synchronized with the null stream: operations issued into the null stream will not commence until all previously issued activity in all blocking streams has completed, and no operation in any blocking stream will commence until all previously issued activity in the null stream finishes. (We will discuss non-blocking streams later in Section 4.1.5.2.)

Streams can be destroyed by calling the routine cudaStreamDestroy(), which takes as its single argument an integer of kind cuda_stream_kind, similar to cudaStreamCreate().

Kernels can by issued into a particular stream by specifying the stream in the execution configuration. Aside from the gridsize and blocksize, there are two optional parameters in the execution configuration, the third parameter is the amount of dynamic shared memory (which will be discussed in Section 4.2.1), and the fourth parameter is the stream. To specify a stream if dynamic shared memory is not needed, we can either specify the default value 0 for the third execution parameter:

```
call kernel<<<gridSize,blockSize,0,stream1 >>>(a_d)
```

or use the keyword stream

```
call kernel<<<gridSize,blockSize,stream=stream1 >>>(a_d)
```

similar to how optional arguments can be specified. This applies to all kernel invocations including CUF kernels.

The following code exhibits the implicit synchronization behavior of kernels submitted to streams created by cudaStreamCreate():

```
1   program twoKernels
2     use cudafor
3     implicit none
4     integer, parameter :: n=100000
5     real, device :: a_d(n,2)
6     real :: a(n,2)
7     integer(kind=cuda_stream_kind) :: stream1, stream2
8     integer :: istat, i
9
10    istat = cudaStreamCreate(stream1)
11    istat = cudaStreamCreate(stream2)
12    a = 1.0
13
14    ! two kernels in the null stream
15
16    a_d = a
17    !$cuf kernel do <<<1,1>>>
18    do i = 1, n
19       a_d(i,1) = a_d(i,1) + i
20    enddo
21    !$cuf kernel do <<<1,1>>>
22    do i = 1, n
23       a_d(i,2) = a_d(i,2) - i
24    enddo
25    a = a_d
26
27    ! one kernel in blocking stream, one in null stream
28
29    a_d = a
30    !$cuf kernel do <<<1,1,stream=stream1 >>>
```

```
31    do i = 1, n
32       a_d(i,1) = a_d(i,1) + i
33    enddo
34    !$cuf kernel do <<<1,1>>>
35    do i = 1, n
36       a_d(i,2) = a_d(i,2) - i
37    enddo
38    a = a_d
39
40    ! two kernels in different, blocking streams
41
42    a_d = a
43    !$cuf kernel do <<<1,1,stream=stream1>>>
44    do i = 1, n
45       a_d(i,1) = a_d(i,1) + i
46    enddo
47    !$cuf kernel do <<<1,1,stream=stream2>>>
48    do i = 1, n
49       a_d(i,2) = a_d(i,2) - i
50    enddo
51    a = a_d
52
53    istat = cudaStreamDestroy(stream1)
54    istat = cudaStreamDestroy(stream2)
55 end program twoKernels
```

Here two different CUF kernels operate on different slices of the same device array. We execute the pair of kernels three different times with different execution configurations. The execution configurations differ here only in the stream that is specified (or not specified). Each kernel launches a single thread to perform all the work – while this is a poor choice in general for such an embarrassingly parallel code, here our goal is to see the overlap of operations on the device. A timeline of the code executed is shown in Fig. 4.2. Here the activity on the device is broken down into streams. The stream enumeration displayed in the profiler timeline differs from what is specified in the code. The first row, labeled `Default stream 7`, corresponds to the null stream, and our two streams created by `cudaStreamCreate()` are `Stream 13` and `Stream 14`. The CUF kernels are labeled with the program name, twoKernels in this case, followed by the line number of the first statement of the CUF kernel, and then "gpu". The host-to-device and device-to-host data transfers are shown by the small, unlabeled sections on the timeline. In the first of three pairs of kernel launches, both kernels are executed in the null stream, and we see that the host-to-device transfer, both kernels, and device-to-host transfer occur consecutively in the same stream. In the second pair of kernel launches, the first CUF kernel is sub-

FIGURE 4.2

Timeline of the twoKernels code showing the synchronization behavior of streams created with `cudaStreamCreate()`. No activity in the null stream (shown here as Default stream 7), including data transfers, can overlap operations in blocking streams. Kernels can overlap if submitted to different, non-null streams.

mitted to stream1. Even though submitted to a different stream, the execution is still sequential due to the synchronization behavior of the null stream with blocking streams: operations issued into the null stream will not commence until all previously issued activity in all blocking streams has completed, and no operation in any blocking stream will commence until all previously issued activity in the null stream finishes. The kernel on line 31 will not begin until the host-to-device on line 29 completes, and the kernel submitted to the null stream on line 35 will not begin until the previous kernel completes. Kernels can overlap when submitted to different, non-null streams. The transfers between host and device still occur in the null stream, and with it still have the synchronization behavior associated with the null stream. This implicit synchronization is beneficial in that it reflects the dependency of the operations: the host-to-device transfer needs to complete before the kernels can begin execution, and the kernels need to finish before the device-to-host transfer can start. But just as we have multiple kernels that operate on different sections of the array, we might also like to have multiple transfers in multiple streams rather than a single monolithic data transfer in each direction. This brings us to our next section.

4.1.3 Asynchronous transfers via cudaMemcpyAsync()

The ability to transfer data between the host and device via assignments statements is very convenient but can be restrictive in terms of having operations overlap. Performing data transfers through the cudaMemcpyAsync() function can allow us to achieve overlap in several ways. This function is most commonly called with four arguments, destination, source, size of the transfer, and stream. An additional optional argument can specify the direction of transfer, but this can be inferred from the type just as the direction is inferred for transfers via assignment statements. The size of transfer is in number of elements, unless the destination and source arguments are instances of type(c_ptr) or type(c_devptr), in which case the size of transfer is in bytes.

The Async in cudaMemcpyAsync() means that the operation is non-blocking with respect to the host: control is returned to the host thread. Therefore we can overlap the data transfer with other activity on the host quite easily, as depicted in the following code snippet:

```
istat = cudaMemcpyAsync(a_d, a, n, 0)
call kernel<<<gridSize,blockSize>>>(a_d)
call cpuRoutine(b)
```

The kernel will not begin execution until the data transfer completes, but because the data transfer and the kernel both return control to the host immediately, the host subroutine cpuRoutine() can overlap their execution.

We can achieve overlap between data transfers and computation on the device by using non-null streams for all data transfers and kernel launches. Additionally, to achieve overlap on the device cudaMemcpyAsync() *requires pinned host memory*. An example code below exhibits such overlap:

```
1   program pipeline
2     use cudafor
3     implicit none
4     integer, parameter :: n=100000
5     integer, parameter :: nStreams=6
6     real, device :: a_d(n,nStreams)
7     real, pinned, allocatable :: a(:,:)
8     integer(kind=cuda_stream_kind) :: streams(nStreams)
```

```
9     integer :: istat, i, j
10
11    do j = 1, nStreams
12       istat = cudaStreamCreate(streams(j))
13    enddo
14
15    allocate(a(n,nStreams))
16    a = 1.0
17
18    do j = 1, nStreams
19       istat = cudaMemcpyAsync(a_d(1,j), a(1,j), n, streams(j))
20       !$cuf kernel do <<<1,1,stream=streams(j)>>>
21       do i = 1, n
22          a_d(i,j) = a_d(i,j) + 1.0
23       enddo
24       istat = cudaMemcpyAsync(a(1,j), a_d(1,j), n, streams(j))
25    enddo
26
27    istat = cudaDeviceSynchronize()
28    if (all(a == 2.0)) print *, 'OK'
29
30    do j = 1, nStreams
31       istat = cudaStreamDestroy(streams(j))
32    enddo
33 end program pipeline
```

After creating the streams on lines 11–13 and allocating and initializing the pinned host array on lines 15 and 16, the loop on line 18 initiates host-to-device transfers, kernels, and device-to-host transfers involving one-dimensional slices of a two-dimensional array. Because the loop index j corresponding to the stream index in the streams array is also used to designate the slices in the two-dimensional array, each iteration of the loop results in the transfers and kernels operating on a single slice in a particular stream. Within a stream, the operations occur in the order submitted, but across streams, the operations are free to overlap as seen from the timeline generated from this code in Fig. 4.3. Because all kernel launches and cudaMemcpyAsync() calls are asynchronous, i.e., they return control to the host thread immediately, this entire loop can finish before the activity in any stream has completed. For this reason, we need the synchronization barrier cudaDeviceSynchronize(), which waits for all previously issued activity on the device to complete before returning control to the CPU, where the result is checked for correctness on the host. Note that on line 7 the host array is declared with the pinned attribute, which is

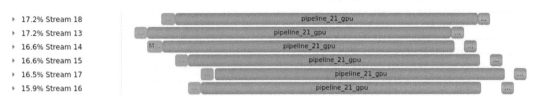

FIGURE 4.3

Timeline of the pipeline code showing overlap between data transfers and kernel execution.

necessary to achieve this overlap. If you were to remove the `pinned` attribute, then the operations would occur in the same streams as depicted in Fig. 4.3, but there would be no overlap between streams.

The routine `cudaMemcpyAsync()` is just one of many runtime routines in the `cudafor` module that perform data transfers. There are synchronous versions, e.g., `cudaMemcpy()`, which behaves similarly to transfers via assignment statements, versions for transfers between multiple devices (`cudaMemcpyPeer()` and `cudaMemcpyPeerAsync()`), version for handling slices in multidimensional arrays (`cudaMemcpy2D()` and `cudaMemcpy2DAsync()`), and many others. In terms of synchronization, all the `Async` versions will behave similarly to what we have seen with `cudaMemcpyAsync()` in this section.

4.1.4 **Synchronization barriers**

Up to this point, we have focused on eliminating unwanted synchronization so that multiple operations on the device can overlap with each other and with other operations on the host. In this section, we discuss host runtime routines that force synchronization. We have seen one such synchronization barrier already, `cudaDeviceSynchronize()`.

4.1.4.1 *cudaDeviceSynchronize()*

In the `pipeline` code above, all transfers and kernels execute asynchronously with the host. Although this is beneficial in terms of achieving overlapping operations, it poses an issue when we want to check the results on the host. How do we ensure that all activity submitted to the streams have completed? The answer is to use `cudaDeviceSynchronize()`. The function `cudaDeviceSynchronize()` will block host code execution until all *previously issued* (rather than *currently executing*) operations involving the device have completed. This applies to any operation issued to the device in any stream, which is exactly what we want in the `pipeline` code. Although ideal for the `pipeline` code, there are other, less severe, synchronization barriers available to the programmer.

4.1.4.2 *cudaStreamSynchronize()*

In asynchronous code, there are occasions where we must ensure that tasks in a particular stream complete before some activity in a different stream commences. This can be accomplished through the `cudaStreamSynchronize()` function. An example of `cudaStreamSynchronize()` use is below:

```
1    program streamSync
2      use cudafor
3      implicit none
4      integer, parameter :: n=100000
5      real, device :: a_d(n), b_d(n), c_d(n)
6      integer(kind=cuda_stream_kind) :: stream1, stream2, stream3
7      integer :: istat, i, j
8
9      istat = cudaStreamCreate(stream1)
10     istat = cudaStreamCreate(stream2)
11     istat = cudaStreamCreate(stream3)
12
13     !$cuf kernel do <<<1,1,stream=stream1>>>
14     do i = 1, n
15        a_d(i) = i
```

```
16    enddo
17
18    !$cuf kernel do <<<1,1,stream=stream2>>>
19    do i = 1, n
20       b_d(i) = i
21    enddo
22
23    !$cuf kernel do <<<1,1,stream=stream3>>>
24    do i = 1, n
25       c_d(i) = 1.0/i
26    enddo
27
28    istat = cudaStreamSynchronize(stream1)
29
30    !$cuf kernel do <<<1,1,stream=stream2>>>
31    do i = 1, n
32       a_d(i) = a_d(i) + b_d(i)
33    enddo
34
35    istat = cudaStreamDestroy(stream1)
36    istat = cudaStreamDestroy(stream2)
37    istat = cudaStreamDestroy(stream3)
38 end program streamSync
```

In this code, three CUF kernels starting on lines 14, 19, and 24 are issued to three streams. A fourth CUF kernel on line 31 is dependent on the data in the first two CUF kernels. Launching the fourth kernel in, say, stream2 will ensure that the second kernel has finished before the fourth commences, but a synchronization barrier is needed to ensure the first kernel has completed. We could use cudaDeviceSynchronize(), but that would require waiting for the third kernel to complete, which we suspect will take longer than the others. On line 28 the cudaStreamSynchronize() function ensures that actions previously submitted in the specified stream, in this case the first kernel, have completed before returning control to the CPU. As a result, we get the timeline in Fig. 4.4, which exhibits optimum overlap for this scenario. We should point out that we do not need any synchronization barrier before invoking cudaStreamDestroy(). A synchronization barrier is not needed because when cudaStreamDestroy() is called, the function will return immediately, and resources associated with the stream will be released once all work in that stream is completed.

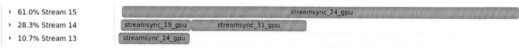

FIGURE 4.4

Timeline of the streamSync code showing how cudaStreamSynchronize() can be used to wait on completion of tasks in the specified stream while allowing work in other streams to continue.

4.1.4.3 cudaEventSynchronize()

In Section 3.1.2, we discussed using CUDA events to measure execution time on the device by inserting CUDA events into a stream using cudaEventRecord(), waiting for the events to be reached in the stream via cudaEventSynchronize(), and then finding the elapsed time between events using cudaEventElapsedTime(). The event mechanism can ensure operations in a stream issued prior to the event being recorded complete before issuing commands from the host. This is useful when multiple operations are issued to a stream and you do not want to block execution with a stream synchronization call, but need to ensure that particular tasks in a stream have completed. An example of stream synchronization is below:

```
1   program eventSync
2     use cudafor
3     implicit none
4     integer, parameter :: n=100000
5     real, device :: a_d(n), b_d(n), c_d(n)
6     integer(kind=cuda_stream_kind) :: stream1, stream2
7     type(cudaEvent) :: event1
8     integer :: istat, i, j
9
10    istat = cudaStreamCreate(stream1)
11    istat = cudaStreamCreate(stream2)
12    istat = cudaEventCreate(event1)
13
14    !$cuf kernel do <<<1,1,stream=stream1>>>
15    do i = 1, n
16       a_d(i) = i
17    enddo
18
19    istat = cudaEventRecord(event1, stream1)
20
21    !$cuf kernel do <<<1,1,stream=stream1>>>
22    do i = 1, n
23       b_d(i) = a_d(i) + 1.0
24    enddo
25
26    istat = cudaEventSynchronize(event1)
27
28    !$cuf kernel do <<<1,1,stream=stream2>>>
29    do i = 1, n
30       c_d(i) = a_d(i) + 2.0
31    enddo
32
33    istat = cudaStreamDestroy(stream1)
34    istat = cudaStreamDestroy(stream2)
35    istat = cudaEventDestroy(event1)
36  end program eventSync
```

In this code the array a_d is initialized in the CUF kernel starting on line 15 and is subsequently used in two other kernels. The second kernel on line 22 is enqueued in the same stream as the first one, and the third kernel on line 29 is submitted to a different stream. To ensure that the first kernel completes before the third kernel commences, an event is inserted after the first kernel into stream1 with cudaEventRecord() on line 19, and the host waits execution in stream1 to reach that event with cudaEventSynchronize() on line 26. The timeline for this code is shown in Fig. 4.5.

FIGURE 4.5

Timeline of the eventSync code showing how cudaEventSynchronize() can be used to wait on completion of certain tasks in the specified stream while allowing work in the specified stream (and other streams) to continue.

If cudaEventSynchronize() is called with an event that was not previously given as an argument to cudaEventRecord(), then the function will return a value of cudaErrorInvalidValue. Note that unlike streams, events are not integers but instances of the derived type cudaEvent. However, similar to streams, they are created and destroyed with calls cudaEventCreate() and cudaEventDestroy().

4.1.4.4 *Querying streams and events*

When the host calls cudaStreamSynchronize() or cudaEventSynchronize() functions, execution of the host thread is blocked until the stream has completed previously enqueued tasks or the event has been recorded, respectively. We can query the status without blocking the host thread by using the cudaStreamQuery() and cudaEventQuery() functions. These functions will return cudaSuccess if all operations in the stream have completed or the event has been recorded. The return value will be cudaErrorNotReady otherwise, except that cudaErrorInvalidValue can be returned from cudaEventQuery() if no cudaEventRecord() has been called for the specified event.

4.1.5 **Advanced stream topics**

Using the approaches described thus far, we can write code where data transfers and kernels overlap to the greatest degree possible. For many, the advanced topics discussed in this section are not necessary, or even desirable, to write well-performing code. We include the following sections to ensure programmers are aware of the tools available to them.

4.1.5.1 *The default stream*

Data transfers and kernels will execute in the null stream unless we specify a different stream as an argument to cudaMemcpyAsync() or as an execution parameter in kernel launches. We can change which stream gets used by default for kernel launches, and in some cases which stream is used for data transfers between host and device, by calling cudaforSetDefaultStream().

The devptr argument to cudaforSetDefaultStream(devptr, stream) is an optional argument that can be a managed or device variable. We give examples of cudaforSetDefaultStream() with and without the optional devptr below.

When cudaforSetDefaultStream() is called with a single stream argument, the specified stream is used by that host thread by default for all subsequent kernel launches and reduction operations such as maxval() that have been overloaded to accommodate device data. For allocatable device or managed variables, the variable is associated with the default stream at the time the variable is allocated, resulting in implicit data transfer and memset operations via assignment statements occurring in that stream. The following code illustrates these concepts:

```
1   program defaultStream
2     use cudafor
3     implicit none
4     integer, parameter :: n=100000
5     real, device, allocatable :: a_d(:), b_d(:)
6     real :: a(n), b(n)
7     integer(kind=cuda_stream_kind) :: stream1
8     integer :: istat, i
9
10    istat = cudaStreamCreate(stream1)
11
12    allocate(a_d(n))
13    a_d = 1.0
14    !$cuf kernel do <<<1,1>>>
15    do i = 1, n
16       a_d(i) = a_d(i) + i
17    enddo
18    a = a_d
19    print *, maxval(a_d)
20
21    istat = cudaforSetDefaultStream(stream1)
22    allocate(b_d(n))
23
24    a_d = 2.0
25    !$cuf kernel do <<<1,1>>>
26    do i = 1, n
27       a_d(i) = a_d(i) + i
28    enddo
29    a = a_d
30    print *, maxval(a_d)
31
32    b_d = 3.0
33    !$cuf kernel do <<<1,1>>>
34    do i = 1, n
35       b_d(i) = b_d(i) + i
36    enddo
37    b = b_d
38    print *, maxval(b_d)
39
40    istat = cudaStreamDestroy(stream1)
41    deallocate(a_d, b_d)
42  end program defaultStream
```

A GPU trace of the code shows the following events and the streams in which they occur:

```
1   Stream   Name
2        7   __pgi_dev_cumemset_16n [328]
3        7   defaultstream_15_gpu [333]
4        7   [CUDA memcpy DtoH]
5        7   cudafor_lib_internals_partialmxvshflshflr4_ [339]
6        7   [CUDA memcpy DtoH]
7        7   __pgi_dev_cumemset_16n [344]
```

```
8     16   defaultstream_26_gpu [348]
9      7   [CUDA memcpy DtoH]
10    16   cudafor_lib_internals_partialmxvshflshflr4_ [351]
11    16   [CUDA memcpy DtoH]
12    16   __pgi_dev_cumemset_16n [355]
13    16   defaultstream_34_gpu [359]
14    16   [CUDA memcpy DtoH]
15    16   cudafor_lib_internals_partialmxvshflshflr4_ [362]
16    16   [CUDA memcpy DtoH]
```

The stream created on line 10 in the code corresponds to stream 16 in the GPU trace output. The operations involving a_d on lines 13–19 of the code are reflected in lines 2–6 of the GPU trace: the memset operation, kernel launch, device-to-host transfer, and reduction. Note that the reduction on line 19 of the code results in two lines in the trace, a kernel on line 5, and the subsequent device-to-host transfer on line 6. All of these occur in the null stream (stream 7 in the profiling output) since no prior call to cudaforSetDefaultStream() has been made. On line 21, cudaforSetDefaultStream() is called, and then the array b_d is allocated. After setting the default stream and allocating b_d, the operations from lines 13–19 are repeated on lines 24–30 using the array a_d again, followed by the same operations using b_d on lines 32–38. The memset from line 24 and the device-to-host transfer on line 29 of the code still occur in the null stream (lines 7 and 9 in the GPU trace) because the variable a_d gets associated with the stream that is the default stream when a_d is allocated. The CUF kernel on line 26 and the reduction on line 30 of the code happen in the stream that is the default stream at the time these operations are launched, which is stream 16 in the GPU trace (lines 8 and 10–11 of the trace output). For the operations on lines 32–38 of the code, everything occurs in stream 16 in the GPU trace.

When calling cudaforSetDefaultStream() with the optional devptr argument, subsequent memset and memcopy operations on the managed or device variable will occur in that stream *if the variable is allocatable*. The following code shows what occurs when both statically declared (a_d) and allocatable (b_d) device arrays are used as arguments to cudaforSetDefaultStream():

```
1   program defaultStreamVar
2     use cudafor
3     implicit none
4     integer, parameter :: n=100000
5     real :: a(n), b(n)
6     real, device :: a_d(n)
7     real, device, allocatable :: b_d(:)
8     integer(cuda_stream_kind) :: s1
9     integer :: istat, i
10
11    istat = cudaStreamCreate(s1)
12
13    a = 1.0
14    allocate(b_d(n))
15
16    istat = cudaforSetDefaultStream(a_d, s1)
17    if (istat /= cudaSuccess) print *, 'a_d stream association error: ', &
18        cudaGetErrorString(istat)
19    istat = cudaforSetDefaultStream(b_d, s1)
```

```
20     if (istat /= cudaSuccess) print *, 'b_d stream association error: ', &
21         cudaGetErrorString(istat)
22
23     a_d = 1.0
24     b_d = 1.0
25
26     !$cuf kernel do <<<*,*>>>
27     do i = 1, n
28         a_d(i) = a_d(i) + b_d(i) + i
29     end do
30
31     print *, minval(a_d)
32     print *, maxval(b_d)
33
34     a = a_d
35     b = b_d
36
37     istat = cudaStreamDestroy(s1)
38     deallocate(b_d)
39 end program defaultStreamVar
```

The output from running the application is

```
a_d stream association error:
invalid argument
    3.000000
    1.000000
```

so the attempt to associate stream s1 with the statically declared array a_d on line 16 returns an `invalid argument` error. A GPU trace of the above code shows which streams are used for the operations on the device:

```
1  Stream   Name
2        7  __pgi_dev_cumemset_16n [330]
3       16  __pgi_dev_cumemset_16n [331]
4        7  defaultstreamvar_27_gpu [336]
5        7  cudafor_lib_internals_partialmnvshflshflr4_ [341]
6        7  [CUDA memcpy DtoH]
7        7  cudafor_lib_internals_partialmxvshflshflr4_ [346]
8        7  [CUDA memcpy DtoH]
9        7  [CUDA memcpy DtoH]
10      16  [CUDA memcpy DtoH]
```

where we observe that all operations occur in the null stream except the memset on line 24 and the device-to-host transfer on line 35, both involving b_d. The CUF kernel on line 27 and reductions on lines 31 and 32 occur in the null stream, as well as the memset and device-to-host transfer involving a_d. Essentially, the variable-stream association for allocatable variables only controls those operations that the user cannot override with optional arguments, i.e., the memset and memcpy operations via overloaded assignment. We can get the kernel and reductions to execute in stream s1 by specifying that stream explicitly:

```
26  !$cuf kernel do <<<*,*,stream=s1>>>
27  do i = 1, n
28      a_d(i) = a_d(i) + b_d(i) + i
29  end do
30
31  print *, minval(a_d, stream=s1)
32  print *, maxval(b_d, stream=s1)
```

which results in

```
1   Stream  Name
2        7  __pgi_dev_cumemset_16n [330]
3       16  __pgi_dev_cumemset_16n [331]
4       16  defaultstreamvarexplicit_27_gpu [336]
5       16  cudafor_lib_internals_partialmnvshflshflr4_ [341]
6       16  [CUDA memcpy DtoH]
7       16  cudafor_lib_internals_partialmxvshflshflr4_ [346]
8       16  [CUDA memcpy DtoH]
9        7  [CUDA memcpy DtoH]
10      16  [CUDA memcpy DtoH]
```

where all operations except the memset and device-to-host transfer of the statically declared a_d occur in stream s1.

Up to this point, we have discussed setting the default stream via cudaforSetDefaultStream(). We can query the default stream through the routine cudaforGetDefaultStream(), which returns the default stream of the host thread or the stream associated with the optional variable argument.

Before leaving this section on the default stream, we should say some comments about how the default stream in CUDA Fortran relates to the default stream in CUDA C and provide some suggestions on how and when the default stream should be changed in CUDA Fortran. In CUDA C, we can change the default stream via a compiler flag or a preprocessor macro to a *per-thread default stream*. When compiled to use the per-thread default stream, all operations involving the device whose invocation does not specify a stream will run in the per-thread default stream rather than the null stream (often called the legacy stream in CUDA C). Otherwise, the legacy or null stream, with its synchronizing behavior, is used by default. Since it is determined at compile time, the default stream in C cannot be modified at runtime, which is why the CUDA Fortran routines cudaforSetDefaultStream() and cudaforGetDefaultStream() use the prefix cudafor and not the prefix cuda; they are specific to CUDA Fortran. From the perspective of CUDA C, the default stream is always the null stream in CUDA Fortran since there is no mechanism to set the default stream at compile time in CUDA Fortran. The default stream in CUDA Fortran is just state handled by the CUDA Fortran runtime. This is why the null stream is always listed as Default stream 7 in the profiler timelines.

In terms of when to change the default stream in CUDA Fortran code, it is best to mimic the behavior in CUDA C as close as possible: create and set the default stream at the beginning of the code, and destroy the stream at the very end of the code. A call to cudaStreamDestroy() only deletes the resources associated with the specified stream and does not clean up any associations made if that stream were used as a default stream. Performing, say, a device-to-host transfer where the device variable was associated with a stream that has been destroyed will result in a runtime error. In general, we prefer using data transfers via cudaMemcpyAsync() and specifying the stream explicitly in the execution configuration of kernels and as an optional argument to reductions. That is enough to achieve overlap between operations on the host and device and between multiple kernels launched on the device, in addition to being explicitly clear regarding which operations occur in which streams. However, we should be aware of how the use of cudaforSetDefaultStream() can affect behavior.

4.1.5.2 *Non-blocking streams*

Up to this point, we have discussed creating, via cudaStreamCreate(), and using *blocking* streams. These streams are blocking in the sense that they synchronize with the null stream, so all operations previously submitted to blocking streams must complete before an operation in the null stream commences, and any operation in the null stream must complete before any operation in a blocking stream can commence.

Say you make use of precompiled code that uses the null stream for all, or even just some, GPU operations. You would like to overlap operations in that precompiled code with other operations involving the GPU. Creating and using blocking streams is not going to accomplish such overlap. But non-blocking streams can solve this problem. Non-blocking streams do not synchronize with the null stream, so an operation in a non-blocking stream can execute concurrently with an operating in the null stream.

Non-blocking streams can be created with the cudaStreamCreateWithFlags() function. The cudaStreamCreateWithFlags() function takes two arguments, the first argument being the stream identifier as in cudaStreamCreate(), and the second argument either cudaStreamDefault or cudaStreamNonBlocking. Use of cudaStreamCreateWithFlags() with cudaStreamDefault is equivalent to cudaStreamCreate(): a blocking stream is created. However, calling cudaStreamCreateWithFlags() with cudaStreamNonBlocking creates a non-blocking stream where activity in that stream can run concurrently with the null stream.

The behavior of different types of streams is illustrated by the following code:

```
 1   program differentStreamTypes
 2     use cudafor
 3     implicit none
 4     integer, parameter :: n=100000
 5     real, device :: a_d(n), b_d(n)
 6     real :: a(n)
 7     integer(kind=cuda_stream_kind) :: stream1, stream2
 8     integer :: istat, i
 9
10     istat = cudaStreamCreate(stream1)
11     istat = cudaStreamCreateWithFlags(stream2, cudaStreamNonBlocking)
12     a = 1.0
13
14     !$cuf kernel do <<<1,1>>>
15     do i = 1, n
16        b_d(i) = i
17     enddo
18     a_d = a
19
20     !$cuf kernel do <<<1,1,stream=stream1>>>
21     do i = 1, n
22        b_d(i) = i
```

```
23    enddo
24    a_d = a
25
26    istat = cudaDeviceSynchronize()
27
28    !$cuf kernel do <<<1,1,stream=stream2>>>
29    do i = 1, n
30       b_d(i) = i
31    enddo
32    a_d = a
33
34    istat = cudaStreamDestroy(stream1)
35    istat = cudaStreamDestroy(stream2)
36
37 end program differentStreamTypes
```

where a host-to-device data transfer in the null stream initializes the a_d array, and a CUF kernel initializes the b_d array. This pair of operations is done multiple times where the CUF kernel occurs in different streams by specifying the optional stream argument in the execution configuration of the CUF kernel. The timeline of this code from nsys-ui is shown in Fig. 4.6, where the CUF kernels are denoted by the label containing the corresponding line number in the main program, and the host-to-device data transfers by the smaller regions with the ellipses. The CUF kernel starting on line 15 occurs in the null stream, and therefore the two operations are sequential on the device. In the second pair of operations beginning at line 21, the CUF kernel occurs in a user created stream, stream1. Because stream1 is a blocking stream with respect to the null stream, execution of the kernel and data transfer once again occur sequentially, even though they occur in different streams. In the third and final pair of operations, the CUF kernel on line 29 occurs in a non-blocking stream, and, as a result, we observe overlap between the data transfer in the null stream and the kernel execution.

FIGURE 4.6

Timeline from nsys-ui of differentStreamTypes code showing the synchronization behavior of non-blocking and blocking streams. Pairs of kernel and host-to-device transfers are issued where the host-to-device transfer occurs in the null stream and the kernel is issued into the null stream, a blocking stream, and a non-blocking stream. Overlap between the transfer and kernel only occurs when the kernel is issued into the non-blocking stream.

FIGURE 4.7

Timeline of differentStreamTypes code with the cudaDeviceSynchronize() call on line 26 commented out. Without this synchronization barrier, the CUF kernel on line 29 in the non-blocking stream overlaps the data transfer on line 24 as well as the transfer on line 32.

Prior to executing the kernel in the non-blocking stream on line 29, cudaDeviceSynchronize() is called. Without this synchronization barrier, the kernel on line 29 would overlap the data transfer on line 24 as well as the transfer on line 32, as seen in Fig. 4.7. (Recall that host-to-device transfers via assignment statements from pageable memory will return control to the host thread after the data has been copied to the pinned buffer.)

Overlapping multiple kernel executions work in the same way. The following code illustrates this behavior:

```fortran
1   program concurrentKernels
2     use cudafor
3     implicit none
4     integer, parameter :: n=100000
5     integer, parameter :: nStreams=6
6     real, device :: a_d(n,nStreams)
7     real :: a(n,nStreams)
8     integer(kind=cuda_stream_kind) :: streams(nStreams)
9     integer :: istat, i, j, flag
10
11    flag = cudaStreamDefault
12    do j = 1, nStreams
13       istat = cudaStreamCreateWithFlags(streams(j), flag)
14    enddo
15    streams(3) = 0
16
17    do j = 1, nStreams
18       !$cuf kernel do <<<1,1,stream=streams(j)>>>
19       do i = 1, n
20          a_d(i,j) = i
21       enddo
22    enddo
23
24    if (flag == cudaStreamNonBlocking) &
25         istat = cudaDeviceSynchronize()
26
27    a = a_d
28
29    do j = 1, nStreams
30       istat = cudaStreamDestroy(streams(j))
31    enddo
32
33  end program concurrentKernels
```

In this code, we launch six kernels in six different streams. Five of the streams are created with cudaStreamCreateWithFlags(), and the remaining stream, the third in the streams array, is set to the null stream. If we create the streams with the cudaStreamDefault flag, then we get a timeline pattern as depicted in top of Fig. 4.8. All kernel activity runs concurrently except when the kernel issued to the null stream is executing. If the streams are created with the cudaStreamNonBlocking flag, then all streams run concurrently as depicted at the bottom of Fig. 4.8. Note that when cudaStreamNonBlocking is used, we need the cudaDeviceSynchronize() call on line 25 to ensure that all of the kernels have completed before we execute the device-to-host data transfer on line 27. If the device synchronization

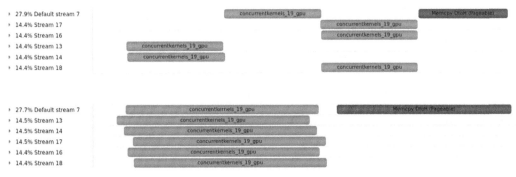

FIGURE 4.8

Timeline of `concurrentKernels` code with the flag set to `cudaStreamDefault` (top) and with the flag set to `cudaStreamNonBlocking` (bottom). (The horizontal axis (time) has been scaled to fill the page width.) With the flag set to `cudaStreamDefault`, kernels overlap except when the kernel issued to the null stream is executing. With the flag set to `cudaStreamNonBlocking`, all kernels overlap.

were not performed, then the device-to-host transfer would begin immediately after the kernel issued to the null stream completed, regardless of the status of other kernels.

4.1.5.3 *Stream priorities*

The `cudaStreamCreateWithPriority()` function takes three arguments, the stream identifier and flag as in `cudaStreamCreateWithFlags()`, and an integer specifying the stream priority as the last argument. The lower the value of the priority argument, the higher the priority of work issued to that stream, where zero represents the default priority. Kernels in a higher-priority stream may preempt kernels already executing in a lower-priority stream. Currently the stream priority affects only kernel execution, not data transfers. The function `cudaDeviceGetStreamPriorityRange()` takes two arguments, integers in which the least and highest priorities supported on the device are returned. The stream priority will be clamped to values in this range if we attempt to create a stream with a priority outside this range.

4.2 Synchronization of kernel threads on the device

In the remainder of this chapter, we deal with synchronization of device threads within a kernel. GPUs have the ability to run many kernel threads concurrently, and although there are cases where threads in a kernel can run completely independent of one another, there are times when device threads can benefit by sharing data. The CUDA programming model has several mechanisms for sharing or exchanging data between threads, each of which requires some type of synchronization.

4.2.1 Shared memory

Perhaps the most common means of sharing data amongst threads is through *shared memory*. In hardware, shared memory resides on the multiprocessor, and all threads of a thread block have access to the same shared memory. Shared memory is declared using the `shared` variable qualifier in device code.

Shared memory can be declared in several ways inside a kernel, depending on whether the amount of memory is known at compile time or at runtime. The following code illustrates various methods of using shared memory:

```
1   module reverse
2   contains
3     attributes(global) subroutine staticReverse(d)
4       implicit none
5       real :: d(*)
6       real, shared :: s(64)
7       integer :: t, tr
8
9       t = threadIdx%x
10      tr = blockDim%x-t+1
11
12      s(t) = d(t)
13      call syncthreads()
14      d(t) = s(tr)
15    end subroutine staticReverse
16
17    attributes(global) subroutine dynamicReverse(d)
18      implicit none
19      real :: d(*)
20      real, shared :: s(*)
21      integer :: t, tr
22
23      t = threadIdx%x
24      tr = blockDim%x-t+1
25
26      s(t) = d(t)
27      call syncthreads()
28      d(t) = s(tr)
29    end subroutine dynamicReverse
30
31    attributes(global) subroutine dynamicReverseAuto(d, n)
32      implicit none
33      real :: d(n)
34      integer, value :: n
35      real, shared :: s(n)
36      integer :: t, tr
37
38      t = threadIdx%x
39      tr = n-t+1
40
41      s(t) = d(t)
42      call syncthreads()
43      d(t) = s(tr)
44    end subroutine dynamicReverseAuto
45  end module reverse
46
47
48  program sharedExample
```

```
49    use cudafor
50    use reverse
51
52    implicit none
53
54    integer, parameter :: n = 64
55    real :: a(n), r(n), d(n)
56    real, device :: d_d(n)
57    integer :: i
58
59    do i = 1, n
60        a(i) = i
61        r(i) = n-i+1
62    enddo
63
64    d_d = a
65    call staticReverse <<<1, n>>>(d_d)
66    d = d_d
67    print *, 'staticReverse max error:', maxval(abs(r-d))
68
69    d_d = a
70    call dynamicReverse <<<1, n, 4*n>>>(d_d)
71    d = d_d
72    print *, 'dynamicReverse max error:', maxval(abs(r-d))
73
74    d_d = a
75    call dynamicReverseAuto <<<1, n, 4*n>>>(d_d, n)
76    d = d_d
77    print *, 'dynamicReverseAuto max error:', maxval(abs(r-d))
78 end program sharedExample
```

This code reverses the data in a 64-element array using shared memory. All of the kernel codes are very similar; the main difference is how the shared memory arrays are declared and how the kernels are invoked. If the shared memory array size is known at compile time, as in the staticReverse kernel, then the array is declared using that value, whether an integer parameter or literal, as is done on line 6 with s(64). In this kernel the two indices representing the original and reverse order are calculated on lines 9 and 10, respectively. On line 12 the data are copied from global memory to shared memory. The reversal is done on line 14, where both indices t and tr are used to copy data from shared memory to global memory.

The other two kernels in this example use dynamic shared memory, where the amount of shared memory is not known at compile time and must be specified (in bytes) when the kernel is invoked in the optional third execution configuration parameter, as is done on lines 70 and 75. The first dynamic shared memory kernel, dynamicReverse, declares the shared memory array on line 20 using an assumed-size array syntax. The size is implicitly determined from the third execution configuration parameter when the kernel is launched. The remainder of the kernel code is identical to the staticReverse kernel.

We can use dynamic shared memory via automatic arrays, as shown in dynamicReverseAuto. In this case the dimension of the dynamic shared memory array is specified by an integer argument. Note that in this case the amount of dynamic memory must still be specified in the third parameter of the execution configuration when the kernel is invoked.

Given these options for declaring dynamic shared memory, which one should be used? If we want to use multiple dynamic shared memory arrays, then using automatic arrays as in the dynamicReverseAuto() routine is preferable. When multiple dynamic shared memory arrays are specified with assumed-size notation, there is no way for the compiler to know how to divide the total dynamic shared memory amongst such arrays. As a result, these arrays are effectively "equivalenced", and we need to supply offsets for all but one of the arrays to avoid the arrays overwriting each others data. For example, the two kernels in the following code declare two dynamic shared memory arrays using automatic array and assumed size notations:

```
1   module m
2   contains
3     attributes(global) subroutine automaticDSM(a, b, n)
4       implicit none
5       real(8) :: a(n)
6       integer :: b(n)
7       integer, value :: n
8
9       real(8), shared :: sa(n)
10      integer, shared :: sb(n)
11      integer :: t, tr
12
13      t = threadIdx%x
14      tr = n-t+1
15
16      sa(t) = a(t)
17      sb(t) = b(t)
18      call syncthreads()
19      a(t) = sa(tr)
20      b(t) = sb(tr)
21    end subroutine automaticDSM
22
23    attributes(global) subroutine assumedSizeDSM(a, b)
24      implicit none
25      real(8) :: a(*)
26      integer :: b(*)
27
28      real(8), shared :: sa(*)
29      integer, shared :: sb(*)
30      integer :: t, tr, offset
31
32      t = threadIdx%x
33      tr = blockDim%x-t+1
34      offset = blockDim%x*sizeof(sa(1))/sizeof(sb(1))
35
36      sa(tr) = a(t)
37      sb(offset+tr) = b(t)
38      call syncthreads()
39      a(t) = sa(t)
40      b(t) = sb(offset+t)
41    end subroutine assumedSizeDSM
42  end module m
```

```
43
44   program main
45     use m
46     implicit none
47     integer, parameter :: n = 512
48     real(8) :: a(n)
49     real(8), device :: a_d(n)
50     integer :: b(n)
51     integer, device :: b_d(n)
52     integer :: i, nerr
53
54     do i = 1, n
55        a(i) = i
56        b(i) = 10*i
57     enddo
58
59     a_d = a; b_d = b
60     call automaticDSM<<<1,n,n*12>>>(a_d, b_d, n)
61     a = a_d; b = b_d
62
63     nerr = 0
64     do i = 1, n
65        if (a(i) /= n-i+1) nerr = nerr+1
66        if (b(i) /= 10*(n-i+1)) nerr = nerr+1
67     end do
68
69     print *, 'automaticDSM errors: ', nerr
70
71     call assumedSizeDSM<<<1,n,n*12>>>(a_d, b_d)
72     a = a_d; b = b_d
73
74     nerr = 0
75     do i = 1, n
76        if (a(i) /= i) nerr = nerr+1
77        if (b(i) /= 10*i) nerr = nerr+1
78     end do
79
80     print *, 'assumeSizeDSM errors: ', nerr
81   end program main
```

Aside from the shared memory declarations, the two kernels are similar except for the argument used to declare the automatic shared memory arrays in the first kernel and the offset needed when accessing elements of the sb array on lines 37 and 40 in the second kernel. The offset is calculated on line 34 taking into account both the number of elements in the sa array and the different word sizes between sa and sb. Because of needing to deal with such offsets, it is simpler and safer to use automatic arrays when using multiple dynamic shared memory arrays.

4.2.2 Synchronizing threads within a block

Before executing line 14 in the staticReverse kernel above, where each thread accesses data in shared memory that was written by another thread, we need to make sure that all threads in the thread block have completed the loads to shared memory on line 12. This is accomplished by the synchronization barrier on line 13, syncthreads(). This synchronization occurs between all threads in a thread block, meaning that no thread can pass this line until all threads in the same thread block have reached it. The same synchronization is used in the other kernels in that module, on lines 27 and 42.

There are several variations of syncthreads(), including the functions syncthreads_and(), syncthreads_or(), and syncthreads_count(). The function syncthreads_and(predicate) performs a block-wise synchronization barrier just as the subroutine syncthreads(), but in addition evaluates the integer or logical predicate for all threads in block and returns a non-zero integer if the integer predicate evaluates to non-zero or the logical predicate evaluates to true by all threads in the block. The function syncthreads_or(predicate) is similar to syncthreads_and(predicate), except that it returns a non-zero integer if the integer predicate for any thread in the block evaluates to non-zero, or if the logical predicate for any thread in the block evaluates to true. The function syncthreads_count(predicate) returns the number of threads whose integer predicate evaluates to nonzero, or whose logical predicate evaluates to true. Examples of these syncthreads_* variants are shown below:

```
1    module m
2    contains
3      attributes(global) subroutine s1(offset)
4        implicit none
5        integer, value :: offset
6        integer :: tid, res
7        tid = threadIdx%x
8
9        res = syncthreads_and(tid > offset)
10       if (tid == 1) print *, 'syncthreads_and(tid > offset):    ', res
11       res = syncthreads_or(tid > offset)
12       if (tid == 1) print *, 'syncthreads_or(tid > offset):    ', res
13       res = syncthreads_count(tid > offset)
14       if (tid == 1) print *, 'syncthreads_count(tid > offset): ', res
15     end subroutine s1
16   end module m
17
18   program syncthreads
19     use m
20     use cudafor
21     implicit none
22     integer :: istat
23
24     print *, 'offset = 0'
25     call s1<<<1, 256>>>(0)
26     istat = cudaDeviceSynchronize()
27
28     print *, 'offset = 4'
29     call s1<<<1, 256>>>(4)
30     istat = cudaDeviceSynchronize()
31   end program syncthreads
```

The output from this code is

```
$ ./a.out
 offset = 0
 syncthreads_and(tid > offset):              1
 syncthreads_or(tid > offset):               1
 syncthreads_count(tid > offset):          256
 offset = 4
 syncthreads_and(tid > offset):              0
 syncthreads_or(tid > offset):               1
 syncthreads_count(tid > offset):          252
```

It should be emphasized that all threads in the thread block need to execute these syncthreads*() routines. If one of these syncthreads*() routines is called in conditional code that does not evaluate uniformly across the thread block, then the behavior is undefined and can produce incorrect results or even hang.

In addition to the variations above, the synchthreads() subroutine has been overloaded for use with cooperative groups, which will be discussed in Section 4.2.6

4.2.3 Warps, warp synchronization, and warp-level primitives

In CUDA's SIMT (Single Instruction, Multiple Thread) architecture, common instructions are issued by groups of 32 threads called *warps*. Each thread has access to its own registers, can load and store date from divergent addresses, and can follow divergent code paths. Different warps may issue and execute different instructions on the device code, and the scheduler coordinates this activity behind the scenes. It is possible to synchronize and exchange data between threads in a warp.

On earlier hardware and CUDA Toolkits, implicit warp-synchronous programming, where threads of a warp execute code in a lock-step fashion, was often assumed. As such, there was no need to synchronize threads within a warp. For current CUDA Toolkits and on hardware of compute capability of 7.0 and higher, this is an unsafe practice, and warp synchronization must be done explicitly or through warp-level routines that have the _sync suffix.

Just as threads launched in a kernel can be identified by the block index within the grid and the thread index within a block, threads in a thread block can be identified based on the warp index within the block and the *lane* within the warp. The generic expressions for the lane and warp IDs for threads in a block with an arbitrary warpsize are

```
warpID = (threadIdx%x-1)/warpsize+1
laneID = threadIdx%x-(warpID-1)*warpsize
```

For a warpsize of 32, the following equivalent expressions are more efficient:

```
warpID = ishft(threadIdx%x-1,-5)+1
laneID = iand(threadIdx%x-1,31)+1
```

Note that these IDs use unit-offset numbering that is standard in Fortran, where the lane values span the range of 1 to 32, as opposed to CUDA C's zero-offset numbering where the lanes take on values from 0 to 31.

Just as a barrier synchronization can be performed by all threads in a thread block by using syncthreads(), it is possible to synchronize at the warp level using syncwarp(mask). The syncwarp(mask) subroutine causes the calling thread to wait until all threads in the mask have executed a syncwarp(mask) call (with the same mask) before proceeding. The mask here is a 32-bit integer where each bit represents a lane in the warp. So while all the threads in a block need to execute the same syncthreads() call, there is greater flexibility with syncwarp(mask) in that only the threads in the specified mask need to participate.

Creating a mask for use in syncwarp(mask) can be done manually with bit manipulation intrinsics or by using the warp-vote functions ballot(predicate) or ballot_sync(mask, predicate) functions. The ballot(predicate) function evaluates the integer or logical predicate for all threads in a warp and returns a 32-bit integer with the Nth bit set if the predicate evaluates to non-zero or true. In ballot_sync(mask, predicate) version, only those threads in mask participate. Note here that in CUDA Fortran, the ballot(predicate) function calls ballot_sync(mask, predicate) with mask=z'ffffffff'. If all threads do not participate in the call due to warp divergence where threads in a warp take different branches of a conditional, then the ballot_sync(mask, predicate) should be used.

An example of use of the warp-vote function is below:

```
 1  module m
 2  contains
 3    attributes(global) subroutine s(a, nWarps)
 4      implicit none
 5      integer :: a(nWarps)
 6      integer, value :: nWarps
 7      integer :: mask, laneID, warpID
 8
 9      warpID = ishft(threadIdx%x-1, -5)+1
10      laneID = iand(threadIdx%x-1,31)+1
11
12      mask = ballot(threadIdx%x > 40)
13      mask = ballot_sync(mask, mod(threadIdx%x,2) == 0)
14      if (laneID == 1) a(warpID) = mask
15    end subroutine s
16  end module m
17
18  program ballot
19    use m
20    implicit none
21    integer, parameter :: nWarps = 3
22    integer :: a(nWarps), i
23    integer, device :: a_d(nWarps)
24
25    call s<<<1,nWarps*32>>>(a_d, nWarps)
26    a = a_d
27    do i = 1, nWarps
28      print "(i0, 1x, B32.32)", i, a(i)
29    enddo
30  end program ballot
```

where two warp-vote calls are done. In the first call on line 12, all threads participate to create a mask with bits set for all threads with a thread index greater than 40. The second call on line 13 returns a mask with bits set for even numbered thread indices for all the participating threads (those specified in the mask from line 12). The output is

```
$ ./a.out
1 00000000000000000000000000000000
2 10101010101010101010101000000000
3 10101010101010101010101010101010
```

4.2.3.1 *SHFL functions*

Data in registers can be exchanged between threads in a warp with the shuffle functions. The __shfl(var, srcLane, width) function returns the value of var returned by the thread whose lane is srcLane (recall that unit-based numbering is used for the lanes). If the optional width argument is specified, which must be a power of two, then the thread's own value is returned if srcLane is outside the range 1:width. There are also __shfl_up(var, delta, width) and __shfl_down(var, delta, width), which subtract or add delta to the caller's laneID to determine the source lane. The function __shfl_xor(var, laneMask, width) determines the source lane as xor(laneID-1, laneMask), where laneID is the caller's unit-based lane. The __shfl_xor(var, laneMask, width) is often used for reductions within a warp:

```
1  module m
2  contains
3    attributes(global) subroutine s(a)
4      implicit none
5      integer :: a(warpsize, 6)
6      integer :: laneMask, stage
7      integer :: var
8
9      var = threadIdx%x
10     a(threadIdx%x,1) = var
11
12     laneMask = 1
13     stage = 2
14     do
15         var = var + __shfl_xor(var, laneMask)
16         laneMask = laneMask*2
17
18         a(threadIdx%x, stage) = var; stage = stage+1
19         if (laneMask > 16) exit
20     enddo
21   end subroutine s
22 end module m
23
24 program shfl
25   use m
26   implicit none
27   integer, device :: a_d(32, 6)
28   integer :: a(32, 6), i
29
30   call s<<<1,32>>>(a_d)
31   a = a_d
```

```
32
33    do i = 1, 6
34        print "(16I4)", a(1:16,i)
35    enddo
36    print *
37    do i = 1, 6
38        print "(16I4)", a(17:32,i)
39    enddo
40
41  end program shfl
```

where at each stage of the sum reduction the values are written to a global array. The resulting output, printed separately for each half warp, show that each thread ends up with the final result

```
$ ./a.out
   1   2   3   4   5   6   7   8   9  10  11  12  13  14  15  16
   3   3   7   7  11  11  15  15  19  19  23  23  27  27  31  31
  10  10  10  10  26  26  26  26  42  42  42  42  58  58  58  58
  36  36  36  36  36  36  36  36 100 100 100 100 100 100 100 100
 136 136 136 136 136 136 136 136 136 136 136 136 136 136 136 136
 528 528 528 528 528 528 528 528 528 528 528 528 528 528 528 528

  17  18  19  20  21  22  23  24  25  26  27  28  29  30  31  32
  35  35  39  39  43  43  47  47  51  51  55  55  59  59  63  63
  74  74  74  74  90  90  90  90 106 106 106 106 122 122 122 122
 164 164 164 164 164 164 164 164 228 228 228 228 228 228 228 228
 392 392 392 392 392 392 392 392 392 392 392 392 392 392 392 392
 528 528 528 528 528 528 528 528 528 528 528 528 528 528 528 528
```

In addition to these shuffle functions, there are versions that take a mask: __shfl_sync(mask, var, srcLane, width), __shfl_up_sync(mask, var, delta, width), __shfl_down_sync(mask, var, delta, width), and __shfl_xor_sync(mask, var, laneMask, width). These versions are in the cooperative_groups module. Similarly to the warp-vote functions, the shuffle functions without the _sync suffix implicitly call the _sync version with mask=z'ffffffff', so there is no need to issue a syncwarp(mask) after a shuffle instruction; the warp synchronization is built into those routines. Just remember that if a shuffle function is called in a warp-divergent section of code, then the versions with the mask must be used.

4.2.4 Atomics

Atomic functions are used when multiple device threads modify the same variable in global or shared memory without any synchronization. They are used in cases where the order of the threads performing the function does not matter, only that race conditions, when threads simultaneously access and modify data, be avoided. To avoid race conditions, thread access to the data is serialized, so each thread's read-modify-write operation is performed without interference from other threads.

As an example, let us have every device thread in a kernel launch increment two counters in global memory:

```
 1  module m
 2  contains
 3    attributes(global) subroutine s1(raceCount, atomicCount)
 4      implicit none
 5      integer :: raceCount, atomicCount
 6      integer :: tmp
 7      raceCount = raceCount + 1
 8      tmp = atomicAdd(atomicCount, 1)
 9    end subroutine s1
10  end module m
11
12  program raceAndAtomic
13    use m
14    implicit none
15    integer, parameter :: nBlocks = 256, nThreads = 256
16    integer, device :: raceCount_d, atomicCount_d
17    integer :: raceCount, atomicCount
18
19    raceCount_d = 0
20    atomicCount_d = 0
21    call s1<<<nBlocks, nThreads>>>(raceCount_d, atomicCount_d)
22    raceCount = raceCount_d
23    atomicCount = atomicCount_d
24    print *, nBlocks*nThreads, raceCount, atomicCount
25  end program raceAndAtomic
```

The global variable raceCount is simply incremented on line 7, whereas the global variable atomicCount is incremented through the atomic function atomicAdd(mem, val). The function atomicAdd(mem, val) will perform the operation

```
old = mem
mem = mem + val
return old
```

without interference from other threads. (Note that atomic functions return the value of the first argument prior to modification.) This kernel is launched on line 21 with 65,536 threads. Running the code gives

```
$ ./a.out
      65536            5          65536
```

The second number representing the result of the race condition will vary from run to run, but the effect of many threads accessing and modifying a single global memory address is clear.

Note that although access to a global or shared memory location by multiple threads through atomic functions is done safely, it does not prevent race conditions involving that variable introduced elsewhere. For example, if we were to change line 8 to

```
      atomicCount = atomicAdd(atomicCount, 1)   ! Don't do this!!
```

the atomicAdd(atomicCount, 1) is performed safely, but we have introduced a race condition via the assignment statement. Running the code with this modification, we get

```
$ ./a.out
        65536           6           24320
```

A version of this kernel using both shared and global memory in the atomic operations is below:

```
3    attributes(global) subroutine s1(raceCount, atomicCount)
4      implicit none
5      integer :: raceCount, atomicCount
6      integer :: tmp
7      integer, shared :: sharedCount
8
9      if (threadIdx%x == 1) sharedCount = 0
10     call syncthreads()
11
12     raceCount = raceCount + 1
13     tmp = atomicAdd(sharedCount, 1)
14     call syncthreads()
15
16     if (threadIdx%x == 1) tmp = atomicAdd(atomicCount, sharedCount)
17   end subroutine s1
```

Here sharedCount is used to count the threads in a block on line 13, and on line 16 the first thread in the block updates the global variable atomicCount with the value of the shared variable sharedCount. This approach reduces the amount of contention for updating the global variable atomicCount, as the number of global variable updates is equal to the number of blocks launched rather than to the number of threads launched.

In addition to atomicAdd(), there are other atomic functions, including atomicSub(), atomicMax(), atomicMin(), atomicAnd(), atomicOr(), atomicXor(), atomicExch(), atomicInc(), atomicDec(), and atomicCAS(). The last function, the atomic Compare And Swap, is used in Section 9.3.2 as part of a reduction, and the atomic exchange function atomicExch() is used in the next section on memory fences.

4.2.5 Memory fences

The CUDA programming model assumes a weakly ordered memory model, that is, the order in which a device thread accesses memory is not necessarily the order in which such memory accesses are observed by another thread. Memory fence functions can be used to obtain a sequentially consistent ordering of memory accesses across threads. There are several memory fence functions that differ by the scope of threads that enforce the consistent ordering of memory accesses.

For all threads in a thread block to observe a consistent ordering of memory accesses, the subroutine threadfence_block() can be used. Memory accesses by the calling thread made prior to threadfence_block() will be observed by all threads in the same thread block as occurring before memory accesses by the calling thread made after the threadfence_block() call. The subroutine threadfence() is similar except that all threads on the device observe the sequentially consistent ordering rather than just threads in the thread block. Increasing the scope further, we have threadfence_system(), where the sequentially consistent ordering is observed by all device threads, host threads, and threads on peer devices (see Section 8.1.1).

The following code demonstrates use of `threadfence()`:

```
 1  module m
 2  contains
 3    attributes(global) subroutine s1(a, b, n, useThreadfence)
 4      implicit none
 5      real :: a(n), b(n)
 6      integer, value :: n
 7      logical, value :: useThreadfence
 8      integer :: tid, i
 9
10      tid = (blockIdx%x-1)*blockDim%x + threadIdx%x
11
12      do i = tid, n, blockDim%x*gridDim%x
13         a(i) = i
14         if (useThreadfence) call threadfence()
15         b(i) = i
16      enddo
17    end subroutine s1
18
19    attributes(global) subroutine s2(a, b, n, flag, useThreadfence)
20      implicit none
21      real :: a(n), b(n), aval, bval
22      integer, value :: n
23      integer :: flag
24      logical, value :: useThreadfence
25      integer :: tid, i, tmp
26
27      tid = (blockIdx%x-1)*blockDim%x + threadIdx%x
28      do i = tid, n, blockDim%x*gridDim%x
29         bval = b(i)
30         if (useThreadfence) call threadfence()
31         aval = a(i)
32         if (aval == 0 .and. bval == i) tmp = atomicExch(flag, 1)
33      enddo
34    end subroutine s2
35
36  end module m
37
38  program threadfence
39    use cudafor
40    use m
41    implicit none
42    integer, parameter :: n=10000*1024
43    integer, parameter :: niter = 2000
44    real, device :: a_d(n), b_d(n)
45    integer, device :: flag_d
46    integer :: flag
47    logical :: useThreadfence
48    integer(cuda_stream_kind) :: stream1, stream2
49    integer :: istat, i, j, icount
50
51    istat = cudaStreamCreate(stream1)
```

```
52    istat = cudaStreamCreate(stream2)
53
54    do j = 1, 2
55       if (j == 1) then
56          useThreadfence = .false.
57          print *, 'Runs without threadfence(): '
58       else
59          useThreadfence = .true.
60          print *, 'Runs with threadfence(): '
61       endif
62
63       icount = 0
64       do i = 1, niter
65          a_d = 0.0
66          b_d = 0.0
67          flag_d = 0
68
69          call s1<<<10,512,0,stream1>>>(a_d, b_d, n, useThreadfence)
70          call s2<<<10,512,0,stream2>>>(a_d, b_d, n, flag_d, useThreadfence)
71          flag = flag_d
72          if (flag == 1) icount = icount+1
73       enddo
74       print "(a, i0,'/',i0)", &
75             '  iterations where out-of-order access observed: ', &
76             icount, niter
77    end do
78
79    istat = cudaStreamDestroy(stream1)
80    istat = cudaStreamDestroy(stream2)
81  end program threadfence
```

where kernel s1 writes values to two global arrays, and kernel s2 reads these values. The argument useThreadfence determines whether or not threadfence() is called between writing a(i) and b(i) on line 14, and between reading b(i) and then a(i) on line 30. With both threadfence() calls, we expect the condition on line 32, which checks for out-of-order accesses, to always evaluate to false. Without the threadfence() calls, the condition on line 32 can evaluate to true, in which case the flag is set to 1 using the atomicExch(mem, val) function. In the host code, the kernels that write and read array values are launched in different streams on lines 69 and 70, so they execute concurrently (you may need to adjust the number of blocks launched by each kernel to fit simultaneously on your device). This is done in a loop over 2000 iterations. The number of iterations where an out-of-order access was observed is recorded. This loop of iterations is done both with and without threadfence() calls. The results obtained are as follows:

```
$ ./a.out
 Runs without threadfence():
  iterations where out-of-order access observed: 318/2000
 Runs with threadfence():
  iterations where out-of-order access observed: 0/2000
```

Note that both threadfence() calls on lines 14 and 30 are required to avoid out-of-order access. If we comment out just the threadfence() call on line 30, in the routine that reads the array values, then out-of-order accesses are much less frequent, but they still can occur. Increasing `niter`, the number of iterations, by an order of magnitude and commenting out the `threadfence()` call on line 30, we have

```
$ ./a.out
 Runs without threadfence():
  iterations where out-of-order access observed: 1760/20000
 Runs with threadfence():
  iterations where out-of-order access observed: 2/20000
```

where 2 out of the 20,000 launches had out-of-order memory access. Uncommenting line 30 returned the last value to zero.

4.2.6 Cooperative groups

Thus far we have used the `syncthreads()` function to perform a synchronization barrier for all threads in a thread block and `syncwarp(mask)` to perform a barrier synchronization amongst the threads in a warp specified by the 32-bit mask. On devices of compute capability 7.0 and higher and with the CUDA 9.0 Toolkit or newer, it is possible to perform a synchronization barrier for these collections of threads, as well as grid-wide synchronizations, using cooperative groups. In addition, on devices of compute capability 9.0 and higher, synchronization can be performed amongst threads in a cluster of thread blocks. Cooperative group definitions, contained in the `cooperative_groups` module, contain the derived types `grid_group`, `cluster_group`, `thread_group`, and `coalesced_group`. The `thread_group` is a generic group, whereas the `grid_group` corresponds to the threads in a kernel launch, and the `coalesced_group` corresponds to threads in a warp. The `cluster_group` corresponds to a cluster of thread blocks that is supported on devices of compute capability 9.0 and higher. Each of these groups has public members `rank` and `size`, where `rank` is the index of the thread within that group, and `size` is the number of total threads in the group. For a `thread_group` set to a block of threads, the `rank` is `threadIdx%x`, and the `size` is `blockDim%x`, assuming a one-dimensional thread block. The `syncthreads()` subroutine has been overloaded to accept instances of these derived types and thus can be used to synchronize across all threads in a grid, block, or warp. For example, the kernel below is from the example of reversing an array in shared memory in Section 4.2.1:

```
31    attributes(global) subroutine dynamicReverseAuto(d, n)
32      implicit none
33      real :: d(n)
34      integer, value :: n
35      real, shared :: s(n)
36      integer :: t, tr
37
38      t = threadIdx%x
39      tr = n-t+1
40
41      s(t) = d(t)
42      call syncthreads()
43      d(t) = s(tr)
44    end subroutine dynamicReverseAuto
```

The cooperative groups equivalent of this kernel is

```
3     attributes(global) subroutine blockReverse(d, n)
4       use cooperative_groups
5       implicit none
6       real :: d(n)
7       integer, value :: n
8       real, shared :: s(n)
9       integer :: t, tr
10      type(thread_group) :: tg
11
12      tg = this_thread_block()
13
14      t = threadIdx%x
15      tr = blockDim%x-t+1
16
17      s(t) = d(t)
18      call syncthreads(tg)
19      d(t) = s(tr)
20    end subroutine blockReverse
```

where the variable tg of type thread_group is initialized using the function this_thread_block() and passes the variable to syncthreads(). There is likewise the function this_warp() that can be used to initialize a coalesced_group instance. Using thread_group in this fashion provides no advantage over the implicit thread block synchronization other than making the scope of the synchronization (all threads in the block) explicit.

4.2.6.1 *Grid synchronization*

With the grid_group type, it is possible to synchronize across all threads in a kernel launch. There is one restriction on the number of threads launched in a kernel for this to take place, namely that all the threads launched in a kernel must actively reside on the device. Therefore we need to determine, for a specific kernel, the number of thread blocks that can concurrently reside on a multiprocessor, multiply that by the number multiprocessors on the device, and launch the kernel with the resulting number of thread blocks. The routine cudaOccupancyMaxActiveBlocksPerMultiprocessor() can be used to determine the number of active blocks that can reside on a particular device for a particular kernel. CUDA Fortran offers a simpler approach however. By using a wildcard "*" as the first parameter in the kernel execution configuration in host code, the compiler will determine the number of blocks to launch on your behalf. Aside from the wildcard used in the first execution parameter, launching a kernel with grid synchronization is no different from launching any other kernel. There are some differences in a kernel that utilizes grid synchronization, which we will explain using the following example:

```
1    module m
2    contains
3      attributes(grid_global) subroutine smooth(a,b,n,radius)
4        use cooperative_groups
5        implicit none
6        real :: a(n), b(n)
7        integer, value :: n, radius
8        integer :: i, j, jj
9        type(grid_group) :: gg
10       real :: bt
```

```
11
12        gg = this_grid()
13        do i = gg%rank, n, gg%size
14            a(i) = i
15        end do
16
17        call syncthreads(gg)
18
19        do i = gg%rank, n, gg%size
20            bt = 0.0
21            do j = i-radius, i+radius
22                jj = j
23                if (j < 1) jj = jj + n
24                if (j > n) jj = jj - n
25                bt = bt + a(jj)
26            enddo
27            b(i) = bt/(2*radius+1)
28        enddo
29
30      end subroutine smooth
31    end module m
32
33    program main
34      use cudafor
35      use m
36      implicit none
37      integer, parameter :: n = 1024*1024
38      real :: a(n), b(n)
39      real, device :: a_d(n), b_d(n)
40      integer :: i, radius
41      radius = 2
42      call smooth<<<*,256>>>(a_d, b_d, n, radius)
43      a = a_d
44      b = b_d
45      print *, 'Filter radius: ', radius
46      do i = 1, n
47          if (abs(b(i)-a(i)) > 0.00010) print *, i, a(i), b(i)
48      enddo
49    end program main
```

This code initializes values in one array and in a separate array and records the values after smoothing by averaging the array elements with their nearest neighbors (assuming periodicity) for a specified radius. Given the linear initialization, the only values affected are those near the (discontinuous) beginning and end of the array, which are printed out in host code. Kernels that use grid synchronization must be declared with the grid_global rather than the global attribute, as is done on line 3. Because the number of threads launched in a kernel with grid synchronization is limited to the number that can reside on the device at one time and because this number is not known in advance, we can not assume that there are enough threads for a one-to-one mapping of threads to array elements. We get around this using a *grid-stride loop*, such as the loop on lines 13–15. If the array size n is equal to or smaller than the number of threads launched by the kernel, then the statement a(i) = i is executed at most once by each thread, but n can be arbitrarily large, and this loop will initialize all elements of the array. Before these array values can be used in the smoothing operation, where each thread uses data written by other threads, we must synchronize across the entire grid to ensure the initialization step has been completed by all threads, as done on line 17. After the synchronization, the smoothing operation can be performed using another grid-stride loop on lines 19–28.

The host code used to launch a kernel that uses grid synchronization is similar to the host code that launches generic kernels, with the exception that an asterisk is used as the first argument in the execution configuration, as on line 42. The output of this code gives the expected results, where only the two values at each end of the array are affected by the smoothing process:

```
$ ./a.out
 Filter radius:                2
              1    1.000000        419431.4
              2    2.000000        209717.2
        1048575    1048575.        838859.8
        1048576    1048576.        629145.6
```

The grid_global kernels can be used to calculate reductions in a single kernel launch without resorting to atomic functions. A reduction using a grid_global kernel is described in detail in Section 9.3.3 of the Monte Carlo chapter.

4.2.6.2 *Thread block clusters*

Devices of compute capability 9.0 and higher contain a *thread block cluster* feature, which represents a level of hierarchy in the architecture between the multiprocessor and device and in the program model between the thread block and grid. In hardware, multiprocessors are grouped into GPU Processing Clusters (GPCs). The multiprocessors in a GPC are physically close together, and there is support for fast access to shared memory between multiprocessors within a cluster, referred to as *distributed shared memory*, as well as hardware-accelerated barriers for synchronization. In the programming model, a thread block cluster is a group of thread blocks guaranteed to be concurrently scheduled on the multiprocessors that make up the GPC. The number of thread blocks in a thread block cluster can be user defined, and a maximum of eight blocks in a cluster is supported as a portable cluster size. The thread block cluster is represented by the cooperative group cluster_group type.

The following code is a simple example of distributed shared memory where a single cluster of two thread blocks uses distributed shared memory to swap halves of an array:

```
1   module m
2      integer, parameter :: nx = 64
3      integer, parameter :: readRemoteSharedMemory = 1
4      integer, parameter :: writeRemoteSharedMemory = 2
5   contains
6      attributes(global) cluster_dims(2,1,1) subroutine swap(a, b, mode)
7         use cooperative_groups
8         implicit none
9         integer, device :: a(nx), b(nx)
10        integer, value :: mode
11
12        type(cluster_group) :: cluster
13        integer, shared :: s(nx/2)
```

```
14      integer, shared :: ds(nx/2); pointer(dsPtr, ds)
15      integer :: i, tibIdx, tibDim, ticIdx, bicIdx
16
17      cluster = this_cluster()
18
19      tibIdx = threadIdx%x    ! thread index in block
20      tibDim = blockDim%x     ! number of threads in block
21      bicIdx = cluster%rank   ! block index in cluster
22      ticIdx = (bicIdx-1)*tibDim + tibIdx   ! thread index in cluster
23
24      s(tibIdx) = 0
25      call syncthreads(cluster)
26
27      ! get pointer to other block's shared memory
28      if (cluster%rank == 1) then
29         dsPtr = cluster_map_shared_rank(s, 2)
30      else
31         dsPtr = cluster_map_shared_rank(s, 1)
32      end if
33
34      if (mode == readRemoteSharedMemory) then
35         s(tibIdx) = a(ticIdx)  ! write to local shared memory
36         call syncthreads(cluster)
37         b(ticIdx) = ds(tibIdx) ! read from remote shared memory
38         call syncthreads(cluster) ! ensure remote read finishes before exit
39      else ! writeRemoteSharedMemory
40         ds(tibIdx) = a(ticIdx) ! write to remote shared memory
41         call syncthreads(cluster)
42         b(ticIdx) = s(tibIdx)  ! read from local shared memory
43      end if
44   end subroutine swap
45 end module m
46
47 program main
48   use m
49   use cudafor
50   implicit none
51   integer :: a(nx), b(nx), gold(nx)
52   integer, device :: a_d(nx), b_d(nx)
53   integer :: i
54
55   do i = 1, nx
56      a(i) = i
57   enddo
58
59   gold(1:nx/2) = a(nx/2+1:nx)
60   gold(nx/2+1:nx) = a(1:nx/2)
61
62   a_d = a
63   b_d = -1
64
65   call swap<<<2,nx/2>>>(a_d, b_d, readRemoteSharedMemory)
```

```
66   b = b_d
67   print *, 'Remote read maxval(abs(gold-b)):  ', maxval(abs(gold-b))
68
69   b_d = -1
70   call swap<<<2,nx/2>>>(a_d, b_d, writeRemoteSharedMemory)
71   b = b_d
72   print *, 'Remote write maxval(abs(gold-b)): ', maxval(abs(gold-b))
73 end program main
```

The kernel attribute cluster_dims(2,1,1) is used on line 6 to indicate that the kernel is to be configured with two blocks per thread block cluster. The cooperative_groups module is used in the kernel on line 7, which contains the definition of the derived type cluster_group used to declare the variable cluster on line 12. On line 13 the local shared memory array s(nx/2) is declared. A Cray pointer to the shared memory of the other block in the thread block cluster is declared on line 14. The cluster variable is initialized using the function this_cluster() on line 17, and various indices are initialized on lines 19–22. When naming variables for the indices, we use acronyms like tibIdx for thread-in-block index to make clear whether the thread index is relative to the thread block or thread block cluster, as both are used in the code. The identity of the thread block within the cluster is determined via the member cluster%rank on line 21.

On line 24 the local shared memory array is initialized to zero, and on line 25 a synchronization barrier acting across the cluster is issued via syncthreads(cluster). A syncthreads(cluster) call such as this is required before any distributed shared memory operation, including mapping, to make sure that all thread blocks have started executing. The function cluster_map_shared_rank() is used to initialize the pointer to the shared memory of the other block in the thread block cluster on lines 29 and 31. After the pointer has been initialized, the other block's shared memory array can be accessed through the pointee array ds().

The block of code on lines 34–43 assigns half of the contents of the global memory array a() to shared memory and then copies shared memory to half of the global array b(), swapping halves of the array somewhere in the process. This is done in one of two ways, either reading from or writing to remote shared memory. When reading from remote shared memory, two syncthreads(cluster) calls, on lines 36 and 38, are used. The syncthreads(cluster) call on line 38 is required to ensure that all remote shared memory accesses have completed before any thread block exits, in addition to the cluster synchronization on line 36, which ensures all blocks in the cluster have written to their local shared memory. When writing to remote shared memory, only a single syncthreads(cluster) call is needed because the remote access occurs first, on line 40, before the local access on line 42. In host code the kernels are invoked, as typically done on lines 65 and 70. Because static shared memory is used in this kernel, we do not specify a dynamic shared memory size as the optional third execution parameter. However, if we had used dynamic shared memory, then the amount of shared memory specified in the execution configuration would correspond to the amount of shared memory used per thread block, not per thread block cluster. Compiling and running this code generate

```
$ nvfortran swap.cuf
$ ./a.out
 Remote read maxval(abs(gold-b)):         0
 Remote write maxval(abs(gold-b)):        0
```

In addition to the integer member `cluster%rank`, which contains the index of the thread block relative to the cluster, the integer member `cluster%size` holds the number of thread blocks in the cluster. The functions `cluster_block_index()` and `cluster_dim_blocks()` return a dim3 instance containing the block index within the cluster and the number of blocks in a cluster, respectively.

Optimization

In the previous chapter, we discussed how we can use timing information to determine the limiting factor of kernel execution. Many science and engineering codes turn out to be bandwidth bound, which is why we devote the majority of this relatively long chapter to memory optimization. CUDA-enabled devices have many different memory types, and to program effectively, we need to use these memory types efficiently.

Data transfers can be broken down into two main categories: data transfers between host and device memories and data transfers between different memories on the device. We begin our discussion with optimizing transfers between the host and device. We then discuss various types of memories on the device and how they can be used effectively. To illustrate many of these memory optimization techniques, we then go through an example of optimizing a matrix transpose kernel.

In addition to memory optimization, in this chapter we also discuss factors in deciding how we should choose execution configurations so that the hardware is efficiently utilized, and finally we discuss instruction optimizations.

5.1 Transfers between host and device

The peak bandwidth between device memory and the GPU is much higher (3352 GB/s on the NVIDIA H100, for example) than the peak bandwidth between host memory and device memory (64 GB/s on PCIe x16 Gen5). Hence, for the best overall application performance, it is important to minimize data transfers between the host and device whenever possible, and when such transfers are necessary make sure they are optimized.

When initially writing or porting an application to CUDA Fortran, typically a few critical sections of code are converted to CUDA Fortran kernels. If these code sections are isolated, then they will require data transfers to and from the host, and overall performance will likely be gated by these data transfers. At this stage of porting code to CUDA Fortran, it is helpful to assess performance both with and without such transfers. The overall time including data transfers is an accurate assessment of the current code performance, and the time without such transfers indicates where performance may be when more of the code is written to run on the device. We should not spend time at this point optimizing transfers between the host and device, because as more host code is converted to kernels, many of these intermediate data transfers will disappear. Of course, there will always be some transfers required between the host and device, and we need to make sure these are performed as efficiently as possible, but optimizing data transfers that will eventually be removed from the code is not well-spent time.

CUDA Fortran for Scientists and Engineers. https://doi.org/10.1016/B978-0-44-321977-1.00014-0
117

There may be some operations that do not demonstrate any speed-up when run on the device in terms of execution time. If executing the operation on the host would require extra transfers between the host and device, then it may be advantageous overall to perform the operation on the device.

There are other circumstances where data transfers between the host and device can be avoided. Intermediate data structures can be created in device memory, operated on by the device, and destroyed without ever being mapped by the host or copied to host memory.

Up to this point, we have discussed how to avoid transfers between the host and device whenever possible. In the remainder of this section, we discuss how to perform necessary transfers between the host and device efficiently. This includes using pinned host memory, batching small transfers together, and performing data transfers asynchronously.

Also note here that in multi-GPU programming, there are ways to avoid data transfers between the host and device in certain frameworks. In Chapter 8, we will discuss multi-GPU programming in depth; in this chapter, we consider only single-GPU applications.

5.1.1 Pinned memory

We have already discussed the distinction between pageable and pinned memory and how to implement use of pinned memory in Section 4.1.1. (If you have not read that section, then now there would be a good time to do so.) In this section, we will quantify the performance differences of pinned versus pageable memory data transfers on a variety of GPUs and platforms using the following code:

```
1   program HDtransfer
2
3     use cudafor
4     implicit none
5
6     integer, parameter :: nElements = 128*1024*1024
7
8     ! host arrays
9     real(4) :: a_pageable(nElements), b_pageable(nElements)
10    real(4), allocatable, pinned :: a_pinned(:), b_pinned(:)
11
12    ! device arrays
13    real(4), device :: a_d(nElements)
14
15    ! events for timing
16    type (cudaEvent) :: startEvent, stopEvent
17
18    ! misc
19    type (cudaDeviceProp) :: prop
20    real(4) :: time
21    integer :: istat, n, i
22    logical :: pinnedFlag
23
24    ! allocate and initialize
25    do i = 1, nElements
26        a_pageable(i) = i
27    end do
28    b_pageable = 0.0
```

```
29
30      allocate(a_pinned(nElements), b_pinned(nElements), &
31          STAT=istat, PINNED=pinnedFlag)
32      if (istat /= 0) then
33         print *, 'Allocation of a_pinned/b_pinned failed'
34         pinnedFlag = .false.
35      else
36         if (.not. pinnedFlag) print *, 'Pinned allocation failed'
37      end if
38
39      if (pinnedFlag) then
40         a_pinned = a_pageable
41         b_pinned = 0.0
42      endif
43
44      istat = cudaEventCreate(startEvent)
45      istat = cudaEventCreate(stopEvent)
46
47      ! output device info and transfer size
48      istat = cudaGetDeviceProperties(prop, 0)
49
50      print "(/, 'Device: ', a)", trim(prop%name)
51
52      ! pageable data transfers
53      print "(/, 'Pageable transfers')"
54      print *, 'size (KB)      H2D (GB/s)        D2H (GB/s)'
55
56      n = 1024
57      do
58         if (n > nElements) exit
59         write(*,'(i8)', advance='no') n*4/1024
60
61         istat = cudaEventRecord(startEvent, 0)
62         a_d(1:n) = a_pageable(1:n)
63         istat = cudaEventRecord(stopEvent, 0)
64         istat = cudaEventSynchronize(stopEvent)
65
66         istat = cudaEventElapsedTime(time, startEvent, stopEvent)
67         write(*,"(f15.2)", advance='no') n*4/time/1.e+6
68
69         istat = cudaEventRecord(startEvent, 0)
70         b_pageable(1:n) = a_d(1:n)
71         istat = cudaEventRecord(stopEvent, 0)
72         istat = cudaEventSynchronize(stopEvent)
73
74         istat = cudaEventElapsedTime(time, startEvent, stopEvent)
75         print "(3x,f15.2)", n*4/time/1.e+6
76
77         if (any(a_pageable(1:n) /= b_pageable(1:n))) &
78             print *, '*** Pageable transfers failed ***'
79
80         n = n*2
81      enddo
```

```
82
83     ! pinned data transfers
84
85     if (pinnedFlag) then
86         print "(/, 'Pinned transfers')"
87         print *, 'size (KB)        H2D (GB/s)          D2H (GB/s)'
88
89         n = 1024
90         do
91             if (n > nElements) exit
92             write(*,"(i8)", advance='no') n*4/1024
93
94
95             istat = cudaEventRecord(startEvent, 0)
96             a_d(1:n) = a_pinned(1:n)
97             istat = cudaEventRecord(stopEvent, 0)
98             istat = cudaEventSynchronize(stopEvent)
99
100            istat = cudaEventElapsedTime(time, startEvent, stopEvent)
101            write(*,"(f15.2)", advance='no') n*4/time/1.e+6
102
103            istat = cudaEventRecord(startEvent, 0)
104            b_pinned(1:n) = a_d(1:n)
105            istat = cudaEventRecord(stopEvent, 0)
106            istat = cudaEventSynchronize(stopEvent)
107
108            istat = cudaEventElapsedTime(time, startEvent, stopEvent)
109            print "(3x,f15.2)", n*4/time/1.e+6
110
111            if (any(a_pinned(1:n) /= b_pinned(1:n))) &
112                    print *, '*** Pinned transfers failed ***'
113
114            n = n*2
115        end do
116
117    end if
118
119    ! cleanup
120    if (allocated(a_pinned)) deallocate(a_pinned)
121    if (allocated(b_pinned)) deallocate(b_pinned)
122    istat = cudaEventDestroy(startEvent)
123    istat = cudaEventDestroy(stopEvent)
124
125 end program HDtransfer
```

The allocation of pinned memory is done on line 30 with error checking on lines 32–37 to determine if the allocation was successful, and if so, whether or not the allocation resulted in pinned memory. Following that, CUDA events are used to time both pageable and pinned data transfers in a loop over various array sizes.

The performance of data transfers between host and device memory depends largely on the generation of PCI Express, or PCIe, available on the motherboard and supported by the device. The current and maximum settings for the PCIe generation can be determined from the `nvidia-smi` utility with the option `--query-gpu=pcie.link.gen.current,pcie.link.gen.max` as follows:

```
$ nvidia-smi --format=csv --query-gpu=pcie.link.gen.current,pcie.link.gen.max
pcie.link.gen.current, pcie.link.gen.max
3, 3
3, 3
3, 3
3, 3
```

which shows a system with four GPUs, with a current and max generation of 3. The maximum PCIe link generation refers to the maximum possible value for the GPU and system configuration. When there is a mismatch between the maximum PCIe generation supported by the device and on the system, the lower of these values is reported. The number reported for the current link generation may be a reduced value if the GPU is idle.

Fig. 5.1 shows the results from the `HDTransfer` code on systems with PCIe Gen3, which has a maximum transfer rate of 1 GB/s per lane or 16 GB/s in one direction for x16 devices. The top figure was obtained with an A100 40GB device, which has support for up to PCIe Gen4, and the bottom figure was obtained with a V100 32GB device, which supports up to PCIe Gen3. Both figures are similar and show data transfer rates above 12 GB/s for large transfers when the host memory is pinned. Pageable transfers observe reduced transfer rates due to the intermediate host copy to a pinned buffer.

Fig. 5.2 shows the results from the same code on a system with PCIe Gen4 support, with a A100 80GB GPU, which also supports up to PCIe Gen4 speeds. PCIe Gen4 has up to double the transfer rate of the previous generation, so 2 GB/s per lane or 32 GB/s unidirectionally on x16 devices. For large pinned transfers, we observe over 25 GB/s. Pageable transfers peak at about half the pinned data transfer rates.

Finally, Fig. 5.3 shows the results of the `HDtransfer` code on a system with PCI Gen5 support and with an H100 80GB device. Once again, the PCIe Gen5 doubles the data transfer rate over the previous generation, so for x16 devices, there is a peak transfer rate of 64 GB/s unidirectionally. In Fig. 5.3, we observe the transfer rates of above 50 GB/s for large pinned transfers. The pageable transfers are less than half the pinned rates.

Two takeaways from the transfer rate plots in Figs. 5.1–5.3 are that the benefits of using pinned memory is substantial, especially for the later PCIe generations, and secondly that large transfers are preferable to smaller transfers. Regarding the latter point, it is often beneficial to copy smaller transfers into a single buffer, preferably pinned, and then execute a single copy on that buffer. This does not apply to non-contiguous slices in a multidimensional array, however. For example, the following code performs a host-to-device transfer of slices in a three-dimensional array:

```
1  program sliceTransfer
2    implicit none
3    integer, parameter :: nx=128, ny=128, nz=128
4    real :: a(nx,ny,nz)
5    real, device :: a_d(nx,ny,nz)
6
7    a = 0.0
8    a_d(2:nx-1,:,:) = a(2:nx-1,:,:)
9
10 end program sliceTransfer
```

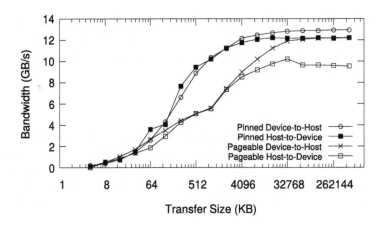

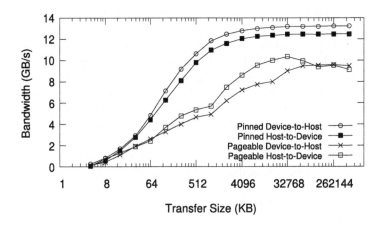

FIGURE 5.1

Transfer rates for pinned and pageable host-to-device and device-to-host transfers of various lengths on systems with PCIe Gen3. The top figure is with an A100 40GB GPU (which can support PCIe Gen4) and the bottom figure is a V100 32GB GPU (PCIe Gen3).

We might guess that the overall transfer is executed by ny*nz individual transfers of nx−2 contiguous elements; it is actually performed by a single call to cudaMemcpy2D() since the arrays are effectively 2D arrays of ny*nz elements in the second dimension, which can be verified by profiling the following code:

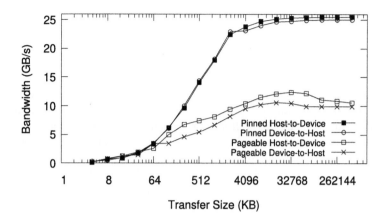

FIGURE 5.2

Transfer rates for pinned and pageable host-to-device and device-to-host transfers of various lengths on a system with PCIe Gen4 and with an A100 80GB GPU (which can support up to PCIe Gen4).

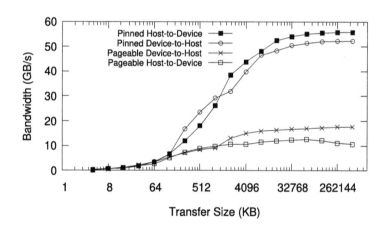

FIGURE 5.3

Transfer rates for pinned and pageable host-to-device and device-to-host transfers of various lengths on a system with PCIe Gen5 and with an H100 80GB GPU (which can support up to PCIe Gen5).

```
$ nvfortran sliceTransfer.cuf
$ nsys profile -o sliceTransfer ./a.out
Generating '/tmp/nsys-report-d352.qdstrm'
[1/1] [=========================100%] sliceTransfer.nsys-rep
Generated:
    sliceTransfer.nsys-rep
$ nsys stats --report cudaapisum sliceTransfer.nsys-rep

 Time (%)  Total Time (ns)  Num Calls        Name
 --------  ---------------  ---------  ----------------------
```

99.6	544,288,933	1	cudaMalloc
0.3	1,768,772	1	cudaMemcpy2D
0.1	481,867	1	cudaFree
0.0	1,109	1	cuModuleGetLoadingMode

While a single large transfer is more efficient than multiple smaller transfers, it can be beneficial to break up one large transfer into multiple smaller transfers to allow the overlapping of transfers between the host and device with each other as well as with computations on the device. This can be accomplished using the techniques mentioned in Section 4.1.3 as demonstrated by the pipeline code, where data transfers and kernels were issued to multiple independent streams, which can overlap execution. A similar code below repeats the transfers of a large array and kernel that modifies the array elements using a varying number of streams while timing the overall execution:

```
1   program async
2     use cudafor
3     implicit none
4     integer, parameter :: maxStreams = 64
5     integer, parameter :: n = maxStreams*1024*1024
6
7     real(8), pinned, allocatable :: a(:), b(:)
8     real(8), device :: a_d(n), b_d(n)
9     real(8) :: gold(n)
10
11    integer(kind=cuda_stream_kind) :: stream(maxStreams)
12    type (cudaEvent) :: startEvent, stopEvent
13
14    real :: time
15    integer :: nStreams, i, j, offset, istat
16
17    block
18      type (cudaDeviceProp) :: prop
19      istat = cudaGetDeviceProperties(prop, 0)
20      print "(' Device: ', a)", trim(prop%name)
21      print "(' Array size (MB): ', f8.2)", real(n)*8/1000/1000
22      print "(/,'          Streams   time (ms)' )"
23    end block
24
25    block
26      logical :: pinnedFlag
27      ! allocate pinned  host memory
28      allocate(a(n), STAT=istat, PINNED=pinnedFlag)
29      if (istat /= 0) then
30         print *, 'Allocation of a failed'
31         stop
32      else
33         if (.not. pinnedFlag) &
34              print *, 'Pinned a allocation failed'
35      end if
36      allocate(b(n), STAT=istat, PINNED=pinnedFlag)
37      if (istat /= 0) then
38         print *, 'Allocation of b failed'
```

```
39         stop
40       else
41         if (.not. pinnedFlag) &
42              print *, 'Pinned b allocation failed'
43       end if
44     end block
45
46     ! create events and streams
47     istat = cudaEventCreate(startEvent)
48     istat = cudaEventCreate(stopEvent)
49
50     do i = 1, maxStreams
51        istat = cudaStreamCreate(stream(i))
52     enddo
53
54     call random_number(a)
55     gold = 0.0
56
57     ! warm up
58     a_d = a
59     !$cuf kernel do <<<*,*>>>
60     do i = 1, n
61        b_d(i) = sin(a_d(i)) + sin(2*a_d(i)) &
62              + sin(3*a_d(i)) + sin(4*a_d(i))
63     enddo
64     gold = b_d
65
66     nStreams = 1
67     do
68        istat = cudaEventRecord(startEvent,0)
69        do j = 1, nStreams
70           offset = (j-1)*(n/nStreams)
71           istat = cudaMemcpyAsync(a_d(offset+1), a(offset+1), &
72                n/nStreams, stream(j))
73
74           !$cuf kernel do <<<*,*,0,stream(j)>>>
75           do i = offset+1, offset+n/nStreams
76              b_d(i) = sin(a_d(i)) + sin(2*a_d(i)) &
77                    + sin(3*a_d(i)) + sin(4*a_d(i))
78           enddo
79
80           istat = cudaMemcpyAsync(b(offset+1), b_d(offset+1), &
81                n/nStreams, stream(j))
82        enddo
83        istat = cudaEventRecord(stopEvent, 0)
84        istat = cudaEventSynchronize(stopEvent)
85        istat = cudaEventElapsedTime(time, startEvent, stopEvent)
86        if (maxval(abs(gold-b)) > 0.0) then
87           print *, n, ' *** Error ***'
88        else
89           print *, nStreams, time
90        end if
```

```
91       nStreams = nStreams*2
92       if (nStreams > maxStreams) exit
93    enddo
94
95    ! cleanup
96    istat = cudaEventDestroy(startEvent)
97    istat = cudaEventDestroy(stopEvent)
98    do j = 1, maxStreams
99       istat = cudaStreamDestroy(stream(j))
100   enddo
101   deallocate(a, b)
102
103 end program async
```

Here the pinned host memory is allocated in the block from lines 25–44, events and streams are created starting at lines 47 and 50, initialization and reference solution are created on lines 54–64, and the loop over the number of streams used, and therefore the number of chunks the array is broken into, on lines 67–93. Note that the first iteration of this loop, where nStreams is 1, corresponds to the case with no overlap of any operations. Typical output for this code is

```
Device: NVIDIA A100-PCIE-40GB
Array size (MB):    536.87

    Streams   time (ms)
          1   89.59411
          2   67.87661
          4   58.23837
          8   53.62685
         16   51.20496
         32   50.72867
         64   53.90893
```

where we see that breaking the array into 32 chunks, which are operated on independently, is the fastest amongst the decompositions used for this problem size on this machine. In general, the optimum number of streams for accomplishing similar tasks, as well as the overall benefit, depends on many factors: the array size (or the size of each chunk), the PCIe generation of the host, the compute capability of the GPU (determines PCIe generations supported and affects kernel execution time), and the complexity of the operations in the kernel. If we parameterize the code as above, then the optimum number of streams can be easily determined with some experimentation.

5.2 Device memory

Up to this point in this chapter, we have focused on efficient means of getting data to and from device DRAM. More precisely, such data are stored in global memory that resides in DRAM. Global memory is accessible by both the device and host and can exist for the lifetime of the application. In addition to global memory, there are other types of data stored in DRAM that have different scopes, lifetimes, and

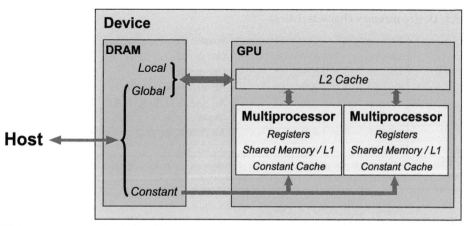

FIGURE 5.4

Schematic of device memory types in DRAM and on-chip.

caching behaviors. There are also several memory types that exist on the chip itself. In this section, we discuss these different memory types and how they can be best used.

The different memory types in CUDA are represented in Fig. 5.4. In device DRAM, there are global, local, and constant memories. On-chip there are registers, shared memory, and various caches (L1, constant).[1]

We will go into details and provide examples for each of these memories in this chapter, but for now, we provide short summaries.

Global memory is the device memory declared with the device attribute in host code. It can be read and written from both the host and device. It is available to all threads launched on the device and persists for the lifetime of the application (or until deallocated if declared allocatable).

Local variables defined in device code are stored in on-chip *registers*, provided that there are sufficient registers available. If there are insufficient registers, then data are stored off-chip in *local memory*. (The adjective "local" in local memory refers to scope, not physical locality.) Both register and local memories have per-thread access.

Shared memory is memory accessible by all threads in a thread-block. It is declared in device code using the shared variable qualifier. It can be used to share data loads and stores and to avoid global memory access patterns that are inefficient. On devices of compute capability 9.0 and higher, distributed shared memory allows thread blocks within a thread block cluster to access each other's shared memory; see the *Thread Block Clusters* subsection of Section 4.2.6.

Constant memory can be read and written from host code but is read-only from any thread in device code. It is allocated using the constant qualifier in a Fortran module and can be used in any code

---

[1] The readers of the previous edition may notice that the read-only texture memory is no longer depicted in this diagram. As of compute capability 5.0 (Maxwell generation), texture memory is unified with L1 memory on the multiprocessor. Any benefit that would come from using texture memory can be realized simply be declaring global memory in kernels with the intent(in) attribute.

Table 5.1 Device memory characteristics.

Memory	Location	Device access	Scope	Lifetime
Register	On-chip	R/W	One thread	Thread
Local	DRAM	R/W	One thread	Thread
Shared	On-chip	R/W	All threads in thread block	Thread block
Distributed shared	On-chip	R/W	All threads in thread block cluster	Thread blocks in cluster
Global	DRAM	R/W	All threads and host	Application
Constant	DRAM	R	All threads and host	Application

Use of distributed shared memory is only available on devices of compute capability 9.0 and higher through the cooperative groups API. Distributed shared memory is physically the same as shared memory; the difference is wider scope of access.

contained in the module as well as in any code that uses the module. Constant data are cached on the chip and are most effective when threads that execute at the same time access the same value.

For reference, Table 5.1 summarizes the characteristics of all the device memory types.

5.2.1 ECC (Error Correcting Code)

Devices with GDDR memory use a portion of the DRAM for ECC (Error Correcting Code) when enabled, which reduces the amount of available global memory as well as the effective bandwidth. Devices with HBM (High-Bandwidth Memory), such as the P100, V100, A100, and H100 GPUs, have native support for ECC and do not reserve a portion of global memory for its use. The ECC is used for single-bit error correction and double-bit error detection. The reply to a single-bit error will cause a slowdown, but these errors are extremely rare, so there is effectively no overhead associated with ECC on these devices. Because we are focused on the performance of GPUs that have HBM, all performance measurements are done with ECC on.

The status of ECC is reported in the ECCEnabled field of the cudaDeviceProp derived type, which is reported by the nvaccelinfo command. Detailed information regarding ECC can be obtained from the nvidia-smi command with the --query --display ECC options, which will generate output similar to the following:

```
    Ecc Mode
        Current                          : Enabled
        Pending                          : Enabled
    ECC Errors
        Volatile
            SRAM Correctable             : 0
            SRAM Uncorrectable           : 0
            DRAM Correctable             : 0
            DRAM Uncorrectable           : 0
        Aggregate
            SRAM Correctable             : 0
            SRAM Uncorrectable           : 0
            DRAM Correctable             : 0
            DRAM Uncorrectable           : 0
```

Here under Ecc Mode the Current and Pending lines indicate whether ECC is currently enabled and what the status will be after a reboot, respectively. Single-bit errors are reported on lines with Correctable, and double-bit errors are reported on lines with Uncorrectable. SRAM refers to static, on-chip memory (registers, on-chip caches, and shared memory), whereas DRAM refers to global, local, and constant memory. Volatile errors are errors since the last time the driver was loaded, whereas Aggregate errors persist indefinitely.

5.2.2 **Global memory**

5.2.2.1 *Declaring global array arguments in kernels*

When declaring global arrays passed as arguments in kernel codes, we have the choice of using known dimensions, assumed-size declarations, where the last dimension can be specified with the asterisk wildcard (*), and assumed-shape declarations, where each dimension can be specified with a colon (:). The following code has two subroutines that perform the same task; they differ in that the first uses assumed-size declarations of the three array arguments, and the second uses assumed-shape declarations:

```
1  module m
2  contains
3    attributes(global) subroutine assumedSizeArrays(a, b, c, nx, ny)
4      implicit none
5      real :: a(nx,ny,*), b(nx,ny,*), c(nx,ny,*)
6      integer, value :: nx, ny
7      integer :: i, j, k
8
9      i = (blockIdx%x-1)*blockDim%x + threadIdx%x
10     j = (blockIdx%y-1)*blockDim%y + threadIdx%y
11     k = (blockIdx%z-1)*blockDim%z + threadIdx%z
12
13     c(i,j,k) = a(i,j,k) + b(i,j,k)
14   end subroutine assumedSizeArrays
15
16   attributes(global) subroutine assumedShapeArrays(a, b, c)
17     implicit none
18     real :: a(:,:,:), b(:,:,:), c(:,:,:)
19     integer :: i, j, k
20
21     i = (blockIdx%x-1)*blockDim%x + threadIdx%x
22     j = (blockIdx%y-1)*blockDim%y + threadIdx%y
23     k = (blockIdx%z-1)*blockDim%z + threadIdx%z
24
25     c(i,j,k) = a(i,j,k) + b(i,j,k)
26   end subroutine assumedShapeArrays
27 end module m
```

It may seem that using assumed-shape declarations is preferable, as the code is shorter, and if needed, the size() function can be used to retrieve the size of each dimension of each array argument. However, if we compile this code with the -gpu=ptxinfo, then we see that resource utilization differs greatly between these two kernels:

```
$ nvfortran -c -gpu=ptxinfo assumedShapeSize.cuf
ptxas info    : 4 bytes gmem
ptxas info    : Compiling entry function
                'm_assumedshapearrays_' for 'sm_75'
ptxas info    : Function properties for m_assumedshapearrays_
    0 bytes stack frame, 0 bytes spill stores,
    0 bytes spill loads
ptxas info    : Used 42 registers, 400 bytes cmem[0]
ptxas info    : Compiling entry function
                'm_assumedsizearrays_' for 'sm_75'
ptxas info    : Function properties for m_assumedsizearrays_
    0 bytes stack frame, 0 bytes spill stores,
    0 bytes spill loads
ptxas info    : Used 10 registers, 384 bytes cmem[0]
```

The kernel with assumed-shape declarations uses over four times the number of registers as the kernel with assumed-size declarations, 42 versus 10 registers. These extra registers are used to hold the array descriptors for the assumed-shape arrays. Note that these registers are not shared amongst threads; every device thread in the thread block will use this many registers. This can greatly limit the number of threads, and therefore thread blocks, that can concurrently reside on a multiprocessor. Best practice in CUDA Fortran is to always use assumed-size rather than assumed-shape declarations.

5.2.2.2 *Coalesced global memory access*

To understand the coalescing of global memory accesses, we should review the concept of a *warp* of threads introduced in Section 4.2.3. Threads in a thread block are partitioned into groups of 32 threads called warps. On a multiprocessor, threads in a warp execute common instructions issued by a warp scheduler. When the threads in a warp execute an instruction that accesses global memory, that memory request for all threads in the warp can be fulfilled by a single transaction if certain alignment and size requirements are met.

All global memory transactions are either 32-, 64-, or 128-byte memory transactions. These transactions are naturally aligned, meaning that they start on an address that is a multiple of the size of the transaction. (When global memory is allocated, the allocation is aligned to 256 bytes.) Furthermore, global memory instructions support reading words of 1, 2, 4, 8, or 16 bytes in length. A global memory request will be compiled to a single instruction if the size is one of the supported word sizes and the data is naturally aligned (the address is a multiple of the word size). If a global memory request gets compiled to a single instruction and if that instruction for a warp of threads addresses a single 32-, 64-, or 128-byte segment of memory, then the memory request for a warp of threads will be *coalesced* into a single memory transaction. For example, if a warp of threads access contiguous 4-byte elements of an array in global memory that reside in a naturally aligned 128-byte segment, then that memory request will be filled in a single 128-byte transaction. If each thread in a warp accesses a 4-byte element in a 32-byte section that contains no other data requested by other threads in the warp, then that warp's memory request will be filled by 32 separate transactions, reducing the effective bandwidth by a factor of eight (only 4 of every 32 bytes transferred are needed).

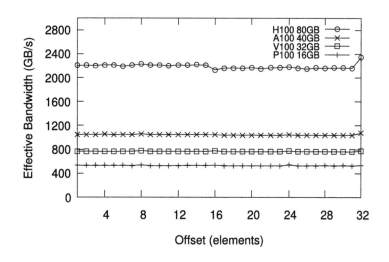

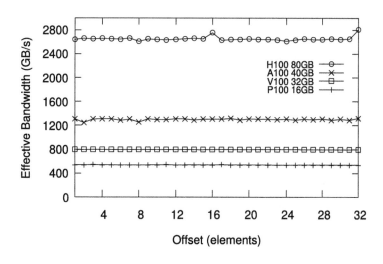

FIGURE 5.5

Effective bandwidth for various degrees of misaligned access of single-precision (top) and double-precision (bottom) arrays in global memory as obtained in the `offset.cuf` code. Performance does not degrade with misalignment since almost all elements transferred are used by some thread in the kernel.

When alignment and size requirements are not met, addition transactions will need to be processed to satisfy the memory request. Because of the advanced memory system with large caches on current GPUs, such extra transactions may not be detrimental to overall performance. Take, for example, the following code that contains a kernel that increments elements of an array, where an offset is applied when calculating the array index:

```fortran
1   module m
2     use, intrinsic :: iso_fortran_env
3     integer, parameter :: fp_kind=real32
4   contains
5     attributes(global) subroutine increment(a, offset)
6       real(fp_kind) :: a(*)
7       integer, value :: offset
8       integer :: i
9       i = blockDim%x*(blockIdx%x-1)+threadIdx%x + offset
10      a(i) = a(i)+1
11    end subroutine increment
12  end module m
13
14  program offset
15    use cudafor
16    use m
17
18    implicit none
19
20    integer, parameter :: nMB = 128   ! transfer size in MB
21    integer, parameter :: n = nMB*1024*1024/fp_kind
22    integer, parameter :: blockSize = 256
23    real(fp_kind), device :: a_d(n+32)
24    type(cudaEvent) :: startEvent, stopEvent
25    type(cudaDeviceProp) :: prop
26    integer :: i, istat
27    real(4) :: time
28
29
30    istat = cudaGetDeviceProperties(prop, 0)
31    print "(/,'Device: ',a)", trim(prop%name)
32    print "('Transfer size (MB): ',i0)", nMB
33
34    if (kind(a_d) == real32) then
35        print "('Single Precision',/)"
36    else
37        print "('Double Precision',/)"
38    endif
39
40    istat = cudaEventCreate(startEvent)
41    istat = cudaEventCreate(stopEvent)
42
43    print *, 'Offset, Bandwidth (GB/s):'
44    do i = 0, 32
45       a_d = 0.0
46       istat = cudaEventRecord(startEvent,0)
47       call increment<<<n/blockSize,blockSize>>>(a_d, i)
48       istat = cudaEventRecord(stopEvent,0)
49       istat = cudaEventSynchronize(stopEvent)
50
51       istat = cudaEventElapsedTime(time, startEvent, &
52           stopEvent)
```

```
53      print *, i, 2*n*fp_kind/time*1.e-6
54    enddo
55
56    istat = cudaEventDestroy(startEvent)
57    istat = cudaEventDestroy(stopEvent)
58  end program offset
```

Fig. 5.5 shows the effective bandwidth as a function of the misalignment for both single-precision and double-precision arrays on various devices. We can clearly see that there is no degradation in effective bandwidth for any misalignment. This is because nearly all of the global data transferred are used in the kernel, perhaps not by the thread in the warp that generated the transaction, but some other thread in the kernel. We could make the argument that in this case, misaligned access actually serves as an efficient prefetching mechanism.

While misaligned access to data may not degrade performance, strided access to data generally does. The following code uses a 2D array to perform strided access to elements of a global array:

```
1  module m
2    use, intrinsic :: iso_fortran_env
3    integer, parameter :: fp_kind=real32
4  contains
5    attributes(global) subroutine increment(a, stride)
6      real(fp_kind) :: a(stride,*)
7      integer, value :: stride
8      integer :: i
9      i = blockDim%x*(blockIdx%x-1)+threadIdx%x
10     a(1,i) = a(1,i)+1
11   end subroutine increment
12 end module m
13
14 program stride
15   use cudafor
16   use m
17
18   implicit none
19
20   integer, parameter :: nMB = 128   ! transfer size in MB
21   integer, parameter :: n = nMB*1024*1024/fp_kind
22   integer, parameter :: blockSize = 256
23   real(fp_kind), device :: a_d(32,n)
24   type(cudaEvent) :: startEvent, stopEvent
25   type(cudaDeviceProp) :: prop
26   integer :: i, istat
27   real(4) :: time
28
29
30   istat = cudaGetDeviceProperties(prop, 0)
31   print "(/,'Device: ',a)", trim(prop%name)
32   print "('Transfer size (MB): ',i0)", nMB
33
34   if (kind(a_d) == real32) then
35      print "('Single Precision',/)"
```

```
36    else
37       print "('Double Precision',/)"
38    endif
39
40    istat = cudaEventCreate(startEvent)
41    istat = cudaEventCreate(stopEvent)
42
43    print *, 'Stride, Bandwidth (GB/s):'
44    do i = 1, 32
45       a_d = 0.0
46       istat = cudaEventRecord(startEvent,0)
47       call increment<<<n/blockSize,blockSize>>>(a_d, i)
48       istat = cudaEventRecord(stopEvent,0)
49       istat = cudaEventSynchronize(stopEvent)
50
51       istat = cudaEventElapsedTime(time, startEvent, &
52             stopEvent)
53       print *, i, 2*n*fp_kind/time*1.e-6
54    enddo
55
56    istat = cudaEventDestroy(startEvent)
57    istat = cudaEventDestroy(stopEvent)
58 end program stride
```

Fig. 5.6 shows the results on various GPUs, where we observe a decrease in effective bandwidth. With a stride of two, the effective bandwidth is essentially halved from the case with contiguous access as half of the data transferred in each transaction is not used in the kernel.

So what can be done when we need to access data in a strided fashion? This is where shared memory comes into play. We can load global memory into the on-chip shared memory in a coalesced, or at least highly contiguous fashion, and then access shared memory in a strided fashion without degrading performance. We will investigate this further in Section 5.2.6.

5.2.3 Local memory

Local memory is so named because its scope is local to the thread, not because of its physical location. In fact, local memory is off-chip in device DRAM along with global memory. A more descriptive moniker would be "thread-local global memory." Hence access to local memory is as expensive as access to global memory.

Local memory can be used to hold automatic variables. This is done by the compiler when it determines that there is insufficient register space to hold the variable. Automatic variables that are likely to be placed in local memory are large structures or arrays, which would consume too much register space and arrays that the compiler determines may be indexed dynamically. Local memory is interleaved so that local memory access is always coalesced.

To illustrate when local memory is used and how to detect when it is used, consider the kernels in the following module:

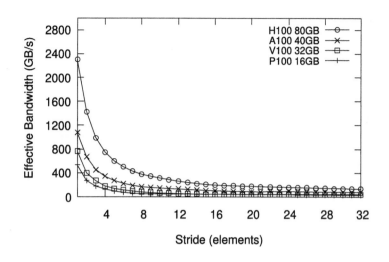

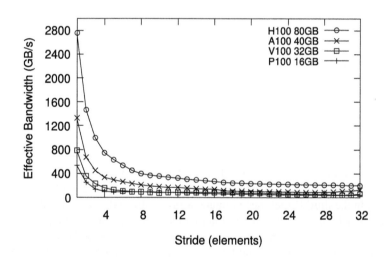

FIGURE 5.6

Effective bandwidth for various degrees of strided access of single-precision (top) and double-precision (bottom) arrays in global memory as obtained in the `stride.cuf` code. The effective bandwidth degrades as the stride increases as a smaller percentage of data transferred is used in the kernel.

```
1   module localmem
2     implicit none
3   contains
4     attributes(global) subroutine k1(a)
5       integer :: a(*)
6       integer :: b(2), i
```

```
 7        i = blockDim%x*(blockIdx%x-1) + threadIdx%x
 8        b = 1
 9        a(i) = b(2)
10     end subroutine k1
11
12     attributes(global) subroutine k2(a, j)
13        integer :: a(*)
14        integer, value :: j
15        integer :: b(2), i
16        i = blockDim%x*(blockIdx%x-1) + threadIdx%x
17        b = 1
18        a(i) = b(j)
19     end subroutine k2
20
21     attributes(global) subroutine k3(a, j)
22        integer :: a(*)
23        integer, value :: j
24        integer :: b(256), i
25        i = blockDim%x*(blockIdx%x-1) + threadIdx%x
26        b = 1
27        a(i) = b(j)
28     end subroutine k3
29
30     attributes(global) subroutine k4(a, j)
31        integer :: a(*), j(*)
32        integer :: b(2), i
33        i = blockDim%x*(blockIdx%x-1) + threadIdx%x
34        b = 1
35        a(i) = b(j(i))
36     end subroutine k4
37  end module localmem
```

Each kernel has an automatic array b(), which is used to assign values to the global array a(). In the first kernel the automatic array b() is indexed by a literal, and in the second kernel the array index is a value argument. In the third kernel the automatic array is also indexed by a value argument, but the automatic array is much larger, and in the last kernel the two-element automatic array is dynamically indexed. Compiling with –gpu=keep and examining the generated .ptx file show loads and stores to local memory for kernels k2(), k3(), and k4(). For example, the k2() kernel's PTX code includes stores to local memory:

```
    st.local.v2.u32        [%rd3], {%r5, %r5};
```

as well as loads from local memory:

```
    ld.local.u32    %r6, [%rd6+-4];
```

However, the PTX code is an intermediate representation that undergoes additional phases of compilation. In compiling PTX to binary the optimizer can decide to use registers instead of local memory, especially for small arrays such as b(2) in the k2() kernel. Compiling the module with the option –gpu=ptxinfo, which provides information resulting from the compilation from PTX to SASS assembly and not about the PTX itself, indicates that the k3() and k4() kernels use 1024 and 8 bytes per thread of local memory for the automatic arrays:

```
ptxas info    : 4 bytes gmem
ptxas info    : Compiling entry function 'localmem_k4_' for 'sm_80'
ptxas info    : Function properties for localmem_k4_
      8 bytes stack frame, 0 bytes spill stores, 0 bytes spill loads
ptxas info    : Used 12 registers, 368 bytes cmem[0]
ptxas info    : Compiling entry function 'localmem_k3_' for 'sm_80'
ptxas info    : Function properties for localmem_k3_
   1024 bytes stack frame, 0 bytes spill stores, 0 bytes spill loads
ptxas info    : Used 11 registers, 364 bytes cmem[0]
ptxas info    : Compiling entry function 'localmem_k2_' for 'sm_80'
ptxas info    : Function properties for localmem_k2_
      0 bytes stack frame, 0 bytes spill stores, 0 bytes spill loads
ptxas info    : Used 10 registers, 364 bytes cmem[0]
ptxas info    : Compiling entry function 'localmem_k1_' for 'sm_80'
ptxas info    : Function properties for localmem_k1_
      0 bytes stack frame, 0 bytes spill stores, 0 bytes spill loads
ptxas info    : Used 10 registers, 360 bytes cmem[0]
```

and that no local memory is used by the k2() kernel. The output of cuobjdump -sass when run on the .bin file generated from -gpu=keep will also indicate local memory loads and stores with lines like

```
    /*00d0*/              LDL R0, [R0+-0x4] ;
```

and

```
    /*00b0*/              STL.64 [R1], R4 ;
```

Finally, we can determine the use of local memory at runtime using the host function cudaFuncGetAttributes(attr, func), which returns attributes of the specified kernel func() in attr, which is an instance of the derived type cudaFuncAttributes defined in the cudafor module. One of these attributes is localSizeBytes, the amount of local memory used per thread in bytes by the kernel. The program below provides an example of its use:

```
40  program localAttribute
41    use localmem
42    use cudafor
43    implicit none
44    type(cudaFuncAttributes) :: attr
45    integer :: istat
46
47    istat = cudaFuncGetAttributes(attr, k1)
48    print "('k1 local memory (bytes/thread): ', i0)", attr%localSizeBytes
49    istat = cudaFuncGetAttributes(attr, k2)
50    print "('k2 local memory (bytes/thread): ', i0)", attr%localSizeBytes
51    istat = cudaFuncGetAttributes(attr, k3)
52    print "('k3 local memory (bytes/thread): ', i0)", attr%localSizeBytes
53    istat = cudaFuncGetAttributes(attr, k4)
54    print "('k4 local memory (bytes/thread): ', i0)", attr%localSizeBytes
55  end program localAttribute
```

which produces:

```
k1 local memory (bytes/thread): 0
k2 local memory (bytes/thread): 0
k3 local memory (bytes/thread): 1024
k4 local memory (bytes/thread): 8
```

The discussion in this section pertains to local memory used for the stack frame. Local memory usage for spilled registers, reflected by the spill stores and spill loads in the -gpu=ptxinfo output, will be discussed in Section 5.2.7 on registers.

5.2.4 Constant memory

All CUDA devices have 64 KB of constant memory. Constant memory is read-only by kernels but can be read and written by the host. Constant memory is located in device DRAM but has a dedicated cache on each multiprocessor. Accesses to different addresses in constant cache by threads in a warp are serialized, so constant cache is most effective when all threads in a warp access the same address. A good example of its use is for physical or mathematical constants, such as π. When access to a single variable by all threads in a warp hits in the constant cache, constant memory can be as fast as register access.

In CUDA Fortran, constant data must be declared in the declaration section of a module, i.e., before the contains, and can be used in any code in the module or any host code that includes the module. Our increment example can be written using constant memory:

```
1  module m
2    integer, constant :: b
3  contains
4    attributes(global) subroutine increment(a)
5      implicit none
6      integer, intent(inout) :: a(*)
7      integer :: i
8
9      i = threadIdx%x
10     a(i) = a(i)+b
11
12   end subroutine increment
13 end module m
14
15
16 program incrementGPU
17   use cudafor
18   use m
19   implicit none
20   integer, parameter :: n = 256
21   integer :: a(n)
22   integer, device :: a_d(n)
23
24   a = 1
25   b = 3
26
```

```
27  a_d = a
28  call increment<<<1,n>>>(a_d)
29  a = a_d
30
31  if (any(a /= 4)) then
32      print *, '**** Program Failed ****'
33  else
34      print *, 'Program Passed'
35  endif
36  end program incrementGPU
```

where the parameter b has been declared as a constant variable using the `constant` attribute on line 2. The kernel no longer passes b as an argument, and it does not need to be declared in the host code. Aside from these changes, the code remains the same as the code used in the introduction.

Constant memory use in kernels can be viewed when compiling via the `-gpu=ptxinfo` flag. Compiling our modified increment example with `-gpu=ptxinfo`, we get

```
ptxas info   : 4 bytes gmem, 4 bytes cmem[3]
ptxas info   : Compiling entry function 'm_increment_'
               for 'sm_80'
ptxas info   : Function properties for m_increment_
    0 bytes stack frame, 0 bytes spill stores,
    0 bytes spill loads
ptxas info   : Used 8 registers, 360 bytes cmem[0]
```

Constant memory is partitioned into multiple banks based on type of use, which in addition to user-defined constant variables includes kernel arguments and compiler generated constants. Different constant memory banks are indicated by the number in square brackets after the cmem. Because user-defined constant variables are declared at module scope rather than within a kernel, user-defined constant data is reported outside any particular kernel's compilation data, as in the first line with cmem[3].[2]

The amount of user-allocated constant memory used by a kernel can be determined at runtime using the function cudaFuncGetAttributes() similar to how it was used to indicate local memory usage in the previous section, but using the attribute constSizeBytes, which indicates the amount of user-allocated constant memory used by the specified kernel. Modifying our host code, we have

```
16  program constantAttribute
17    use cudafor
18    use m
19    implicit none
20    type(cudaFuncAttributes) :: attr
21    integer :: istat
22
23    istat = cudaFuncGetAttributes(attr, increment)
24    print "('Constant memory used (bytes): ', i0)", attr%constSizeBytes
25  end program constantAttribute
```

---

[2] The gmem reported here is global memory reserved by the compiler for various purposes, including character strings and coefficients used in calculating sine and cosine, but not the amount of global memory associated with kernel arguments.

Table 5.2 Caching behavior of loads from global and local memory.

	L1	L2
Global memory		
intent(in)	✓	
__ldca()	✓	✓
__ldcg()		✓
__ldcv()		
-gpu=loadcache:L1	✓	✓
-gpu=loadcache:L2		✓
Default (CC$\geq$6.0)	✓	✓
Default (CC<6.0)		✓
Local memory		
CC$\geq$6.0	✓	✓
CC<6.0		✓

The caching behavior can be modified through use of the variable qualifier intent(in), *the cache load functions* __ldc[a|g|v](), *and compiler option* -gpu=loadcache:[L1|L2].

which generates

```
Constant memory used (bytes): 4
```

5.2.5 L1 and L2 caches

The L1 and L2 caches are hardware-managed caches. Each multiprocessor has its own L1 cache, whereas the L2 cache is on-chip but shared amongst multiprocessors (see Fig. 5.4). While the L1 and L2 caches are hardware-managed, the programmer can affect the path that data takes through the cache hierarchy through load and store functions, variable attributes, and compiler options. These are summarized for loads in Table 5.2.

Loads from global memory will be cached in L1 as well as L2 by default on devices of compute capability 6.0 and higher. On earlier architectures loads from global memory are cached only in the L2 cache by default.

Devices of compute capability 5.0 and higher combined separate L1 and texture caches into a single cache. In previous architectures, we could bypass the L2 cache and route read-only data from global memory through the texture cache. This required declaring a texture pointer at module scope and using Fortran pointer assignment to bind the texture pointer to the global array prior to kernel invocation. On devices of compute capability 5.0 and higher, global data passed as kernel arguments can be routed directly through the combined L1/texture cache (bypassing the L2 cache) simply by declaring such data with the intent(in) qualifier, as is done on line 14 in the code below:

```
1  module m
2  contains
3    attributes(global) subroutine k(b,a)
```

```
 4         implicit none
 5         real :: b(*), a(*)
 6         integer :: i
 7         i = (blockIdx%x-1)*blockDim%x + threadIdx%x
 8         b(i) = a(i)
 9       end subroutine k
10
11       attributes(global) subroutine k_ii(b,a)
12         implicit none
13         real :: b(*)
14         real, intent(in) :: a(*)
15         integer :: i
16         i = (blockIdx%x-1)*blockDim%x + threadIdx%x
17         b(i) = a(i)
18       end subroutine k_ii
19
20       attributes(global) subroutine k_ca(b,a)
21         implicit none
22         real :: b(*), a(*)
23         integer :: i
24         i = (blockIdx%x-1)*blockDim%x + threadIdx%x
25         b(i) = __ldca(a(i))
26       end subroutine k_ca
27
28       attributes(global) subroutine k_cg(b,a)
29         implicit none
30         real :: b(*), a(*)
31         integer :: i
32         i = (blockIdx%x-1)*blockDim%x + threadIdx%x
33         b(i) = __ldcg(a(i))
34       end subroutine k_cg
35
36       attributes(global) subroutine k_cv(b,a)
37         implicit none
38         real :: b(*), a(*)
39         integer :: i
40         i = (blockIdx%x-1)*blockDim%x + threadIdx%x
41         b(i) = __ldcv(a(i))
42       end subroutine k_cv
43     end module m
```

The generated PTX code for the kernel that declares the array argument with the intent(in) attribute contains the following load instruction:

```
        ld.global.nc.f32        %f1, [%rd6];
```

where nc indicates a non-coherent or read-only load. The kernel on lines 3–9 that does not use the intent(in) attribute generates a load instruction in PTX without nc:

```
        ld.global.f32   %f1, [%rd6];
```

Similar differences can be seen in the disassembled code via cuobjdump -sass, where the non-coherent load in PTX translates to

```
    LDG.E.CONSTANT.SYS R3, [R2] ;
```

as opposed to the normal load from global memory:

```
    LDG.E.SYS R3, [R2] ;
```

The cache load functions __ldca(), __ldcg(), and __ldcv() used on lines 25, 33, and 41 are hints to the compiler to cache loads at all levels (L1 and L2), the global level (L2) only, and at no levels (volatile access), respectively. These functions offer a fine-grained approach to specifying the caching behavior on a per-use basis. Typical PTX instructions generated from these three cache load functions are

```
    ld.global.ca.f32 %f1, [%rd1];
    ld.global.cg.f32 %f1, [%rd1];
    ld.global.cv.f32 %f1, [%rd1];
```

and the corresponding instructions from disassembled code are

```
    LDG.E.STRONG.CTA R3, [R2+-0x4] ;
    LDG.E.STRONG.GPU R3, [R2+-0x4] ;
    LDG.E.STRONG.SYS R3, [R2+-0x4] ;
```

respectively. There are two other cache hint functions for loads, cache streaming, __ldcs(), and last use, __ldlu(). The first of these, cache streaming, is for data likely to be accessed once or twice and uses an evict-first policy to limit cache pollution by the streaming data. The last use function avoids write-backs of cache lines that will not be used again.

On a per-compilation unit basis, the use of caches for global loads can be controlled to the extent possible for the specific architecture by the -gpu=loadcache:[L1|L2] option, where -gpu=loadcache:L1 will cache loads in L1 as well as L2, and -gpu=loadcache:L2 will cache global loads in L2 but not in L1. If we compile the above module with -gpu=loadcache:L1, only the load in the first kernel on lines 3–9 will be affected. The PTX will remain unchanged from before:

```
    ld.global.f32    %f1, [%rd6];
```

but the disassembled code will indicate caching behavior similar to using __ldca():

```
    LDG.E.STRONG.CTA R3, [R2+-0x4] ;
```

Likewise, compiling with -gpu=loadcache:L2 will also not affect the generated PTX code, but the disassembled object code for the kernel on lines 3–9 will indicate caching behavior similar to __ldcg():

```
    LDG.E.STRONG.GPU R3, [R2+-0x4] ;
```

Because the generated PTX is not affected by the compiler option -gpu=loadcache:[L1|L2], code execution from JIT-compiled PTX will not observe the caching behavior specified by the -gpu=loadcache:[L1|L2] option.

Local memory caching is similar to the default global memory caching behavior. On devices of compute capability 6.0 and higher, loads from local memory are cached in L1 and L2. On devices with compute capabilities less than 6.0, loads from local memory are cached only in L2.

Table 5.3 Preferred shared memory carveouts as percentages of maximum shared memory capacity, which are supported on devices of different compute capabilities rounded up to the nearest integer percentage.

Compute capability	Unified data cache (KB)	Max shared memory (KB)	Shared memory capacities (KB in header, % in table)										
			0	8	16	32	64	96	100	132	164	196	228
7.0	128	96	0	9	17	33	67	100					
7.5	96	64				50	100						
8.0, 8.7	192	164	0	8	16	32	64		100				
9.0	256	228	0	4	8	15	29		44	58	72	86	100

Hints for the caching behavior of stores to global memory can be specified with the subroutines __stwb(), __stcg(), __stcs(), and __stwt(). The default store instruction is the write-back instruction __stwb(), which writes back cache lines at all coherent levels. The cache at global level store instruction __stcg() caches in L2 but not in L1. The cache streaming store instruction __stcs() is intended for data likely accessed only once and sets an evict-first cache line policy. The write-through store instruction __stwt() writes data to system global memory through the L2 cache.

On devices of compute capability 7.0 and greater, the same memory is used for L1 and shared memory. The amount dedicated to each can be specified by the cudaFuncSetAttribute() function, which is described in the following section on shared memory.

5.2.6 Shared memory

Shared memory, as its name implies, allows threads in a thread block to exchange data. Because shared memory allows exchange of data between threads, safe use of shared memory requires synchonization between threads of a thread block, which we have discussed in detail in Section 4.2.1 of the Synchronization chapter. This section focuses on using shared memory efficiently in kernels. Before we get to using shared memory in device code, there are some configurations of shared memory from host code that may be useful in optimizing performance.

5.2.6.1 Configuring shared memory

Devices of compute capabilities 5.0 and 6.0 have a dedicated shared memory space. On devices of compute capability 7.0 and higher, a unified data cache is used for both L1 cache and shared memory. How much of this unified data cache is dedicated to L1 cache and shared memory is configurable on a per kernel basis. The values supported for each architecture are given in Table 5.3. The driver automatically configures the shared memory capacity for each kernel and in most cases will provide optimal performance. However, there may be some cases where the driver cannot evaluate the workload optimally. In such cases, additional hints regarding the shared memory capacity can be specified with the cudaFuncSetAttribute() function.

The cudaFuncSetAttribute(function, attribute, value) routine assigns the specified value to the specified attribute for the particular kernel given by function. The attribute cudaFuncAttributePreferredSharedMemoryCarveout allows specification of a preferred amount of the unified data cache to be used as shared memory, referred to as the shared memory carveout, as an integer percentage of the maximum supported shared memory size for that architecture. The percentages of maximum shared memory size supported for each architecture are given in Table 5.3. These preferred sizes are hints, and the driver may choose a different configuration if needed for the kernel to run or if the preferred carveout is not supported for the architecture. When a specified integer percentage does not map to a supported capacity, the next larger capacity is used. In addition to an integer percentage, the constants cudaSharedmemCarveoutDefault, cudaSharedmemCarveoutMaxL1, and cudaSharedmemCarveoutMaxShared can be used to specify the carveout.

Kernels relying on shared memory allocations over 48 KB per thread block must use dynamic shared memory rather than statically sized arrays and require an explicit opt-in using cudaFuncSetAttribute() to specify the attribute cudaFuncAttributeMaxDynamicSharedMemorySize. An example that reserves the maximum allowable shared memory per block is given below:

```
1    module m
2    contains
3      attributes(global) subroutine increment(a, b)
4        implicit none
5        integer, intent(inout) :: a(*)
6        integer, shared :: s(*)
7        integer, value :: b
8        integer :: i, il
9
10       il = threadIdx%x
11       i = (blockIdx%x-1)*blockDim%x + threadIdx%x
12       s(il) = a(i)
13       call syncthreads()
14       a(i) = s(il)+b
15     end subroutine increment
16   end module m
17
18
19   program maxSharedMemory
20     use cudafor
21     use m
22     implicit none
23
24     integer, parameter :: n = 1024*1024
25     integer :: a(n)
26     integer, device :: a_d(n)
27     type(cudaFuncAttributes) :: attr
28     type(cudaDeviceProp) :: prop
29     integer :: istat, smBytes
30
31     istat = cudaGetDeviceProperties(prop, 0)
32     print "(/,'Device Name: ',a)", trim(prop%name)
33     print "('Compute Capability: ',i0,'.',i0)", &
34         prop%major, prop%minor
35
36     print "(/,'sharedMemPerBlock: ', i0)", prop%sharedMemPerBlock
37     print "('sharedMemPerBlockOptIn: ', i0)", &
38         prop%sharedMemPerBlockOptIn
39     print "('sharedMemPerMultiprocessor: ', i0)", &
```

```
40          prop%sharedMemPerMultiprocessor
41
42     smBytes = prop%sharedMemPerBlockOptIn
43     istat = cudaFuncSetAttribute(increment, &
44          cudaFuncAttributeMaxDynamicSharedMemorySize, &
45          smBytes)
46
47     a_d = 1
48     call increment<<<n/32, 32, smBytes>>>(a_d, 2)
49     a = a_d
50     if (all(a==3)) then
51        print "(/,'Passed')"
52     else
53        print "(/,'*** Failed ***')"
54     end if
55  end program maxSharedMemory
```

where on line 43 the dynamic shared memory accessible per block is set to the maximum allowable, which is given by the sharedMemPerBlockOptIn member of the cudaDeviceProp derived type. The kernel is launched with this amount of dynamic shared memory specified in the third execution configuration argument on line 48. Typical output is

```
Device Name: NVIDIA A100-PCIE-40GB
Compute Capability: 8.0

sharedMemPerBlock: 49152
sharedMemPerBlockOptIn: 166912
sharedMemPerMultiprocessor: 167936

Passed
```

5.2.6.2 *Global memory coalescing through shared memory*

One of the most common uses of shared memory is to facilitate global memory coalescing. We have seen in Section 5.2.2 that strided memory access has a detrimental effect on performance. We can use shared memory to load data from global memory to shared memory in a coalesced manner and then redistribute the data amongst threads via shared memory. Provided that shared memory bank conflicts are avoided (more on this later), such redistribution is very fast in relation to global memory access since shared memory is on-chip.

We will illustrate how shared memory can be used to facilitate global memory coalescing by writing a kernel that performs an out-of-place matrix transpose. Let us begin with the simplest approach to performing a transpose:

```
53  attributes(global) subroutine transposeNaive(matOut, matIn)
54     implicit none
55     real, intent(out) :: matOut(nCols, nRows)
56     real, intent(in) :: matIn(nRows, nCols)
57
58     integer :: row, col, j
59
```

```
60        row = (blockIdx%x-1)*nTile + threadIdx%x
61        col = (blockIdx%y-1)*nTile + threadIdx%y
62
63        do j = 0, nTile-1, blockCols
64            matOut(col+j,row) = matIn(row,col+j)
65        end do
66    end subroutine transposeNaive
```

The declaration section of the module containing this kernel defines the following parameters:

```
2    integer, parameter :: nRows=1024, nCols=1024
3    integer, parameter :: blockRows = 32, blockCols = 8
4    integer, parameter :: nTile = blockRows
```

We launch this kernel with a thread block of blockRows × blockCols or 32 × 8 threads. Each thread block transposes an nTile×nTile or 32 × 32 tile of the nRows×nCols matrix. The row and col calculations on lines 60 and 61 correspond to the row and column indices of the upper left corner of the tile of the input matrix that is being transposed. Using a thread block with fewer threads than tile elements means that each thread transposes several matrix elements, four in this case, which is the purpose of the loop on line 63. Loading data from the input matrix on line 64 is done in a coalesced manner: contiguous threads in a warp read contiguous words from global memory, corresponding to a column of the tile being transposed. However, writing the data to the output matrix is uncoalesced as the threads in a warp write to global memory in a strided manner across columns in the output matrix. This is depicted in Fig. 5.7.

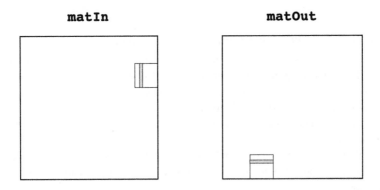

matIn   **matOut**

FIGURE 5.7

Transpose as performed by the transposeNaive() kernel. The small square represents one of the tiles that each thread block transposes. Within that tile, the elements transposed by a warp of threads (for one iteration of the do loop in j) are depicted by the rectangle. Contiguous threads in a warp read contiguous words from global memory, representing a section of a column of the input matrix, and as such the loads from global memory are coalesced. However, contiguous threads in a warp write in a strided manner to global memory, across columns of the output matrix, and thus the stores to global memory are not coalesced.

It is useful to compare performance of the transpose kernel to that of a kernel that performs a copy:

```
9    attributes(global) subroutine copyMat(matOut, matIn)
10     implicit none
11     real, intent(out) :: matOut(nRows, nCols)
12     real, intent(in) :: matIn(nRows, nCols)
13
14     integer :: row, col, j
15
16     row = (blockIdx%x-1)*nTile + threadIdx%x
17     col = (blockIdx%y-1)*nTile + threadIdx%y
18
19     do j = 0, nTile-1, blockCols
20        matOut(row, col+j) = matIn(row, col+j)
21     enddo
22    end subroutine copyMat
```

where on line 20, both the loads from and stores to global memory are coalesced. Averaging over 100 invocations of these kernels with 1024×1024 matrices on various devices gives

	Effective Bandwidth (GB/s)			
	P100	V100	A100	H100
Kernel	(16GB)	(32GB)	(80GB)	(80GB)
copyMat	469	719	1736	2464
transposeNaive	115	158	275	399

where we observe the penalty for uncoalesced writes to global memory. This is not unexpected, as we have seen the performance degradation due to strided global memory access earlier in this chapter in Fig. 5.6.

We can avoid strided access to global memory using the approach in the following code, which is graphically depicted in Fig. 5.8:

```
75    attributes(global) subroutine transposeCoalesced(matOut, matIn)
76     implicit none
77     real, intent(out) :: matOut(nCols, nRows)
78     real, intent(in) :: matIn(nRows, nCols)
79
80     real, shared :: tile(nTile, nTile)
81     integer :: row, col, j
82
83     row = (blockIdx%x-1)*nTile + threadIdx%x
84     col = (blockIdx%y-1)*nTile + threadIdx%y
85
86     do j = 0, nTile-1, blockCols
87        tile(threadIdx%x, threadIdx%y+j) = matIn(row,col+j)
88     end do
89
90     call syncthreads()
91
92     row = (blockIdx%y-1)*nTile + threadIdx%x
93     col = (blockIdx%x-1)*nTile + threadIdx%y
```

```
94
95      do j = 0, nTile-1, blockCols
96        matOut(row,col+j) = tile(threadIdx%y+j, threadIdx%x)
97      end do
98    end subroutine transposeCoalesced
```

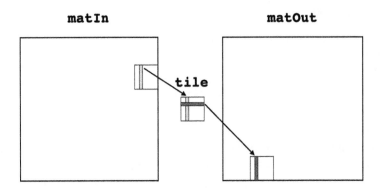

FIGURE 5.8

Transpose as performed by the `transposeCoalesced()` kernel. The small square represents a tile that each thread block transposes. The shaded rectangles represent the data movement by a warp of threads (for one iteration of the j loops). A warp reads contiguous words from the `matIn` matrix in global memory and writes that data to a column in the shared memory tile. After all of the writes to the shared memory tile have completed, a warp reads a row of the shared memory tile and writes that data to contiguous words in the output matrix in global memory. As such, all access to global memory is coalesced.

In this kernel, we declare a shared memory tile on line 80. Data are loaded from global memory and stored to the shared memory on line 87 in a coalesced manner (a warp of threads reads contiguous words from global memory and writes those data to a column of the shared memory tile). Because each thread will access data in shared memory written by other threads, we require the `syncthreads()` call on line 90 to perform a block-wide synchronization to ensure all writes to the shared memory tile have completed. On line 96 a warp of threads reads a row of data from the shared memory tile and writes those data to contiguous words in the output matrix in global memory, where the global memory access is once again coalesced. Adding the performance of this coalesced kernel to our table, we have

| Kernel | Effective Bandwidth (GB/s) | | | |
	P100 (16 GB)	V100 (32 GB)	A100 (80 GB)	H100 (80 GB)
copyMat	469	719	1736	2464
transposeNaive	115	158	275	399
transposeCoalesced	363	416	723	1165

Here we notice a large improvement in performance over the case with uncoalesced global memory access, but the results still fall short of the copyMat kernel. We may think that this performance difference is due to the overhead of shared memory, but this can be easily checked by a kernel that performs a copy through shared memory:

```
26    attributes(global) subroutine copySharedMem(matOut, matIn)
27      implicit none
28      real, intent(out) :: matOut(nRows, nCols)
29      real, intent(in) :: matIn(nRows, nCols)
30
31      real, shared :: tile(nTile, nTile)
32      integer :: row, col, j
33
34      row = (blockIdx%x-1)*nTile + threadIdx%x
35      col = (blockIdx%y-1)*nTile + threadIdx%y
36
37      do j = 0, nTile-1, blockCols
38        tile(threadIdx%x, threadIdx%y+j) = matIn(row,col+j)
39      end do
40
41      call syncthreads()
42
43      do j = 0, nTile-1, blockCols
44        matOut(row,col+j) = tile(threadIdx%x, threadIdx%y+j)
45      end do
46    end subroutine copySharedMem
```

Updating our table with results of the shared memory copy, we have

	Effective Bandwidth (GB/s)			
	P100	V100	A100	H100
Kernel	(16 GB)	(32 GB)	(80 GB)	(80 GB)
copyMat	469	719	1736	2464
copySharedMem	468	709	1689	2364
transposeNaive	115	158	275	399
transposeCoalesced	363	416	723	1165

which indicates that the overhead of using shared memory is not responsible for the performance difference between the coalesced transpose and copy kernels. To understand this difference, we need to discuss how shared memory is organized.

5.2.6.3 *Shared memory bank conflicts*

To achieve high memory bandwidth for concurrent accesses, shared memory is divided into equally sized memory modules (banks) that can be accessed simultaneously. Therefore any memory load or store of n addresses that spans n distinct memory banks can be serviced simultaneously, yielding an effective bandwidth that is n times as high as the bandwidth of a single bank. However, if multiple addresses of a memory request map to the same memory bank, then the accesses are serialized. The hardware splits a memory request that has bank conflicts into as many separate conflict-free requests as necessary, decreasing the effective bandwidth by a factor equal to the number of separate memory requests. The one exception here is when multiple threads access the same word, which results in a broadcast.

To minimize bank conflicts, it is important to understand how memory addresses map to memory banks and how to optimally schedule memory requests. Shared memory banks are organized so that successive 32-bit words are assigned to successive banks and each bank has a bandwidth of 32 bits per clock cycle.

Returning to our matrix transpose code, we see that reading a row in the shared memory tile represents a worst-case scenario for bank conflicts, as all the elements in a row of a 32×32 tile map to the same memory bank, which results in a 32-way bank conflict for a warp of threads. Fortunately, we can eliminate bank conflicts entirely by padding the first dimension of the shared memory tile:

```
105    attributes(global) subroutine transposeNoBankConflicts(matOut, matIn)
106      implicit none
107      real, intent(out) :: matOut(nCols, nRows)
108      real, intent(in) :: matIn(nRows, nCols)
109
110      real, shared :: tile(nTile+1, nTile)
111      integer :: row, col, j
112
113      row = (blockIdx%x-1)*nTile + threadIdx%x
114      col = (blockIdx%y-1)*nTile + threadIdx%y
115
116      do j = 0, nTile-1, blockCols
117          tile(threadIdx%x, threadIdx%y+j) = matIn(row,col+j)
118      end do
119
120      call syncthreads()
121
122      row = (blockIdx%y-1)*nTile + threadIdx%x
123      col = (blockIdx%x-1)*nTile + threadIdx%y
124
125      do j = 0, nTile-1, blockCols
126          matOut(row,col+j) = tile(threadIdx%y+j, threadIdx%x)
127      end do
128    end subroutine transposeNoBankConflicts
```

Other than modifying the declaration of the shared memory tile on line 110, this kernel is the same as transposeCoalesced(). This simple change has a substantial effect on performance:

	Effective Bandwidth (GB/s)			
	P100	V100	A100	H100
Kernel	(16 GB)	(32 GB)	(80 GB)	(80 GB)
copyMat	469	719	1736	2464
copySharedMem	468	709	1689	2364
transposeNaive	115	158	275	399
transposeCoalesced	363	416	723	1165
transposeNoBankConflicts	464	713	1703	2340

where the transposeNoBankConflicts() kernel has achieved (in some cases, marginally surpassed) the copySharedMem() kernel.

Before leaving the topic of shared memory, we should comment on the path that data transfers from global memory to shared memory take when performed as done on line 117 of the transposeNoBankConflicts() kernel. Although a single statement in source code, line 117 compiles to two separate instructions, a load from global memory to registers and a store from registers to shared memory. The load from global memory to registers will not block execution of the device thread; however, the first use of those data will block until the load completes. Unfortunately, the first use is the subsequent store to shared memory. On devices of compute capability 8.0 and higher, it is possible to transfer data from global memory to shared memory without the use of registers in one instruction using the asynchronous memory copies via the pipeline primitives interface. The use of the pipeline primitives interface is discussed in Section 5.3.2.1.

5.2.7 Registers

In general, accessing a register consumes zero extra clock cycles per instruction, but latencies may occur due to register read-after-write dependencies. This latency depends on the instruction and hardware. If an instruction has a four-cycle latency, and the multiprocessor has four warp schedulers, then 16 warps are required to hide this latency. If a warp has instruction-level parallelism, for example, the do-loops over j in the transpose examples of Section 5.2.6, then the number of warps required to hide register latency will be less by a factor of the instruction-level parallelism. Note that the number of warps here refers to the number of active warps per multiprocessor, not the number of warps per block.

Because the number of registers per multiprocessor is fixed (64 K 32-bit registers) and is shared amongst all active threads, it is important to be aware of the number of registers used per thread for kernels. The number of registers used per thread is reported by the -gpu=ptxinfo compiler option. The maximum number of registers that can be used per thread is 255, but problems can arrive well before reaching that limit. If one were to launch a kernel that uses 65 registers per thread with an execution configuration that specifies 1024 threads per thread block, then the number of registers required by a single thread block would exceed the total numbers of registers available on a multiprocessor, and the kernel would not launch.

The programmer has some control over register usage through the -gpu=maxregcount:n compiler option and the
launch_bounds(maxThreadsPerBlock, minBlocksPerMultiprocessor, maxBlocksPerCluster) specifier in the definition of the global subroutine. The maximum number of registers per thread specified in the compiler option -gpu=maxregcount:n will apply to all kernels in the compilation unit. The launch_bounds() specifier allows finer control as it applies to individual kernels. The first argument, maxThreadsPerBlock, is a required argument and specifies the maximum number of threads per block with which the kernel will be invoked. The second argument, minBlocksPerMultiprocessor, is optional and specifies the minimum number of thread blocks that will simultaneously reside on a multiprocessor. The third argument, maxBlocksPerCluster, is also optional and specifies the maximum number of thread blocks per thread block cluster that a kernel will ever be invoked with for kernels that use distributed shared memory on devices of compute capability 9.0 or higher. An example of how launch_bounds() is used is shown in the following module:

```
1   module spill
2   contains
3     attributes(global) subroutine k(a, n)
4       integer :: a(*)
5       integer, value :: n
6       integer, parameter :: nb = 32
7       integer :: b(nb), tid, i
8       tid = blockDim%x*(blockIdx%x-1) + threadIdx%x
```

```
 9        do i = 1, nb
10          b(i) = a(mod(tid-1+i,n)+1)
11        enddo
12        do i = 2, nb
13          b(1) = b(1) + b(i)
14        enddo
15        a(tid) = b(1)
16      end subroutine k
17
18
19      attributes(global) launch_bounds(1024,2) subroutine klb(a, n)
20        integer :: a(*)
21        integer, value :: n
22        integer, parameter :: nb = 32
23        integer :: b(nb), tid, i
24        tid = blockDim%x*(blockIdx%x-1) + threadIdx%x
25        do i = 1, nb
26          b(i) = a(mod(tid-1+i,n)+1)
27        enddo
28        do i = 2, nb
29          b(1) = b(1) + b(i)
30        enddo
31        a(tid) = b(1)
32      end subroutine klb
33    end module spill
```

where the two kernels differ only in the launch_bound() specification. By specifying a maximum number of threads per block as 1024 and a minimum of two blocks to simultaneously reside on a multiprocessor, the 64 K registers must be divided amongst the 2048 threads, resulting in a maximum of 32 registers per thread for the second kernel. This is reflected in the information provided by –gpu=ptxinfo:

```
ptxas info    : 4 bytes gmem
ptxas info    : Compiling entry function 'spill_klb_' for 'sm_60'
ptxas info    : Function properties for spill_klb_
    112 bytes stack frame, 144 bytes spill stores, 144 bytes spill loads
ptxas info    : Used 32 registers, 332 bytes cmem[0]
ptxas info    : Compiling entry function 'spill_k_' for 'sm_60'
ptxas info    : Function properties for spill_k_
    0 bytes stack frame, 0 bytes spill stores, 0 bytes spill loads
ptxas info    : Used 40 registers, 332 bytes cmem[0]
```

where for this compute capability (6.0), the kernel without the launch_bounds() specification uses 40 registers per thread, and the kernel with launch_bounds uses 32 registers per thread. As a result, when the kernel that uses 40 registers per thread is invoked with a thread block of 1024 threads, only a single kernel can reside on a multiprocessor due to register usage. When the kernel that uses 32 registers per thread is invoked with a thread block of 1024 threads, two thread blocks can coexist on a multiprocessor, as requested. Although limiting the number of threads used in this manner can increase the number of blocks that can concurrently reside on a multiprocessor, it can cause register spilling, which is reported in the -gpu=ptxinfo output under bytes spill stores and bytes spill

Table 5.4 Thread block and multiprocessor (SM) limits for various CUDA architectures.

Compute capability	6.0	6.1	6.2	7.0	7.2	7.5	8.0	8.6	8.7	8.9	9.0
Max threads/block	1024										
Max blocks/SM	32					16	32	16		24	32
Max warps/SM	64					32	64	48			64
Threads/warp	32										
Max threads/SM	2048					1024	2048	1536			2048
32-bit registers/SM	64K										
Max 32-bit registers/block	64 K		32 K	64 K							
Max 32-bit registers/thread	255										

loads numbers. Because local memory is cached in the on-chip L1 cache, some spilling may not be too detrimental to performance, but the further spills extend down the memory hierarchy the more performance will deteriorate. As a result of these two opposing factors (higher occupancy and register spilling), some experimentation is often needed to obtain the optimal situation.

5.2.7.1 *Exchanging register data between threads in a warp*

In Section 5.2.6, we discussed how shared memory can be used to exchange data between threads in a thread block. This was used in the transpose example to facilitate global memory coalescing. Data in registers can be exchanged between warps of a thread using the warp shuffle functions. These shuffle functions are described in Section 4.2.3, where a simple example of a reduction using `__shfl_xor()` is provided, and in Section 9.3.1 of the Monte Carlo chapter, where a more elaborate reduction is performed using shuffle functions.

5.3 **Execution configuration**

Even if a kernel has been optimized so that all global memory accesses are perfectly coalesced, we still have to deal with the issue that such memory accesses have a latency of several hundred cycles. To get good overall performance, we have to ensure that there is enough parallelism on a multiprocessor so that stalls for memory accesses are hidden as best as possible. There are two ways to achieve this parallelism: through the number of concurrent threads on a multiprocessor and through the number of independent operations issued per thread. The first of these we call thread-level parallelism, and the second we refer to as instruction-level parallelism.

5.3.1 **Thread-level parallelism**

Thread-level parallelism can be controlled to some degree in the execution configuration specified in the host code used to launch kernels. In the execution configuration, we specify the number of threads per block and the number of blocks in the kernel launch. The number of thread blocks that can reside on a multiprocessor for a given kernel then becomes an important consideration and can be limited by a variety of factors, some of which are given in Table 5.4 for different compute capabilities. There is a hard limit of 16 to 32 thread blocks per multiprocessor depending on the compute capability. There are also limits on the number of threads per block and the number of resident threads per multiprocessor. Note that GPUs of compute capabilities *.0 have the same values for each category in the table, so P100, V100, A100, and H100 GPUs have the same limits. The number of resident blocks per multiprocessor can also be limited by resource utilization, such as the number of registers required per thread and the amount of shared memory used per thread block.

The metric *occupancy* is used to help assess the thread-level parallelism of a kernel on a multi-processor. *Occupancy* is the ratio of the number of active warps per multiprocessor to the maximum number of possible active warps. Warps are used in the definition, but we can equivalently think of this metric in terms of threads. A higher occupancy does not necessarily lead to higher performance, as we can express a fair amount of instruction-level parallelism in kernel code. But if we rely on thread-level parallelism to hide latencies, then the occupancy should not be very small. The theoretical occupancy can be calculated from data returned by the cudaOccupancyMaxActiveBlocksPerMultiprocessor() and cudaDeviceProperties() functions. The first of these functions returns the maximum number of thread blocks of a specified size that can simultaneously reside on a multiprocessor, and the instance of the derived type returned by cudaDeviceProperties() contains a member with the maximum number of threads that can reside on a multiprocessor. The occupancy calculated in this manner is an upper limit based on the limits in Table 5.4 as well as the shared memory utilization per block and register usage per thread. The achieved occupancy for a kernel invocation can be lower as the actual number of active warps on a multiprocessor varies over time.

To illustrate how choosing different execution configurations can affect performance, we can look at simple kernels that copy elements from one array to another. The first kernel we investigate is

```
11      attributes(global) subroutine copy(odata, idata)
12        implicit none
13        real(fpKind) :: odata(*), idata(*), tmp
14        integer :: i
15
16        i = (blockIdx%x-1)*blockDim%x + threadIdx%x
17        tmp = idata(i)
18        odata(i) = tmp
19      end subroutine copy
```

Running this kernel on an A100 80GB GPU with various thread block sizes, we get

```
Multiple Blocks per Multiprocessor
    Threads/Block         Bandwidth (GB/s)      Occupancy (%)
               32              254.31                50.00
               64              423.86               100.00
              128              693.58               100.00
              256              953.67               100.00
              512              953.67               100.00
             1024              953.67               100.00
```

The occupancy here is the theoretical occupancy calculated by

```
116       istat = cudaOccupancyMaxActiveBlocksPerMultiprocessor( &
117          maxBlocks, copy, i, 0)
118       occupancy = 100.*maxBlocks*i/prop%maxThreadsPerMultiprocessor
```

where the variable i on line 117 is the number of threads per block. For a device of compute capability 8.0, the maximum number of blocks that can reside on multiprocessor at once is 32. In the first row of results with a block size equal to a warp of threads, that translates to 32 warps, which is half of the 64 allowable warps per multiprocessor (or 1024 out of the possible 2048 threads), hence the 50% occupancy. Doubling the block size to 64 threads per block doubles the occupancy, and nearly doubles the bandwidth. Increasing the block size further does not increase the theoretical occupancy, which is already 100%, but it does increase the achieved occupancy and results in higher bandwidth.

Shared memory can be helpful in several situations, such as helping to coalesce or eliminate redundant access to global memory. However, it also can act as a constraint on occupancy. Our example code above does not use shared memory in the kernel; however, we can determine the sensitivity of performance to occupancy by specifying an amount of dynamic shared memory when launching the kernel. We can opt-in to the maximum amount of shared memory available for a single thread block with

```
130    smBytes = prop%sharedMemPerBlockOptIn
131    istat = cudaFuncSetAttribute(copy, &
132        cudaFuncAttributeMaxDynamicSharedMemorySize, &
133        smBytes)
```

where smBytes is used in the execution configuration:

```
144        call copy<<<grid, threadBlock, smBytes>>>(b_d, a_d)
```

By specifying the maximum amount of shared memory in this way (without modifying the kernel), it is possible to reduce the occupancy to a point where only a single block can run on a multiprocessor at a time. The output from these runs is

```
Single Block per Multiprocessor
     Threads/Block         Bandwidth (GB/s)      Occupancy (%)
               32               64.11               1.56
               64              125.07               3.13
              128              224.39               6.25
              256              401.55              12.50
              512              544.96              25.00
             1024              762.94              50.00
```

The theoretical occupancy numbers indicate that only a single thread block resides at any one time on a multiprocessor. Because of the reduced occupancy, there are not enough memory requests being issued to cover the latency, and the performance degrades as a result. This exercise prompts the question what can be done in more complicated kernels where either register or shared memory use limits the occupancy? The solution to poor performance in such cases is to use instruction-level parallelism.

5.3.2 Instruction-level parallelism

We have already seen an example of instruction-level parallelism in this book, in the transpose example in Section 5.2.6. Here is the transposeNoBankConflicts() kernel again:

```
105  attributes(global) subroutine transposeNoBankConflicts(matOut, matIn)
106    implicit none
107    real, intent(out) :: matOut(nCols, nRows)
108    real, intent(in) :: matIn(nRows, nCols)
109
110    real, shared :: tile(nTile+1, nTile)
111    integer :: row, col, j
112
113    row = (blockIdx%x-1)*nTile + threadIdx%x
114    col = (blockIdx%y-1)*nTile + threadIdx%y
115
116    do j = 0, nTile-1, blockCols
117       tile(threadIdx%x, threadIdx%y+j) = matIn(row,col+j)
118    end do
119
120    call syncthreads()
121
122    row = (blockIdx%y-1)*nTile + threadIdx%x
123    col = (blockIdx%x-1)*nTile + threadIdx%y
124
125    do j = 0, nTile-1, blockCols
126       matOut(row,col+j) = tile(threadIdx%y+j, threadIdx%x)
127    end do
128  end subroutine transposeNoBankConflicts
```

where the parameters nTile and blockCols are 32 and 8, respectively. With these parameters, each thread block transposes a tile of 32 × 32 elements, but rather than launching this kernel with a thread block of 32 × 32 threads, we used a thread block of 32 × 8 threads, where each thread transposes four elements, which is accomplished in the loops on lines 116 and 125. By changing the blockCols parameter in the declaration section of the module we can experiment with different block sizes and, consequently, with the amount of instruction-level parallelism used in the kernels. The following table compares the transpose results of all kernels for various thread block sizes on an A100 80GB GPU:

Kernel	Effective Bandwidth (GB/s)			
	32 × 4 thread block	32 × 8 thread block	32 × 16 thread block	32 × 32 thread block
copyMat	1675	1736	1710	1478
copySharedMem	1629	1689	1603	1369
transposeNaive	281	275	287	290
transposeCoalesced	730	723	690	638
transposeNoBankConflicts	1678	1703	1606	1365

Using a thread block of 32 × 32 or 1024 threads, a maximum of two thread blocks can reside at one time on a multiprocessor on this device. As the number of threads per block is halved for each configuration, twice as many blocks can reside on a multiprocessor, and the amount of instruction-level parallelism doubles as well, so for a 32 × 4 thread block 16 blocks can simultaneously reside on a multiprocessor, and we have an eight-fold instruction level parallelism. The theoretical occupancy for all these cases on this device is 100%.[3] Because the same number of elements are transposed per thread block in all cases, having a larger number of thread blocks per multiprocessor results in an increase in the number of memory transactions in flight, which helps cover the memory latency. At some point, other factors, such as scheduling overhead, can affect the achieved occupancy and usually some experimentation with parameters such as blockCols is required to find the optimum configuration.

Returning to our copy example, we can modify the kernel to use instruction-level parallelism:

```
25   attributes(global) subroutine copy_ILP(odata, idata)
26      implicit none
27      real(fpKind) :: odata(*), idata(*), tmp(ILP)
28      integer :: i,j
29
30      i = (blockIdx%x-1)*blockDim%x*ILP + threadIdx%x
31
32      do j = 1, ILP
33         tmp(j) = idata(i+(j-1)*blockDim%x)
34      enddo
35
36      do j = 1, ILP
37         odata(i+(j-1)*blockDim%x) = tmp(j)
38      enddo
39   end subroutine copy_ILP
```

In addition to having each thread copy multiple elements, we group or batch all the loads together in the loop from lines 32–34 through use of a thread-private array tmp(ILP), which resides in register memory. The reason we do this *load batching* is because in CUDA a load command will not block further independent execution, but the first use of the data requested by a load will block until that load completes. If we use nvdisasm to disassemble the binary code for copy_ILP, then we observe the following sequence of instructions:

```
1     LDG.E R3, [R2.64] ;
2     IMAD.WIDE R6, R17.reuse, c[0x0][0x0], R4 ;
3     LDG.E R5, [R4.64] ;
4     IMAD.WIDE R8, R17, c[0x0][0x0], R6 ;
5     LDG.E R7, [R6.64] ;
6     LDG.E R9, [R8.64] ;
7     IMAD.WIDE R10, R0, R17, c[0x0][0x160] ;
8     IMAD.WIDE R12, R17, c[0x0][0x0], R10 ;
9     IMAD.WIDE R14, R17, c[0x0][0x0], R12 ;
10    IMAD.WIDE R16, R17, c[0x0][0x0], R14 ;
11    STG.E [R10.64], R3 ;
12    STG.E [R12.64], R5 ;
13    STG.E [R14.64], R7 ;
14    STG.E [R16.64], R9 ;
```

Here the LDG.E instructions on lines 1, 3, 5, and 6 are the loads from global memory to registers, the IMAD instructions perform integer multiply and add used for index calculations, and the STG.E

---

[3] The 4KB of shared memory per block and register usage per thread do not limit occupancy for these cases.

instructions on lines 11–14 are stores from register to global memory. The term *load-use separation* is used to describe the amount of time or the number of instructions between when a load is issued and when the requested data are used. For example, for the first load of this kernel from global memory to the register R3 on line 1 of the disassembled code, there are nine operations performed before that register is used in the store operation on line 11. The load on the first line will not block execution (neither will the other loads), and execution is stalled only on line 11 when register R3 is used. The larger the load-use separation, the better in terms of hiding load latencies. If we once again use dynamically allocated shared memory to restrict the occupancy to a single block per multiprocessor, then for this kernel, we get

```
Register ILP=4, Single Block per Multiprocessor
   Threads/Block        Bandwidth (GB/s)      Occupancy (%)
            32               217.98                 1.56
            64               381.47                 3.13
           128               586.88                 6.25
           256               762.94                12.50
           512               953.67                25.00
          1024              1089.91                50.00
```

where through instruction-level parallelism, we have surpassed the same performance as when shared memory does not restrict occupancy.

The approach of using a single thread to process multiple elements of a shared memory array can be beneficial even if occupancy is not an issue. This is because some operations common to each element can be performed by the thread once, amortizing the cost over the number of shared memory elements processed by the thread.

One drawback of instruction-level parallelism via thread-private arrays like tmp(ILP) is that such arrays consume registers and, consequently, can further add to register pressure. As a result, determining how much instruction-level parallelism to use is a balancing act and often requires some experimentation to achieve optimal results.

As long as we are allocating dynamic shared memory to restrict occupancy to one thread block per multiprocessor, we can make use of this allocation by using shared memory for the load-batching array:

```
45    attributes(global) subroutine copy_ILP_shared(odata, idata)
46      implicit none
47      real(fpKind) :: odata(*), idata(*)
48      real(fpKind), shared :: tmp(blockDim%x, ILP)
49      integer :: i,j
50
51      i = (blockIdx%x-1)*blockDim%x*ILP + threadIdx%x
52
53      do j = 1, ILP
54         tmp(threadIdx%x,j) = idata(i+(j-1)*blockDim%x)
55      enddo
56
57      do j = 1, ILP
58         odata(i+(j-1)*blockDim%x) = tmp(threadIdx%x,j)
59      enddo
60    end subroutine copy_ILP_shared
```

where rather than having a thread-private array tmp(ILP), we have a shared memory array tmp(blockDim%x, ILP). Since each thread writes only data it reads, no synchronization barrier is needed. This approach produces

```
Shared Memory ILP=4, Single Block per Multiprocessor
     Threads/Block          Bandwidth (GB/s)        Occupancy (%)
               32                 100.39                   1.56
               64                 186.08                   3.13
              128                 331.71                   6.25
              256                 544.96                  12.50
              512                 693.58                  25.00
             1024                 847.71                  50.00
```

which shows improvement over the case with no instruction-level parallelism but is not as fast as the case where a thread-private array is used. Look at the disassembled code for copy_ILP_shared, we observe the following sequence of instructions:

```
1     LDG.E R12, [R2.64] ;
2     IMAD.WIDE R4, R0, c[0x0][0x0], R2 ;
3     LDG.E R14, [R4.64] ;
4     IMAD.WIDE R6, R0, c[0x0][0x0], R4 ;
5     LDG.E R15, [R6.64] ;
6     IMAD.WIDE R8, R0, c[0x0][0x0], R6 ;
7     LDG.E R17, [R8.64] ;
8     LOP3.LUT R11, RZ, c[0x0][0x0], RZ, 0x33, !PT ;
9     IADD3 R10, R19, 0x1, RZ ;
10    IADD3 R25, R10, c[0x0][0x0], R11 ;
11    IADD3 R23, R25, c[0x0][0x0], RZ ;
12    IADD3 R16, R23, c[0x0][0x0], RZ ;
13    IADD3 R10, R16, c[0x0][0x0], RZ ;
14    IMAD.WIDE R2, R13, R0, c[0x0][0x160] ;
15    IMAD.WIDE R4, R0, c[0x0][0x0], R2 ;
16    IMAD.WIDE R6, R0, c[0x0][0x0], R4 ;
17    IMAD.WIDE R8, R0, c[0x0][0x0], R6 ;
18    STS [R25.X4+'(S14_3)], R12 ;
19    STS [R23.X4+'(S14_3)], R14 ;
20    STS [R16.X4+'(S14_3)], R15 ;
21    STS [R10.X4+'(S14_3)], R17 ;
22    LDS R11, [R25.X4+'(S14_3)] ;
23    LDS R19, [R23.X4+'(S14_3)] ;
24    LDS R21, [R16.X4+'(S14_3)] ;
25    STG.E [R2.64], R11 ;
26    STG.E [R4.64], R19 ;
27    STG.E [R6.64], R21 ;
28    STG.E [R8.64], R17 ;
```

where in addition to the loads from global memory to registers on lines 1, 3, 5, and 7 and the store from registers to global memory on line 25–28, there are stores to shared memory from registers via the STS instruction on lines 18–21 and loads from shared memory to registers via the LDS instruction on lines 22–24. Once again execution is not blocked at the load instructions on lines 1, 3, 5, and 7, but execution will stall at the stores to shared memory on lines 18–21 until the loads complete. Since the load-use separation is larger in this case compared to when a register array was used to hold the temporary value, the round trip from registers to shared memory results in slower overall performance. As long as register pressure is not an issue, using temporary arrays in registers is faster than using shared memory in such cases. Note that in the case of the matrix transpose, data are being shared between threads, and as such use of shared memory (along with a synchronization barrier between threads of a thread block) is required.

On devices of compute capability 8.0 and higher, the process of loading data from global memory to shared memory can be made more efficient using the asynchronous data transfers.

5.3.2.1 *Asynchronous data transfers between global and shared memory*

We have seen in the previous section that data transfers from global memory to shared memory, such as

```
aShared(is) = aGlobal(i)
```

where aShared and aGlobal are arrays in shared and global memory, translate to two instructions: a load from global memory to registers and a store from registers to shared memory. Thread execution will not block on load of data from global memory to registers, but rather stalls on the first use of such data, which in this case will be the store operation from registers to shared memory.

On devices of compute capability 8.0 and higher, it is possible to bypass the use of registers entirely when loading data from global memory to shared memory using the pipeline primitives interface. The pipeline primitives interface is a small set of routines contained in the wmma module that includes

```
call pipelineMemcpyAsync(aShared(is), aGlobal(i))
call pipelineCommit()
call pipelineWaitPrior(D)
```

The pipelineMemcpyAsync() routine submits requests for data transfers from global memory to shared memory to the pipeline, pipelineCommit() commits submitted requests as the current batch, and pipelineWaitPrior(D) waits for a prior batch or batches as specified by its argument. If {0, 1, 2, ..., N} is the sequence of invocations of pipelineCommit(), then calling pipelineWaitPrior(D) will wait for the completion of batches up to and including N-D. So pipelineWaitPrior(0) will wait for all previously committed batches to complete, pipelineWaitPrior(1) will wait for all but the most recent committed batch to complete, and so forth.

In addition to bypassing registers when transferring global data to shared memory, such transfers are asynchronous and allow the device thread to continue execution until encountering a pipelineWaitPrior() that requires otherwise. This is analogous to how cudaMemcpyAsync() is used to asynchronously transfer data between the host and device global memory so that one can overlap data transfers between the host and device with kernel execution.

We can modify the copy kernel to use the asynchronous data transfer from global to shared memory rather than the assignment statement version that will stall on the load from registers to shared memory:

```
66    attributes(global) subroutine copy_ILP_sharedAsync(odata, idata)
67      use wmma
68      implicit none
69      real(fpKind) :: odata(*), idata(*)
70      real(fpKind), shared :: tmp(blockDim%x, ILP)
71      integer :: i,j
72
73      i = (blockIdx%x-1)*blockDim%x*ILP + threadIdx%x
74
75      do j = 1, ILP
76          call pipelineMemcpyAsync(tmp(threadIdx%x,j), &
77              idata(i+(j-1)*blockDim%x))
78          call pipelineCommit()
79      enddo
80
81      do j = 1, ILP
82          call pipelineWaitPrior(ILP-j)
83          odata(i+(j-1)*blockDim%x) = tmp(threadIdx%x,j)
84      enddo
85    end subroutine copy_ILP_sharedAsync
```

Looking at the disassembled code for copy_ILP_sharedAsync(), we see that in place of the LDG.E instruction that loads data from global memory to registers and the STS instruction that stores data in registers to shared memory, we have

```
LDGSTS.E [R19], [R2.64+-0x4] ;
```

which is the fused load-store instruction that performs the load of global data directly to shared memory. The pipelineCommit() call generates the dependency barrier:

```
LDGDEPBAR ;
```

which is a fence for completion of the LDGSTS instructions that otherwise might complete out of order with respect to one another. The pipelineWaitPrior() command produces the dependency barrier:

```
DEPBAR.LE SB0, 0x3 ;
```

which occurs before the LDS and STG.E instructions that load the data from shared memory to registers and then store the data from registers to global memory.

The benefit from using this approach would be realized if we had some independent computation between the two do loops in the copy_ILP_sharedAsync() kernel, which would be executed immediately after issuing the loads from global memory in the first loop without stalling on the stores to shared memory. As is, for this simple kernel, there is no perfomance advantage in implementing asynchronous copies to shared memory. However, this does illustrate how the asynchronous copies are implemented.

5.3.2.2 *Instruction-level parallelism in CUF kernels*

We can achieve instruction-level parallelism in CUF kernels by explicitly specifying thread block and grid parameters, which are not sufficient to cover all elements of the array. The compiler will then generate a kernel where each thread processes multiple elements. For example, if we return to our first

CUF kernel code and explicitly specify the grid size in addition to the block size in the directive, then we have

```
1   program ilp
2     implicit none
3     integer, parameter :: n = 1024*1024
4     integer :: a(n), i, b
5     integer, device :: a_d(n)
6     integer, parameter :: tPB = 256
7
8     a = 1
9     b = 3
10
11    a_d = a
12
13    !$cuf kernel do <<<1024,tPB>>>
14    do i = 1, n
15        a_d(i) = a_d(i) + b
16    enddo
17
18    a = a_d
19
20    if (any(a /= 4)) then
21        write(*,*) '**** Program Failed ****'
22    else
23        write(*,*) 'Program Passed'
24    endif
25  end program ilp
```

Here the 1024 blocks of 256 threads cannot process the 1024^2 elements if each thread processes a single element, so the compiler generates a loop, which results in each thread processing 4 array elements.

Note that when the compiler encounters wildcards in execution configurations and generates a launch configuration, it may by default generate instruction-level parallelism. It is wise to profile the application first and see if specifying values rather than wildcards in the execution configuration is needed.

5.4 Instruction optimization

Up to this point, we have addressed optimization from the perspective of data movement, both between the host and device and within the device. We have also spoken about ensuring that there is enough parallelism exposed to keep the device busy, either through thread-level parallelism (execution configuration and occupancy) or though instruction-level parallelism. When a code is not memory bound and there is sufficient parallelism exposed on the device, then we need to address the instruction throughput of kernels to increase performance.

The arithmetic throughput of various native instructions on devices of different compute capabilities is listed in Table 5.5. (A more complete version of this table can be found in the *CUDA C++ Programming Guide*.) Other instructions map to multiple native instructions, with the exception of certain device intrinsics.

Table 5.5 Native arithmetic instruction throughput in results per clock cycle per multiprocessor. The entry MI implies the operation gets translated to multiple instructions.

Compute capability	\multicolumn{9}{c}{Arithmetic instruction throughput (Results/clock cycle/multiprocessor)}

Compute capability	6.0	6.1	6.2	7.0, 7.2	7.5	8.0	8.6	8.9	9.0
Floating-point operations									
16-bit floating point add, multiply, multiply–add	128	2	256	128	128	256	256	128	256
32-bit floating point add, multiply, multiply–add	64	128	128	64	64	64	128	128	128
32-bit floating point reciprocal, reciprocal square root	16	32	32	16	16	16	16	16	16
64-bit floating point add, multiply, multiply–add	32	4	4	32	2	32	2	2	64
Integer operations									
32-bit integer add, subtract	64	128	128	64	64	64	64	64	64
32-bit integer multiply, multiply–add	MI	MI	MI	64	64	64	64	64	64
32-bit integer ishift()	32	64	64	64	64	64	64	64	64
32-bit iand(), ieor(), ior()	64	128	128	64	64	64	64	64	64
Warp operations									
warp shuffle	32	32	32	32	16	32	32	32	32
warp reduce	MI	MI	MI	MI	MI	16	16	16	16
warp vote	64	64	64	64	64	64	64	64	64
Type conversions									
8- and 16-bit to 32-bit integer type conversions	16	32	32	64	64	64	64	64	64
type conversions to and from 64-bit types	16	4	4	16	2	16	2	2	16
other type conversions	16	32	32	16	16	16	16	16	16

5.4.1 Device intrinsics

CUDA Fortran allows access to many of the built-in device functions through the use of the cudadevice module in device code. A full list of the built-in functions available to CUDA Fortran is included in the *CUDA Fortran Programming and Reference Guide*. Here we briefly discuss a few classes of these functions.

5.4.1.1 Directed rounding

Directed rounding in CUDA is available through additional instructions rather than by setting a rounding mode. The suffixes _ru, _rd, _rn, and _rz imply rounding upward, downward, to nearest even, and to zero. For example, 32-bit and 64-bit floating-point addition functions are available in various rounding modes using __fadd_[rn,rz,ru,rd] and __dadd_[rn,rz,ru,rd].

5.4.1.2 C intrinsics

There are some C intrinsics available through the cudadevice module that are not available in Fortran. In particular, sincos(x, s, c) calculates both sine and cosine of the argument x. This function nearly doubles the throughput relative to calling sine and cosine separately, without any loss of precision.

5.4.1.3 *Fast math intrinsics*

CUDA has a set of fast, but less accurate, intrinsics for 32-bit floating-point data, which can be enabled per compilation unit through the -gpu=fastmath compiler option or selectively by using the cudadevice module and explicitly calling __fdividef(x,y), __sinf(x), __cosf(x), __tanf(x), __sincosf(x,s,c), __logf(x), __log2f(x), __log10f(x), __expf(x), __exp10f(x), and __powf(x,y).

5.4.1.4 *Compiler options*

We have already discussed the compiler option -gpu=fastmath used to invoke faster, but less accurate, intrinsics for 32-bit floating point data. There are some other compiler options that affect instruction throughput.

The option -gpu=[no]fma toggles the use of fusing multiply–add instructions. If we compile the code

```
1  module m
2  contains
3    attributes(global) subroutine k(a, b, c)
4      real :: a, b, c
5      c = a*b+c
6    end subroutine k
7  end module m
```

with the -gpu=keep and inspect the generated PTX code, then we will find

```
          fma.rn.ftz.f32   %f4, %f2, %f3, %f1;
```

which is an IEEE-754(2008) compliant fused-multiply add instruction where the full-width product is used in the addition, followed by a single rounding step. Contrast this to the case where -gpu=nofma is specified, where the PTX contains the two instructions:

```
          mul.rn.ftz.f32   %f4, %f2, %f3;
          add.rn.ftz.f32   %f5, %f1, %f4;
```

The FMA instruction will execute faster than separate MUL and ADD instructions as there is dedicated hardware for those operations. In terms of accuracy, the lack of any truncation or rounding of the product prior to the addition in FMA means that the FMA will in general yield a more accurate result than separate MUL and ADD instructions.

The option -gpu=[no]flushz controls single-precision denormals support. By default (or with -gpu=flushz) denormals are flushed to zero and will generally execute faster than code with -gpu=noflushz, where denormals are supported. PTX instructions will contain ftz when denormals are flushed to zero, as in the FMA, MUL, and ADD instructions above.

5.4.2 Divergent warps

Another instruction optimization is minimizing the number of divergent warps. Consider the following segment of device code:

```
1      i = blockDim%x*(blockIdx%x-1) + threadIdx%x
2      if (mod(i,2) == 0) then
3        x(i) = 0
4      else
5        x(i) = 1
6      endif
```

which sets x(i) to zero or one if the index i is even or odd. Because instructions are issued warp-wise, if a branch of a conditional is satisfied by any thread in a warp, then all threads in a warp must execute that branch. The different execution paths are serialized, and the instruction count per thread increases accordingly. The results for threads that do not satisfy the branch are effectively masked out, but the performance implications are that every thread in a warp executes every branch that is satisfied by one thread in the warp.

In our example above, because half the threads in a warp satisfy each branch, all threads execute both branches. The performance penalty is not severe for this simple example, but if there are many branches to an if or case construct, or multiple levels of nesting of such control flow statements, then warp divergence can become a problem. On the other hand, if a condition evaluates uniformly over a warp of threads, then at most a single branch is executed, as in the following example:

```
i = blockDim%x*(blockIdx%x-1) + threadIdx%x
if (mod((i-1)/warpsize,2) == 0) then
  x(i) = 0
else
  x(i) = 1
endif
```

which sets x(i) to zero or one if it belongs to an even or odd warp. Here each thread only executes one branch.

If a considerable amount of computations are to be performed on only a portion of array elements that results in substantial warp divergence, then it may be beneficial to pack those participating elements into an array, perform the operations on the array in a non-divergent manner, and then scatter the resulting values back to the original array. Section 6.5 on array compaction discusses how to do so efficiently.

Porting tips and techniques

This chapter contains material that is helpful in porting applications to CUDA Fortran. The techniques presented here are not optimization techniques in the sense of making codes run faster, rather they are coding styles and techniques that can reduce the effort involved in porting applications to CUDA Fortran.

One goal we pursue when porting code to CUDA Fortran is to leave the CPU code intact, so that the same source code can be compiled to run on either the CPU or GPU by the absence or presence of the -cuda compiler option. This can be easily done with preprocessor macros, but we also strive to minimize code that gets duplicated and therefore minimize the maintenance headaches that results from such code duplication.

6.1 CUF kernels

When porting codes to CUDA Fortran, CUF kernels can be a tremendous asset. If a loop or region of tightly nested loops allows acceleration via a CUF kernel, then by all means use the CUF kernel directive to do so, especially as a first pass at porting the code. If a particular CUF kernel becomes a performance bottleneck, then an explicit kernel for the loop can be written at a later time, but if that loop is not in the critical path for performance, then there is no reason to spend time writing kernel code for what can be accomplished with a simple CUF kernel directive.

Let us start with a very simple example that we will extend throughout this chapter to illustrate the various techniques. Say we have the host code

```
1  program main
2    implicit none
3    integer, parameter :: n=8
4    real :: a(n), b(n)
5    integer :: i
6
7    do i = 1, n
8       a(i) = i+1
9    enddo
10
11   do i = 1, n
12      b(i) = a(i)+1
13   enddo
14
15   print *, a
16   print *, b
```

```
17   end program main
```

Both loops have an independence between iterations that allows the use of CUF kernels, so we can port the code simply by declaring the arrays as managed and using CUF kernels:

```
1    program main
2      use cudafor
3      implicit none
4      integer, parameter :: n=8
5      real, managed :: a(n), b(n)
6      integer :: i
7
8      !$cuf kernel do <<<*,*>>>
9      do i = 1, n
10         a(i) = i+1
11     enddo
12
13     !$cuf kernel do <<<*,*>>>
14     do i = 1, n
15         b(i) = a(i)+1
16     enddo
17
18     i = cudaDeviceSynchronize()
19
20     print *, a
21     print *, b
22   end program main
```

where in addition to declaring the arrays with the managed attribute and adding the CUF kernel directives, the cudafor module is used, and after the last do loop, a call to cudaDeviceSynchronize is made. If we use device rather managed variables, then more changes are required:

```
1    program main
2      implicit none
3      integer, parameter :: n=8
4      real :: a(n), b(n)
5      real, device :: a_d(n), b_d(n)
6      integer :: i
7
8      !$cuf kernel do <<<*,*>>>
9      do i = 1, n
10         a_d(i) = i+1
11     enddo
12
13     !$cuf kernel do <<<*,*>>>
14     do i = 1, n
15         b_d(i) = a_d(i)+1
16     enddo
17
18     a = a_d; b = b_d
19
20     print *, a
```

```
21    print *, b
22  end program main
```

Here the use cudafor statement is not required since a call to cudaDeviceSynchronize() is not needed as the explicit data transfers perform the synchronization. However, device versions of the arrays are needed, in declaration statements, within the loops, and in data transfers from the device to host before printing the results.

While these changes are relatively basic, the issue in both these versions of this code is that now we have separate codes to maintain, one for the host and either the managed or device version of the codes. By using conditional inclusion of source code described in the next section we can compile for execution on the host or device from a single source file.

6.2 **Conditional inclusion of code**

When porting code to CUDA Fortran, we inevitably run across sections of code that we wish only to be used when compiling for the CPU or GPU. Conditional inclusion of code can be done in several ways: by defining a preprocessor symbol at compile time, using the predefined symbol _CUDA when code is compiled with CUDA Fortran extensions, and using the sentinel !@cuf.

The following version of our example code with managed memory uses the _CUDA symbol to conditionally include code that will allow execution on the device:

```
1   program main
2   #ifdef _CUDA
3      use cudafor
4   #endif
5      implicit none
6      integer, parameter :: n=8
7      real :: a(n), b(n)
8   #ifdef _CUDA
9      attributes(managed) :: a, b
10  #endif
11     integer :: i
12
13     !$cuf kernel do <<<*,*>>>
14     do i = 1, n
15        a(i) = i+1
16     enddo
17
18     !$cuf kernel do <<<*,*>>>
19     do i = 1, n
20        b(i) = a(i)+1
21     enddo
22
23  #ifdef _CUDA
24     i = cudaDeviceSynchronize()
25     print *, 'GPU version'
26  #endif
27
```

```
28      print *, a
29      print *, b
30   end program main
```

Three preprocessor #ifdef _CUDA statements are used here: one to include the cudafor module, one to add the managed attribute to the arrays, and one to include the device synchronization and also print a statement indicating that the code is executing on the GPU. When the source code is in a file with the .F90 extension, then the preprocessor is invoked automatically, and the code is compiled as normal Fortran:

```
$ nvfortran portingManaged_CUDA.F90
$ ./a.out
    2.000000         3.000000         4.000000         5.000000
    6.000000         7.000000         8.000000         9.000000
    3.000000         4.000000         5.000000         6.000000
    7.000000         8.000000         9.000000         10.00000
```

If the -cuda flag is used, then the _CUDA symbol is defined, and the CUDA Fortran version is compiled:

```
$ nvfortran portingManaged_CUDA.F90 -cuda
$ ./a.out
 GPU version
    2.000000         3.000000         4.000000         5.000000
    6.000000         7.000000         8.000000         9.000000
    3.000000         4.000000         5.000000         6.000000
    7.000000         8.000000         9.000000         10.00000
```

The device version of the code can be modified similarly:

```
1    program main
2      implicit none
3      integer, parameter :: n=8
4      real :: a(n), b(n)
5   #ifdef _CUDA
6      attributes(device) :: a, b
7      real :: a_h(n), b_h(n)
8   #endif
9      integer :: i
10
11     !$cuf kernel do <<<*,*>>>
12     do i = 1, n
13        a(i) = i+1
14     enddo
15
16     !$cuf kernel do <<<*,*>>>
17     do i = 1, n
18        b(i) = a(i)+1
19     enddo
20
21   #ifdef _CUDA
22     a_h = a; b_h = b
```

```
23    print *, 'GPU version'
24    print *, a_h
25    print *, b_h
26  #else
27    print *, a
28    print *, b
29  #endif
30
31  end program main
```

although here the changes are a bit more extensive than in the managed case as we need both host and device versions of the arrays. To minimize changes in the body of the CUF kernels, we make the arrays a() and b() the device version and declare additional host arrays use for output.

The sentinel !@cuf can be used rather than preprocessor directives to accomplish the same conditional inclusion of code. A line that begins with the !@cuf sentinel will appear as a statement (minus the !@cuf sentinel) when CUDA Fortran is enabled in compilation; otherwise, the entire line is a comment. Using this technique, the managed code becomes

```
1   program main
2     !@cuf use cudafor
3     implicit none
4     integer, parameter :: n=8
5     real :: a(n), b(n)
6     !@cuf attributes(managed) :: a, b
7     integer :: i
8
9     !$cuf kernel do <<<*,*>>>
10    do i = 1, n
11       a(i) = i+1
12    enddo
13
14    !$cuf kernel do <<<*,*>>>
15    do i = 1, n
16       b(i) = a(i)+1
17    enddo
18
19    !@cuf i = cudaDeviceSynchronize()
20    !@cuf print *, 'GPU version'
21
22    print *, a
23    print *, b
24  end program main
```

In addition to being shorter, the code does not require the preprocessor and can be named with a lower-case extension:

```
$ nvfortran portingManagedSent.f90
$ ./a.out
      2.000000        3.000000        4.000000        5.000000
      6.000000        7.000000        8.000000        9.000000
      3.000000        4.000000        5.000000        6.000000
```

```
     7.000000        8.000000        9.000000      10.00000
$ nvfortran portingManagedSent.f90 -cuda
$ ./a.out
 GPU version
     2.000000        3.000000        4.000000       5.000000
     6.000000        7.000000        8.000000       9.000000
     3.000000        4.000000        5.000000       6.000000
     7.000000        8.000000        9.000000      10.00000
```

The sentinel can also be used in the device variable version:

```
1  program main
2    implicit none
3    integer, parameter :: n=8
4    real :: a(n), b(n)
5    !@cuf attributes(device) :: a, b
6    !@cuf real :: a_h(n), b_h(n)
7    integer :: i
8
9    !$cuf kernel do <<<*,*>>>
10   do i = 1, n
11      a(i) = i+1
12   enddo
13
14   !$cuf kernel do <<<*,*>>>
15   do i = 1, n
16      b(i) = a(i)+1
17   enddo
18
19   !@cuf a_h = a; b_h = b
20   !@cuf print *, 'GPU version'
21
22 #ifdef _CUDA
23   print *, a_h
24   print *, b_h
25 #else
26   print *, a
27   print *, b
28 #endif
29
30 end program main
```

but there is need for a preprocessor directive due to the #else clause when writing out results. For a small code such as this, the changes needed to accommodate host and device version of the same array are minor, but in a larger code, such duplication can become error prone and difficult to maintain. There are several options at our disposal to temporarily rename variables, so that such duplication can be avoided entirely, which we explore next.

6.3 **Renaming variables**

When porting applications to CUDA Fortran, the ability to temporarily rename variables so that code written for host variables can be used for device variables can greatly reduce the effort involved in porting, code maintainability, and code legibility – especially when used in conjunction with CUF kernels. We will discuss two ways to accomplish renaming, the first via use statements and the second using associate blocks.

6.3.1 **Renaming via use statements**

Many large Fortran codes place large arrays shared by several program units in modules that are accessed through use statements in the relevant subprograms. When such program units contain loops that can be converted into CUF kernels, these program units can be ported to CUDA Fortran without altering the contents of such loops by using the renaming option in the use statement along with placing a CUF kernel directive before the loop. In addition to enabling a CUDA Fortran port with minimal effort, this programming convention preserves the regular Fortran code, so we can compile host Fortran or CUDA Fortran simply by omitting or including -cuda on the compile line. To illustrate this technique, we will port the following CPU code that solves the 2D Laplace equation via finite difference method:

```
1   module parameters
2     use, intrinsic :: iso_fortran_env
3     integer, parameter :: nx = 4096, ny = 4096
4     integer, parameter :: iterMax = 100
5     integer, parameter :: reportInterval = 10
6     integer, parameter :: fp_kind = real32
7     real(fp_kind), parameter :: tol = 1.0e-5_fp_kind
8   end module parameters
9
10  module arrays
11    use parameters
12    real(fp_kind) :: a(nx,ny), aNew(nx,ny), absResidual(2:nx-1,2:ny-1)
13  end module arrays
14
15  module laplaceRoutines
16  contains
17    subroutine initialize()
18      use parameters
19      use arrays
20      implicit none
21      real(fp_kind), parameter :: &
22           pi = 2.0_fp_kind*asin(1.0_fp_kind)
23      real(fp_kind) :: y0(nx)
24      integer :: i
25
26      do i = 1, nx
27         y0(i) = sin(pi*(i-1)/(nx-1))
28      enddo
29      a = 0.0_fp_kind
30      a(:,1) = y0
```

```
31        a(:,ny) = y0*exp(-pi)
32        aNew = a
33     end subroutine initialize
34
35
36     subroutine laplaceSolution()
37       use parameters
38       use arrays
39       implicit none
40       real(fp_kind) :: maxResidual = 2*tol
41       integer :: iter
42
43       iter=0
44       do while ( maxResidual > tol .and. iter <= iterMax )
45          iter = iter + 1
46          call jacobiIteration()
47          maxResidual = maxval(absResidual)
48          if(mod(iter,reportInterval) == 0) &
49               print '(i8,3x,f10.6)', iter, maxResidual
50          a = aNew
51       end do
52     end subroutine laplaceSolution
53
54
55     subroutine jacobiIteration()
56       use parameters
57       use arrays
58       implicit none
59       integer :: i, j
60
61       do j=2,ny-1
62          do i=2,nx-1
63             aNew(i,j) = 0.2_fp_kind * &
64                  (a(i,j-1)+a(i-1,j)+a(i+1,j)+a(i,j+1)) + &
65                  0.05_fp_kind * &
66                  (a(i-1,j-1)+a(i+1,j-1)+a(i-1,j+1)+a(i+1,j+1))
67             absResidual(i,j) = abs(aNew(i,j)-a(i,j))
68          end do
69       end do
70     end subroutine jacobiIteration
71
72  end module laplaceRoutines
73
74
75  program main
76     use parameters
77     use arrays
78     use laplaceRoutines
79     implicit none
80     real :: startTime, stopTime
81
82     print '(/,a,i0,a,i0,a)', &
```

```
83            'Relaxation calculation on ', nx, ' x ', ny, ' mesh'
84     print *, 'Iteration   Max Residual'
85
86     call initialize()
87
88     call cpu_time(startTime)
89     call laplaceSolution()
90
91     call cpu_time(stopTime)
92     print '(a,f10.3,a)', '  Completed in ', &
93          stopTime-startTime, ' seconds'
94  end program main
```

A variant of this code is discussed in the finite difference method case study later in this book, but this simplified version is useful in demonstrating this porting technique.

The CUDA Fortran version of the code only has a few changes. The parameters module on lines 1–8 requires no modification to run on the device. The arrays module in the ported code

```
10  module arrays
11    use parameters
12    real(fp_kind) :: a(nx,ny), aNew(nx,ny), absResidual(2:nx-1,2:ny-1)
13    !@cuf real(fp_kind), device :: a_d(nx,ny), aNew_d(nx,ny)
14    !@cuf attributes(device) :: absResidual
15  end module arrays
```

uses the !@cuf sentinel to conditionally include code when compiled for CUDA Fortran. When compiling for CUDA Fortran, the arrays a_d() and aNew_d(), which are device counterparts to the host arrays a() and aNew(), are declared on line 13, and the device attribute is assigned to the array absResidual() on line 14. Note the different treatment when porting these arrays. When compiling for CUDA Fortran, both host and device arrays are needed for a() and aNew() and therefore the additional declaration of device arrays on line 13, whereas the array absResidual() is needed only on the device, and hence the addition of the device attribute.

In the laplaceRoutines module, the initialize() subroutine becomes

```
19    subroutine initialize()
20      use parameters
21      use arrays
22      implicit none
23      real(fp_kind), parameter :: &
24            pi = 2.0_fp_kind*asin(1.0_fp_kind)
25      real(fp_kind) :: y0(nx)
26      integer :: i
27
28      do i = 1, nx
29         y0(i) = sin(pi*(i-1)/(nx-1))
30      enddo
31      a = 0.0_fp_kind
32      a(:,1) = y0
33      a(:,ny) = y0*exp(-pi)
34      aNew = a
35      !@cuf aNew_d = aNew
```

```
36        !@cuf a_d = a
37     end subroutine initialize
```

This routine initializes the arrays on the host and then uses statements with the !@cuf sentinel to transfer the results to the device. We could have easily ported the initialization routine to the device; however, in many codes, it is common to do initialization on the host and then transfer the results to the device, so we mimic that tendency here.

In the laplaceSolution() subroutine

```
40     subroutine laplaceSolution()
41        use parameters
42  #ifdef _CUDA
43        use arrays, only: a => a_d, aNew => aNew_d, absResidual
44  #else
45        use arrays
46  #endif
47        !@cuf use cudafor
48        implicit none
49        real(fp_kind) :: maxResidual = 2*tol
50        integer :: iter
51
52        iter=0
53        do while ( maxResidual > tol .and. iter <= iterMax )
54           iter = iter + 1
55           call jacobiIteration()
56           maxResidual = maxval(absResidual)
57           if(mod(iter,reportInterval) == 0) &
58                print '(i8,3x,f10.6)', iter, maxResidual
59           a = aNew
60        end do
61     end subroutine laplaceSolution
```

we see the first use of module variable renaming via the only: localName => moduleName option to the use statement on line 43. In this subroutine, we only need the device versions of arrays a() and aNew(), but rather than modify the executable statements of the code by appending _d suffix to the arrays, on line 43, we rename the device arrays declared in the module so that they can be locally accessed by the names without the _d suffix. The host arrays defined in the arrays module are not accessible in this routine due to the only option, so there is no conflict when renaming the module device arrays in this fashion. Note that we also need to conditionally include the cudafor module, which contains the code that overloads the maxval() intrinsic for device data that is used on line 56. Note that by using this renaming technique all the changes made in porting this subroutine occur before the implicit none statement, whereas the executable statements remain unaltered. For this particular code, changing the executable statements would not be a burden, but in a larger code, this renaming approach reduces the amount of changes needed in porting and maintaining the code – the same executable statements are used for both CPU and GPU codes.

The jacobiIteration() subroutine

```
64    subroutine jacobiIteration()
65       use parameters
66  #ifdef _CUDA
67       use arrays, only: a => a_d, aNew => aNew_d, absResidual
68  #else
69       use arrays
70  #endif
71       implicit none
72       integer :: i, j
73
74       !$cuf kernel do(2) <<<*,*>>>
75       do j=2,ny-1
76          do i=2,nx-1
77             aNew(i,j) = 0.2_fp_kind * &
78                   (a(i,j-1)+a(i-1,j)+a(i+1,j)+a(i,j+1)) + &
79                   0.05_fp_kind * &
80                   (a(i-1,j-1)+a(i+1,j-1)+a(i-1,j+1)+a(i+1,j+1))
81             absResidual(i,j) = abs(aNew(i,j)-a(i,j))
82          end do
83       end do
84    end subroutine jacobiIteration
```

also makes use of module variable renaming on line 67. In this routine, which contains a doubly nested loop that performs the update to all interior points, aside from the variable renaming, we only need include a CUF kernel directive to port the code, which is ignored when compiled for regular Fortran. The contents of the loop are unaltered. We could have left the main program unaltered but included some conditional output indicating when the code is compiled for execution on the GPU:

```
89   program main
90      use parameters
91      use arrays
92      use laplaceRoutines
93      implicit none
94
95      real :: startTime, stopTime
96
97      !@cuf print '(/,a,/)', 'GPU version'
98      print '(/,a,i0,a,i0,a)', &
99            'Relaxation calculation on ', nx, ' x ', ny, ' mesh'
100
101     print *, 'Iteration   Max Residual'
102
103     call initialize()
104
105     call cpu_time(startTime)
106     call laplaceSolution()
107
108     call cpu_time(stopTime)
109     print '(a,f10.3,a)', '   Completed in ', &
110           stopTime-startTime, ' seconds'
```

```
111  end program main
```

which we strongly encourage. This can be extended further by printing the device name using the device API routines as done in the introduction.

We have ported several large codes using this variable renaming technique, for example the CFD code AFiD available at https://github.com/PhysicsofFluids/AFiD_GPU_opensource, where many subroutines consisting of many nested loops were unmodified except for module variable renaming and CUF kernel directives. This porting strategy cannot make use of certain kernel optimizations, such as shared memory, but if needed, explicit kernels with such optimizations can be added on a case-by-case basis. But as is, this technique can port a lot of code quickly provided loops satisfy the criteria for porting via CUF kernels.

Compiling and executing the ported code, we have

```
$ nvfortran -O3 laplace2DUse.F90
$ ./a.out

Relaxation calculation on 4096 x 4096 mesh
 Iteration    Max Residual
       10     0.023564
       20     0.011931
       30     0.008061
       40     0.006065
       50     0.004811
       60     0.004040
       70     0.003442
       80     0.003029
       90     0.002685
      100     0.002420
   Completed in      2.124 seconds
$ nvfortran -O3 -cuda laplace2DUse.F90
$ ./a.out

GPU version


Relaxation calculation on 4096 x 4096 mesh
 Iteration    Max Residual
       10     0.023564
       20     0.011931
       30     0.008061
       40     0.006065
       50     0.004811
       60     0.004040
       70     0.003442
       80     0.003029
       90     0.002685
      100     0.002420
   Completed in      0.145 seconds
```

where we have named the file with the .F90 extension, which invokes the preprocessor by default. We could have an .f90 extension and explicitly specify -Mpreprocess on the compile line as well.

6.3.2 **Renaming via the** `associate` **construct**

The associate construct allows us to associate a name with a variable for the duration of the associate block. Here is our example code used earlier in this section, which uses variable renaming via associate blocks to allow compilation for execution on either the host or device:

```
1   program main
2     implicit none
3     integer, parameter :: n=8
4
5     real :: a(n), b(n)
6     !@cuf   real, device :: a_d(n), b_d(n)
7     integer :: i
8
9     !@cuf associate(a => a_d)
10    !$cuf kernel do
11    do i = 1, n
12       a(i) = i+1
13    enddo
14    !@cuf associate(b => b_d)
15    !$cuf kernel do
16    do i = 1, n
17       b(i) = a(i)+1
18    enddo
19    !@cuf end associate ! b ...
20    !@cuf end associate ! a ...
21    !@cuf a = a_d; b = b_d
22
23    !@cuf print *, 'GPU run'
24    print *, a
25    print *, b
26  end program main
```

On line 9 the name a is associated with the device array a_d for the duration of the associate block (the end associate statement on line 20), and similarly for the name b and device array b_d between lines 14 and 19. Within these blocks, the host arrays are unavailable; however, both host and device arrays are available outside the blocks, as in the device-to-host transfer statements on line 21. As you can see from this example, associate blocks can be nested.

The Laplace code using associate blocks is

```
1   module parameters
2     use, intrinsic :: iso_fortran_env
3     integer, parameter :: nx = 4096, ny = 4096
4     integer, parameter :: iterMax = 100
5     integer, parameter :: reportInterval = 10
6     integer, parameter :: fp_kind = real32
7     real(fp_kind), parameter :: tol = 1.0e-5_fp_kind
8   end module parameters
9
10  module arrays
11    use parameters
12    real(fp_kind) :: a(nx,ny), aNew(nx,ny), absResidual(2:nx-1,2:ny-1)
```

```fortran
13       !@cuf real(fp_kind), device :: a_d(nx,ny), aNew_d(nx,ny)
14       !@cuf attributes(device) :: absResidual
15  end module arrays
16
17  module laplaceRoutines
18  contains
19    subroutine initialize()
20      use parameters
21      use arrays
22      implicit none
23      real(fp_kind), parameter :: &
24            pi = 2.0_fp_kind*asin(1.0_fp_kind)
25      real(fp_kind) :: y0(nx)
26      integer :: i
27
28      do i = 1, nx
29          y0(i) = sin(pi*(i-1)/(nx-1))
30      enddo
31      a = 0.0_fp_kind
32      a(:,1) = y0
33      a(:,ny) = y0*exp(-pi)
34      aNew = a
35      !@cuf aNew_d = aNew
36      !@cuf a_d = a
37    end subroutine initialize
38
39
40    subroutine laplaceSolution()
41      use parameters
42      !@cuf use cudafor
43      use arrays
44      implicit none
45      real(fp_kind) :: maxResidual = 2*tol
46      integer :: iter
47
48      iter=0
49      !@cuf associate(a=>a_d, aNew=>aNew_d)
50      do while ( maxResidual > tol .and. iter <= iterMax )
51         iter = iter + 1
52         call jacobiIteration()
53         maxResidual = maxval(absResidual)
54         if(mod(iter,reportInterval) == 0) &
55              print '(i8,3x,f10.6)', iter, maxResidual
56         a = aNew
57      end do
58      !@cuf end associate
59    end subroutine laplaceSolution
60
61
62    subroutine jacobiIteration()
63      use parameters
64      use arrays
```

```
65      implicit none
66      integer :: i, j
67
68      !@cuf associate(a=>a_d, aNew=> aNew_d)
69      !$cuf kernel do(2) <<<*,*>>>
70      do j=2,ny-1
71         do i=2,nx-1
72            aNew(i,j) = 0.2_fp_kind * &
73                  (a(i,j-1)+a(i-1,j)+a(i+1,j)+a(i,j+1)) + &
74                  0.05_fp_kind * &
75                  (a(i-1,j-1)+a(i+1,j-1)+a(i-1,j+1)+a(i+1,j+1))
76            absResidual(i,j) = abs(aNew(i,j)-a(i,j))
77         end do
78      end do
79      !@cuf end associate
80    end subroutine jacobiIteration
81
82 end module laplaceRoutines
83
84
85 program main
86   use parameters
87   use arrays
88   use laplaceRoutines
89   implicit none
90
91   real :: startTime, stopTime
92
93   !@cuf print '(/,a,/)', 'GPU associate version'
94   print '(/,a,i0,a,i0,a)', &
95        'Relaxation calculation on ', nx, ' x ', ny, ' mesh'
96
97   print *, 'Iteration   Max Residual'
98
99   call initialize()
100
101   call cpu_time(startTime)
102   call laplaceSolution()
103
104   call cpu_time(stopTime)
105   print '(a,f10.3,a)', ' Completed in ', &
106        stopTime-startTime, ' seconds'
107 end program main
```

Note that here we have avoided the need of the preprocessor completely, and all conditional inclusion of code is done with the !@cuf sentinel. The only clause is not needed in any of the use statements, as all renaming is done via associate blocks.

```
$ nvfortran -O3 laplace2DAssoc.f90
$ ./a.out

Relaxation calculation on 4096 x 4096 mesh
```

```
 Iteration    Max Residual
        10       0.023564
        20       0.011931
        30       0.008061
        40       0.006065
        50       0.004811
        60       0.004040
        70       0.003442
        80       0.003029
        90       0.002685
       100       0.002420
  Completed in        2.134 seconds
$ nvfortran -O3 -cuda laplace2DAssoc.f90
$ ./a.out

GPU associate version


Relaxation calculation on 4096 x 4096 mesh
 Iteration    Max Residual
        10       0.023564
        20       0.011931
        30       0.008061
        40       0.006065
        50       0.004811
        60       0.004040
        70       0.003442
        80       0.003029
        90       0.002685
       100       0.002420
  Completed in        0.147 seconds
```

We should spend some time for discussion of the relative merits of use statement renaming versus associate block renaming. First of all, use statement renaming is restricted to variables that are declared in modules, whereas associate block renaming can be used to rename any variable that is in scope. Both associate block and use statement renaming allow control over the extent of the renaming since the end associate statement can be placed anywhere, and likewise the scope of use statement can be controlled by placing the statement just after the block statement of a block-end block section of code. One downside of associate block renaming is that there can be some overhead on the host with its use, similarly to the overhead associated with pointers. From our Laplace example, however, no such overhead is observed.

6.4 Minimizing memory footprint for work arrays

While GPUs are available with large amounts of memory, the desire to run larger and larger simulations along with requiring compatibility with older hardware makes the minimization of a application's device memory footprint on GPUs a significant factor in code design. Many codes in CUDA Fortran require large amounts scratch or work arrays on the device in addition to the device memory used for the main arrays, and efficient reuse of the such work arrays becomes a key factor in minimizing the memory footprint. One issue that comes up often when reusing scratch space due to Fortran's strong typing is a means of using a work array as an array of a different type, rank, and/or kind. This section describes several methods of how we can accomplish such work array reuse.

The following code declares a real device array r_d and uses it both as a real and complex array as arguments to explicit kernels as well as in a CUF kernel:

```
1   module m
2   contains
3
4     attributes(global) subroutine r1(x, n)
5       implicit none
6       real :: x(*)
7       integer, value :: n
8       integer :: i
9       i = threadIdx%x + (blockIdx%x-1)*blockDim%x
10      if (i <= n) x(i) = i
11    end subroutine r1
12
13    ! can use ignore_tkr if you have access to the routine
14    attributes(global) subroutine c1(x, n)
15      implicit none
16      !dir$ ignore_tkr x
17      complex :: x(*)
18      integer, value :: n
19      integer :: i
20      i = threadIdx%x + (blockIdx%x-1)*blockDim%x
21      if (i <= n) x(i) = cmplx(-i, -1.0)
22    end subroutine c1
23
24    attributes(global) subroutine c2(x, n)
25      implicit none
26      complex :: x(*)
27      integer, value :: n
28      integer :: i
29      i = threadIdx%x + (blockIdx%x-1)*blockDim%x
30      if (i <= n) x(i) = cmplx(-i*2, -2.0)
31    end subroutine c2
32
33    ! use a wrapper with ignore_tkr
34    subroutine wrap_c2(x, n, g, b)
35      implicit none
36      !dir$ ignore_tkr x
37      complex, device :: x(*)
38      integer, value :: n, g, b
39      call c2<<<g,b>>>(x, n)
40    end subroutine wrap_c2
41
42  end module m
43
44
45  program main
```

```
46   use m
47   use union
48   use cudafor
49   implicit none
50   integer, parameter :: blks=2, tpb = 16, n = blks*tpb
51   real :: r(n)
52   real, device :: r_d(n)
53   complex, device, pointer :: ptr(:)
54   integer :: i
55
56   ! use r_d as real
57   call r1<<<blks, tpb>>>(r_d, n)
58   r = r_d
59   print *, r(1:4)
60
61   ! OK since ignore_tkr is in the kernel
62   call c1<<<blks/2,tpb>>>(r_d, n/2)
63   r = r_d
64   print *, r(1:4)
65
66   ! OK since ignore_tkr is in the wrapper to c2
67   call wrap_c2(r_d, n/2, blks/2, tpb)
68   r = r_d
69   print *, r(1:4)
70
71   r_d = 0.0
72
73   call union(r_d, ptr)
74   ! OK since ptr is complex
75   call c2<<<blks/2,tpb>>>(ptr, n/2)
76   r = r_d
77   print *, r(1:4)
78
79   !for use in CUF kernel as a complex, use pointer
80   !$cuf kernel do
81   do i = 1, n/2
82      ptr(i) = conjg(ptr(i))
83   end do
84   r = r_d
85   print *, r(1:4)
86
87   end program main
```

The first kernel invocation

```
57   call r1<<<blks, tpb>>>(r_d, n)
```

uses the real array r_d as a real array in kernel r1(), so there is no problem with type matching. The second kernel invocation on line 62 passes a real array to the c1() kernel, which has the array argument declared as a complex array. The type mismatch is avoided in this case by use of the ignore_tkr directive on line 16 of the kernel, informing the compiler to ignore the type, kind, and rank of argument x(*). The invocation of the kernel with a real argument only needs modification of the number of elements in the second argument and execution configuration (here the number of blocks, but could also be the number of threads per block) relative to the first kernel due to different sizes of real and complex data:

```
62    call c1<<<blks/2,tpb>>>(r_d, n/2)
```

This works as long as the programmer has access to the code. But when using `ignore_tkr` realize that the specified type/kind/rank checking is turned off for all invocations of this routine. If we have no access to the kernel code, or we want to avoid type checking only for certain invocations, then another approach is needed. A wrapper function that contains the `ignore_tkr` directive, such as `wrap_c2()`,

```
34    subroutine wrap_c2(x, n, g, b)
35      implicit none
36      !dir$ ignore_tkr x
37      complex, device :: x(*)
38      integer, value :: n, g, b
39      call c2<<<g,b>>>(x, n)
40    end subroutine wrap_c2
```

can be used if the programmer has no access to the kernel (in this case `c2()`) or if the user wants to keep type checking for other kernel invocations. This approach works fine, but if the number of routines requiring wrappers is large, then it can be burdensome. Ideally, we want the equivalent to a C union, which we can achieve using device pointers. The code for the `union()` function is in the union module used in the main program, but before we delve into the implementation, let us show how it is used:

```
73    call union(r_d, ptr)
74    ! OK since ptr is complex
75    call c2<<<blks/2,tpb>>>(ptr, n/2)
76    r = r_d
77    print *, r(1:4)
```

The call to the union function on line 73 associates the pointer `ptr` in the second argument, declared as

```
53    complex, device, pointer :: ptr(:)
```

with the memory in the first argument, in this case `r_d`. This pointer can then be used as the first argument in the kernel `c2()` without any need of the `ignore_tkr` directive. When we wish to use a work array as a different type or kind in a CUF kernel located in the same program unit in which the array is declared, then use the union technique as there is no mechanism to specify `ignore_tkr` in a CUF kernel:

```
79    !for use in CUF kernel as a complex, use pointer
80    !$cuf kernel do
81    do i = 1, n/2
82       ptr(i) = conjg(ptr(i))
83    end do
84    r = r_d
85    print *, r(1:4)
```

Now let us look into the implementation of the `union()` function:

```
1   module union
2
3      interface union
4          module procedure union_r4c4, union_r4dc4d
5      end interface union
6
7   contains
8
9      subroutine union_r4c4(s, d_ptr)
10        use iso_c_binding
11        implicit none
12        real(4) :: s(:)
13        complex(4), pointer :: d_ptr(:)
14        type(c_ptr) :: s_cptr
15        integer :: d_shape(1)
16
17        d_shape(1) = size(s)/2
18        s_cptr = transfer(loc(s), s_cptr)
19        call c_f_pointer(s_cptr, d_ptr, d_shape)
20     end subroutine union_r4c4
21
22     subroutine union_r4dc4d(s, d_ptr)
23        use cudafor
24        implicit none
25        real(4), device :: s(:)
26        complex(4), device, pointer :: d_ptr(:)
27        type(c_devptr) :: s_cptr
28        integer :: d_shape(1)
29
30        d_shape(1) = size(s)/2
31        s_cptr = c_devloc(s)
32        call c_f_pointer(s_cptr, d_ptr, d_shape)
33     end subroutine union_r4dc4d
34
35   end module union
```

Here union is a generic interface to two routines, one that points a complex rank-one pointer to a real rank-one array for host data and another for device data. This can be extended to any type, rank, and kind arguments easily, but for brevity, we limit the implementation to these two routines, which are very similar. The host version uses the loc() function that returns the address as an integer and then uses the transfer function to initialize a type(c_ptr) instance pointing to the real first argument, followed by the c_f_pointer() routine that associates Fortran pointer of complex type with the same memory. In the device version of this, the c_devptr() function in the cudafor module is used to initialize an instance of type(c_devptr), followed by a call to an overloaded version of c_f_pointer() that accepts device data.

Now that we have gone through all the code, let us compile and run it:

```
$ nvfortran -c union_m.cuf
$ nvfortran test_union.cuf union_m.o
test_union.cuf:
```

```
$ ./a.out
      1.000000          2.000000          3.000000          4.000000
     -1.000000         -1.000000         -2.000000         -1.000000
     -2.000000         -2.000000         -4.000000         -2.000000
     -2.000000         -2.000000         -4.000000         -2.000000
     -2.000000          2.000000         -4.000000          2.000000
```

which is the expected result. This union interface can be extended to share the same memory amongst variables with any combination of type, kind, and rank to facilitate minimizing the footprint of both host and device memory.

6.5 **Array compaction**

In codes where by computation array elements are predicated on array values meeting certain criteria, performance may suffer from branch divergence and non-coalescing, depending on the granularity of the array elements that satisfy the condition and the amount of computation performed on the elements. If the cost of branch divergence and noncoalesced data access is severe, then a preferable option may be to gather the data that satisfy the criteria into an array, perform the calculations on that compacted array, and then scatter the results back to the original array. This can be performed using the compact module described in this section.

The following code does an array compaction on the host (lines 43–53) and on the device using the compact() routine:

```
1   program main
2     use compact
3     use cudafor
4     implicit none
5     integer, parameter :: n=1024*1024*8
6     real(8) :: a(n), threshold
7     real(8), device :: a_d(n)
8     integer, device :: mask_d(n)
9     real(8), device, allocatable :: ac_d(:)
10    integer, device, allocatable :: ic_d(:)
11    real(8), allocatable :: ac(:), ach(:)
12    integer, allocatable :: ic(:), ich(:)
13    integer :: nc, nch, i, j, nerri, nerra, iter
14    real :: t1, t2
15
16
17    print *, 'Array size: ', n
18    print *, 'Block size: ', compact_tpb
19
20    threshold = 0.5d0
21    call random_number(a)
22    a_d = a
23
24    mask_d = 0
25    !$cuf kernel do <<<*,*>>>
```

```
26   do i = 1, n
27      if (a_d(i) <= threshold) mask_d(i) = 1
28   enddo
29
30   call cpu_time(t1)
31   call compact(a_d, mask_d, n, ac_d, ic_d, nc)
32   call cpu_time(t2)
33
34   print *, 'elapsed time gpu:', t2-t1
35
36   allocate(ac(nc), ic(nc))
37   ac = ac_d
38   ic = ic_d
39
40   ! do on host
41
42   call cpu_time(t1)
43   nch = count(a <= threshold)
44   allocate(ach(nch), ich(nch))
45   j = 0
46   do i = 1, n
47      if (a(i) <= threshold) then
48         j = j+1
49         ach(j) = a(i)
50         ich(j) = i
51      end if
52      if (j == nch) exit
53   enddo
54   call cpu_time(t2)
55
56   print *, 'elapsed time host:', t2-t1
57
58   if (nc /= nch) then
59      print *, 'Error: nc from host and device: ', nch, nc
60   else
61      print *, 'nc: ', nc
62   end if
63
64   nerri = 0
65   nerra = 0
66   do i = 1, min(nc,nch)
67      if (ic(i) /= ich(i)) nerri = nerri+1
68      if (ac(i) /= ach(i)) nerra = nerra+1
69   end do
70   print *, 'Errors in index array: ', nerri
71   print *, 'Errors in data array: ', nerra
72
73 end program main
```

This is similar to Fortran's PACK intrinsic, except that in addition to the compacted data array, the index array is calculated, which can be used to scatter the data from the compacted array to the original array in parallel. The original array is assigned random numbers on line 21, and mask array elements are either one or zero based on whether or not the corresponding array values are less than or equal to the specified threshold. The arguments to the compact() routine are a_d, the device input array (of various intrinsic types); mask_d, the integer device mask array; n, the number of elements in a_d and mask_d; ac_d, the allocatable device array containing the elements in a_d where mask_d is one; ic_d, the array of indices into a_d where mask_d is one; and nc, the number of elements in the compacted array. The compact() routine is a generic interface used to accommodate a variety of intrinsic types; the specific routine for an array of 64-bit reals is

```
125   subroutine compactReal8(a_d, mask_d, n, ac_d, ic_d, nc)
126     use cudafor
127     implicit none
128     real(8), device, intent(in) :: a_d(n)
129     integer, device, intent(in) :: mask_d(n)
130     integer, intent(in) :: n
131     real(8), device, allocatable :: ac_d(:)
132     integer, device, allocatable :: ic_d(:)
133     integer, intent(out) :: nc
134
135     integer, device, allocatable :: index_d(:)
136     integer :: i, nBlocks, nMask
137
138     nBlocks = (n-1)/(2*compact_tpb)+1
139     nMask = nBlocks*(2*compact_tpb)
140     allocate(index_d(0:nMask))
141
142     call indexCalculations(index_d, mask_d, n, nMask, nBlocks)
143     nc = index_d(n)
144     allocate(ac_d(nc), ic_d(nc))
145     !$cuf kernel do <<<*,*>>>
146     do i = 1, n
147        if (mask_d(i) == 1) then
148           ic_d(index_d(i)) = i
149           ac_d(index_d(i)) = a_d(i)
150        end if
151     end do
152     deallocate(index_d)
153   end subroutine compactReal8
```

where the routine indexCalculations() performs a parallel prefix sum on the mask array. Because the mask array uses values of one to indicate true, the parallel prefix sum on the mask array results in the indices into the compacted array to which the data are transferred, as indicated on lines 148–149. We should mention here that in the kernels that follow, thread blocks of compact_tpb threads perform parallel prefix sums on 2*compact_tpb elements, which is why the factor of two appears on lines 138 and 139.

The indexCalculations() code is

```
219   subroutine indexCalculations(index_d, mask_d, n, nMask, nBlocks)
220     implicit none
221     integer, device :: index_d(:)
222     integer, device :: mask_d(:)
223     integer :: n, nMask, nBlocks
```

```
224
225        integer, device, allocatable :: partialSum_d(:)
226        integer :: i, j
227
228        !$cuf kernel do <<<*,*>>>
229        do i = 1, n
230           index_d(i) = mask_d(i)
231        end do
232
233        allocate(partialSum_d(nBlocks))
234
235        ! do block-wise (exclusive) scan
236        call scan<<<nBlocks, compact_tpb>>>(index_d, partialSum_d)
237
238        ! calculate (exclusive) cumulative block sum from partial sums
239        call singleBlockScan<<<1,compact_tpb>>>(partialSum_d, nBlocks)
240
241        ! add in the cumulative block sums
242        !$cuf kernel do <<<*,*>>>
243        do i = 2*compact_tpb+1, nMask
244           j = (i-1)/(2*compact_tpb)+1
245           index_d(i) = index_d(i) + partialSum_d(j)
246        enddo
247
248        ! exclusive to inclusive scan, add last element and
249        ! ignore the first
250        !$cuf kernel do <<<1,1>>>
251        do i = n, n
252           index_d(i+1) = index_d(i) + mask_d(i)
253        end do
254
255        deallocate(partialSum_d)
256     end subroutine indexCalculations
```

The first scan kernel invoked on line 236 calculates the blockwise prefix sum for all elements while writing the sum of each block to a global array. The global array of partial sums then undergoes its own scan on line 239 to determine the cumulative block sums. The cumulative block sums are then added to the blockwise prefix sums, giving the prefix sum of the mask array on lines 243–246.

We now delve into the parallel prefix sum or scan algorithm. The scan algorithm used here is based on the work of Harris et al. (2007). The CUDA Fortran blockwise scan is

```
329     attributes(global) subroutine scan(a, pSum)
330        implicit none
331        integer :: a(*), pSum(*)
332
333        integer, shared :: s(2*compact_tpb)
334        integer :: tid, gid, stride, nr, i1, i2, t
335
336        tid = threadIdx%x
337        gid = (blockIdx%x-1)*blockDim%x*2 + tid
338
339        s(tid) = a(gid)
```

```
340        s(tid+compact_tpb) = a(gid+compact_tpb)
341
342        stride = 1
343        nr = compact_tpb
344        do
345           call syncthreads()
346           if (nr == 0) exit
347           if (tid <= nr) then
348              i1 = stride*(2*(tid-1)+1)
349              i2 = stride*(2*(tid-1)+2)
350              s(i2) = s(i2)+s(i1)
351           endif
352           stride = stride*2
353           nr = nr/2
354        end do
355
356        if (tid == compact_tpb) then
357           pSum(blockIdx%x) = s(2*compact_tpb)
358           s(2*compact_tpb) = 0
359        endif
360        call syncthreads()
361
362        stride = compact_tpb
363        nr = 1
364        do
365           if (tid <= nr) then
366              i1 = stride*(2*(tid-1)+1)
367              i2 = stride*(2*(tid-1)+2)
368              t = s(i1)
369              s(i1) = s(i2)
370              s(i2) = s(i2)+t
371           end if
372           stride = stride/2
373           call syncthreads()
374           if (stride == 0) exit
375           nr=nr*2
376        enddo
377        a(gid) = s(tid)
378        a(gid+compact_tpb) = s(tid+compact_tpb)
379     end subroutine scan
```

The loop on lines 344–354 is the upsweep or reduce phase of the scan where partial sums are calculated and stored in a shared memory array. The process is depicted in the top part of Fig. 6.1. On lines 356–359, one thread writes the last element in shared memory containing the sum of all compact_tpb*2 elements that this block processes to a partial sum array in global memory. The loop on lines 364–376 is the downsweep phase of the scan where the intermediate partial sums are combined to produce the blockwise result.

The second scan in indexCalculations() is launched with a single thread block and offsets all of the blockwise prefix sums with the sums from the prior blocks, giving the final result:

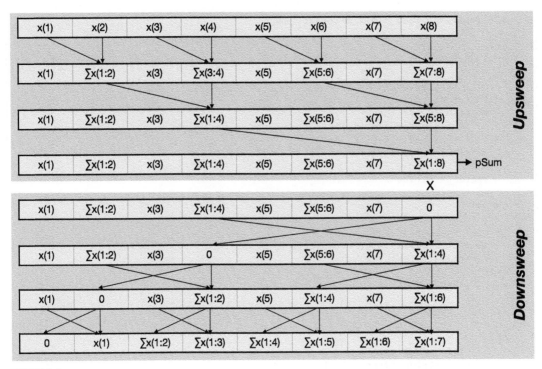

FIGURE 6.1

Depiction of the exclusive scan for an array of eight elements, consisting of an upsweep or reduction phase where the last element is the sum, and a downsweep phase where partial sums are combined to produce the final result.

```
265   attributes(global) subroutine singleBlockScan(a, n)
266      implicit none
267      integer :: a(*)
268      integer, value :: n  ! size of a_d in elements
269      integer, shared :: s(2*compact_tpb)
270      integer :: tid, gid, stride, nr, i1, i2, t
271      integer :: blockIdx_x, blockSum, cumulativeSum
272
273      tid = threadIdx%x
274      cumulativeSum = 0
275      blockIdx_x = 1
276      do
277         gid = (blockIdx_x -1)*blockDim%x*2 + tid
278         s(tid) = a(gid)
279         s(tid+compact_tpb) = a(gid+compact_tpb)
280
281         stride = 1
282         nr = compact_tpb
```

```
283        do
284            call syncthreads()
285            if (nr == 0) exit
286            if (tid <= nr) then
287                i1 = stride*(2*(tid-1)+1)
288                i2 = stride*(2*(tid-1)+2)
289                s(i2) = s(i2)+s(i1)
290            endif
291            stride = stride*2
292            nr = nr/2
293        end do
294
295        blockSum = s(2*compact_tpb)
296        call syncthreads()
297        if (tid == compact_tpb) then
298            s(2*compact_tpb) = 0
299        endif
300        call syncthreads()
301
302        stride = compact_tpb
303        nr = 1
304        do
305            if (tid <= nr) then
306                i1 = stride*(2*(tid-1)+1)
307                i2 = stride*(2*(tid-1)+2)
308                t = s(i1)
309                s(i1) = s(i2)
310                s(i2) = s(i2)+t
311            end if
312            stride = stride/2
313            call syncthreads()
314            if (stride == 0) exit
315            nr=nr*2
316        enddo
317        a(gid) = s(tid) + cumulativeSum
318        a(gid+compact_tpb) = s(tid+compact_tpb) + cumulativeSum
319        if (blockIdx_x*compact_tpb*2 >= n) exit
320        blockIdx_x = blockIdx_x + 1
321        cumulativeSum = cumulativeSum + blockSum
322      end do
323    end subroutine singleBlockScan
```

One last issue needs to be addressed: the memory bank conflicts encountered in the scan() and singleBlockScan() kernels. As the stride variable doubles with each iteration in the upsweep stage of the scan, so does the degree of memory bank conflicts. The downsweep phase also encounters bank conflicts, only in reverse. The remedy for the bank conflicts is the same as we have seen before: pad the shared memory array. In compactOpt_m.cuf, we define two module scope parameters

```
 9    ! to avoid bank conflicts, pad shared memory array by compact_pad
10    ! in scan kernels and use padi() function to generate indices
11    ! used to access shared memory array
12
```

```
13    integer, parameter :: compact_bankSize = 32
14    integer, parameter :: compact_pad = (2*compact_tpb-1)/compact_bankSize
```

as well as a function to return padded indices:

```
23    ! shift index i to account for padding in shared memory in scan kernels
24    ! used to avoid shared memory bank conflicts
25
26    attributes(device) function padi(i) result(res)
27      integer :: i, res
28      res = i + (i-1)/compact_bankSize
29    end function padi
```

The scan function then becomes

```
344   attributes(global) subroutine scan(a, pSum)
345     implicit none
346     integer :: a(*), pSum(*)
347
348     integer, shared :: s(2*compact_tpb + compact_pad)
349     integer :: tid, gid, stride, nr, i1, i2, t
350
351     tid = threadIdx%x
352     gid = (blockIdx%x-1)*blockDim%x*2 + tid
353
354     s(padi(tid)) = a(gid)
355     s(padi(tid+compact_tpb)) = a(gid+compact_tpb)
356
357     stride = 1
358     nr = compact_tpb
359     do
360        call syncthreads()
361        if (nr == 0) exit
362        if (tid <= nr) then
363           i1 = padi(stride*(2*(tid-1)+1))
364           i2 = padi(stride*(2*(tid-1)+2))
365           s(i2) = s(i2)+s(i1)
366        endif
367        stride = stride*2
368        nr = nr/2
369     end do
370
371     if (tid == compact_tpb) then
372        pSum(blockIdx%x) = s(padi(2*compact_tpb))
373        s(padi(2*compact_tpb)) = 0
374     endif
375     call syncthreads()
376
377     stride = compact_tpb
378     nr = 1
379     do
380        if (tid <= nr) then
381           i1 = padi(stride*(2*(tid-1)+1))
```

```
382              i2 = padi(stride*(2*(tid-1)+2))
383              t = s(i1)
384              s(i1) = s(i2)
385              s(i2) = s(i2)+t
386           end if
387           stride = stride/2
388           call syncthreads()
389           if (stride == 0) exit
390           nr=nr*2
391        enddo
392        a(gid) = s(padi(tid))
393        a(gid+compact_tpb) = s(padi(tid+compact_tpb))
394     end subroutine scan
```

where the shared memory array declared on line 348 contains padded values, and any index to this shared memory array is done through calling the padi() function, as on lines 354–365, 363–364, and elsewhere.

Interfacing with CUDA C code and CUDA libraries

7

This chapter covers how to interface CUDA Fortran with CUDA C, including both CUDA C source code and many of the CUDA libraries distributed with the NVIDIA HPC SDK. As far as the CUDA libraries are concerned, in this chapter we cover: cuBLAS, a CUDA implementation of the Basic Linear Algebra Subprograms (BLAS) library; cuSPARSE, a library of linear algebra routines that accommodates sparse matrices; cuSOLVER, which contains LAPACK-like routines for dense matrix factorizations and triangular solves, sparse least-squares, and eigenvalue solvers; and cuTENSOR, which contains a set of primitives for tensor manipulation. In addition, this chapter gives examples of how to interface with Thrust, a C++ template library that provides data parallel primitives such as scan, sort, and reduce.

There are several CUDA libraries that are not addressed in this chapter because they are discussed in detail elsewhere in this book. cuFFT, a fast Fourier transform library, is discussed at length in Chapter 11 on spectral methods. cuRAND, a random number generation library, is discussed in Chapter 9 on Monte Carlo methods. The NVIDIA Tools Extension (NVTX) library used to customize profiling has been discussed in Section 3.1.4. Details of the Fortran APIs for all the CUDA libraries are contained in the online documentation *NVIDIA Fortran CUDA Interfaces*.

Some of the CUDA C libraries, such as cuBLAS and cuSPARSE, have precompiled CUDA Fortran modules, and access to these routines from CUDA Fortran is done by using the relevant module. Because of some differences between Fortran and C, primarily the strong typing in Fortran, the interfaces to the C library routines have been overloaded to make use from Fortran simpler. We will go over such cases in the cuBLAS and cuSPARSE libraries later in this chapter, but we will first discuss how we can interface with user-written CUDA C code.

7.1 Calling user-written CUDA C code

The introduction of the `iso_c_binding` module in Fortran 2003 provided a standardized method of interoperating with C. The `iso_c_binding` module defines named constants holding kind type parameter values, the `value` attribute to designate pass-by-value arguments, and the `bind` attribute used to make procedures interoperable. The use of these features can be demonstrated by defining an interface to the following CUDA C code, which contains both a CUDA C kernel and a CUDA C device function:

```
1   extern "C" __global__ void Ckernel(float *a, float b)
2   {
3     a[threadIdx.x] = b;
4   }
5
```

```
6  extern "C" __device__ float Cdevicefun(float a)
7  {
8    return 2*a;
9  }
```

CUDA C and Fortran kernel codes share quite a bit in common: both have automatically defined variables blockIdx, blockDim, and threadIdx, though with different offsets. The __global__ and __device__ in CUDA C are equivalent to CUDA Fortran's attributes(global) and attributes(device). Of note here is the extern "C", which is required for CUDA Fortran to interface with this routine as it prevents name mangling.

The following CUDA Fortran code contains a module with an interface to the CUDA C kernel on lines 3–10, an interface to the CUDA C function on lines 12–19, and a CUDA Fortran kernel on lines 23–28, which calls the CUDA C device function on line 27:

```
1   module m
2
3      interface
4         attributes(global) subroutine kernel(x, v) &
5              bind(C,name='Ckernel')
6           use iso_c_binding
7           real(c_float), device :: x(*)
8           real(c_float), value :: v
9         end subroutine kernel
10     end interface
11
12     interface
13        attributes(device) function devicefun(x) result(res) &
14             bind(C,name='Cdevicefun')
15          use iso_c_binding
16          real(c_float) :: res
17          real(c_float), value :: x
18        end function devicefun
19     end interface
20
21   contains
22
23     attributes(global) subroutine Fkernel(x, v)
24       implicit none
25       real, device :: x(*)
26       real, value :: v
27       x(threadIdx%x) = devicefun(v)
28     end subroutine Fkernel
29
30   end module m
31
32   program main
33     use m
34     implicit none
35     real :: x(1), f(1)
36     real, device :: x_d(1), f_d(1)
37     integer :: i
```

```
38
39      call kernel<<<1,1>>>(x_d, 1.0)
40      x = x_d
41      if (x(1) == 1.0) print *, 'Calling C Kernel -- OK'
42
43      !$cuf kernel do <<<*,*>>>
44      do i = 1, 1
45          f_d(i) = devicefun(x_d(i))
46      end do
47      f = f_d
48      if (f(1) == 2.0) print *, 'CUF Kernel Calling C Function -- OK'
49
50      call Fkernel<<<1,1>>>(x_d, 4.0)
51      x = x_d
52      if (x(1) == 8.0) print *, 'Fortran Kernel Calling C Function -- OK'
53   end program main
```

The interface on line 3 defines a Fortran kernel kernel that is bound to our CUDA C kernel Ckernel via the bind() attribute. The bind attribute is used similarly on line 14 to define the function devicefun, which is bound to the CUDA C device function Cdevicefun. The bind() attribute is used here with two arguments: the first is the language in which the routine being called is written, in this case C, and the second is the name of the routine being called. The kind type parameter value c_float is defined in the iso_c_binding module. The use of the device variable qualifier for the array argument declaration on line 7 is optional as this is the default for kernel arguments, whereas the value attribute used on line 8 is required for the scalar argument that is passed by value.

With the interfaces to the CUDA C routines defined in the module, the host code on lines 32–53 looks identical to host code that calls CUDA Fortran routines. On line 39 the CUDA C kernel is called, the CUF kernel on lines 43–46 calls the CUDA C device function, and the CUDA Fortran kernel is called on line 50, which in turn calls the CUDA C device function.

Compiling and running the code is done as follows:

```
$ nvcc -c -rdc=true -arch=sm_70 c.cu
$ nvfortran -gpu=cc70 callingC.cuf c.o
callingC.cuf:
$ ./a.out
 Calling C Kernel -- OK
 CUF Kernel Calling C Function -- OK
 Fortran Kernel Calling C Function -- OK
```

There are several issues to be aware of when compiling the source code. The version of the CUDA toolkit used in the linking step should be the same or more recent than that invoked by the nvcc command. This can be facilitated in CUDA Fortran via the -gpu option. When calling CUDA C device functions from CUDA Fortran, the relocatable device code flag -rdc=true must be used as an option to nvcc. Relocatable device code is also required in the CUDA Fortran code, but -gpu=rdc is the default case. When interfacing only with CUDA C kernels, relocatable device code is not needed.

7.1.1 The `ignore_tkr` directive

Fortran's strong typing can be a great asset in developing interfaces to C routines. As we will see in the following sections, generic interfaces can be written that will resolve to either host or device routines based on whether arguments reside on the host or device. However, there can be times where strong typing is not desired, and in such cases we can use the `ignore_tkr` directive. This directive instructs the compiler to ignore a variable's type, kind, rank, and in addition the presence or absence of the device and managed attributes, in any combination. The `ignore_tkr` directive was used in developing interfaces to certain routines in the cuBLAS and cuSPARSE libraries where scalar arguments can reside either on the host or device:

```
!dir$ ignore_tkr (d) alpha, (d) beta
real(c_float) :: alpha, beta
```

where the presence or absence of the `device` variable attribute is ignored in argument matching due to the (d) before each variable name. The parenthesized list applies only to a single variable, so (d) is required before both variables above. If the second (d) were omitted, then the default case corresponding to (tkrdm) would apply to `beta` indicating its type, kind, rank, as well as device and managed attributes, are to be ignored.

7.2 cuBLAS

cuBLAS is the CUDA version of the well-known Basic Linear Algebra Subprograms (BLAS) library. The NVIDIA HPC SDK comes with a `cublas` module, which contains two APIs, a legacy API and a new API.

7.2.1 Legacy cuBLAS API

The legacy cuBLAS API corresponds closely to the traditional BLAS API. The following code illustrates use of the legacy cuBLAS API in performing a matrix multiplication:

```
1   program sgemmLegacy
2     use cublas
3     use cudafor
4     implicit none
5     integer, parameter :: m = 100, n = 100, k = 100
6     real :: a(m,k), b(k,n), c(m,n)
7     real, device :: a_d(m,k), b_d(k,n), c_d(m,n)
8     real, parameter :: alpha = 1.0, beta = 0.0
9     integer :: lda = m, ldb = k, ldc = m
10    integer :: istat
11
12    a = 1.0; b = 2.0; c = 0.0
13
14    call sgemm('n', 'n', m, n, k, &
15          alpha, a, lda, b, ldb, beta, c, ldc)
16    print *, 'sgemm(host data) error =', &
17          maxval(c-k*2.0)
```

```
18
19    istat = cublasInit()
20    if (istat /= CUBLAS_STATUS_SUCCESS) & 
21        print *, 'Error initializing CUBLAS'
22
23    a_d = a; b_d = b; c_d = 0.0
24
25    call cublasSgemm('n', 'n', m, n, k, &
26        alpha, a_d, lda, b_d, ldb, beta, c_d, ldc)
27    c = c_d
28    print *, 'cublasSgemm error =', maxval(c-k*2.0)
29
30    c_d = 0.0
31    call sgemm('n', 'n', m, n, k, &
32        alpha, a_d, lda, b_d, ldb, beta, c_d, ldc)
33    c = c_d
34    print *, 'sgemm(device data) error =', &
35        maxval(c-k*2.0)
36
37    istat = cublasShutdown()
38    if (istat /= CUBLAS_STATUS_SUCCESS) & 
39        print *, 'Error shutting down CUBLAS'
40  end program sgemmLegacy
```

On line 14 the host BLAS sgemm() routine is called with host arguments. The equivalent cuBLAS routine can be called in two ways, using either cublasSgemm() as on line 25 or the overloaded sgemm() name as on line 31. The interface for sgemm() resolves to either the host sgemm() or cublasSgemm() depending on whether the matrix arguments reside on the host or device. Successful execution of the initialization and shutdown routines, cublasInit() and cublasShutdown(), can be checked by comparing their return values to the parameter CUBLAS_STATUS_SUCCESS.

Compilation of this program is done simply by adding the cuBLAS and host BLAS libraries. CUDA libraries are added via the -cudalib=... option.

```
$ nvfortran sgemmLegacy.cuf -cudalib=cublas -lblas
$ ./a.out
 sgemm(host data) error =      0.000000
 cublasSgemm error =      0.000000
 sgemm(device data) error =      0.000000
```

7.2.2 New cuBLAS API

The new cuBLAS API was introduced to allow additional functionality over the legacy API. Using the new cuBLAS API, our sgemm example becomes

```
1  program sgemmNew
2    use cublas
3    use cudafor
4    implicit none
5    integer, parameter :: m = 100, n = 100, k = 100
6    real :: a(m,k), b(k,n), c(m,n)
```

```
 7    real, device :: a_d(m,k), b_d(k,n), c_d(m,n)
 8    real, parameter :: alpha = 1.0, beta = 0.0
 9    real, device :: alpha_d, beta_d
10    integer :: lda = m, ldb = k, ldc = m
11    type(cublasHandle) :: h
12    integer :: istat
13
14    a = 1.0; b = 2.0; c = 0.0
15    a_d = a; b_d = b; c_d = 0.0
16
17    istat = cublasCreate(h)
18    if (istat /= CUBLAS_STATUS_SUCCESS) &
19        print *, 'Error initializing CUBLAS'
20
21
22    istat = cublasSgemm_v2(h, CUBLAS_OP_N, CUBLAS_OP_N, m, n, k, &
23        alpha, a_d, lda, b_d, ldb, beta, c_d, ldc)
24    c = c_d
25    print *, 'cublasSgemm error =', maxval(c-k*2.0)
26
27    alpha_d = alpha; beta_d = beta
28
29    istat = cublasSgemm_v2(h, CUBLAS_OP_N, CUBLAS_OP_N, m, n, k, &
30        alpha_d, a_d, lda, b_d, ldb, beta_d, c_d, ldc)
31    c = c_d
32    print *, 'cublasSgemm error =', maxval(c-k*2.0)
33
34
35    istat = cublasDestroy(h)
36    if (istat /= CUBLAS_STATUS_SUCCESS) &
37        print *, 'Error shutting down CUBLAS'
38 end program sgemmNew
```

which when compiled and run produces

```
$ nvfortran sgemmNew.cuf -cudalib=cublas
$ ./a.out
 cublasSgemm error =    0.000000
 cublasSgemm error =    0.000000
```

An additional argument of type cublasHandle is required as the first argument of all cuBLAS routines in the new API and allows more control over the library setup when using multiple host threads and multiple GPUs. This handle is created and destroyed using the routines cublasCreate() and cublasDestroy(), which replace the cublasInit() and cublasShutdown() of the legacy API.

All of the routines in the new CUBLAS API return a status value, which can be checked against CUBLAS_STATUS_SUCCESS for errors. The character arguments used to indicate the non-transpose, transpose, and conjugate transpose operations to be performed on input arrays in the legacy interface are replaced with integer arguments in the new interface that can take on values CUBLAS_OP_N, CUBLAS_OP_T, and CUBLAS_OP_C.

Some scalar parameters, such as alpha and beta, can reside on either the host or device. In CUDA C a call to cublasSetPointerMode() is required to determine where such data reside; however, in CUDA

Fortran, there is no need to use this function due to strong typing. A generic interface for these functions is defined in the cublas module, which calls one of two wrapper functions based on where such data reside. These wrapper functions set the pointer mode, call the cuBLAS routine, and then reset the pointer mode.

With the statement use cublas on line 2, the calls to SGEMM on lines 22 and 29 require the _v2 suffix for the new API. Alternatively, we could have the statement use cublas_v2 on line 2 and remove the suffix _v2 from the SGEMM calls.

Using the new interface, the stream in which a cuBLAS operation executes can be set using the routine cublasSetStream(handle, stream). This function sets the cuBLAS library stream for all subsequent cuBLAS calls using the specified handle. By default the null stream is used where the stream's blocking behavior prohibits any overlap with other computation or data transfers.

Some additional routines have been added to the new API, such as batched cuBLAS routines, which we present next.

7.2.3 Batched cuBLAS routines

When dealing with small arrays and matrices, one method of exposing parallelism on the GPU is to execute the same cuBLAS call on multiple independent systems simultaneously. While you can do this manually by calling multiple cuBLAS kernels across multiple CUDA streams, batched cuBLAS routines enable such parallelism automatically for certain operations (GEMM, GETRF, GETRI, and TRSM). We discuss how to interface with these C routines, which require some special attention when called from CUDA Fortran.

The C batched cuBLAS functions use an array of pointers as one of their arguments, where each pointer in the array points to an independent matrix. This poses a problem for Fortran, which does not allow arrays of pointers. To accommodate this argument, we can make use of the c_devptr type defined in the cudafor module. The c_devptr type is the device analogue of the c_ptr type from the iso_c_binding module.

We will illustrate how to call batched cuBLAS routines using cublasSgetrfBatched(). This routine has the following arguments:

- h, the cuBLAS handle obtained from cublasCreate()
- n, the size of the n×n matrices
- Aarray, the array pointers to the matrices
- lda, the leading dimension of the matrices
- ipvt, an output array containing pivot information
- info, another output array containing factorization information
- batchSize, the number of independent n×n matrices on which to perform factorization

The cuBLAS handle h, the size of the matrices n, the leading dimensions lda, and the number of matrices batchSize are all scalar parameters declared in host memory and passed by value. The integer arrays ipvt and info are output arrays allocated on the device. Of special note is the array of pointers Aarray. The Fortran language does not allow array of pointers, which is where the c_devptr type comes in. It is best to discuss how the derived type c_devptr is used in a complete code:

```fortran
1   program testgetrfBatched
2     use cudafor
3     use cublas
4     implicit none
5
6     integer, parameter :: n=2, nbatch=3, lda=n
7     real :: a(n,n,nbatch)
8     real, device :: a_d(n,n,nbatch)
9     type(c_devptr) :: devPtrA(nbatch)
10    type(c_devptr), device :: devPtrA_d(nbatch)
11    type(cublasHandle) :: h1
12    integer   :: ipvt(n*nbatch), info(nbatch)
13    integer, device :: ipvt_d(n*nbatch), info_d(nbatch)
14    integer :: i, k, istat
15
16    ! intitialize arrays and transfer to device
17    do k = 1, nbatch
18       a(1,1,k) = 6.0*k
19       a(2,1,k) = 4.0*k
20       a(1,2,k) = 3.0*k
21       a(2,2,k) = 3.0*k
22    end do
23    a_d = a
24
25    print "(/,'Input:')"
26    do k = 1, nbatch
27       print "(2x,'Matrix: ', i0)", k
28       do i=1, n
29          print *, a(i,:,k)
30       enddo
31    enddo
32
33    ! build an array of pointers
34    do k = 1, nbatch
35       devPtrA(k) = c_devloc(a_d(1,1,k))
36    end do
37    devPtrA_d = devPtrA
38
39    ! create handle, call cublasSgetrfBatched, and destroy handle
40    istat = cublasCreate(h1)
41    if (istat /= CUBLAS_STATUS_SUCCESS) &
42        write(*,*) 'cublasCreate failed'
43    istat= cublasSgetrfBatched(h1, n, devPtrA_d, lda, &
44        ipvt_d, info_d, nbatch)
45    if (istat /= CUBLAS_STATUS_SUCCESS) &
46        write(*,*) 'cublasSgetrfBatched failed: ', istat
47    istat = cublasDestroy(h1)
48    if (istat /= CUBLAS_STATUS_SUCCESS) &
49        write(*,*) 'cublasDestroy failed'
50
51    a = a_d
52
```

```
53 | print "(/, 'LU Factorization:')"
54 | do k = 1, nbatch
55 |    print "(2x,'Matrix: ', i0)", k
56 |    do i = 1, n
57 |       print *, a(i,:,k)
58 |    enddo
59 | enddo
60 |
61 | end program testgetrfBatched
```

Note that two variables are declared of type c_devptr: on line 9, devPtrA is declared as a host array of device pointers, and on line 10, devPtrA_d is a device array of device pointers. The batched cuBLAS routines require a device array of device pointers, but initialization is done using the host array. The host function c_devloc() used on line 35 determines the address of the nbatch matrices stored in the three-dimensional array a_d. In general, the matrices can be distributed across multiple variables, but we use a single three-dimensional array for convenience. The results from c_devloc() are first stored in the host array devPtrA and then transferred to the device array devPtrA_d on line 37. devPtrA_d is used a few lines later in the call to cublasSgetrfBatched().

7.2.4 GEMM with tensor cores

Tensor cores are specialized matrix-multiply-and-accumulate units, which first appeared in V100 GPUs with support for half precision (real(2)) multiplicands. Support for single and double precision multiplicands was added in A100 GPUs. Tensor cores are essentially dedicated GEMM units that operate on small matrices but can be used as building blocks for larger GEMM operations. The cuBLAS library leverages the performance of tensor cores in GEMM operations whenever possible by default starting in cuBLAS 11.0.

We should be aware that tensor core support for 32-bit floating point data makes use of the Tensor Float 32 (TF32) format, which uses the same 8-bit exponent as an FP32 format but uses a mantissa of 10 rather than 23 bits. In the TF32 matrix-multiply-and-accumulate, the operands are rounded to TF32 before multiplication, and the accumulation is done in FP32. This allows for greater performance at the expense of some accuracy. Because of the loss of accuracy, we need to opt in to using tensor cores when performing SGEMMs by calling cublasSetMathMode(), as is done in the following code:

```
1  | program main
2  |    use cudafor
3  |    use cublas_v2
4  |    implicit none
5  |    integer, parameter :: m=3200, n=3200, k=3200
6  |
7  |    type(cublasHandle) :: handle
8  |    type(cudaDeviceProp) :: prop
9  |    type(cudaEvent) :: startEvent, stopEvent
10 |    real :: err, time
11 |    integer :: istat
12 |
13 |    istat = cudaGetDeviceProperties(prop, 0)
14 |    print "(' Device: ', a)", trim(prop%name)
15 |    print "(' m = ', i0, ', n = ', i0, ', k = ', i0)", m, n, k
```

```
16
17     istat = cublasCreate(handle)
18     istat = cudaEventCreate(startEvent)
19     istat = cudaEventCreate(stopEvent)
20
21     block
22       real(8) :: a(m,k), b(k,n), c(m,n), cref(m,n)
23       real(8), device :: a_d(m,k), b_d(k,n), c_d(m,n)
24
25       call random_number(a)
26       call random_number(b)
27       cref = matmul(a,b)
28
29       a_d = a; b_d = b; c_d = 0.0
30       istat = cudaDeviceSynchronize()
31       istat = cudaEventRecord(startEvent, 0)
32       istat = cublasDGemm(handle, CUBLAS_OP_N, CUBLAS_OP_N, &
33             m, n, k, 1.0_8, a_d, m, b_d, k, 0.0_8, c_d, n)
34       istat = cudaEventRecord(stopEvent, 0)
35       istat = cudaEventSynchronize(stopEvent)
36       c = c_d
37       istat = cudaEventElapsedTime(time, startEvent, stopEvent)
38
39       print *, 'DGEMM maxval(abs(cref-c)): ', maxval(abs(cref-c))
40       print *, 'DGEMM TFlops: ', 2.*k*m*n/(time/1000.)/1.0E+12
41       print *
42     end block
43
44     block
45       real(4) :: a(m,k), b(k,n), c(m,n), cref(m,n)
46       real(4), device :: a_d(m,k), b_d(k,n), c_d(m,n)
47
48       call random_number(a)
49       call random_number(b)
50       cref = matmul(a,b)
51
52       a_d = a; b_d = b; c_d = 0.0
53       istat = cudaDeviceSynchronize()
54       istat = cudaEventRecord(startEvent, 0)
55       istat = cublasSGemm(handle, CUBLAS_OP_N, CUBLAS_OP_N, &
56             m, n, k, 1.0, a_d, m, b_d, k, 0.0, c_d, n)
57       istat = cudaEventRecord(stopEvent, 0)
58       istat = cudaEventSynchronize(stopEvent)
59       c = c_d
60       istat = cudaEventElapsedTime(time, startEvent, stopEvent)
61
62       print *, 'SGEMM (FP32) maxval(abs(cref-c)): ', maxval(abs(cref-c))
63       print *, 'SGEMM (FP32) TFlops: ', 2.*k*m*n/(time/1000.)/1.0E+12
64       print *
65     end block
66
67     block
```

```
68    real(4) :: a(m,k), b(k,n), c(m,n), cref(m,n)
69    real(4), device :: a_d(m,k), b_d(k,n), c_d(m,n)
70
71    istat = cublasSetMathMode(handle, CUBLAS_TF32_TENSOR_OP_MATH)
72
73    call random_number(a)
74    call random_number(b)
75    cref = matmul(a,b)
76
77    a_d = a; b_d = b; c_d = 0.0
78    istat = cudaDeviceSynchronize()
79    istat = cudaEventRecord(startEvent, 0)
80    istat = cublasSGemm(handle, CUBLAS_OP_N, CUBLAS_OP_N, &
81          m, n, k, 1.0, a_d, m, b_d, k, 0.0, c_d, n)
82    istat = cudaEventRecord(stopEvent, 0)
83    istat = cudaEventSynchronize(stopEvent)
84    c = c_d
85    istat = cudaEventElapsedTime(time, startEvent, stopEvent)
86
87    print *, 'SGEMM (TF32) maxval(abs(cref-c)): ', maxval(abs(cref-c))
88    print *, 'SGEMM (TF32) TFlops: ', 2.*k*m*n/(time/1000.)/1.0E+12
89  end block
90
91  istat = cublasDestroy(handle)
92  istat = cudaEventDestroy(startEvent)
93  istat = cudaEventDestroy(stopEvent)
94 end program main
```

This code contains three blocks where a GEMM is performed. The first block performs DGEMM, the second performs an SGEMM using the default FP32 format, and in the third block a call to cublasSetMathMode() on line 71 with the flag CUBLAS_TF32_TENSOR_OP_MATH opts into using tensor cores for the SGEMM. We can disable the use of tensor cores for SGEMM by calling cublasSetMathMode() with the CUBLAS_PEDANTIC_MATH flag. All of the GEMM calculations are timed, and the TFlops are calculated. Compiling and running this code we get

```
$ nvfortran -O3 gemmPerf.cuf -cudalib=cublas
$ ./a.out
 Device: NVIDIA A100 80GB PCIe
 m = 3200, n = 3200, k = 3200
 DGEMM maxval(abs(cref-c)):     6.7075234255753458E-012
 DGEMM TFlops:      16.81997

 SGEMM (FP32) maxval(abs(cref-c)):     3.8452148E-03
 SGEMM (FP32) TFlops:      17.15358

 SGEMM (TF32) maxval(abs(cref-c)):     6.1279297E-02
 SGEMM (TF32) TFlops:      100.0000
```

where we observe the accuracy and performance differences when the tensor cores are used for the SGEMM. We can verify that tensor cores are used by profiling the application, where a GPU trace shows the following activities on the device:

```
[CUDA memcpy HtoD]
[CUDA memcpy HtoD]
__pgi_dev_cumemset_16n
void cutlass::Kernel<cutlass_80_tensorop_d884gemm_...
[CUDA memcpy DtoH]
[CUDA memcpy HtoD]
[CUDA memcpy HtoD]
__pgi_dev_cumemset_16n
ampere_sgemm_128x128_nn
[CUDA memcpy DtoH]
[CUDA memcpy HtoD]
[CUDA memcpy HtoD]
__pgi_dev_cumemset_16n
void cutlass::Kernel<cutlass_80_tensorop_s1688gemm_...
[CUDA memcpy DtoH]
```

Here the CUTLASS C++ template library is used to interface with the tensor cores. The ampere_sgemm_128x128_nn line refers to the sgemm using FP32 representation.

On a final note, matrix multiplication for complex data via CGEMM and ZGEMM are handled in the same way as SGEMM and DGEMM as far as tensor core usage goes.

7.3 cuSPARSE

The cuSPARSE library is a sparse matrix analog to the cuBLAS library. The cuSPARSE library contains routines callable from the host for operations between sparse and dense vectors (level 1), sparse matrices and dense vectors (level 2), and sparse matrices and dense matrices (level 3), along with conversion routines between various sparse formats. Many sparse formats are available, such as coordinate (COO), compressed sparse column (CSC), compressed sparse row (CSR), and block compressed sparse row (BSR), amongst others, though not all operations are available in all sparse formats.

Just as with cuBLAS, CUDA Fortran contains a module defining CUDA Fortran interfaces to the cuSPARSE library. Access to these routines is simply a matter of including use cusparse and linking with the cuSPARSE library. Below is an example of a sparse matrix-vector multiplication using cuSPARSE:

```fortran
1   program sparseMatVec
2     use cudafor
3     use cusparse
4
5     implicit none
6
7     integer, parameter :: n = 5    ! # rows/cols in matrix
8     integer, parameter :: nnz = 5 ! # nonzeros in matrix
9
10    type(cusparseHandle) :: h
11
12    ! CSR matrix
13    type(cusparseSpMatDescr) :: descrA
```

```
14    real(4), device :: csrValues_d(nnz)
15    integer(4), device :: csrRowOffsets_d(n+1), csrColInd_d(nnz)
16
17    ! dense vectors
18    type(cusparseDnVecDescr) :: descrX, descrY
19    real, device :: x_d(n), y_d(n)
20    real :: y(n)
21
22    ! parameters
23    real(4) :: alpha = 1.0, beta = 0.0
24
25    integer :: status, i
26
27    ! initalize cusparse
28    status = cusparseCreate(h)
29
30    ! CSR representation for upper circular shift matrix
31    csrValues_d = 1.0
32    csrColInd_d = [2, 3, 4, 5, 1]
33    csrRowOffsets_d = [1, 2, 3, 4, 5, 6]
34
35    ! vectors
36    x_d = [11.0, 12.0, 13.0, 14.0, 15.0]
37    y_d = 0.0
38
39    y = x_d
40    print *, 'Original vector'
41    print "(5(1x,f7.2))", y
42
43    ! initialize sparse matrix descriptor A in CSR format
44    status = cusparseCreateCsr(descr = descrA, &
45        rows = n, &
46        cols = n, &
47        nnz = nnz, &
48        csrRowOffsets = csrRowOffsets_d, &
49        csrColInd = csrColInd_d, &
50        csrValues = csrValues_d, &
51        csrRowOffsetsType = CUSPARSE_INDEX_32I, &
52        csrColIndType = CUSPARSE_INDEX_32I, &
53        idxBase = CUSPARSE_INDEX_BASE_ONE, &
54        valueType = CUDA_R_32F)
55
56    ! initialize the dense vector descriptors for X and Y
57    status = cusparseCreateDnVec(descrX, n, x_d, valueType = CUDA_R_32F)
58    status = cusparseCreateDnVec(descrY, n, y_d, valueType = CUDA_R_32F)
59
60    ! y = alpha*A*x + beta*y
61
62    block
63      integer(8) :: bufferSize
64      integer(1), allocatable, device :: buffer_d(:)
65
66      status = cusparseSpMV_buffersize(h, &
```

```
67            CUSPARSE_OPERATION_NON_TRANSPOSE , &
68            alpha, descrA, descrX, beta, descrY, &
69            CUDA_R_32F, &
70            CUSPARSE_SPMV_ALG_DEFAULT , &
71            buffersize)
72
73       allocate(buffer_d(buffersize))
74
75       status = cusparseSpMV(h, &
76            CUSPARSE_OPERATION_NON_TRANSPOSE , &
77            alpha, descrA, descrX, beta, descrY, &
78            CUDA_R_32F, &
79            CUSPARSE_SPMV_ALG_DEFAULT , &
80            buffer_d)
81
82       deallocate(buffer_d)
83     end block
84
85     y = y_d
86     print *, 'Shifted vector'
87     print "(5(1x,f7.2))", y
88
89     ! shift down and subtract original
90     ! x = alpha*(A')*y - x
91
92     beta = -1.0
93
94     block
95       integer(8) :: bufferSize
96       integer(1), allocatable, device :: buffer_d(:)
97
98       status = cusparseSpMV_buffersize(h, &
99            CUSPARSE_OPERATION_TRANSPOSE , &
100           alpha, descrA, descrY, beta, descrX, &
101           CUDA_R_32F, &
102           CUSPARSE_SPMV_ALG_DEFAULT , &
103           buffersize)
104
105      allocate(buffer_d(buffersize))
106
107      status = cusparseSpMV(h, &
108           CUSPARSE_OPERATION_TRANSPOSE , &
109           alpha, descrA, descrY, beta, descrX, &
110           CUDA_R_32F, &
111           CUSPARSE_SPMV_ALG_DEFAULT , &
112           buffer_d)
113
114      deallocate(buffer_d)
115    end block
116
117    y = x_d
118    print *, 'Max error: ', maxval(abs(y))
```

```
119
120    ! cleanup
121
122    status = cusparseDestroySpMat(descrA)
123    status = cusparseDestroyDnVec(descrX)
124    status = cusparseDestroyDnVec(descrY)
125    status = cusparseDestroy(h)
126
127 end program sparseMatVec
```

Here the cusparse handle, matrix, and vector descriptors are initialized on lines 28, 44–54, and 57–58. The CSR arrays used to define the matrix are initialized on lines 31–33. This matrix is the 5×5 upper circular shift matrix

$$
A = \begin{bmatrix}
0 & 1 & 0 & 0 & 0 \\
0 & 0 & 1 & 0 & 0 \\
0 & 0 & 0 & 1 & 0 \\
0 & 0 & 0 & 0 & 1 \\
1 & 0 & 0 & 0 & 0
\end{bmatrix}.
$$

An upward shift of the vector x_d is performed in the block from lines 62–83 via the routines cusparseSpMV_buffersize() and cusparseSpMV(). The first routine determines the size of a work array required by the second routine. The shifted vector is transferred to the host and printed out, which is followed by a downward shift via the transpose the matrix in the block from lines 94–115. The call to cusparseSpMV on line 75 also subtracts the original vector from the result of the matrix–vector multiplication. Compiling and running the code we obtain the expected results:

```
$ nvfortran cusparseMV.cuf -cudalib=cusparse
$ ./a.out
 Original vector
    11.00    12.00    13.00    14.00    15.00
 Shifted vector
    12.00    13.00    14.00    15.00    11.00
 Max error:    0.000000
```

From the perspective of the Fortran language, the arguments to the cuSPARSE API have a degree of redundancy, which is not only cumbersome but also error prone. For example, when initializing the dense vector descriptors

```
57    status = cusparseCreateDnVec(descrX, n, x_d, valueType = CUDA_R_32F)
58    status = cusparseCreateDnVec(descrY, n, y_d, valueType = CUDA_R_32F)
```

the second and fourth arguments, n and CUDA_R_32F, can be inferred from the arrays x_d and y_d themselves. In what follows, we present extensions of the cudafor and cusparse modules that eliminate such redundancy in the API arguments. The first item we address is how to deal with the CUDA data type enumerations such as CUDA_R_32F that are defined in the cudafor module. We create a module cudaforEx that extends the cudafor module with the routine cudaforGetDataType():

```
1   module cudaforEx
2     use cudafor
3
4   contains
5
6     function cudaforGetDataType(x) result(res)
7       use cudafor
8       !dir$ ignore_tkr (rd) x
9       class(*) :: x
10      integer :: res
11      select type (x)
12      type is (real(2))
13          res = CUDA_R_16F
14      type is (real(4))
15          res = CUDA_R_32F
16      type is (real(8))
17          res = CUDA_R_64F
18      type is (integer(4))
19          res = CUDA_R_32I
20      type is (complex(4))
21          res = CUDA_C_32F
22      type is (complex(8))
23          res = CUDA_C_64F
24      class default
25          res = -1
26      end select
27    end function cudaforGetDataType
28
29  end module cudaforEx
```

which makes use of *unlimited polymorphism* and select type to return the correct value for the type and kind of argument. The ignore_tkr directive is used to ignore the rank and presence of the device attribute of the argument. Similarly, we define in a cusparseEx module a routine that returns the index type:

```
21    function cusparseGetIndexType(x) result(res)
22      use cusparse
23      implicit none
24      !dir$ ignore_tkr (rd) x
25      class(*) :: x
26      integer :: res
27      select type(x)
28      type is (integer(4))
29          res = CUSPARSE_INDEX_32I
30      type is (integer(8))
31          res = CUSPARSE_INDEX_64I
32      class default
33          res = -1
34      end select
35    end function cusparseGetIndexType
```

We could use these routines when calling cusparseCreateCsr(), cusparseCreateDnVec(), cusparseSpMV_buffersize(), and cusparseSpMV(), but our approach is to extend the cuSPARSE API through generic interfaces with routines that have fewer arguments and in these wrapper functions, call the cuSPARSE functions. Let us start with the simplest case, cusparseCreateDnVec(). We can define a generic interface

```
 9    interface cusparseCreateDnVec
10        module procedure :: &
11            cusparseCreateDnVec_abr
12    end interface cusparseCreateDnVec
```

with a single module procedure that handles both single and double precision through unlimited polymorphism:

```
71    function cusparseCreateDnVec_abr(descr, x_d) result(status)
72        use cudaforEx
73        use cusparse
74        implicit none
75        type(cusparseDnVecDescr) :: descr
76        class(*), device :: x_d(:)
77        integer :: status
78
79        status = cusparseCreateDnVec(descr, &
80            size(x_d), x_d, cudaforGetDataType(x_d))
81    end function cusparseCreateDnVec_abr
```

where on line 76, x_d is declared as an unlimited polymorphic variable, and size(x_d) and cudaforGetDataType(x_d) are used to generate two of the arguments. The invocations of cusparseCreateDnVec() now become

```
56    ! initialize the dense vector descriptors for X and Y
57    status = cusparseCreateDnVec(descrX, x_d)
58    status = cusparseCreateDnVec(descrY, y_d)
```

Note that the original function call with four arguments is still available to the programmer, since we have not replaced the original function but have simply extended the interface.

The routine to initialize a CSR matrix descriptor is handled in a similar fashion with the generic interface:

```
 4    interface cusparseCreateCsr
 5        module procedure :: &
 6            cusparseCreateCsr_abr
 7    end interface cusparseCreateCsr
```

where the specific routine is

```
39    function cusparseCreateCsr_abr(descr, cols, &
40        csrRowOffsets_d, csrColInd_d, csrValues_d, idxBase) &
41        result(status)
42      use cudaforEx
43      use cusparse
```

```
44      implicit none
45      type(cusparseSpMatDescr) :: descr
46      integer(4) :: cols
47      class(*), device :: csrRowOffsets_d(:), csrColInd_d(:)
48      class(*), device :: csrValues_d(:)
49      integer, optional :: idxBase
50      integer :: status
51
52      integer :: rows, nnz
53      integer :: idxBaseLocal = CUSPARSE_INDEX_BASE_ONE
54
55      if (present(idxBase)) idxBaseLocal = idxBase
56
57      rows = size(csrRowOffsets_d)-1
58      nnz = size(csrValues_d)
59
60      status = cuSparseCreateCsr(descr, &
61          rows, cols, nnz, &
62          csrRowOffsets_d, csrColInd_d, csrValues_d, &
63          cusparseGetIndexType(csrRowOffsets_d), &
64          cusparseGetIndexType(csrColInd_d), &
65          idxBaseLocal, &
66          cudaforGetDataType(csrValues_d))
67    end function cusparseCreateCsr_abr
```

In this wrapper function the rows argument is obtained from the size of csrRowsOffsets_d on line 57, the nnz argument is obtained from the size of csrValues_d on line 58, the idxBase is an optional argument by default set to CUSPARSE_INDEX_BASE_ONE, the valueType argument is once again obtained from cudaforGetDataType() function, and the index types for csrRowOffsets_d and csrColInd_d arrays are obtained from the function cusparseGetIndexType() defined in this module. As a result, the invocation becomes

```
53    status = cusparseCreateCsr(descrA, &
54        n, csrRowOffsets_d, csrColInd_d, csrValues_d)
```

For the actual sparse matrix/dense vector multiplication wrapper functions, we have two optional arguments, alg, which is by default set to CUSPARSE_SPMV_ALG_DEFAULT, and the buffer argument:

```
85    function cusparseSpMV_abr(h, opA, alpha, A, x, beta, y, alg, buffer) &
86          result(status)
87      use cudaforEx
88      use cusparse
89      implicit none
90      type(cusparseHandle) :: h
91      type(cusparseSpMatDescr) :: A
92      integer :: opA
93      type(cusparseDnVecDescr) :: x, y
94      class(*) :: alpha, beta
95      integer, optional :: alg
96      integer(1), device, optional :: buffer(*)
97      integer :: status
98
```

```
99      ! valueType determined by alpha/beta
100     integer :: algLocal = CUSPARSE_SPMV_ALG_DEFAULT
101
102     if (present(alg)) algLocal = alg
103
104     if (present(buffer)) then
105        status = cusparseSpMV(h, &
106             opA, alpha, A, X, beta, Y, &
107             cudaforGetDataType(alpha), &
108             algLocal, buffer)
109     else
110        block
111           integer(8) :: bufferSize
112           integer(1), allocatable, device :: buffer_d(:)
113
114           status = cusparseSpMV_buffersize(h, &
115                opA, alpha, A, x, beta, y, &
116                cudaforGetDataType(alpha), &
117                algLocal, &
118                buffersize)
119           if (status /= CUSPARSE_STATUS_SUCCESS) return
120
121           allocate(buffer_d(buffersize))
122
123           status = cusparseSpMV(h, &
124                opA, alpha, A, X, beta, Y, &
125                cudaforGetDataType(alpha), &
126                algLocal, &
127                buffer_d)
128
129           deallocate(buffer_d)
130        end block
131     endif
132  end function cusparseSpMV_abr
```

If a buffer argument is present, then a call to cusparseSpMV is made using buffer without calling cusparseSpMV_buffersize() and allocating a temporary buffer. If the buffer argument is not present, then buffersize is determined in a call to cusparseSpMV_buffersize(), buffer is allocated and used in the cusparseSpMV() call, and then buffer is deallocated. The computeType argument is determined from the data type of the alpha and beta parameters.

7.4 cuSOLVER

The cuSOLVER library contains LAPACK-like routines like matrix factorizations and triangular solves that are built on top of cuBLAS and cuSPARSE. The cusolverDN module contains two APIs for dense matrices, a legacy API and a generic API similar to the API we discussed in the cuSPARSE section. We use the generic API in this section.

The following code illustrates how to solve a linear system of equations using Cholesky decomposition of the symmetric positive definite matrix via cusolverDnXpotrf(), followed by a triangular solve via cusolverDnXpotrs():

```fortran
1   program main
2     use cudaforEx
3     use cublas
4     use cusolverDN
5     implicit none
6     integer, parameter :: n=3
7     real(8) :: a(n,n), b(n)
8     real(8), device :: a_d(n,n), b_d(n)
9     integer, device :: devInfo_d
10    integer(8) :: wsSizeH, wsSizeD
11    integer(1), allocatable :: buffer(:)
12    integer(1), device, allocatable :: buffer_d(:)
13    integer, device :: info_d
14    integer :: istat, i
15
16    type(cusolverDnHandle) :: h
17    type(cusolverDnParams) :: params
18
19    a = reshape([25, 15, -5, 15, 18, 0, -5, 0, 11], shape=[3,3])
20    print *, 'A:'
21    do i = 1, n
22       print *, a(i,:)
23    enddo
24    a_d = a
25    b = [40, 51, 28]
26    b_d = b
27    print *, 'b:'
28    print *, b
29
30    istat = cusolverDnCreate(h)
31    istat = cusolverDnCreateParams(params)
32    istat = cusolverDnXpotrf_buffersize(handle = h, &
33          params = params, &
34          uplo = CUBLAS_FILL_MODE_UPPER, &
35          n = n, &
36          dataTypeA = cudaDataType(cudaforGetDataType(a_d)), &
37          A = a_d, &
38          lda = n, &
39          computeType = cudaDataType(cudaforGetDataType(a_d)), &
40          workspaceinBytesOnDevice = wsSizeD, &
41          workspaceinBytesOnHost = wsSizeH)
42
43    allocate(buffer(wsSizeH), buffer_d(wsSizeD))
44
45    istat = cusolverDnXpotrf(handle = h, &
46          params = params, &
47          uplo = CUBLAS_FILL_MODE_UPPER, &
48          n = n, &
```

```
49      dataTypeA = cudaDataType(cudaforGetDataType(a_d)), &
50      A = a_d, &
51      lda = n, &
52      computeType = cudaDataType(cudaforGetDataType(a_d)), &
53      bufferOnDevice = buffer_d, &
54      workspaceinBytesOnDevice = wsSizeD, &
55      bufferOnHost = buffer, &
56      workspaceinBytesOnHost = wsSizeH, &
57      devinfo = info_d)
58
59  a = a_d
60
61  print *, 'Cholesky factorization:'
62  do i = 1, n
63     print *, a(i,:)
64  enddo
65
66  istat = cusolverDnXpotrs(handle = h, &
67      params = params, &
68      uplo = CUBLAS_FILL_MODE_UPPER, &
69      n = n, &
70      nrhs = 1, &
71      dataTypeA = cudaDataType(cudaforGetDataType(a_d)), &
72      A = a_d, &
73      lda = n, &
74      dataTypeB = cudaDataType(cudaforGetDataType(b_d)), &
75      B = b_d, &
76      ldb = n, &
77      devinfo = info_d)
78
79  b = b_d
80
81  print *, 'x:'
82  print *, b
83
84  ! cleanup
85
86  deallocate(buffer, buffer_d)
87  istat = cusolverDnDestroyParams(params)
88  istat = cusolverDnDestroy(h)
89 end program main
```

Similar to cuBLAS and cuSPARSE, cuSolverDN requires a handle of type cusolverDnHandle that is created and destroyed on lines 30 and 88, and used as the first argument to all cuSolverDN calls. Instances of the type cusolverDnParams are used to hold information on which algorithms are used in which cuSolverDN routines. In general, such parameters can be configured by calling cusolverDnSetAdvOptions(), but Cholesky factorization only supports the default algorithm, which is set when initialized on line 31. The call to cusolverDnXpotrf_buffersize() on line 32 is used to determine the size of host and device buffers required for the factorization.

Similar to the cuSPARSE generic API, the data type used to store the matrix A and the type used for computation are passed as arguments on lines 36 and 39. For these arguments, we used the cudaforGetDataType() routine from the cudaforEx module we created in the cuSPARSE section. Unlike cuSPARSE, where the datatype arguments are of integer(4) type and kind, cuSolverDN requires such arguments to be instances of the derived type cudaDataType. We can either modify the cudaforGetDataType() routine to an instance of cudaDataType or just use the constructor as on lines 36 and 39.

After the host and device buffer sizes are determined and allocated, we call cusolverDnXpotrf() to do the factorization. Because we specify CUBLAS_FILL_MODE_UPPER, only the upper triangular portion of the input matrix will be modified. We transfer the matrix to the host and print it and then solve the system of equations with cusolverDnXpotrs(). The last argument to both cusparseDnXpotrf() and cusparseDnXpotrs() is a device variable indicating the success (0) or failure (non-zero) of the factorization and matrix solve.

Compiling and running the code we have

```
$ nvfortran cudaforEx.cuf potr.cuf -cudalib=cusolver
cudaforEx.cuf:
potr.cuf:
$ ./a.out
 A:
     25.00000000000000       15.00000000000000      -5.000000000000000
     15.00000000000000       18.00000000000000       0.000000000000000
     -5.000000000000000       0.000000000000000      11.00000000000000
 b:
     40.00000000000000       51.00000000000000      28.00000000000000
 Cholesky factorization:
     5.000000000000000       3.000000000000000      -1.000000000000000
     15.00000000000000       3.000000000000000       1.000000000000000
     -5.000000000000000       0.000000000000000      3.000000000000000
 x:
     1.000000000000000       2.000000000000000      3.000000000000000
```

In addition to the Cholesky factorization, cuSolverDN also has routines for LU and QR factorizations, as well as for SVD and bidiagonalization routines.

7.5 cuTENSOR

Tensors can be thought of as a generalization of matrices to higher dimensions. The cuTENSOR library is a CUDA library with routines that perform operations such as contractions, reductions (including partial reductions), and element-wise operations on tensors of up to 64 dimensions.

In CUDA Fortran, there are two sets of interfaces to cuTENSOR, a low-level set of interfaces defined in the cutensor module that maps directly to the cuTENSOR library API and the cutensorEx module where Fortran intrinsic functions are overloaded to use cuTENSOR routines. For example, matrix multiplication is a type of tensor contraction, and in the cutensorEx module, the Fortran intrinsic matmul() has been overloaded to accept arguments with the device attribute, where the matrix multiplication is done with the cutensorContraction() routine in the cuTENSOR library. Furthermore, if the targeted architecture has tensor cores that support the type and kind of arguments, then the tensor contraction will be performed using tensor cores. The following code demonstrates how matmul() is overloaded to use tensor cores on an A100 GPU:

```fortran
program main
  use cudafor
  use cutensorEx
  implicit none
  integer, parameter :: m=3200, n=3200, k=3200
  real(8) :: a(m,k), b(k,n)
  real(8) :: c(m,n), cref(m,n)
  real(8), device :: a_d(m,k), b_d(k,n)
  real(8), device :: c_d(m,n)
  integer :: istat

  type(cudaDeviceProp) :: prop
  type(cudaEvent) :: startEvent, stopEvent
  real :: err, time

  istat = cudaGetDeviceProperties(prop, 0)
  print "(' Device: ', a)", trim(prop%name)
  print "(' m = ', i0, ', n = ', i0, ', k = ', i0)", m, n, k

  istat = cudaEventCreate(startEvent)
  istat = cudaEventCreate(stopEvent)

  call random_number(a)
  call random_number(b)

  ! on host
  cref = matmul(a,b)

  a_d = a; b_d = b
  ! for overhead
  c_d = matmul(a_d, b_d)

  c_d = 0.0
  istat = cudaDeviceSynchronize()
  istat = cudaEventRecord(startEvent, 0)
  c_d = matmul(a_d, b_d)
  istat = cudaEventRecord(stopEvent, 0)
  istat = cudaEventSynchronize(stopEvent)
  c = c_d
  istat = cudaEventElapsedTime(time, startEvent, stopEvent)

  print *, 'cuTensor matmul maxval(abs(cref-c)): ', maxval(abs(cref-c))
  print *, 'cuTensor matmul TFLOPS: ', 2.*k*m*n/(time/1000.)/1.0E+12

  block
    use cublas_v2
    type(cublasHandle) :: handle

    istat = cublasCreate(handle)
    c_d = 0.0
```

```
51        istat = cudaDeviceSynchronize()
52        istat = cudaEventRecord(startEvent, 0)
53        istat = cublasDGemm(handle, CUBLAS_OP_N, CUBLAS_OP_N, &
54              m, n, k, 1.0_8, a_d, m, b_d, k, 0.0_8, c_d, n)
55        istat = cudaEventRecord(stopEvent, 0)
56        istat = cudaEventSynchronize(stopEvent)
57        c = c_d
58        istat = cudaEventElapsedTime(time, startEvent, stopEvent)
59
60        print *, 'cublasDGemm maxval(abs(cref-c)): ', maxval(abs(cref-c))
61        print *, 'cublasDGemm TFLOPS: ',  2.*k*m*n/(time/1000.)/1.0E+12
62
63        istat = cublasDestroy(handle)
64    end block
65
66 end program main
```

where for comparison, we have also performed the matrix multiplication with the cuBLAS DGEMM routine, which also utilizes tensor cores. The code is compiled and run with

```
$ nvfortran -O3 matmulTC.cuf -cudalib=cublas,cutensor
$ ./a.out
  Device: NVIDIA A100 80GB PCIe
  m = 3200, n = 3200, k = 3200
  cuTensor matmul maxval(abs(cref-c)):     6.7075234255753458E-012
  cuTensor matmul TFLOPS:       15.92436
  cublasDGemm maxval(abs(cref-c)):     6.7075234255753458E-012
  cublasDGemm TFLOPS:       17.46248
```

The cuBLAS DGEMM performs better, but there is much more to the `cutensorEx` than matrix multiplication. In addition to `matmul`, `cutensorEx` has functions that overload `reshape()`, `transpose()`, `spread()`, and `dot_product()`. Furthermore, there is support for converting expressions involving multiple source arrays into cuTENSOR calls. For example, the matrix multiplication of the transpose of the matrices on line 28 occurs in a single cuTENSOR contraction kernel:

```
1  program main
2    use cudafor
3    use cutensorEx
4    implicit none
5    integer, parameter :: m=3200, n=m, k=3200
6    real(8) :: a(m,k), b(k,n)
7    real(8) :: c(m,n), cref(m,n)
8    real(8), device :: a_d(m,k), b_d(k,n)
9    real(8), device :: c_d(m,n)
10   integer :: istat
11
12   type(cudaDeviceProp) :: prop
13
14   istat = cudaGetDeviceProperties(prop, 0)
15   print "(' Device: ', a)", trim(prop%name)
16   print "(' m = ', i0, ', n = ', i0, ', k = ', i0)", m, n, k
17
```

```
18 │   call random_number(a)
19 │   call random_number(b)
20 │
21 │   ! transpose(A*B) = tranpose(B)*transpose(A)
22 │   ! LHS on host
23 │   cref = matmul(a,b)
24 │   cref = transpose(cref)
25 │
26 │   ! RHS on device
27 │   a_d = a; b_d = b
28 │   c_d = matmul(transpose(b_d), transpose(a_d))
29 │   c = c_d
30 │   print *, 'maxval(abs(tr(AB)-tr(B)tr(A))): ', &
31 │         maxval(abs(cref-c))
32 │ end program main
```

Output from this code is

```
$ nvfortran -O3 matmulTranspose.cuf -cudalib=cutensor
$ ./a.out
 Device: NVIDIA A100 80GB PCIe
 m = 3200, n = 3200, k = 3200
 maxval(abs(tr(AB)-tr(B)tr(A))):    6.7075234255753458E-012
```

See the cuTENSOR Fortran Extensions in the *Nvidia Fortran CUDA Interfaces Guide* for more detail on what expressions are supported in this manner.

7.5.1 Low-level cuTENSOR interfaces

We will go through how to use the low-level cuTENSOR interfaces to calculate the matrix multiplication that we performed with the overloaded `matmul()` intrinsic in the previous section. Using the low-level interface is more involved, but it is also far more flexible.

Our matrix multiplication in tensor notation can be written as

$$C_{m,n} = A_{m,k}B_{k,n},$$

where indices such as k here that appear twice in a single term are contracted or summed over all values of that index. The indices m, n, and k are referred to as modes of the tensors.

Here is the code for matrix multiplication using the cuTENSOR API:

```
 1 │ program main
 2 │   use cudafor
 3 │   use cutensor_v2
 4 │   implicit none
 5 │   integer, parameter :: m=3200, n=3200, k=3200
 6 │   real(8) :: a(m,k), b(k,n), c(m,n), cref(m,n)
 7 │   real(8), device :: a_d(m,k), b_d(k,n), c_d(m,n)
 8 │   real(8) :: alpha = 1.0, beta = 0.0
 9 │
10 │   type(cudaDeviceProp) :: prop
11 │
12 │   type(cutensorHandle) :: handle
```

```
13    type(cutensorTensorDescriptor) :: Adesc, Bdesc, Cdesc
14    type(cutensorOperationDescriptor) :: opDesc
15    type(cutensorPlan) :: plan
16    type(cutensorPlanPreference) :: pref
17    integer(4) :: aMode(2), bMode(2), cMode(2)
18
19    integer :: istat
20    type(cutensorStatus) :: ctStat
21
22    istat = cudaGetDeviceProperties(prop, 0)
23    if (istat /= cudaSuccess) &
24        print *, cudaGetErrorString(istat)
25    print "(' Device : ', a)", trim(prop%name)
26    print "(' m = ', i0, ', n = ', i0, ', k = ', i0)", m , n , k
27
28    call random_number(a); call random_number(b)
29    a_d = a; b_d = b; c_d = 0.0
30
31    ! host reference
32    cref = matmul(a,b)
33
34    ! Initialize cutensor library
35    ctStat = cutensorCreate(handle)
36    if (ctStat /= CUTENSOR_STATUS_SUCCESS) &
37        print *, cutensorGetErrorString(ctStat)
38
39    ! Create tensor descriptors
40    block
41      integer(8) :: extent(2), stride(2)
42      integer(4) :: nModes
43      integer(4) :: ialign
44
45      ! A
46
47      nModes=2
48      extent = shape(a)
49      stride = [1, m]
50      Amode = [ichar('m'), ichar('k')]
51      ialign = 128
52
53      ctStat = cutensorCreateTensorDescriptor(handle, Adesc, &
54          nModes, extent, stride, CUTENSOR_R_64F, ialign)
55
56      ! B
57
58      nModes=2
59      extent = shape(b)
60      stride = [1, k]
61      Bmode = [ichar('k'), ichar('n')]
62      ialign = 128
63
64      ctStat = cutensorCreateTensorDescriptor(handle, Bdesc, &
```

```
65              nModes, extent, stride, CUTENSOR_R_64F, ialign)
66
67      ! C
68
69      nModes=2
70      extent = shape(c)
71      stride = [1, m]
72      Cmode = [ichar('m'), ichar('n')]
73      ialign = 128
74
75      ctStat = cutensorCreateTensorDescriptor(handle, Cdesc, &
76          nModes, extent, stride, CUTENSOR_R_64F, ialign)
77    end block
78
79    ctStat = cutensorCreateContraction(handle, opDesc, &
80        Adesc, Amode, CUTENSOR_OP_IDENTITY, &
81        Bdesc, Bmode, CUTENSOR_OP_IDENTITY, &
82        Cdesc, Cmode, CUTENSOR_OP_IDENTITY, &
83        Cdesc, Cmode, CUTENSOR_COMPUTE_DESC_64F)
84
85    ctStat = cutensorCreatePlanPreference(&
86        handle, pref, CUTENSOR_ALGO_DEFAULT, CUTENSOR_JIT_MODE_NONE)
87
88    ! create work buffer
89    block
90      integer(8) :: worksize
91      integer(1), device, allocatable :: workspace_d(:)
92
93      ctStat = cutensorEstimateWorkspaceSize(handle, opDesc, pref, &
94          CUTENSOR_WORKSPACE_DEFAULT, worksize)
95      print *,"Estimated workspace size (B): ", worksize
96
97      ctStat = cutensorCreatePlan(handle, plan, opDesc, pref, worksize)
98      allocate(workspace_d(worksize))
99
100     ! now do contraction
101     block
102       type(cudaEvent) :: startEvent, stopEvent
103       real(4) :: time
104
105       istat = cudaEventCreate(startEvent)
106       istat = cudaEventCreate(stopEvent)
107
108       istat = cudaDeviceSynchronize()
109       istat = cudaEventRecord(startEvent, 0)
110
111       ctStat = cutensorContract(handle, plan, alpha, a_d, b_d, &
112           beta, c_d, c_d, workspace_d, worksize, 0)
113
114       istat = cudaEventRecord(stopEvent, 0)
115       istat = cudaEventSynchronize(stopEvent)
116       istat = cudaEventElapsedTime(time, startEvent, stopEvent)
```

```
117          istat = cudaEventDestroy(startEvent)
118          istat = cudaEventDestroy(stopEvent)
119
120          c = c_d
121          print *, 'maxval(abs(c-cref))', maxval(abs(c-cref))
122          print *, 'TFLOPS: ', 2.*k*m*n/(time/1000.)/1.0E+12
123        end block
124        deallocate(workspace_d)
125      end block
126
127      ! cleanup
128
129      ctStat = cutensorDestroy(handle)
130      ctStat = cutensorDestroyPlan(plan)
131      ctStat = cutensorDestroyOperationDescriptor(opDesc)
132      ctStat = cutensorDestroyTensorDescriptor(Adesc)
133      ctStat = cutensorDestroyTensorDescriptor(Bdesc)
134      ctStat = cutensorDestroyTensorDescriptor(Cdesc)
135
136    end program main
```

Similar to other CUDA libraries, cuTENSOR uses types for its handle and various descriptors. The return values of cuTENSOR functions are of type type(cutensorStatus), as the variable ctStat declared on line 20 indicates. The parameter CUTENSOR_STATUS_SUCCESS is an instance of type(cutensorStatus) as well. Comparisons between the return values from cuTENSOR calls can be made with CUTENSOR_STATUS_SUCCESS directly since the comparison operators have been overloaded to handle these types.

After initializing the cuTENSOR library (line 35), the tensor descriptors are created for our order-2 tensors, or matrices, in the block from lines 40–77. Each of our tensors has two modes. We specify the extent, the number of elements in each mode, and the stride, the distance in physical memory (in units of elements) between two successive elements, for each mode. The modes for each tensor are "labeled" with integer values in the arrays Amode, Bmode, and Cmode. Any integer value can be used for any mode, but usage must be consistent across all tensors. On lines 50, 61, and 72, we assign the modes using the ichar() intrinsic, which allows us to essentially keep the symbolic notation of the tensor equations. Next, the routine that creates the tensor contraction descriptor is called on line 79, and the plan preference is set on line 85. Workspace is determined on line 93, the tensor contraction plan is created on line 97, and workspace is allocated on line 98. Finally, the tensor contraction is performed on line 111. Compiling and executing the code we obtain

```
$ nvfortran cutensorContraction.cuf -cudalib=cutensor
cutensorContraction.cuf:
$ ./a.out
 Device : NVIDIA A100 80GB PCIe
 m = 3200, n = 3200, k = 3200
 Estimated workspace size (B):                    4194560
 maxval(abs(c-cref))   6.7075234255753458E-012
 TFLOPS:     18.29094
```

7.6 Thrust

Thrust is a C++ template library that provides a set of parallel primitives such as scan, reduce, and sort. In Section 6.5 on array compaction, we implemented a prefix sum or scan routine in CUDA Fortran. We could have used Thrust to accomplish the same. Thrust header files are included in the CUDA Toolkit include directory.

The first step in using Thrust from CUDA Fortran is to create C wrapper functions that CUDA Fortran can interface with. Here are wrapper functions for the sort algorithm:

```
1   #include <thrust/device_vector.h>
2   #include <thrust/sort.h>
3
4
5   extern "C" {
6     void sort_int_wrapper(int *data, int N)
7     {
8       // C ptr to device_vector container
9       thrust::device_ptr <int> dev_ptr(data);
10      // Use device_ptr in Thrust sort algorithm
11      thrust::sort(dev_ptr, dev_ptr+N);
12    }
13
14    //Sort for float arrays
15    void sort_float_wrapper(float *data, int N)
16    {
17      thrust::device_ptr <float> dev_ptr(data);
18      thrust::sort(dev_ptr, dev_ptr+N);
19    }
20
21    //Sort for double arrays
22    void sort_double_wrapper(double *data, int N)
23    {
24      thrust::device_ptr <double> dev_ptr(data);
25      thrust::sort(dev_ptr, dev_ptr+N);
26    }
27  }
```

Thrust has two vector types, one for host and one for device variables. Here we make use of a pointer to the device vector type via `thrust::device_ptr` in declaring our arguments to `thrust::sort()`. The `thrust::sort()` routine is overloaded to accommodate a variety of arguments; here we specify pointers to the first and last elements.

The next step is to create Fortran interfaces to these C routines. The `thrust.cuf` file contains a thrust module with the generic interface `thrustsort` that contains bindings to the three specific routines in the CUDA C file we created above:

```
1   module thrust
2
3     interface thrustsort
4        subroutine sort_int(input, N) bind(C, name="sort_int_wrapper")
5           use iso_c_binding
6           integer(c_int), device :: input(*)
```

```
7        integer(c_int), value :: N
8      end subroutine sort_int
9
10     subroutine sort_float(input, N) bind(C, name="sort_float_wrapper")
11       use iso_c_binding
12       real(c_float), device :: input(*)
13       integer(c_int), value :: N
14     end subroutine sort_float
15
16     subroutine sort_double(input, N) bind(C, name="sort_double_wrapper")
17       use iso_c_binding
18       real(c_double), device :: input(*)
19       integer(c_int), value :: N
20     end subroutine sort_double
21   end interface thrustsort
22
23 end module thrust
```

The last piece of code needed is the CUDA Fortran code that includes the thrust module and calls thrustsort() on device arrays:

```
1  program testsort
2    use thrust
3    implicit none
4    integer, parameter :: n = 10
5    real :: cpuData(n)
6    real, device :: gpuData(n)
7
8    call random_number(cpuData)
9    cpuData(5)=100.
10
11   print *, "Before sorting", cpuData
12
13   gpuData=cpuData
14   call thrustsort(gpuData, size(gpuData))
15   cpuData=gpuData
16
17   print *, "After sorting", cpuData
18 end program testsort
```

Compilation and execution of the codes are done as follows:

```
$ nvcc -c -arch=sm_75 -o thrust.C.o thrust.cu
$ nvfortran -gpu=cc75 thrust.cuf testSort.cuf thrust.C.o -c++libs
thrust.cuf:
testSort.cuf:
$ ./a.out
 Before sorting    0.9079230       0.1906921      6.7165293E-02   0.8000845
         100.0000       0.6368300       0.5887827       0.1590656
       0.3206477       0.4481761
 After sorting   6.7165293E-02      0.1590656       0.1906921       0.3206477
       0.4481761       0.5887827       0.6368300       0.8000845
       0.9079230       100.0000
```

Here we compile the C wrapper functions in thrust.cu with nvcc and save the result to thrust.C.o rather than to the default thrust.o, which would be overwritten when compiling thrust.cuf in the next line. Note that the option -c++libs is used to append the C++ libraries required by Thrust.

Multi-GPU programming

There are many configurations in which multiple GPUs can be used by an application, based on the number of host threads used and whether or not resources are distributed across multiple compute nodes, as in a cluster. CUDA is compatible with any host threading model, such as OpenMP and MPI, and each host thread can access single or multiple GPUs. In this chapter, we explore two common scenarios: using multiple GPUs from a single host thread and using MPI where each MPI process uses a separate GPU. We discuss these two multi-GPU approaches in the following sections.

8.1 CUDA multi-GPU features

Management of multiple GPUs from a single host thread is quite simple: switching to another device is simply done with cudaSetDevice(). All CUDA calls are issued to the *current* GPU, and cudaSetDevice() sets the current GPU. We give a simple example of its use in the following code, which assigns values to arrays on different devices:

```
1  module kernel
2  contains
3    attributes(global) subroutine assign(a, v)
4      implicit none
5      real :: a(*)
6      real, value :: v
7      a(threadIdx%x) = v
8    end subroutine assign
9  end module kernel
10
11 program minimal
12   use cudafor
13   use kernel
14   implicit none
15   integer, parameter :: n=32
16   real :: a(n)
17   real, device, allocatable :: a0_d(:), a1_d(:)
18   integer :: nDevices, istat
19
20   istat = cudaGetDeviceCount(nDevices)
21   if (nDevices < 2) then
22     print *, 'This program requires at least two GPUs'
23     stop
24   end if
```

```
25
26    istat = cudaSetDevice(0)
27    allocate(a0_d(n))
28    call assign<<<1,n>>>(a0_d, 3.0)
29    a = a0_d
30    deallocate(a0_d)
31    print *, 'Device 0: ', a(1)
32
33    istat = cudaSetDevice(1)
34    allocate(a1_d(n))
35    call assign<<<1,n>>>(a1_d, 4.0)
36    a = a1_d
37    deallocate(a1_d)
38    print *, 'Device 1: ', a(1)
39 end program minimal
```

The kernel code used to assign values on lines 3–8 does not differ from the kernel code for single GPU use; all the differences between single- and multi-GPU codes occur in the host code. The declaration of device arrays on line 17 uses the allocatable variable attribute. Device arrays that are not declared with the allocatable attribute are implicitly allocated on the default device (device 0). To declare arrays intended to reside on other devices, the allocation must be done after the current device is set to the appropriate device, and hence the variable attribute allocatable is needed. Lines 20–24 ensure that there are at least two CUDA-capable GPUs on the system and terminate the program if that is not the case.

The current device is set to device 0 on line 26. This is not necessary as the default device is 0, but we include this for clarity. In this code the allocation, kernel launch, device to host transfer, and deallocation of device data on lines 27–30 all require the current device to be set to the device where the array a0_d resides. On lines 34–37, similar operations are performed with a device array allocated on device 1.

Compilation and execution of this code are as simple as

```
% nvfortran  minimal.cuf -o minimal
% ./minimal
Device 0:      3.000000
Device 1:      4.000000
```

8.1.1 Peer-to-peer communication

Up to this point, we have discussed multi-GPU programming where the GPUs operate independently using local data. If data from one GPU are needed by another, we could stage the transfer through the host using two transfers, one device-to-host transfer from the GPU where the data resides, followed by a host-to-device transfer to the destination GPU.

CUDA allows, under certain conditions, peer-to-peer access, where such transfers are not staged through the CPU. With peer-to-peer access enabled between two devices, we can transfer data between GPUs as simply as we can transfer data between the host and device:

```
a1_d = a0_d
```

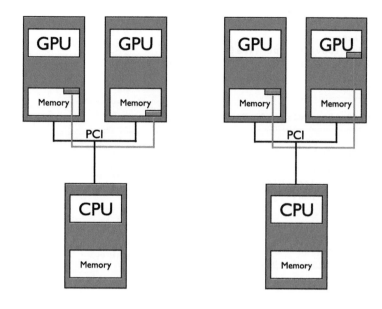

FIGURE 8.1

Depiction of *direct transfer* (left) and *direct access* (right) via peer-to-peer communication.

Not only is the coding easier in this case, but there can be significant performance gains as such *direct transfers* occur across the PCIe bus or even faster NVLink connection, without any interaction from the host (aside from initiating the transfer), as depicted on the left of Fig. 8.1. In addition to *direct transfers*, it is possible for a kernel executing on one GPU to access data from another GPU, a feature called *direct access*. All of this is made possible by a feature called *Unified Virtual Addressing*, or *UVA*. In UVA the host and all GPU memories are combined into a single virtual address space, where memory of each device occupies a contiguous set of addresses in this virtual space. Based on the value of the virtual address for a given variable, the runtime is able to determine where the data reside.

8.1.1.1 *Requirements for peer-to-peer communication*

There are some requirements that must be met to use peer-to-peer features: the pair or pairs of GPUs must be of the same generation and located on the same I/O Hub (IOH) chipset. This last requirement might not be as readily verified as the others, but we can use the peer-to-peer API to determine which GPUs are capable of peer access with each other, as is done in the following code:

```
1  program checkP2pAccess
2    use cudafor
3    implicit none
4    integer, allocatable :: p2pOK(:,:)
5    integer :: nDevices, i, j, istat
6    type (cudaDeviceProp) :: prop
7
8    istat = cudaGetDeviceCount(nDevices)
9    print "('Number of CUDA-capable devices: ', i0,/)", &
10        nDevices
```

```
11
12    do i = 0, nDevices -1
13       istat = cudaGetDeviceProperties(prop, i)
14       print "('Device ', i0, ': ', a)", i, trim(prop%name)
15    enddo
16    print *
17
18    allocate(p2pOK(0:nDevices -1, 0:nDevices -1))
19    p2pOK = 0
20
21    do j = 0, nDevices -1
22       do i = j+1, nDevices -1
23          istat = cudaDeviceCanAccessPeer(p2pOK(i,j), i, j)
24          p2pOK(j,i) = p2pOK(i,j)
25       end do
26    end do
27
28    do i = 0, nDevices -1
29       write(*, "(3x,i3)", advance='no') i
30    enddo
31    print *
32
33    do j = 0, nDevices -1
34       write(*,"(i3)", advance='no') j
35       do i = 0, nDevices -1
36          if (i == j) then
37             write(*,"(2x,'-',3x)", advance='no')
38          else if (p2pOK(i,j) == 1) then
39             write(*,"(2x, 'Y',3x)",advance='no')
40          else
41             write(*,"(6x)",advance='no')
42          end if
43       end do
44       print *
45    end do
46 end program checkP2pAccess
```

In this code, after listing all the CUDA-capable devices in the loop from lines 12–15, the code performs a double-nested loop on lines 21–26, which evaluates whether GPUs can access each others memories:

```
21    do j = 0, nDevices -1
22       do i = j+1, nDevices -1
23          istat = cudaDeviceCanAccessPeer(p2pOK(i,j), i, j)
24          p2pOK(j,i) = p2pOK(i,j)
25       end do
26    end do
```

The function cudaDeviceCanAccessPeer() on line 23 determines if device i is capable of accessing the memory of device j and sets p2pOK(i,j) to either one or zero if this is possible or not, respectively. Although there is a directionality of transfer implied by this function, any of the restrictions that would prevent peer access does not relate to the direction of transfer. In essence, the cudaDeviceCanAccessPeer() call can be interpreted as generally determining whether or not peer access is possible between the devices specified in the last two arguments. For this reason, the loop for i on line 22 is set up to determine accessibility when i>j, and line 24 applies the result to the cases where j>i.

The remainder of the code prints out a matrix reflecting peer-to-peer accessibility. On a DGX A100, a system with 8 GPUs all capable of peer-to-peer access we will see

```
% nvfortran p2pAccess.cuf -o p2pAccess
%  ./p2pAccess
Number of CUDA-capable devices: 8

Device 0: NVIDIA A100-SXM4-80GB
Device 1: NVIDIA A100-SXM4-80GB
Device 2: NVIDIA A100-SXM4-80GB
Device 3: NVIDIA A100-SXM4-80GB
Device 4: NVIDIA A100-SXM4-80GB
Device 5: NVIDIA A100-SXM4-80GB
Device 6: NVIDIA A100-SXM4-80GB
Device 7: NVIDIA A100-SXM4-80GB


        0    1    2    3    4    5    6    7
   0    -    Y    Y    Y    Y    Y    Y    Y
   1    Y    -    Y    Y    Y    Y    Y    Y
   2    Y    Y    -    Y    Y    Y    Y    Y
   3    Y    Y    Y    -    Y    Y    Y    Y
   4    Y    Y    Y    Y    -    Y    Y    Y
   5    Y    Y    Y    Y    Y    -    Y    Y
   6    Y    Y    Y    Y    Y    Y    -    Y
   7    Y    Y    Y    Y    Y    Y    Y    -
```

which shows that each GPU is capable of accessing the others memory. It is important to remember that device ordering is zero-based to be compatible with the underlying CUDA C runtime.

We can use the environment variable CUDA_VISIBLE_DEVICES to enumerate which devices are available to CUDA programs and in what order, for example, by continuing in the above shell:

```
% export CUDA_VISIBLE_DEVICES=2,4,1,3
% ./p2pAccess
Number of CUDA-capable devices: 4

Device 0: NVIDIA A100-SXM4-80GB
Device 1: NVIDIA A100-SXM4-80GB
Device 2: NVIDIA A100-SXM4-80GB
Device 3: NVIDIA A100-SXM4-80GB


        0    1    2    3
   0    -    Y    Y    Y
   1    Y    -    Y    Y
   2    Y    Y    -    Y
   3    Y    Y    Y    -
```

In addition to using the CUDA API to determine which pairs of cards in a system are capable of peer-to-peer communication, the nvidia-smi topo command can be used to provide this and additional information about the topology of GPUs on a system (see Section A.2.4), and the Linux command /sbin/lspci -tv can be used to print the PCI-e tree.

8.1.2 Peer-to-peer direct transfers

We begin our discussion of peer-to-peer direct transfers using the following code that copies data from an array from one device to another using three different methods: transfer via assignment which implicitly uses cudaMemcpy(), transfer via cudaMemcpyPeer() with peer access enabled, and transfer via cudaMemcpyPeer() with peer access disabled. The code also times the transfers twice using events on each device. The code is listed below, followed by a discussion:

```
1   program directTransfer
2     use cudafor
3     implicit none
4     integer, parameter :: N = 4*1024*1024
5     real, pinned, allocatable :: a(:), b(:)
6     real, device, allocatable :: a_d(:), b_d(:)
7
8     ! these hold free and total memory before and after
9     ! allocation, used to verify allocation is happening
10    ! on proper devices
11    integer(cuda_count_kind), allocatable :: &
12          freeBefore(:), totalBefore(:), &
13          freeAfter(:), totalAfter(:)
14
15    integer :: istat, nDevices, i, accessPeer, timingDev
16    type (cudaDeviceProp) :: prop
17    type (cudaEvent) :: startEvent, stopEvent
18    real :: time
19
20    istat = cudaGetDeviceCount(nDevices)
21    if (nDevices < 2) then
22        print *, 'Need at least two CUDA capable devices'
23        stop
24    endif
25    print "('Number of CUDA-capable devices: ', i0,/)", &
26          nDevices
27
28    ! allocate host arrays
29    allocate(a(N), b(N))
30    allocate(freeBefore(0:nDevices-1), &
31          totalBefore(0:nDevices-1))
32    allocate(freeAfter(0:nDevices-1), &
33          totalAfter(0:nDevices-1))
34
35    ! get device info (including total and free memory)
36    ! before allocating a_d and b_d on devices 0 and 1
37    do i = 0, nDevices-1
38        istat = cudaGetDeviceProperties(prop, i)
```

```
39      istat = cudaSetDevice(i)
40      istat = cudaMemGetInfo(freeBefore(i), totalBefore(i))
41   enddo
42   istat = cudaSetDevice(0)
43   allocate(a_d(N))
44   istat = cudaSetDevice(1)
45   allocate(b_d(N))
46
47   ! print out free memory before and after allocation
48   print "('Allocation summary')"
49   do i = 0, nDevices-1
50      istat = cudaGetDeviceProperties(prop, i)
51      print "('  Device ', i0, ': ', a)", &
52           i, trim(prop%name)
53      istat = cudaSetDevice(i)
54      istat = cudaMemGetInfo(freeAfter(i), totalAfter(i))
55      print "('    Free memory before: ', i0, &
56           ', after: ', i0, ', difference: ',i0,/)", &
57           freeBefore(i), freeAfter(i), &
58           freeBefore(i)-freeAfter(i)
59   enddo
60
61   ! check whether devices 0 and 1 can use P2P
62   if (nDevices > 1) then
63      istat = cudaDeviceCanAccessPeer(accessPeer, 0, 1)
64      if (accessPeer == 1) then
65         print *, 'Peer access available between 0 and 1'
66      else
67         print *, 'Peer access not available between 0 and 1'
68      endif
69   endif
70
71   ! initialize
72   a = 1.0
73   istat = cudaSetDevice(0)
74   a_d = a
75
76   ! perform test twice, timing on both sending GPU
77   ! and receiving GPU
78   do timingDev = 0, 1
79      write(*,"(/,'Timing on device ', i0, /)") timingDev
80
81      ! create events on the timing device
82      istat = cudaSetDevice(timingDev)
83      istat = cudaEventCreate(startEvent)
84      istat = cudaEventCreate(stopEvent)
85
86      if (accessPeer == 1) then
87         ! enable P2P communication
88         istat = cudaSetDevice(0)
89         istat = cudaDeviceEnablePeerAccess(1, 0)
90         istat = cudaSetDevice(1)
```

```
91          istat = cudaDeviceEnablePeerAccess(0, 0)
92
93          ! transfer (implicitly) across devices
94          b_d = -1.0
95          istat = cudaSetDevice(timingDev)
96          istat = cudaEventRecord(startEvent,0)
97          b_d = a_d
98          istat = cudaEventRecord(stopEvent,0)
99          istat = cudaEventSynchronize(stopEvent)
100         istat = cudaEventElapsedTime(time, &
101             startEvent, stopEvent)
102         b = b_d
103         if (any(b /= a)) then
104            print "('Transfer failed')"
105         else
106            print "('b_d=a_d transfer (GB/s): ', f)", &
107                N*4/time/1.0E+6
108         endif
109      end if
110
111      ! transfer via cudaMemcpyPeer()
112      if (accessPeer == 0) istat = cudaSetDevice(1)
113      b_d = -1.0
114
115      istat = cudaSetDevice(timingDev)
116      istat = cudaEventRecord(startEvent,0)
117      istat = cudaMemcpyPeer(b_d, 1, a_d, 0, N)
118      istat = cudaEventRecord(stopEvent,0)
119      istat = cudaEventSynchronize(stopEvent)
120      istat = cudaEventElapsedTime(time, startEvent, &
121          stopEvent)
122      if (accessPeer == 0) istat = cudaSetDevice(1)
123      b = b_d
124      if (any(b /= a)) then
125         print "('Transfer failed')"
126      else
127         print "('cudaMemcpyPeer transfer (GB/s): ', f)", &
128             N*4/time/1.0E+6
129      endif
130
131      ! cudaMemcpyPeer with P2P disabled
132      if (accessPeer == 1) then
133         istat = cudaSetDevice(0)
134         istat = cudaDeviceDisablePeerAccess(1)
135         istat = cudaSetDevice(1)
136         istat = cudaDeviceDisablePeerAccess(0)
137         b_d = -1.0
138
139         istat = cudaSetDevice(timingDev)
140         istat = cudaEventRecord(startEvent,0)
141         istat = cudaMemcpyPeer(b_d, 1, a_d, 0, N)
142         istat = cudaEventRecord(stopEvent,0)
```

```
143        istat = cudaEventSynchronize(stopEvent)
144        istat = cudaEventElapsedTime(time, startEvent, &
145            stopEvent)
146
147        istat = cudaSetDevice(1)
148        b = b_d
149        if (any(b /= a)) then
150            print "('Transfer failed')"
151        else
152            print "('cudaMemcpyPeer transfer w/ P2P', &
153                ' disabled (GB/s): ', f)", N*4/time/1.0E+6
154        endif
155      end if
156
157      ! destroy events associated with timingDev
158      istat = cudaEventDestroy(startEvent)
159      istat = cudaEventDestroy(stopEvent)
160    end do
161
162    ! clean up
163    deallocate(freeBefore, totalBefore, freeAfter, totalAfter)
164    deallocate(a, b, a_d, b_d)
165  end program directTransfer
```

After declaring and allocating host data, the device management API is used to determine the number and types of GPUs on the system from lines 29–41. Of special note here is

```
40        istat = cudaMemGetInfo(freeBefore(i), totalBefore(i))
```

which is used to determine the available memory on each device before array allocations. The device arrays are allocated on lines 43 and 45. After the device allocations, cudaMemGetInfo() is used again on line 54 to determine the available memory on all devices after allocations, and the difference in available memory before and after is printed out. We do this to verify that arrays are being allocated on the intended devices.

Whether peer access is possible between devices 0 and 1 is determined on lines 62–69, which is followed by initialization of host data and a loop that performs and times the data transfers between devices. If we were enabling bidirectional peer access between two devices, two calls to cudaDeviceEnablePeerAccess() would be required. But here we only need to determine whether peer access is possible between two devices, so a single call to cudaDeviceCanAccessPeer() suffices.

The main loop starting at line 78 is over the timing device, timingDev, as both device 0 and 1 are used to time execution. We time on each device not because we expect different answers, rather we do this to demonstrate some features of using events in multi-GPU code. CUDA events use the GPU clock and are therefore associated with the current device at the time the events are created. For this reason, the events are created within the timing device loop on lines 83–84 after the current device is set to the timing device on line 82. After this, if peer access between devices 0 and 1 is possible, then it is enabled on lines 88–91, and the direct transfer of data via assignment statement is performed on line 97. Before any call to the CUDA event API, the current device must be set to timingDev.

Note that before the transfer of b_d from device 1 to the host on line 102, we do not need to set the current device, which is timingDevice, to device 1. The current device does not need to be on the sending or receiving end of a data transfer; it only needs to have peer access to the device, or devices, involved in such a transfer. For this reason, we enable bidirectional access between devices 0 and 1 on lines 89 and 91 to accommodate device-to-host transfers when the current device is not sending or receiving data. The same logic applies to data transfers between two devices. The transfer is a valid operation as long as the current device has peer access to the memory of both devices involved in a data transfer.

Data transfer by explicitly calling cudaMemcpyPeer() can be done whether peer access is enabled or not. If peer access is enabled, then the transfer is done without being staged through the CPU, and we should obtain a similar transfer rate to as the above implicit transfer via assignment. When peer access is not enabled, cudaMemcpyPeer() issues a device-to-host transfer from the device on which the source array resides followed by a host-to-device transfer to the device on which the destination array resides. In addition, when peer access is not enabled, we must be careful that the current device is set properly when initializing device data as on line 113:

```
112     if (accessPeer == 0) istat = cudaSetDevice(1)
113     b_d = -1.0
```

and also when retrieving the results on line 123. When peer access is enabled, we do not need to set the current device as long as the current device has access to devices involved in the transfer.

Finally, we time the transfer after explicitly disabling peer-to-peer communication on lines 134 and 136. Once again, here we use cudaMemcpyPeer() on line 141. The results of running this program on a system with two peer-to-peer capable cards is

```
Number of CUDA-capable devices: 2

Allocation summary
  Device 0: NVIDIA A100-SXM4-80GB
  Free memory before: 84751286272, after: 84734509056, difference: 16777216

  Device 1: NVIDIA A100-SXM4-80GB
  Free memory before: 84751286272, after: 84734509056, difference: 16777216

  Peer access available between 0 and 1

Timing on device 0

b_d=a_d transfer (GB/s):       130.7451477
cudaMemcpyPeer transfer (GB/s):       241.4960785
cudaMemcpyPeer transfer w/ P2P disabled (GB/s):       14.6285715


Timing on device 1

b_d=a_d transfer (GB/s):       109.8445435
cudaMemcpyPeer transfer (GB/s):       192.1172638
cudaMemcpyPeer transfer w/ P2P disabled (GB/s):       14.5667925
```

As we expect, the transfer rates for transfers with peer-to-peer disabled are substantially slower than those where it is enabled; on this particular system the P2P traffic will route through the NVLink connections, whereas the normal traffic will route through the PCI-e links.

In the beginning of this chapter, we developed a code that printed a matrix indicating which pairs of devices are capable of peer-to-peer communication. The code just above printed out the bandwidth of data transfers between two devices. We can combine these features in one code to print a matrix of bandwidth between two devices:

```fortran
 1  program p2pBandwidth
 2    use cudafor
 3    implicit none
 4    integer, parameter :: N = 4*1024*1024
 5    type distributedArray
 6       real, device, allocatable :: a_d(:)
 7    end type distributedArray
 8    type (distributedArray), allocatable :: distArray(:)
 9
10    real, allocatable :: bandwidth(:,:)
11    real :: array(N), time
12    integer :: nDevices, access, i, j, istat
13    type (cudaDeviceProp) :: prop
14    type (cudaEvent) :: startEvent, stopEvent
15
16    istat = cudaGetDeviceCount(nDevices)
17    print "('Number of CUDA-capable devices: ', i0,/)", &
18         nDevices
19
20    do i = 0, nDevices-1
21       istat = cudaGetDeviceProperties(prop, i)
22       print "('Device ', i0, ': ', a)", i, trim(prop%name)
23    enddo
24    print *
25
26    allocate(distArray(0:nDevices-1))
27
28    do j = 0, nDevices-1
29       istat = cudaSetDevice(j)
30       allocate(distArray(j)%a_d(N))
31       distArray(j)%a_d = j
32       do i = j+1, nDevices-1
33          istat = cudaDeviceCanAccessPeer(access, j, i)
34          if (access == 1) then
35             istat = cudaSetDevice(j)
36             istat = cudaDeviceEnablePeerAccess(i, 0)
37             istat = cudaSetDevice(i)
38             istat = cudaDeviceEnablePeerAccess(j, 0)
39          endif
40       enddo
41    end do
42
43    allocate(bandwidth(0:nDevices-1, 0:nDevices-1))
44    bandwidth = 0.0
45
46    do j = 0, nDevices-1
47       istat = cudaSetDevice(j)
```

```
48      istat = cudaEventCreate(startEvent)
49      istat = cudaEventCreate(stopEvent)
50      do i = 0, nDevices-1
51         if (i == j) cycle
52         istat = cudaMemcpyPeer(distArray(j)%a_d, j, &
53              distArray(i)%a_d, i, N)
54         istat = cudaEventRecord(startEvent,0)
55         istat = cudaMemcpyPeer(distArray(j)%a_d, j, &
56              distArray(i)%a_d, i, N)
57         istat = cudaEventRecord(stopEvent,0)
58         istat = cudaEventSynchronize(stopEvent)
59         istat = cudaEventElapsedTime(time, &
60              startEvent, stopEvent)
61
62         array = distArray(j)%a_d
63         if (all(array == i)) bandwidth(j,i) = N*4/time/1.0E+6
64      end do
65      distArray(j)%a_d = j
66      istat = cudaEventDestroy(startEvent)
67      istat = cudaEventDestroy(stopEvent)
68   enddo
69
70   print "('Bandwidth (GB/s) for transfer size (MB): ', &
71         f9.3,/)", N*4.0/1024**2
72   write (*,"(' S\\R    0')", advance='no')
73   do i = 1, nDevices-1
74      write(*,"(5x,i3)", advance='no') i
75   enddo
76   print *
77
78   do j = 0, nDevices-1
79      write(*,"(i3)", advance='no') j
80      do i = 0, nDevices-1
81         if (i == j) then
82            write(*,"(4x,'-',3x)", advance='no')
83         else
84            write(*,"(f8.2)",advance='no') bandwidth(j,i)
85         end if
86      end do
87      write(*,*)
88   end do
89
90   ! cleanup
91   do j = 0, nDevices-1
92      deallocate(distArray(j)%a_d)
93   end do
94   deallocate(distArray,bandwidth)
95
96 end program p2pBandwidth
```

where we use cudaMemcpyPeer() for all transfers, with peer access enabled if possible. Most of the content of this code appeared in one of the two aforementioned codes, the exception being how the device arrays are organized in this code. We define a derived type `distributedArray` on lines 5–7, which contains an allocatable device array `a_d`. On line 8, we declare an allocatable host array of this type as `distArray`. After determining the number of devices on the system, the host array `distArray` is allocated on line 26 using zero offset to correspond to the way CUDA enumerates devices. We then loop over devices and allocate `distArray(j)%a_d` on device j on line 30. Using derived types in this manner is a convenient and general way to deal with data that are distributed across multiple devices. Peer access is enabled if possible in the loop on lines 32–40, the transfers are performed and timed on lines 46–68, and the bandwidth matrix is printed out on lines 70-88. Running this code on the DGX A100 system, we obtain

```
Number of CUDA-capable devices: 8

Device 0: NVIDIA A100-SXM4-80GB
...
Device 7: NVIDIA A100-SXM4-80GB

Bandwidth (GB/s) for transfer size (MB):    16.000

  S\R    0       1       2       3       4       5       6       7
   0     -     199.58  220.85  199.80  200.49  199.65  200.03  199.80
   1   199.96    -     199.80  199.88  199.80  199.88  199.80  199.96
   2   199.88  224.25    -     199.80  199.80  200.57  199.80  199.88
   3   224.44  199.73  199.80    -     199.80  199.88  199.80  199.80
   4   197.99  199.80  199.80  197.40    -     199.05  199.80  199.80
   5   199.96  199.80  199.80  199.80  199.80    -     199.80  199.80
   6   199.73  199.80  199.80  199.73  199.80  221.78    -     197.99
   7   199.88  199.80  199.80  199.80  199.80  199.80  199.80    -
```

The rows in the output correspond to the sending devices, and the columns are the receiving devices for the transfers. If we now run the same code on a DGX H100, then we will see a speed increase due to the faster NVLink available on the Hopper generation GPUs:

```
Number of CUDA-capable devices: 8

Device 0: NVIDIA H100 80GB HBM3
...
Device 7: NVIDIA H100 80GB HBM3
Bandwidth (GB/s) for transfer size (MB):    16.000

  S\R    0       1       2       3       4       5       6       7
   0     -     292.41  293.39  293.39  294.05  293.55  289.34  294.05
   1   293.72    -     293.39  293.23  284.94  293.39  294.21  293.72
   2   289.18  293.39    -     293.55  289.18  293.72  288.70  293.72
   3   293.39  293.39  293.23    -     317.94  292.90  252.91  294.88
   4   294.05  293.88  294.05  293.88    -     294.88  294.05  293.23
   5   294.05  293.88  294.05  293.88  294.21    -     293.55  293.39
   6   293.88  293.88  293.88  293.88  294.71  293.39    -     293.23
   7   289.66  293.72  293.88  289.18  294.21  293.39  293.39    -
```

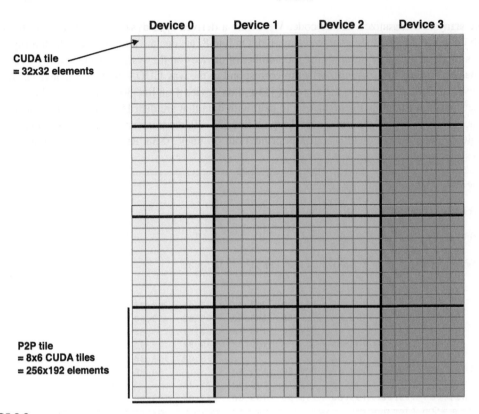

CUDA tile = 32x32 elements

P2P tile = 8x6 CUDA tiles = 256x192 elements

Device 0   Device 1   Device 2   Device 3

FIGURE 8.2

Device data layout for peer-to-peer transpose with an nRows × nCols = 1024 × 768 matrix on four devices. Each device holds a 1024 × 192 vertical slice of input matrix shown above (as well as a 768 × 256 vertical slice of the output matrix). Each of these slices of the input matrix is broken into four tiles of 256 × 192 elements, which are used for peer-to-peer transfers. The CUDA kernel transposes this tile using 48 thread blocks, each of which processes a 32 × 32 tile.

8.1.3 Peer-to-peer transpose

In this section, we extend the matrix transpose example of Section 5.2.6.2 to operate on a matrix distributed across multiple GPUs. The data layout is shown in Fig. 8.2 for an nRows × nCols = 1024 × 768 element matrix distributed amongst four devices. Each device contains a vertical slice of the input matrix shown in the figure and a vertical slice of the output matrix. These input matrix slices of 1024 × 192 elements are divided into four tiles containing 256 × 192 elements each, which are referred to as a p2pTile in the code. As the name indicates, the p2pTiles are used for peer-to-peer transfers. After a p2pTile has been transferred to the appropriate device if necessary (tiles on the block diagonal do not need to be transferred as the input and output tiles are on the same device), a CUDA transpose kernel launch transposes the elements within the p2pTile using thread blocks that process smaller tiles of 32 × 32 elements.

We start the discussion of the code with the transpose kernel:

```
14    attributes(global) subroutine cudaTranspose( &
15         matOut, ldOut, matIn, ldIn)
16      implicit none
17      real, intent(out) :: matOut(ldOut, *)
18      real, intent(in) :: matIn(ldIn, *)
19      integer, value, intent(in) :: ldOut, ldIn
20      real, shared :: tile(nTile+1, nTile)
21      integer :: row, col, j
22
23      row = (blockIdx%x-1)*nTile + threadIdx%x
24      col = (blockIdx%y-1)*nTile + threadIdx%y
25
26      do j = 0, nTile-1, blockCols
27         tile(threadIdx%x, threadIdx%y+j) = matIn(row, col+j)
28      end do
29
30      call syncthreads()
31
32      row = (blockIdx%y-1)*nTile + threadIdx%x
33      col = (blockIdx%x-1)*nTile + threadIdx%y
34
35      do j = 0, nTile-1, blockCols
36         matOut(row,col+j) = tile(threadIdx%y+j, threadIdx%x)
37      end do
38    end subroutine cudaTranspose
```

This transpose kernel is basically the same as the `transposeNoBankConlficts()` kernel we developed in Section 5.2.6.2 for the single-GPU transpose, with the exception that two additional arguments are passed to the kernel, `ldOut` and `ldIn`, the leading dimensions of `matOut` and `matIn` arrays. Because the full matrix will be distributed amongst multiple devices in the multi-GPU case, we accommodate variable partition sizes in this manner.

These matrix dimensions were declared at module scope in the single-GPU example; here they are declared in the main code and passed as kernel arguments. In addition, since only a slice of the full array will reside on each device, the matrix declarations use assumed-size notation as on lines 17 and 18.

Most of the host code performs mundane tasks such as getting the number and types of devices:

```
85    ! determine number of devices
86
87    istat = cudaGetDeviceCount(nDevices)
88    print "('Number of CUDA-capable devices: ', i0,/)", nDevices
89
90    do i = 0, nDevices-1
91       istat = cudaGetDeviceProperties(prop, i)
92       print "('  Device ', i0, ': ', a)", i, trim(prop%name)
93    end do
```

and checking that all devices are peer-to-peer capable and enabling peer-to-peer communication:

```
95    ! check to make sure all devices are P2P accessible with
96    ! each other and enable peer access, if not exit
```

```
97
98    do j = 0, nDevices -1
99       do i = j+1, nDevices -1
100         istat = cudaDeviceCanAccessPeer(access, j, i)
101         if (access /= 1) then
102            print *, &
103                  'Not all devices are P2P accessible ', &
104                  'with each other.'
105            print *, &
106                  'Use the p2pAccess code to determine ', &
107                  'a subset that can do P2P and set'
108            print *, &
109                  'the environment variable ', &
110                  'CUDA_VISIBLE_DEVICES accordingly'
111            stop
112         end if
113         istat = cudaSetDevice(j)
114         istat = cudaDeviceEnablePeerAccess(i, 0)
115         istat = cudaSetDevice(i)
116         istat = cudaDeviceEnablePeerAccess(j, 0)
117      end do
118   end do
```

as well as verifying that the matrix divides evenly into the various tile sizes, printing out the various sizes, and initializing host data and transposing on the host.

Because we want to overlap the execution of the transpose kernel with the data transfer between GPUs, we want to avoid using the default stream for peer-to-peer communication and kernel execution. We want each device to have nDevices streams, one for each transpose call. Since there are nDevices devices, each requiring nDevices streams, we use a two-dimensional variable to hold the stream IDs:

```
176   allocate(streamID(0:nDevices -1,0:nDevices -1))
177   do p = 0, nDevices -1
178      istat = cudaSetDevice(p)
179      do stage = 0, nDevices -1
180         istat = cudaStreamCreate(streamID(p,stage))
181      enddo
182   enddo
```

where the first index to streamID corresponds to the particular device the stream is associated with, and the second index refers to the stages of the calculation.

The stages of the transpose, enumerated zero to nDevices-1, are organized as follows. In the zeroth stage, each device transposes the submatrix that lies along the block diagonal of the global matrix, which is depicted in the top diagram of Fig. 8.3. This is done first as no peer-to-peer communication is involved, and the kernel execution can overlap data transfers in the first stage.

In stage one, data from what is primarily the first block-superdiagonal of the input matrix is sent to the devices that hold the corresponding first block-subdiagonal, as depicted in Fig. 8.3. After the transfer completes, the receiving device performs the transpose. Note that one of the blocks transferred during stage one is not on the superdiagonal, as we wrap the pattern so that all devices both send and receive data during each stage. The following stages do similar operations on additional block super- and sub-diagonals until all the data from blocks have been transposed. The wrapping during these

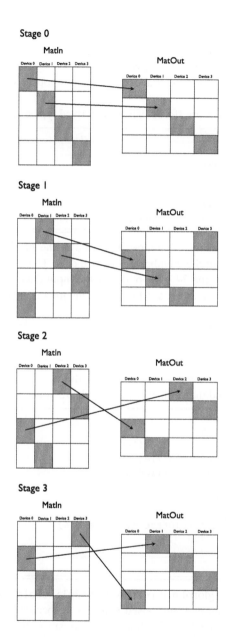

FIGURE 8.3

Stages of the matrix transpose. In stage zero, each device transposes the block along the global matrix block diagonal, which requires no peer-to-peer communication. In stage one, blocks from the first super-diagonal of the input matrix are transferred to the device holding the respective block sub-diagonal, after which the transpose is performed on the receiving device. Subsequent stages (such as stage 2) do the same for subsequent super- and sub-diagonals.

stages becomes more pronounced, so that in the final stage, data from blocks in the first sub-diagonal of the input matrix transfer to blocks in the first super-diagonal of the output matrix. In using this arrangement, during each stage other than the zeroth, each device sends and receives a block of data, and both of these transfers can overlap if transferred asynchronously since the devices have separate send and receive copy engines.

The distributed global matrices are stored using the derived type deviceArray:

```
68    ! distributed arrays
69    type deviceArray
70       real, device, allocatable :: v(:,:)
71    end type deviceArray
72
73    type (deviceArray), allocatable :: &
74         matIn_da(:), matOut_da(:), matRec_da(:)   ! (0:nDevices-1)
```

The same technique was used in the p2pBandwidth code in the previous section. Instances of this derived type will be host data, but the member v is device data. There are three allocatable array declarations of this derived type on line 74: matIn_da for the input data, matRec_da, which is a receive buffer used in the transfers, and matOut_da, which holds the final transposed data. These variables are allocated by

```
186    allocate(matIn_da(0:nDevices-1),&
187         matOut_da(0:nDevices-1), matRec_da(0:nDevices-1))
```

which represents decomposition of the global array into the vertical slices depicted in Fig. 8.2. The members of the derived type hold the vertical slices, which are allocated and initialized by

```
189    do p = 0, nDevices-1
190        istat = cudaSetDevice(p)
191        allocate(matIn_da(p)%v(nRows,p2pTileCols), &
192             matRec_da(p)%v(nRows,p2pTileCols), &
193             matOut_da(p)%v(nCols,p2pTileRows))
194
195        colOffset = p*p2pTileCols
196        matIn_da(p)%v(:,:) = &
197             matIn(:,colOffset+1:colOffset+p2pTileCols)
198        matRec_da(p)%v(:,:) = -1.0
199        matOut_da(p)%v(:,:) = -1.0
200    enddo
```

where nRows and nCols are the global matrix sizes, and p2pTileCols and p2pTileRows are the sizes of the vertical slices of the input and transposed matrices, respectively. Note that the current device is set on line 190 before each member v is allocated. Also, since the matrix on the host is stored in matIn(nRows,nCols), the offset colOffset is used when initializing matIn_da on lines 196–197.

The code that performs the various transpose stages is

```
212    ! Stage 0:
213    ! transpose diagonal blocks (local data) before kicking off
214    ! transfers and transposes of other blocks
215
```

```
216   do p = 0, nDevices-1
217      istat = cudaSetDevice(p)
218      if (asyncVersion) then
219         call cudaTranspose &
220               <<<dimGrid, dimBlock, 0, streamID(p,0)>>> &
221               (matOut_da(p)%v(p*p2pTileCols+1,1), nCols, &
222               matIn_da(p)%v(p*p2pTileRows+1,1), nRows)
223      else
224         call cudaTranspose<<<dimGrid, dimBlock>>> &
225               (matOut_da(p)%v(p*p2pTileCols+1,1), nCols, &
226               matIn_da(p)%v(p*p2pTileRows+1,1), nRows)
227      endif
228   enddo
229
230   ! now send data to blocks to the left of diagonal
231   ! (using mod for wrapping) and transpose
232
233   do stage = 1, nDevices-1     ! stages = offset diagonals
234      do rDev = 0, nDevices-1  ! device that receives
235         sDev = mod(stage+rDev, nDevices)  ! dev that sends
236
237         if (asyncVersion) then
238            istat = cudaSetDevice(rDev)
239            istat = cudaMemcpy2DAsync( &
240                  matRec_da(rDev)%v(sDev*p2pTileRows+1,1), nRows, &
241                  matIn_da(sDev)%v(rDev*p2pTileRows+1,1), nRows, &
242                  p2pTileRows, p2pTileCols, &
243                  stream=streamID(rDev,stage))
244         else
245            istat = cudaMemcpy2D( &
246                  matRec_da(rDev)%v(sDev*p2pTileRows+1,1), nRows, &
247                  matIn_da(sDev)%v(rDev*p2pTileRows+1,1), nRows, &
248                  p2pTileRows, p2pTileCols)
249         end if
250
251         istat = cudaSetDevice(rDev)
252         if (asyncVersion) then
253            call cudaTranspose &
254                  <<<dimGrid, dimBlock, 0, streamID(rDev,stage)>>>  &
255                  (matOut_da(rDev)%v(sDev*p2pTileCols+1,1), nCols, &
256                  matRec_da(rDev)%v(sDev*p2pTileRows+1,1), nRows)
257         else
258            call cudaTranspose<<<dimGrid, dimBlock>>> &
259                  (matOut_da(rDev)%v(sDev*p2pTileCols+1,1), nCols, &
260                  matRec_da(rDev)%v(sDev*p2pTileRows+1,1), nRows)
261         endif
262      enddo
263   enddo
```

Stage 0 occurs in the loop on lines 216–228. After the device is set on line 217, the transpose of the diagonal block is performed either using the default, blocking stream on line 224, or in a non-default stream on line 219, depending on the value of the parameter asyncVersion. The execution configuration used in the kernel launches is determined by

```
141   dimGrid = dim3(p2pTileRows/nTile, p2pTileCols/nTile, 1)
142   dimBlock = dim3(nTile, blockCols, 1)
```

where the thread block is the same as in the single-GPU case, and each kernel launch operates on a submatrix of size p2pTileRows×p2pTileCols.

The other stages are performed in the loop on lines 233–263. After the sending and receiving devices are determined on lines 234 and 235, the peer-to-peer transfer is performed using either cudaMemcpy2DAsync() or cudaMemcpy2D(), depending on the value of asyncVersion. If the asynchronous version is used, then the device is set to the receiving device on line 238, and accordingly the non-default stream used for the transfer is the stream associated with the receiving device. We use the stream associated with the device receiving the data rather than the device sending the data because we want to block the launch of the transpose kernel on the receiving device until the transfer is complete. This is accomplished by default when the same stream is used for the transfer and transpose. For the synchronous data transfer, the device does not need to be specified via cudaSetDevice(). Note that the array receiving the data is matRec_da. The out-of-place transpose from matRec_da to matOut_da is then performed by the kernel launch on line 253 or 258. Regardless of whether the default stream is used or not, the device must be set as done on line 251.

The remainder of the code transfers the data back to the host, checks for correctness, and reports the effective bandwidth. Timing in this case is done using a wall-clock timer. This code uses the C function gettimeofday():

```
1   #include <time.h>
2   #include <sys/types.h>
3   #include <sys/times.h>
4   #include <sys/time.h>
5
6   double wallclock()
7   {
8       struct timeval tv;
9       struct timezone tz;
10      double t;
11
12      gettimeofday(&tv, &tz);
13
14      t = (double)tv.tv_sec;
15      t += ((double)tv.tv_usec)/1000000.0;
16
17      return t;
18  }
```

which is accessed in the Fortran code using the timing module:

```
1   module timing
2     interface wallclock
3        function wallclock() result(res) bind(C, name='wallclock')
4           use iso_c_binding
5           real (c_double) :: res
```

```
6        end function wallclock
7      end interface wallclock
8    end module timing
```

Whenever this routine is called, we explicitly check to make sure there are no pending or executing operations on the device:

```
265    ! wait for execution to complete and get wallclock
266    do p = 0, nDevices-1
267       istat = cudaSetDevice(p)
268       istat = cudaDeviceSynchronize()
269    enddo
270    timeStop = wallclock()
```

Note that most of this multi-GPU code is overhead associated with declaring and initializing arrays and enabling peer-to-peer communication. The actual data transfers and kernel launches are contained in approximately 50 lines of code, which contains branches for synchronous and asynchronous execution. The transpose kernel itself is only slightly modified from the single-GPU transpose to allow for arbitrary matrix sizes.

We use a compute node with two devices for running this transpose code. To compare to the single-GPU transpose results in Section 5.2.6.2, which used 1024×1024 matrices, we choose an overall matrix size of 2048×2048. In this case, each transpose kernel processes a 1024×1024 submatrix, the same as in the single-GPU case. When using blocking transfers, we obtain the following results:

```
Number of CUDA-capable devices: 2

  Device 0: NVIDIA A100-SXM4-80GB
  Device 1: NVIDIA A100-SXM4-80GB

Array size: 2048x2048

CUDA block size: 32x8,   CUDA tile size: 32x32
dimGrid: 32x32x1,    dimBlock: 32x8x1

nDevices: 2, Local input array size: 2048x1024
p2pTileDim: 1024x1024

async mode:   F

Bandwidth (GB/s):   175.70
```

and when using asynchronous transfers, we have

```
Number of CUDA-capable devices: 2

  Device 0: NVIDIA A100-SXM4-80GB
  Device 1: NVIDIA A100-SXM4-80GB


Array size: 2048x2048
```

```
CUDA block size: 32x8,  CUDA tile size: 32x32
dimGrid: 32x32x1,   dimBlock: 32x8x1

nDevices: 2, Local input array size: 2048x1024
p2pTileDim: 1024x1024

async mode:  T

Bandwidth (GB/s):  212.27
```

Although both these numbers fall short of the effective bandwidth achieved in the single-GPU case, we must take into account that half of the data is being transferred over NVLink or the PCIe bus, which is over an order of magnitude (NVLink) or almost two orders (PCIe) slower than the global memory bandwidth within a GPU. In light of this, the use of asynchronous transfers that overlap kernel execution is advantageous as can be seen from the results. In addition, typically, the transpose is used as a means to some other operation that can be done in parallel, in which case cost of the transfer is further amortized.

8.2 Multi-GPU programming with MPI

In the preceding section, we explored using multiple GPUs from a single host thread. Toggling between GPUs using cudaSetDevice() provides a convenient way to distribute data and processing amongst several GPUs. As problems scale up, however, this approach reaches a limit in how many GPUs can be attached to a single node. When this limit is reached, we can program for multiple nodes using MPI. MPI can be used in conjunction with the multi-GPU techniques described above, where MPI can be used to transfer data between nodes, and the CUDA multi-GPU features can be used to distribute and process data amongst the GPUs attached to that node. This is analogous to how OpenMP and MPI are used on CPUs in clusters. We can even combine MPI, OpenMP, and multi-GPU models in an application.

We will briefly discuss the MPI library calls used in this section as they are introduced in the text. For those new to MPI, a more detailed discussion of the API routines can be found in *MPI – The Complete Reference* by Snir et al. (1996) and *Using MPI: Portable Parallel Programming with the Message-Passing Interface* by Gropp et al. (1999). Before we jump into MPI code, we should mention some high-level aspects of the MPI programming model. Just as all device threads in a kernel execute the same device code, all host threads (usually called *ranks*) in an MPI application execute the same host code. In CUDA, we use predefined variables to identify the individual device threads in device code, and in MPI, individual MPI ranks are identified through the library call MPI_COMM_RANK(). However, although the CUDA programming model benefits from fine-grained parallelism (e.g., coalescing), MPI generally benefits from coarse-grained parallelism, where each MPI rank operates on a large partition of the data.

Compilation of MPI CUDA Fortran code is performed using the MPI wrapper mpif90 supplied with numerous MPI distributions. Execution of MPI programs is typically performed with the command mpirun, where the program executable and the number of MPI ranks used are provided on the command line. There are now several MPI implementations (OpenMPI, MVAPICH, Spectrum MPI, Cray MPI, MPICH) that support CUDA-aware features, which will be discussed later in this section.

There are many ways to use CUDA Fortran in conjunction with MPI in terms of how devices are mapped to MPI ranks. In this section, we opt for a simple, versatile approach where each MPI rank is associated with a single GPU. In this configuration, we can still use multiple GPUs per node simply by using multiple MPI ranks per node, which is determined by how the application is launched rather than from within the code. If the nature of the application merits a different mapping of GPUs to MPI ranks, then we can add this later using the techniques discussed earlier in this chapter, but in general the one GPU per MPI rank model is a good first approach.

8.2.1 Assigning devices to MPI ranks

One of the first issues arising in multi-GPU MPI codes using the configuration where each MPI rank has a unique device is how to ensure that no device is assigned to multiple MPI ranks. How devices are associated with CPU processes and threads depends on how the system is configured via nvidia-smi. NVIDIA's System Management Interface (nvidia-smi) is a tool distributed with the driver that allows users to display and administrators to modify settings of devices attached to the system.[1] We can use this utility to simply print the devices attached to the system:

```
% nvidia-smi -L
GPU 0: Tesla V100-DGXS-16GB (UUID: GPU-xxxxx)
GPU 1: Tesla V100-DGXS-16GB (UUID: GPU-xxxxx)
GPU 2: Tesla V100-DGXS-16GB (UUID: GPU-xxxxx)
GPU 3: Tesla V100-DGXS-16GB (UUID: GPU-xxxxx)
```

as well as getting detailed information about temperature, power, and various settings. The setting we are concerned with here is the compute mode. The compute mode determines if multiple processes or threads can use the same GPU. The three modes, from least to most restrictive, are as follows:

default: 0   In this mode, multiple host threads can use the same device via calls to cudaSetDevice();
exclusive process: 3   In this mode, only a single context can be created by a single process system-wide, and this context can be current to all threads of that process;
prohibited: 2   In this mode, no contexts can be created on the device.

We can query the compute mode as follows:

```
% nvidia-smi -q -d COMPUTE
==============NVSMI LOG==============

Timestamp                           : Thu Apr 13 01:56:04 2023
Driver Version                      : 525.60.13
CUDA Version                        : 12.0

Attached GPUs                       : 4
GPU 00000000:07:00.0
    Compute Mode                    : Default
GPU 00000000:08:00.0
    Compute Mode                    : Default
```

---

[1] nvidia-smi is discussed in more detail in Appendix A.

```
GPU 00000000:0E:00.0
    Compute Mode                        : Default
GPU 00000000:0F:00.0
    Compute Mode                        : Default
```

which indicates that all the devices on this DGX Station are in the default compute mode. Changing the compute mode requires administrator privileges; on shared resources or supercomputer centers, it is usually impossible to change it.

To illustrate the different behavior of these modes, we use the following simple program:

```
1   program mpiDevices
2     use cudafor
3     use mpi
4     implicit none
5
6     ! global array size
7     integer, parameter :: n = 1024*1024
8     ! MPI  variables
9     integer :: myrank, nprocs, ierr
10    ! device
11    type(cudaDeviceProp) :: prop
12    integer(int_ptr_kind()) :: freeB, totalB, freeA, totalA
13    real, device, allocatable :: d(:)
14    integer :: i, j, istat
15
16    ! MPI initialization
17    call MPI_Init(ierr)
18    call MPI_Comm_rank(MPI_COMM_WORLD, myrank, ierr)
19    call MPI_Comm_size(MPI_COMM_WORLD, nProcs, ierr)
20
21    ! print compute mode for device
22    istat = cudaGetDevice(j)
23    istat = cudaGetDeviceProperties(prop, j)
24    do i = 0, nprocs-1
25       call MPI_Barrier(MPI_COMM_WORLD, ierr)
26       if (myrank == i) print "('[',i0,'] using device: ', &
27             i0, ' in compute mode: ', i0)", &
28             myrank, j, prop%computeMode
29    enddo
30
31    ! get memory use before large allocations,
32    call MPI_Barrier(MPI_COMM_WORLD, ierr)
33    istat = cudaMemGetInfo(freeB, totalB)
34
35    ! now allocate arrays, one rank at a time
36    do j = 0, nProcs-1
37
38       ! allocate on device associated with rank j
39       call MPI_Barrier(MPI_COMM_WORLD, ierr)
40       if (myrank == j) allocate(d(n))
41
42       ! Get free memory after allocation
```

```
43        call MPI_Barrier(MPI_COMM_WORLD, ierr)
44        istat = cudaMemGetInfo(freeA, totalA)
45
46        if (myrank == j) print "('  [',i0,'] after allocation on rank: ', &
47            i0, ', device arrays allocated: ', i0)", &
48            myrank, j, (freeB-freeA)/n/4
49
50     end do
51
52     deallocate(d)
53     call MPI_Finalize(ierr)
54  end program mpiDevices
```

In this code, each MPI rank allocates a device array and reports the memory usage on each device as the allocations are performed. The module containing all the MPI interfaces and parameters is included on line 3. The typical MPI initialization occurs on lines 17–20. The call to MPI_Init() on line 17 initializes MPI, the call to MPI_Comm_rank() on line 18 returns the MPI rank in the myrank variable, and the call to MPI_Comm_size() returns the number of ranks launched by the application. The device number each rank uses and its compute mode are printed in lines 22–29. The loop used for printing on line 24 is not technically needed but is used along with the MPI_Barrier() call to avoid collisions in output from different ranks. The synchronization barrier MPI_Barrier() blocks execution of all MPI processes until every MPI process has reached that point in the code, similar to CUDA's syncthreads() used in device code. After printing the device number and compute mode, the amount of free space on each device is determined on line 33. In each iteration of the loop on lines 36–50, a device array is allocated on the device associated with a particular rank (line 40), the free memory after allocation is determined (line 44), and the number of arrays allocated on each device is printed out (line 46).

When run using two MPI processes on a single node with two devices in exclusive mode, we obtain

```
[0] using device: 0 in compute mode: 3
[1] using device: 1 in compute mode: 3
  [0] after allocation on rank: 0, device arrays allocated: 1
  [1] after allocation on rank: 1, device arrays allocated: 1
```

which indicates that two separate devices are used by the two ranks from the devices listed in the first two lines, which is verified from the memory utilization in the remainder of the output.

On a node with devices in default compute mode, a two-MPI process run results in

```
[0] using device: 0 in compute mode: 0
[1] using device: 0 in compute mode: 0
  [0] after allocation on rank: 0, device arrays allocated: 1
  [1] after allocation on rank: 1, device arrays allocated: 2
```

which indicates that device 0 is being used for both MPI ranks, which is verified in the allocation summary where after each allocation stage, the free memory on all ranks decreases.

Relying on the compute mode setting is not a very portable approach for configuring the mapping between MPI ranks and GPUs, since it is often impossible to change the compute mode settings. There are more portable ways to ensure that each MPI rank has a unique device regardless of the compute mode setting. These include running in a wrapper script that exposes a single unique GPU to each

MPI rank and alternately using MPI to determine the number of ranks running on each node and then selecting the proper device. In the wrapper script approach, the environment variable CUDA_VISI-BLE_DEVICES is set to expose a single unique GPU to each MPI rank. In the wrapper script below, how LOCAL_RANK is set will depend on the MPI implementation; here it is done via the variable provided by OpenMPI:

```
$ cat wrapper.sh
#!/bin/bash
export LOCAL_RANK=$OMPI_COMM_WORLD_LOCAL_RANK #OpenMPI specific
export CUDA_VISIBLE_DEVICES=$LOCAL_RANK
exec $*
```

and then invoke mpirun with

```
mpirun -np 2 ./wrapper.sh mpiDevice
```

The approach of using MPI to determine the number of ranks running on each node and then selecting the proper device is the most generic and robust way to map MPI ranks to devices. The following module shows one way of implementing this approach[2]:

```
1  module mpiDeviceUtil
2  contains
3    ! assign a different GPU to each MPI rank
4    ! note: all the memory allocations should be dynamic,
5    ! otherwise all the arrays will be allocated on device 0
6    subroutine assignDevice(dev)
7      use mpi
8      use cudafor
9      implicit none
10     integer :: dev
11     integer :: local_comm, ierr
12
13     dev=0
14     call MPI_Comm_split_type(MPI_COMM_WORLD, MPI_COMM_TYPE_SHARED, 0, &
15          MPI_INFO_NULL, local_comm, ierr)
16     call MPI_Comm_rank(local_comm, dev, ierr)
17     ierr = cudaSetDevice(dev)
18   end subroutine assignDevice
19 end module mpiDeviceUtil
```

where the subroutine assignDevice() is responsible for finding and setting a unique device. The MPI_Comm_split_type() call with MPI_COMM_TYPE_SHARED as the second argument returns a new communicator local_comm with all the MPI ranks on each node, and a call to MPI_Comm_rank() returns the new rank with respect to the new communicator. This new rank is used to set the current device on line 17. Once again, we emphasize that this routine can be used regardless of the compute mode setting. The code can be modified to select only GPUs with certain characteristics, such as devices with a certain amount of memory, by adding more logic before the cudaSetDevice() call. The following code shows how this module is used:

---

[2] This version uses an MPI-3 API call, which greatly simplifies the code used in the first edition.

```
1   program main
2     use mpi
3     use mpiDeviceUtil
4     use cudafor
5     implicit none
6
7     ! global array size
8     integer, parameter :: n = 1024*1024
9     ! mpi
10    character (len=MPI_MAX_PROCESSOR_NAME) :: hostname
11    integer :: myrank, nprocs, ierr, namelength
12    ! device
13    type(cudaDeviceProp) :: prop
14    integer(cuda_count_kind) :: freeB, totalB, freeA, totalA
15    real, device, allocatable :: d(:)
16    integer :: deviceID, i, istat
17
18    call MPI_Init(ierr)
19    call MPI_Comm_rank(MPI_COMM_WORLD, myrank, ierr)
20    call MPI_Comm_size(MPI_COMM_WORLD, nProcs, ierr)
21
22    ! get and set unique device
23    call assignDevice(deviceID)
24
25    ! print hostname and device ID for each rank
26    call MPI_Get_processor_name(hostname, namelength, ierr)
27    do i = 0, nProcs-1
28       call MPI_Barrier(MPI_COMM_WORLD, ierr)
29       if (i == myrank) &
30           print "('[',i0,'] host: ', a, ',  device: ', i0)", &
31           myrank, trim(hostname), deviceID
32    enddo
33
34    ! get memory use before large allocations,
35    call MPI_Barrier(MPI_COMM_WORLD, ierr)
36    istat = cudaMemGetInfo(freeB, totalB)
37
38    ! allocate memory on each device
39    call MPI_Barrier(MPI_COMM_WORLD, ierr)
40    allocate(d(n))
41
42    ! Get free memory after allocation
43    call MPI_Barrier(MPI_COMM_WORLD, ierr)
44    istat = cudaMemGetInfo(freeA, totalA)
45
46    do i = 0, nProcs-1
47       call MPI_Barrier(MPI_COMM_WORLD, ierr)
48       if (i == myrank) &
49           print "(' [', i0, '] ', &
50           'device arrays allocated: ', i0)", &
51           myrank, (freeB-freeA)/n/4
52    end do
```

```
53
54    deallocate(d)
55    call MPI_Finalize(ierr)
56  end program main
```

We simply need to use `mpiDeviceUtil`, as on line 3, and call `assignDevice()`, as on line 23, after the `MPI_Init()` subroutine is called, as on line 18. When run using five MPI ranks across three nodes, the code produces

```
% mpirun -np 5 -host c0-7,c0-2,c0-7,c0-3,c0-7 assignDevice
[0] host: compute-0-7.local,  device: 0
[1] host: compute-0-7.local,  device: 1
[2] host: compute-0-7.local,  device: 2
[3] host: compute-0-2.local,  device: 0
[4] host: compute-0-3.local,  device: 0
   [0] device arrays allocated: 1
   [1] device arrays allocated: 1
   [2] device arrays allocated: 1
   [3] device arrays allocated: 1
   [4] device arrays allocated: 1
```

where to save space in the output, the code prints the arrays allocated on each device only after all allocations are made. The code is successful at assigning different devices to the MPI ranks.

8.2.2 MPI transpose

The MPI transpose code shares much in common with the peer-to-peer transpose code discussed previously in this chapter: the domain decomposition, the transpose kernel, execution configuration, and the communication pattern and stages are the same. One small difference is the code needed to initialize MPI and assign the device to the MPI rank:

```
71    call MPI_Init(ierr)
72    call MPI_Comm_rank(MPI_COMM_WORLD, myrank, ierr)
73    call MPI_Comm_size(MPI_COMM_WORLD, nProcs, ierr)
74
75    ! get and set device
76
77    call assignDevice(deviceID)
```

where we use the routine `assignDevice()` from the `mpiDeviceUtil` module introduced in the previous section to assign a unique device to the MPI rank. Parameter checking and initialization are similar in both codes. Timing in the MPI code is done using the MPI function `MPI_Wtime()` after a call to `MPI_Barrier()`.

The main difference between the peer-to-peer and MPI codes occurs within the loop over communication stages:

```
173       do stage = 1, nProcs-1
174          ! sRank = the rank to which myrank sends data
175          ! rRank = the rank from which myrank receives data
176          sRank = modulo(myrank-stage, nProcs)
```

```
177          rRank = modulo(myrank+stage, nProcs)
178
179          call MPI_Barrier(MPI_COMM_WORLD, ierr)
180
181          ! D2H transfer - pack into contiguous host array
182          ierr = cudaMemcpy2D(sTile, mpiTileRows, &
183                  matIn_d(sRank*mpiTileRows+1,1), nRows, &
184                  mpiTileRows, mpiTileCols)
185
186          ! MPI transfer
187          call MPI_Sendrecv(sTile, mpiTileRows*mpiTileCols, &
188                  MPI_REAL, sRank, myrank, &
189                  rTile, mpiTileRows*mpiTileCols, MPI_REAL, &
190                  rRank, rRank, MPI_COMM_WORLD, status, ierr)
191
192          ! H2D transfer
193          rTile_d = rTile
194
195          ! do transpose from receive tile into final array
196          call cudaTranspose<<<dimGrid, dimBlock>>> &
197                  (matOut_d(rRank*mpiTileCols+1,1), nCols, &
198                  rTile_d, mpiTileRows)
199
200        end do ! stage
```

The cudaMemcpy2d() or cudaMemcpy2dAsync() calls that transfer data between devices in the peer-to-peer code are replaced by a device-to-host transfer (line 182), an MPI transfer between hosts (line 187), and a host-to-device transfer (line 193). Running this code with 2 MPI ranks on a DGX Station V100 with an overall matrix of 2048 × 2048, we obtain

```
Array size: 2048x2048

CUDA block size: 32x8,  CUDA tile size: 32x32
dimGrid: 32x32x1,    dimBlock: 32x8x1

nprocs: 2,  Local input array size: 2048x1024
mpiTile: 1024x1024

Bandwidth (GB/s):    18.54
```

which is considerably under the performance of the synchronous peer-to-peer code even though both MPI ranks, and therefore devices, were on the same node. This is not surprising, however, given that the transfers are staged through the host. When performing a parallel transpose on devices distributed across multiple nodes, we would expect to incur the cost of transfers between host and device. However, when MPI transfers occur between device on the same node that are peer-to-peer capable, we would like to take advantage of the peer-to-peer capability in such cases. Luckily, there are MPI implementations, such as OpenMPI, MVAPICH, Spectrum MPI, Cray MPI, and MPICH, that do exactly that. In the following section, we show how the GPU-aware capabilities can be leveraged in the transpose code.

8.2.3 GPU-aware MPI transpose

GPU-aware MPI implementations overload some of the MPI calls[3] so that device and host arrays can be passed as arguments. When array arguments are device arrays that reside on different GPUs that are peer-to-peer capable, the transfer is done using the peer-to-peer mechanism in a non-default stream. Otherwise, data transfers are staged through the host similar to how the transfers were performed in the previous section, but these transfers are taken care of behind the scenes.

The main loop over communication stages can now operate directly on device arrays without the need to copy the array to CPU memory before invoking data transfers:

```
171    do stage = 1, nProcs-1
172        ! sRank = the rank to which myrank sends data
173        ! rRank = the rank from which myrank receives data
174        sRank = modulo(myrank-stage, nProcs)
175        rRank = modulo(myrank+stage, nProcs)
176
177        call MPI_Barrier(MPI_COMM_WORLD, ierr)
178
179        ! pack tile so data to be sent are contiguous
180
181        !$cuf kernel do(2) <<<*,*>>>
182        do j = 1, mpiTileCols
183            do i = 1, mpiTileRows
184                sTile_d(i,j) = matIn_d(sRank*mpiTileRows+i,j)
185            enddo
186        enddo
187
188        call MPI_Sendrecv(sTile_d, mpiTileRows*mpiTileCols, &
189            MPI_REAL, sRank, myrank, &
190            rTile_d, mpiTileRows*mpiTileCols, MPI_REAL, &
191            rRank, rRank, MPI_COMM_WORLD, status, ierr)
192
193        ! do transpose from receive tile into final array
194        ! (no need to unpack)
195
196        call cudaTranspose<<<dimGrid, dimBlock>>> &
197            (matOut_d(rRank*mpiTileCols+1,1), nCols, &
198            rTile_d, mpiTileRows)
199
200    end do ! stage
```

where the MPI_Sendrecv() call on line 188 uses two device arrays, sTile_d and rTile_d. To facilitate the transfer, the sent data are packed into the contiguous array sTile_d using the CUF kernel on lines 181–196.

When run on the same system (DGX Station V100) and devices as the previous MPI transpose code, we obtain

---

[3] For a complete list of the GPU-aware calls, we refer to the documentation of the relevant MPI implementation.

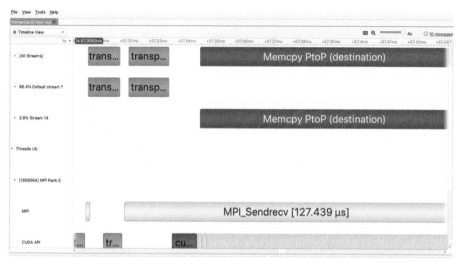

FIGURE 8.4

nsys GUI showing that the `MPI_Sendrecv()` is performed via peer-to-peer communication.

```
Array size: 2048x2048

CUDA block size: 32x8,  CUDA tile size: 32x32
dimGrid: 32x32x1,   dimBlock: 32x8x1

nprocs: 2,  Local input array size: 2048x1024
mpiTile: 1024x1024

Bandwidth (GB/s):  148.71
```

which shows a considerable performance boost. We could also use nsys to trace MPI calls, taking care of generating different profiler output files for each MPI rank with the special %q{OMPI_COMM_WORLD_RANK} syntax and specifying the profiling of MPI events:

```
$ mpirun -np 2 --bind-to none nsys profile -o transpose.%q{OMPI_COMM_WORLD_RANK}
-t cuda,mpi  ./transposeCAMPI
```

Fig. 8.4 shows that, as expected, the MPI_Sendrecv() is translated to a peer-to-peer call, since both ranks are on the same system and the GPUs are capable of peer-to-peer communications.

PART

Case studies

2

Monte Carlo method

9

A book on high performance and parallel computing is not complete without an example that shows how to compute π. Instead of using the classic example of numerical integration of the function $\int_0^1 \frac{4}{1+x^2} dx$, we use a Monte Carlo method.

Calculating π using a Monte Carlo method is quite simple. In a unit square, we generate a sequence of N points (x_i, y_i), $i = 1, \ldots, N$, where each component is a random number with uniform distribution (Fig. 9.1). We then count the number of points M that lie on or inside the unit circle (i.e., satisfy the relationship $x_i^2 + y_i^2 \leq 1$). The ratio of M to N will give us an estimate of $\pi/4$, which is the ratio of the area of a quarter of the unit circle, $\pi/4$, to the area of the unit square, 1. The method is inherently parallel, as every point can be evaluated independently, so we expect good performance and scalability on the GPU.

The accuracy of the ratio depends on the number of points used. The convergence to the real value is very slow: simple Monte Carlo methods like the one just presented have a convergence rate of $O(1/\sqrt{N})$. There are algorithmic improvements like importance sampling and the use of low-discrepancy sequences (quasi-Monte Carlo methods) to improve the convergence speed, but these are beyond the scope of this book.

When writing a CUDA Fortran code to solve this problem, the first issue we face is how to generate the random numbers on the GPU. Parallel random number generation is a fascinating subject, but we

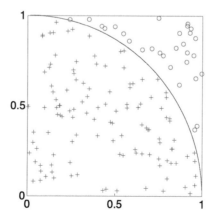

FIGURE 9.1

Monte Carlo method: π is computed as the ratio between the points inside the circle and the total number of points.

CUDA Fortran for Scientists and Engineers. https://doi.org/10.1016/B978-0-44-321977-1.00019-X

are going to take a shortcut and use CURAND, the library for random number generation provided by CUDA. CURAND provides a high-quality, high-performance series of random and pseudo-random number generators.

9.1 CURAND

The basic operations we need to perform in CURAND to generate a sequence of random numbers are:

- Create a generator using curandCreateGenerator();
- Set a random number seed with curandSetPseudoRandomGeneratorSeed();
- Generate the data from a distribution using the functions curandGenerateUniform(), curandGenerateNormal(), or curandGenerateLogNormal() depending on the distribution required;
- Destroy the generator with curandDestroyGenerator().

Before applying this procedure to generate random numbers in our Monte Carlo code, we demonstrate how CURAND is used from CUDA Fortran in a simple application that generates N random numbers on the GPU, copies the results back to the CPU, and prints the first four values. The main code is in the file generate_randomnumbers.cuf:

```
1   ! Generate N random numbers on GPU, copy them back to CPU
2   ! and print the first 4
3
4   program curand_example
5     use precision_m
6     use curand
7     implicit none
8     real(fp_kind), allocatable:: hostData(:)
9     real(fp_kind), allocatable, device:: deviceData(:)
10    type(curandGenerator) :: gen
11    integer ::  N, istat
12    integer(kind=8) :: seed
13
14    ! Define how many numbers we want to generate
15    N=20
16
17    ! Allocate array on CPU
18    allocate(hostData(N))
19
20    ! Allocate array on GPU
21    allocate(deviceData(N))
22
23    if (fp_kind == singlePrecision) then
24       write(*,"('Generating random numbers in single precision')")
25    else
26       write(*,"('Generating random numbers in double precision')")
27    end if
28
29    ! Create pseudonumber generator
```

```
30    istat = curandCreateGenerator(gen, CURAND_RNG_PSEUDO_DEFAULT)
31
32    ! Set seed
33    seed=1234
34    istat= curandSetPseudoRandomGeneratorSeed( gen, seed)
35
36    ! Generate N floats or double on device
37    istat= curandGenerate(gen, deviceData, N)
38
39    ! Copy the data back to CPU
40    hostData=deviceData
41
42    ! print the first 4 of the sequence
43    write(*,*) hostData(1:4)
44
45    ! Deallocate data on CPU and GPU
46    deallocate(hostData)
47    deallocate(deviceData)
48
49    ! Destroy the generator
50    istat = curandDestroyGenerator(gen)
51
52    end program curand_example
```

This code uses the precision_m module (line 5) to facilitate toggling between singe and double precision. This module is contained in the precision_m.f90 file listed at the end of Section 1.4.2. The code also uses the curand module (line 6), which contains the interfaces that allow CUDA Fortran to call the CURAND library functions. (In the first edition of this book, a custom module was used.)

CURAND contains different routines for single and double precision. While we can use the precision_m module to toggle between single and double precision variables in our code, we need to use generic interfaces in curand to effectively toggle between functions. The new module provides a generic interface curandGenerate(), which will map to curandGenerateUniform(), curandGenerateUniformDouble(), curandGenerateNormal(), or curandGenerateNormalDouble().

The correct version will be called depending on whether curandGenerate() is called with single- or double-precision arguments and on the number of arguments.

The two source files code can be compiled with

```
$ nvfortran -O3 -o rng_gpu_sp precision_m.F90 \
  generate_randomnumbers.cuf  -cudalib=curand
```

Here we need to add the CURAND library (-cudalib=curand) to link the proper functions. We also renamed the precision module file precision_m.F90 so that the -Mpreprocess compiler option is not needed. If we execute rng_gpu_sp, then we will see the following output:

```
$ ./rng_gpu_sp
  Generating random numbers in single precision
    0.1454676       0.8201809       0.5503992       0.2948303
```

To create a double precision executable, we compile the code using

```
$ nvfortran -DDOUBLE -O3 -o rng_gpu_dp precision_m.F90 \
  generate_randomnumbers.cuf -cudalib=curand
```

where the option -DDOUBLE was added. If we execute rng_gpu_dp, then we will see that the code is now using double precision:

```
$ ./rng_gpu_dp
  Generating random numbers in double precision
  0.4348988043884129  0.9264169202024377  0.8118452111300192  0.3085554246353980
```

The two sequences are different; they are not just the same sequence with different precision.

9.2 Computing π with CUF kernels

Having established how to generate the random numbers in parallel on the GPU, we turn our attention to writing a Monte Carlo code to test if points are inside the circle and count the number of points that satisfy this criterion. To accomplish this, we will first use kernel loop directives, or CUF kernels. As described briefly in the introduction in Section 1.3.6 and in more detail in the Porting Tips and Techniques chapter in Section 6.1, CUF kernels are directives that tell the compiler to generate a kernel from a loop or tightly nested loops when the data in the loop reside on the GPU. These directives can greatly simplify the job of writing many trivial kernels and in addition are able to recognize reduction operations, such as counting the number of points that lie within the unit circle in our example.

If the random numbers are stored in two arrays X(N) and Y(N), then the CPU code to determine the number of points that lie inside the unit circle is

```
inside=0
do i=1,N
  if (  (X(i)**2 + Y(i)**2 ) <= 1._fpkind ) inside=inside+1
end do
```

If we denote by X_d and Y_d the two corresponding arrays on the GPU, then the compiler is able to generate a kernel that performs the same operations on the GPU simply by adding the directive

```
inside=0
!$cuf kernel do <<< *, * >>>
do i=1,N
  if (  (X_d(i)**2 + Y_d(i)**2 ) <= 1._fpkind ) inside=inside+1
end do
```

This directive instructs the compiler to generate a kernel for the do loop that follows. Moreover, the compiler is able to detect that the host variable inside is the result of a reduction operation. Without the use of CUF kernels, reductions in CUDA need to be expressed using either atomic operations or a sequence of two kernels: the first kernel generates partial sums, and the second kernel uses a single block to compute the final sum. We present these methods of performing the reduction later in this chapter. Although not difficult, getting all the details right can be time consuming.

Putting together the random number generation with the CUF kernel that counts the number of points that lie in the unit circle, we have a fully functional Monte Carlo code. We also perform the same operation on the CPU to check the results. When the counting variable is an integer, we should get exactly the same result on both platforms, since integer addition is commutative. We will see later on that when the accumulation is done on floating-point variables, there may be differences due to the different order of accumulation.

```
1   ! Compute pi using a Monte Carlo method
2
3   program compute_pi
4     use precision_m
5     use curand
6     implicit none
7     real(fp_kind), allocatable:: hostData(:)
8     real(fp_kind), allocatable, device:: deviceData(:)
9     real(fp_kind) :: pival
10    type(curandGenerator):: gen
11    integer :: inside_gpu, inside_cpu, i, istat
12    integer(kind=8) :: twoN, seed, N
13
14    ! Define how many numbers we want to generate
15    N=100000
16    twoN=N*2
17
18    ! Allocate array on CPU
19    allocate(hostData(twoN))
20
21    ! Allocate array on GPU
22    allocate(deviceData(twoN))
23
24    if (fp_kind == singlePrecision) then
25       write(*,"('Compute pi in single precision')")
26    else
27       write(*,"('Compute pi in double precision')")
28    end if
29
30    ! Create pseudonumber generator
31    istat = curandCreateGenerator(gen, CURAND_RNG_PSEUDO_DEFAULT)
32
33    ! Set seed
34    seed=1234
35    istat = curandSetPseudoRandomGeneratorSeed( gen, seed)
36
37    ! Generate N floats or double on device
38    istat = curandGenerate(gen, deviceData, twoN)
39
40    ! Copy the data back to CPU to check result later
41    hostData=deviceData
42
43    ! Perform the test on GPU using CUF kernel
44    inside_gpu=0
45    !$cuf kernel do <<<*,*>>>
46    do i=1,N
47       if( (deviceData(i)**2+deviceData(i+N)**2) <= 1._fp_kind ) &
```

```
48              inside_gpu=inside_gpu+1
49      end do
50
51      ! Perform the test on CPU
52      inside_cpu=0
53      do i=1,N
54          if( (hostData(i)**2+hostData(i+N)**2) <= 1._fp_kind ) &
55              inside_cpu=inside_cpu+1
56      end do
57
58      ! Check the results
59      if (inside_cpu .ne. inside_gpu) &
60          write(*,*) "Mismatch between CPU/GPU"
61
62      ! Print the value of pi and the error
63      pival= 4._fp_kind*real(inside_gpu,fp_kind)/real(N,fp_kind)
64      write(*,"(t3,a,i10,a,f10.8,a,e11.4)") "Samples=", N, &
65          " Pi=", pival, &
66          " Error=", abs(pival-2.0_fp_kind*asin(1.0_fp_kind))
67
68      ! Deallocate data on CPU and GPU
69      deallocate(hostData)
70      deallocate(deviceData)
71
72      ! Destroy the generator
73      istat = curandDestroyGenerator(gen)
74  end program compute_pi
```

In this code, rather than generate two sequences of N random numbers for the x and y coordinates, we generate only one set of twoN random numbers, which can be interpreted as containing all the x coordinates first followed by all the y coordinates. Compiling the code similarly to rng_gpu_sp, for single precision, typical output will be

```
$ ./pi_sp
 Compute pi  in single precision
  Samples=    100000   Pi=3.13631988  Error= 0.5273E-02
```

which gives a reasonable result for the number of samples used in the calculation. We can add a simple do loop to study the convergence of the solution:

```
Compute pi  in single precision
  Samples=      10000   Pi=3.11120009  Error= 0.3039E-01
  Samples=     100000   Pi=3.13632011  Error= 0.5273E-02
  Samples=    1000000   Pi=3.14056396  Error= 0.1029E-02
  Samples=   10000000   Pi=3.14092445  Error= 0.6683E-03
  Samples=  100000000   Pi=3.14158082  Error= 0.1192E-04
```

From these results, which span several orders of magnitude of sample size, we observe $O(1/\sqrt{N})$ convergence of the method, as expected. We need to increase the sample size by two orders of magnitude to lower the error by an order of magnitude. Using double precision would not alter the convergence rate as the rate is determined solely by the number of points: the test of whether a point it is inside or outside the unit circle is not affected by precision. A typical result in double precision is

```
Compute pi  in double precision (seed = 1234)
  Samples=       10000  Pi=3.13440000  Error= 0.7193E-02
  Samples=      100000  Pi=3.13716000  Error= 0.4433E-02
  Samples=     1000000  Pi=3.14028800  Error= 0.1305E-02
  Samples=    10000000  Pi=3.14155360  Error= 0.3905E-04
  Samples=   100000000  Pi=3.14141980  Error= 0.1729E-03
```

where the apparent better precision of the double sequence is a consequence of a lucky seed. Changing the seed will produce a new series that will generate different results. For example, doing a simulation in double precision with a seed=1234567 will give lower accuracy than the simulation with single precision with seed=1234:

```
Compute pi  in double precision (seed=1234567)
  Samples=       10000  Pi=3.12880000  Error= 0.1279E-01
  Samples=      100000  Pi=3.14676000  Error= 0.5167E-02
  Samples=     1000000  Pi=3.14274000  Error= 0.1147E-02
  Samples=    10000000  Pi=3.14062480  Error= 0.9679E-03
  Samples=   100000000  Pi=3.14148248  Error= 0.1102E-03
```

9.2.1 IEEE-754 precision

CPUs have been following the IEEE Standard for Floating-Point Arithmetic, also known as IEEE 754 standard, for quite some time: the original standard was published in 1985 and was updated in 2008 to IEEE 754-2008. This standard made it possible to write algorithms using floating-point arithmetic that produce identical results when executed on a variety of platforms. A detailed description is outside the scope of this book, but one of the main additions to the updated standard was the introduction of a Fused Multiply-Add (FMA) instruction. FMA computes $a \times b + c$ with only one rounding operation and has been available on several computer architectures, including IBM Power architecture and Intel Itanium. All recent mainstream x86-64 CPUs also support FMA instructions (but sometimes it depends on whether the operation is performed in the FPU or in the vector units). When implemented in hardware, the equivalent instruction takes about the same time as a multiply, resulting in a performance advantage for many applications. Whereas an unfused multiply–add would compute the product $a \times b$, round it to P significant bits, add the result to c, and round back to P significant bits, a fused multiply–add would compute the entire sum $a \times b + c$ to its full precision before rounding the final result down to P significant bits.

NVIDIA GPUs have support for the IEEE 754-2008 FMA both in single and double precision. In CUDA Fortran, it is possible to disable generating FMA instructions using the compiler option -gpu=nofma. There is also a flag to disable FMA on the CPU, -Mnofma (it is important to note that this is a global compiler flag, and to keep generating FMA instructions on the GPU, we would need to explicitly specify -gpu=fma).

If we revisit our calculation of π, then we realize that the result of the test to see if the points are inside the unit circle is dependent on whether FMA is used or not. The test is summing the square of the coordinates of each point and comparing this value to the unity. If the value computed by the CPU and GPU is off by only one bit, then the test will give different results if the point is exactly on the unit circle. The probability of finding points exactly on the unit circle is small but non-zero. If we rerun the previous code with seed=1234567, then we observe a discrepancy between the number of interior points detected by the CPU and the one detected by the GPU when the number of samples is equal to 100 million.

```
Compute pi  in single precision
  (seed=1234567 FMA enabled on GPU, disabled on CPU)
   Samples=     10000   Pi=3.16720009   Error= 0.2561E-01
   Samples=    100000   Pi=3.13919997   Error= 0.2393E-02
   Samples=   1000000   Pi=3.14109206   Error= 0.5007E-03
   Samples=  10000000   Pi=3.14106607   Error= 0.5267E-03
 Mismatch between CPU/GPU          78534862        78534859
   Samples= 100000000   Pi=3.14139414   Error= 0.1986E-03
```

There are 3 out of 100 million points for which the test gives different results. We will analyze the error in detail for the first point; however, the same analysis applies to the other points. To analyze the error, we look at results obtained by rearranging the order of the multiplications and additions. Using the notation FMA(a,b,c)=a*b+c, we could compute $x^2 + y^2$ in one of three ways (the results on the left are in floating-point notation, and the ones on the right in hexadecimal notation):

1. Compute x*x, compute y*y, and then add the two squares:
   (x*x + y*y) = 1.000000000e+00 3f800000.
2. Compute y*y, use FMA(x,x,y*y):
   FMA(x,x,y*y)= 1.000000000e+00 3f800000.
3. Compute x*x, use FMA(y,y,x*x):
   FMA(y,y,x*x)= 1.000000119e+00 3f800001.

In theory, the last way should be the most accurate, as in this case $y > x$, and therefore we are using the full precision for the bigger term. To confirm this, we could try the following experiment: What would it happen if we recompute the distance on the CPU in double precision?

The following code performs this experiment. It loads the hex values of x and y, computes the distance with the single-precision values, casts the values of x and y to double precision, recomputes the distance in double, and finally recasts the double-precision value of the distance to single precision:

```
 1  program test_accuracy
 2    real :: x, y, dist
 3    double precision:: x_dp, y_dp, dist_dp
 4
 5    x=Z'3F1DC57A'
 6    y=Z'3F499AA3'
 7    dist= x**2 +y**2
 8
 9    x_dp=real(x,8)
10    y_dp=real(y,8)
11    dist_dp= x_dp**2 +y_dp**2
12
13    print *, 'Result with operands in single precision:'
14    print '((2x,z8)) ', dist
15
```

Table 9.1 Coordinates of the points and distance from the origin with results different between CPU and GPU. Values are in floating-point (top) and hexadecimal (bottom) representations.

N	x	y	x^2+y^2 CPU	x^2+y^2 GPU with FMA
2377069	6.162945032e-01	7.875158191e-01	1.000000000	1.000000119
	3F1DC57A	3F499AA3	3F800000	3F800001
33027844	2.018149495e-01	9.794237018e-01	1.000000000	1.000000119
	3E4EA894	3F7ABB83	3F800000	3F800001
81541078	6.925099492e-01	7.214083672e-01	1.000000000	1.000000119
	3F314855	3F38AE38	3F800000	3F800001

```
16   print *, 'Result in double precision with operands'
17   print *, 'promoted to double precision:'
18   print '((2x,z16))', dist_dp
19
20   print *, 'Result in single precision with operands'
21   print *, 'promoted to double precision:'
22   print '((2x,z8))', real(dist_dp,4)
23
24   end program test_accuracy
```

The results of the code are shown below, and the same analysis on all three points is summarized in Table 9.1.

```
Result with operands in single precision:
 3F800000
Result in double precision with operands
promoted to double precision:
 3FF0000015781ED0
Result in single precision with operands
promoted to double precision:
 3F800001
```

The result from fmaf(y,y,x*x)   in single precision on the GPU matches the result on the CPU when the operands are promoted to double precision, all the operations are performed in double precision, and the final result is casted back to single.

The following detailed analysis shows why the third result differs by one *ULP* (unit in the last place or unit of least precision, the spacing between floating-point numbers) from the other two results:

```
   x   = 3f1dc57a
   y   = 3f499aa3
   x*x = 3ec277a0
   fma(y,y,x*x) =
           3f1ec431_5e83c90
         + 3ec277a0_0000000
         --------------------
           9ec431_5e83c90   // align mantissas for add
```

```
                  613bd0_0000000
                  -------------------
                  1000001_5e83c90   // sum
                  800000_af41e48    // normalized mantissa
                  -------------------
                = 3f800000_af41e48  // result before rounding
                = 3f800001          // rounded result
```

As Einstein said: "A man with a watch knows what time it is. A man with two watches is never sure." Now that we have two outputs, we may get different results and need to understand the source of the possible difference. In the context of finite precision math, the difference is extremely slight. FMA instructions are now present in x86 processors too, so this kind of behavior can be observed on mainstream CPUs as well. Recompiling the code disabling the FMA instruction (-Mnofma) will generate the same value on the GPU as on the CPU, as we expected from our analysis:

```
Compute pi in single precision
  (seed=1234567 FMA disabled on CPU and GPU)
  Samples=      10000  Pi=3.16720009  Error= 0.2561E-01
  Samples=     100000  Pi=3.13919997  Error= 0.2393E-02
  Samples=    1000000  Pi=3.14109206  Error= 0.5007E-03
  Samples=   10000000  Pi=3.14106607  Error= 0.5267E-03
  Samples=  100000000  Pi=3.14139462  Error= 0.1981E-03
```

9.3 Computing π with reduction kernels

The use of CUF kernels to calculate π was advantageous in that we did not need to write explicit code for a reduction; the compiler performed the reduction on our behalf. However, circumstances may arise where we need to write a reduction in CUDA Fortran, so in this section, we explore how this is done in the context of our Monte Carlo code.

The most common reduction operation computes the sum of a large array of values. Other reduction operations that are often encountered are the computation of the minimum or maximum value of an array. Before describing the approach, we should remember that the properties of a reduction operator $\otimes$:

- The operator is *commutative*: $a \otimes b = b \otimes a$;
- The operator is *associative*: $a \otimes (b \otimes c) = (a \otimes b) \otimes c$.

With these two properties, we can rearrange and combine the elements in any order. We should point out that the second property is not always true when performed on a computer: whereas integer addition is always associative, floating-point addition is not: if we change the order of the partial sums and the operands are expressed as floating-point numbers, then we may get different results.

We have seen that the fundamental programming paradigms of CUDA are that each block is independent and that the same shared memory is visible only to threads within a thread block. How could we perform a global operation like a reduction using multiple blocks with these two constraints? There are several ways of doing this, which we discuss in this and the following sections. The approach we

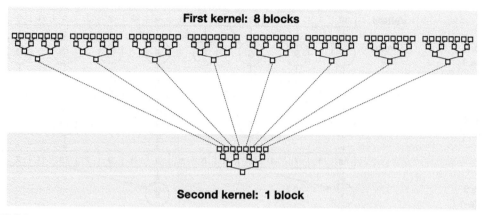

FIGURE 9.2

Two-stage reduction: multiple blocks perform a local reduction in a first stage. A single block performs the final reduction in a second stage.

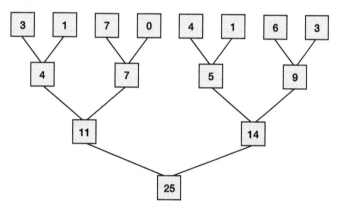

FIGURE 9.3

Tree reduction in a single block.

take in this section is to use two different kernels to perform the reduction. In the first kernel, each block computes its partial sum and writes the result back to global memory. After the first kernel is completed, a second kernel consisting of a single block is launched, which reads the partial sums and performs the final reduction. The code used for these two stages is quite similar, as the operations performed by a block in both stages are almost identical.

If each block would calculate a partial sum with a single accumulator (like we would do on the CPU), then there will only be a single thread out of the entire thread block working, and the rest would be idle. Although this is still legal CUDA code, it will give very poor performance since the hardware utilization would be sub-optimal. Luckily, there is a very well-known work-around to perform a parallel summation: a tree reduction. Figs. 9.2 and 9.3 depict tree reductions. To sum N values using a tree reduction, we will first sum them in pairs ending up with $N/2$ values, and we will keep repeating the

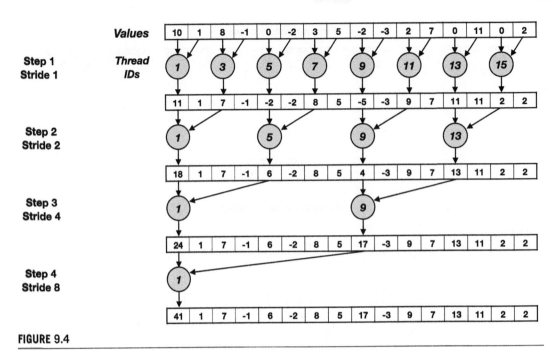

FIGURE 9.4

Tree reduction in a single block with divergence.

procedure until there is a single value left. The level of parallelism decreases for each iteration, but it is still better than the sequential alternative.

We are going to analyze a case in which $N = 16$, assuming a block with 16 threads for illustrative purposes; in reality, we want to use many more threads in a block to hide latencies. After we load the values in shared memory, each active thread at step M ($M = 1, \ldots, \log N$) will sum its value to the one with stride 2^{M-1}, such as in Fig. 9.4. If we look carefully at Fig. 9.4, then we notice that there is room for improvement. The issue here is thread divergence. For cases where a large number of threads per block are used, a warp of threads in the latter stages of the reduction may have only one active thread. We would like to have all the active threads in as few warps as possible to minimize divergence within a warp. This can be achieved by storing the result of one step of the reduction so that all the active threads for the next step are contiguous. This is accomplished by the scenario in Fig. 9.5.

With the reduction pattern of Fig. 9.5 in mind, we are now ready to write the kernel to perform the final reduction, where a single thread block is launched. The code to calculate the final sum is

```
3    attributes(global) subroutine final_pi_shared(partial)
4      implicit none
5      integer :: partial(*)
6
7      integer, shared :: p_s(*)
8      integer :: index, inext
9
10     index=threadIdx%x
11
```

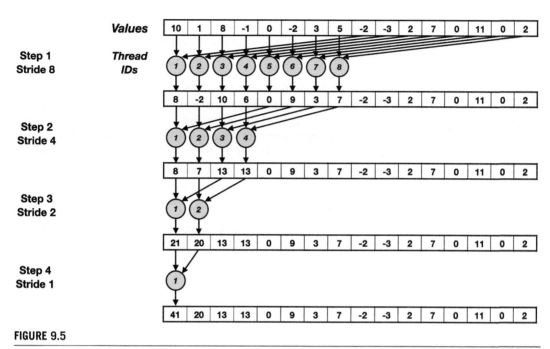

FIGURE 9.5

Tree reduction in a single block without divergence.

```
12        p_s(index)=partial(index)
13        call syncthreads()
14
15        inext=blockDim%x/2
16        do while ( inext >=1 )
17           if (index <=inext) &
18                 p_s(index)=p_s(index)+p_s(index+inext)
19           inext = inext/2
20           call syncthreads()
21        end do
22        if (index == 1) partial(1)=p_s(1)
23     end subroutine final_pi_shared
```

On line 12, each thread loads a value of the partial sum array from global memory into the shared memory array p_s. To ensure that all the threads have completed this task, a call to syncthreads() forces a barrier (the control flow will resume when all the threads in a thread block have reached this point). This will ensure a consistent view of the shared memory array for all the threads. We are now ready to start the reduction. For the first stage of reduction, a thread pool composed of half the threads (inext) will sum the value at index with value at index+inext and store the result at index. For each subsequent stage, inext is halved, and the procedure repeated until there is only one thread left in the pool.

When the while loop beginning on line 16 has completed, the final answer is in the first element of the shared memory array, p_s(1), and gets written to partial(1) in global memory on line 22, which can be accessed from host code. The only limitation in the kernel is the requirement for the total number of threads used to be a power of 2. It will be easy to pad the array in shared memory up to the next power of two with values that are neutral to the reduction operation (for the sum, the neutral value is 0).

Having written the kernel for the final reduction, we now turn to writing the kernel to calculate the partial reduction that generates the input to the final reduction kernel. In the Monte Carlo code, to compute π, the number of points used was quite large (up to 100 million). We could use a 1D grid of blocks and a 1:1 mapping between threads and elements of the array (old generations of GPU had some limitations on the maximum number of blocks $\approx 33M - 66M$, but in current generations, this limit is very high). We could use a 2D grid of blocks to increase the total number of threads available on older generations of GPUs, but there is another, simpler strategy. We can have each thread add up multiple elements of the array in serial fashion and start the tree reduction when each thread has exhausted the work. This approach uses a *grid-stride loop*, where all threads stride through the input data by the number of threads launched in the grid. This will be beneficial for performance since all the threads will be active throughout this loop, instead of losing half of the active threads at each step of the reduction. The code containing this approach is as follows:

```
25    attributes(global) &
26          subroutine partial_pi_shared(input, partial, twoN)
27       use precision_m
28       implicit none
29       real(fp_kind) :: input(twoN)
30       integer :: partial(*)
31       integer, value :: twoN
32
33       integer, shared :: p_s(*)
34       integer :: N
35       integer :: i, index, inext,interior
36
37       N = twoN/2 ! x=input(1:N), y=input(N+1:twoN)
38
39       ! grid-stride loop over data
40       index=threadIdx%x+(blockIdx%x-1)*blockDim%x
41       interior=0
42       do i=index, N, BlockDim%x*GridDim%x
43          if( (input(i)**2 + input(i+N)**2) <= 1._fp_kind ) &
44                interior=interior+1
45       end do
46
47       ! Local reduction within block
48       index=threadIdx%x
49       p_s(index)=interior
50       call syncthreads()
51
52       inext=blockDim%x/2
53       do while ( inext >=1 )
54          if (index <=inext) &
55                p_s(index)=p_s(index)+p_s(index+inext)
56          inext = inext/2
57          call syncthreads()
```

```
58        end do
59        if (index == 1) partial(blockIdx%x)=p_s(1)
60      end subroutine partial_pi_shared
```

The partial reduction is very similar to the final reduction. In the partial reduction, instead of reading the partial sum from global memory, we start from the input data. The first N values in the input array are values for x, and the next N values of input are the y values. The variable interior stores the number of points each thread determines is inside the circle. The loop starting on line 42 is the grid-stride loop over the input data. The rest of the code follows exactly the same logic as the kernel that computes the final sum, with the only difference that thread 1 will write its partial sum in the global array partial at the position corresponding to the block index.

Now that we have the two custom kernels, the only missing piece is their invocation. In the code below, we call the first kernel that computes the partial sums (using, for example, 256 blocks of 256 threads), followed by the kernel that computes the final result (using 1 block with 256 threads):

```
95      call partial_pi_shared<<<gridSize,blockSize,blockSize*4>>> &
96           (deviceData, partial_d, twoN)
97      call final_pi_shared<<<1,gridSize,gridSize*4>>>(partial_d)
98      inside_shared=partial_d(1)
```

Once again, the size of the grid and thread block are independent of the number of points we process, as the grid-stride loop on line 41 in the partial reduction accommodates any amount of data. We can use different block and grid sizes; the only requirement is that the number of blocks in the partial reduction must correspond to the number of threads used in the one block of the final reduction. To accommodate different block sizes, dynamic shared memory is used as is indicated by the third configuration parameter argument.

9.3.1 Reductions with SHFL instructions

In Section 4.2.3, we discussed how data in registers can be exchanged between threads in a warp by using the shuffle functions. Just to refresh terminology, in the discussion that follows, the term *lane* is the unit-based thread ID within a warp (takes on values from 1 to 32). The shuffle functions are as follows:

- __shfl(var,srcLane, width): returns the value of var held by the thread whose index is given by srcLane;
- __shfl_up(var, delta, width): var is shifted up the warp by delta lanes;
- __shfl_down(var, delta, width): var is shifted down the warp by delta lanes;
- __shfl_xor(var, laneMask, width): this mode implements a butterfly addressing pattern such as is used in tree reduction and broadcast. Using 0-based lane numbering (e.g., from 0 to 31), it performs a bitwise XOR of the caller's (0-based) lane with the laneMask. The value of var held by the resulting (0-based) lane is returned. If the resulting lane falls outside the range permitted by width, then the thread's own value of var is returned.

The width argument is optional in all shuffle functions and has a default value of 32, the current warp size. The source lane index will not wrap around the value of width, so the lower or upper delta lanes are unchanged.

There are two advantages of using these instructions. Firstly, by not using or reducing the amount of shared memory used you can increase the occupancy. Secondly, a shuffle instruction is faster than accessing shared memory, since it does not require the three steps incurred by shared memory operations (write, synchronize, read). Aside from reductions, shuffle instructions can be used for scan, transpose, and sorting operations.

The following code computes the sum of each thread's variable within a warp (using only 8 threads to better visualize the data flow in Fig. 9.6):

```
1   module shuffle_m
2   contains
3     attributes(global) subroutine shuffle_xor(len)
4       integer:: i,n,depth
5       integer,value:: len
6
7       i=threadIdx%x
8       depth=bit_size(len)-leadz(len)-1    !log2(len)
9       do n=depth,1,-1
10        i=i+__shfl_xor(i,ishft(len,-n),len)
11        print*,threadIdx%x,ishft(len,-n),i
12      end do
13    end subroutine shuffle_xor
14
15    attributes(global) subroutine shuffle_down(len)
16      integer:: i,n,depth
17      integer,value:: len
18
19      i=threadIdx%x
20      depth=bit_size(len)-leadz(len)-1    !log2(len)
21      do n=depth,1,-1
22        i=i+__shfl_down(i,ishft(len,-n),len)
23        print*,threadIdx%x,ishft(len,-n),i
24      end do
25    end subroutine shuffle_down
26  end module shuffle_m
27
28  program test_shuffle
29    use cudafor
30    use shuffle_m
31    integer:: depth
32    print *," Thread id"," laneMask  "," __shfl_xor"
33    len=8
34    call shuffle_xor<<<1,len>>>(len)
35    istat=cudaDeviceSynchronize()
36    print *," Thread id"," delta  "," __shfl_down"
37    call shuffle_down<<<1,len>>>(len)
38    istat=cudaDeviceSynchronize()
39  end program test_shuffle
```

Each thread in the __shfl_xor version will contain the sum, whereas in the __shfl_down version, only the first thread will contain the sum.

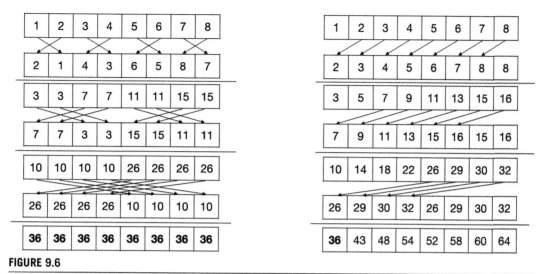

FIGURE 9.6

Reduction in a single warp with 8 elements with shfl instructions. On the left, using `__shfl_xor`, on the right with `__shfl_down`.

The subroutine to compute the partial reduction is very similar to the one we have seen in the previous section:

```
module pi_shfl_m
contains
  attributes(global) subroutine partial_pi_shfl(input, partial, twoN)
    use precision_m
    implicit none
    real(fp_kind) :: input(twoN)
    integer :: partial(*)
    integer, value :: twoN

    integer, shared :: p_s(32)
    integer :: N, interior
    integer :: i, tid, width, warpID, laneID

    N = twoN/2
    tid = threadIdx%x+(BlockIdx%x-1)*BlockDim%x

    interior=0
    do i = tid, N, BlockDim%x*GridDim%x
       if( (input(i)**2+input(i+N)**2) <= 1._fp_kind ) &
           interior=interior+1
    end do

    ! Local reduction per warp
    i = 1
    do while (i < warpsize)
       interior = interior + __shfl_xor(interior,i)
```

```
27        i = i*2
28     end do
29
30     ! first element of a warp writes to shared memory
31     warpID = (threadIdx%x-1)/warpsize+1        ! warp ID within block
32     laneID = threadIdx%x-(warpID-1)*warpsize  ! thread ID within warp
33     if (laneID == 1) p_s(warpID)=interior
34     call syncthreads()
35
36     ! reduction of shared memory values by first warp
37     if (warpID == 1) then
38        interior = p_s(laneID)
39        width = blockDim%x/warpsize
40        i = 1
41        do while (i < width)
42           interior = interior + __shfl_xor(interior, i, width)
43           i = i*2
44        end do
45        if (laneID == 1) partial(blockIdx%x) = interior
46     end if
47  end subroutine partial_pi_shfl
48
49  attributes(global) subroutine final_pi_shfl(partial)
50     implicit none
51     integer :: partial(*)
52
53     integer, shared :: p_s(32)
54     integer :: val
55     integer :: i, warpID, laneID, width
56
57     warpID = (threadIdx%x-1)/warpsize+1
58     laneID = threadIdx%x - (warpID-1)*warpsize
59
60     val = partial(threadIdx%x)
61     i = 1
62     do while (i < warpsize)
63        val = val + __shfl_xor(val, i)
64        i = i*2
65     enddo
66
67     ! if more than one warp, reduce amongst warps
68     if (blockDim%x > warpsize) then
69        if (laneID == 1) p_s(warpID) = val
70        call syncthreads()
71
72        if (warpID == 1) then
73           val = p_s(laneID)
74           width = blockDim%x/warpsize
75           i = 1
76           do while (i < width)
77              val = val + __shfl_xor(val, i, width)
78              i=i*2
```

```
79              enddo
80            end if
81        endif
82
83        if (warpID == 1 .and. laneID == 1) partial(1) = val
84      end subroutine final_pi_shfl
85
86    end module pi_shfl_m
```

In the variable interior, each thread will sum the number of points inside the unit circle from a grid-stride loop on line 18. Once the grid-stride loop is completed, __shfl_xor is used to sum the values of interior within the warp in the loop starting on line 25. At this point, we have the first thread in each warp transfer the value of interior to the shared memory array p_s at the location of the warpID at line 33. The first warp then performs a reduction on the values in shared memory. On line 38 the values in shared memory transferred to the variable interior by all threads in the first warp, and the while loop on line 41 uses __shfl_xor() to perform the reduction. The variable width represents the number of warps in the thread block. The sum within the block is then written to the global array partial at the blockIdx%x location. The final reduction kernel beginning on line 49 takes a similar approach.

The calling sequence is similar to before, with the exception that there is no need to specify an amount of dynamic shared memory, since only 32 elements in shared memory are needed (1024 threads divided by a warp size of 32):

```
113      call partial_pi_shfl<<<gridSize,blockSize>>> &
114           (deviceData, partial_d, twoN)
115      call final_pi_shfl<<<1,gridSize>>>(partial_d)
116      inside_shfl=partial_d(1)
```

9.3.2 Reductions with atomic locks

In the previous sections, we have used a two-kernel approach to circumvent this issue of independence of thread blocks, where the second kernel consists of a single thread block. An alternative to the two-kernel approach is to use atomic locks within a single kernel launch to share and update data safely for certain operations. The reduction code using atomic locks will be nearly identical to the code that performs the partial reduction in the two-kernel approach. The only difference is that instead of having each block, store its partial sum to global memory:

```
59      if (index == 1) partial(blockIdx%x)=p_s(1)
```

and then run a second kernel to add these partial sums; a single value in global memory is updated using an atomic lock to ensure that only one block at a time updates the final sum:

```
37      if (index == 1) then
38         do while (atomiccas(lock,0,1) == 1)
39         end do
40         partial(1)=partial(1)+p_s(1)
41         call threadfence()
42         lock = 0
43      end if
```

Outside of this code, the integer variable lock is declared in global memory and initialized to 0. To set the lock, the code uses the atomicCAS (atomic Compare And Swap) instruction. atomicCAS(mem,comp,val) compares mem to comp and atomically stores back the value val in mem if they are equal. The function returns the argument mem. The logic is equivalent to the following code:

```
old = mem
if (mem == comp ) then
   mem = val
end if
return old
```

with the addition of the atomic update, i.e., only one block at a time will be able to acquire the lock. Another important routine is threadfence(), which ensures that the global memory access made by the calling thread prior to threadfence() is visible to all the threads in the device. We also need to be sure that the variable that is going to store the final sum (in this case, we reuse the first element of the partial array from the previous kernel) is initialized to zero:

```
104       partial_d(1) = 0
105       call pi_lock<<<gridSize,blockSize,blockSize*4>>> &
106            (deviceData,partial_d,twoN)
107       inside_lock=partial_d(1)
```

As a final note in this section, we should elaborate on the degree to which atomic functions can provide cooperation between blocks. Atomic operations can only be used when the order of the operations is not important, as in the case of reductions. This is because the order in which the blocks are scheduled cannot be determined – there is no guarantee, for example, that block 1 starts before block N. If we were to assume any particular order, then the code might cause deadlock. Deadlocks, along with race conditions, are the most difficult bugs to diagnose and fix, since their occurrence may be sporadic and/or may cause the computer or GPU to lock. The code for the atomic lock does not rely on a particular scheduling of the blocks; it only ensures that one block at the time updates the variable but the order of the blocks does not matter. One drawback of using atomics is the non-deterministic value of the final sum. CUF kernels now use atomics by default (in the very earlier editions of the compiler, they used a two-kernel approach).

9.3.3 Reductions using the grid_group cooperative group

The grid_group cooperative group discussed in Section 4.2.6.1 allows us to synchronize across all threads of a kernel launch. As such, we can perform a reduction across in a single kernel launch without having to resort to atomic locks as in the previous section.

We will modify the code in Section 9.3.1, maintaining the grid-stride loop, reductions within a warp and block, and writing intermediate results to a global array. Being able to synchronize across all threads in a kernel launch means that we can combine the partial and final kernels into a single kernel. In addition to changes in device code, we need to modify the host code to determine an appropriate execution configuration for launching a kernel that synchronizes across an entire grid. To synchronize across all threads in the kernel launch, all of the thread blocks in the launch must be active on the device, meaning that all threads blocks must be assigned to multiprocessors and not queued by the scheduler waiting for other threads blocks to complete. We can determine the number of thread blocks that will concurrently fit on a device using the following lines of code:

```
44    type(cudaDeviceProp) :: prop
45    istat = cudaGetDeviceProperties(prop, 0)
46    istat = cudaOccupancyMaxActiveBlocksPerMultiprocessor( &
47         nBlocks, pi_gg, blockSize, 0)
48    nBlocks = nBlocks * prop%multiProcessorCount
```

Here the function on line 46 returns in nBlocks the number of thread blocks of blockSize threads that can simultaneously reside on a multiprocessor for the kernel pi_gg. The last argument, 0, of the call on line 47 specifies that 0 bytes of dynamic shared memory are used. On line 48 the value of nBlocks is multiplied by the number of multiprocessors on the device to determine the overall number of blocks to launch. It is worth noting here that this number of blocks may not be a power of two and that care in the kernel code must be taken to accommodate this generality.

The kernel code that performs the reduction using grid-wide synchronization is

```
3     attributes(grid_global) subroutine pi_gg(input, partial, twoN)
4        use cooperative_groups
5        use precision_m
6        implicit none
7        real(fp_kind) :: input(twoN)
8        integer :: partial(*)
9        integer, value :: twoN
10
11       integer, shared :: p_s(32)
12       type(grid_group) :: gg
13       integer :: N, interior
14       integer :: i, warpID, laneID, width
15
16       warpID = ishft(threadIdx%x-1,-5)+1
17       laneID = iand(threadIdx%x-1,31)+1
18       N = twoN/2
19
20       gg = this_grid()
21
22       interior=0
23       do i = gg%rank, N, gg%size
24          if( (input(i)**2+input(i+N)**2) <= 1._fp_kind ) &
25             interior=interior+1
26       end do
27
28       ! Local reduction per warp
29       i = 1
30       do while (i < warpsize)
31          interior = interior + __shfl_xor(interior,i)
32          i = i*2
33       end do
34
35       ! first element of a warp writes to shared memory
36       if (laneID == 1) p_s(warpID)=interior
37
38       call syncthreads(this_thread_block())
```

```
39
40     ! reduction of shared memory values by first warp
41     if (warpID == 1) then
42         interior = p_s(laneID)
43         width = blockDim%x/warpsize
44         i = 1
45         do while (i < width)
46             interior = interior + __shfl_xor(interior, i, width)
47             i = i*2
48         end do
49         if (laneID == 1) partial(blockIdx%x) = interior
50     end if
51
52     call syncthreads(gg)
53
54     if (blockIdx%x == 1) then
55
56         ! block-stride loop (if gridDim%x > blockDim%x)
57         interior = 0
58         do i = threadIdx%x, gridDim%x, blockDim%x
59             interior = interior + partial(i)
60         enddo
61
62         i = 1
63         do while (i < warpsize)
64             interior = interior + __shfl_xor(interior, i)
65             i = i*2
66         enddo
67
68         ! if more than one warp, reduce amongst warps
69         if (gridDim%x > warpsize) then
70             if (warpID == 1) p_s(laneID) = 0
71             call syncthreads(this_thread_block())
72             if (laneID == 1) p_s(warpID) = interior
73             call syncthreads(this_thread_block())
74
75             if (warpID == 1) then
76                 interior = p_s(laneID)
77                 i = 1
78                 do while (i < warpsize)
79                     interior = interior + __shfl_xor(interior, i)
80                     i=i*2
81                 enddo
82             end if
83         endif
84
85         if (warpID == 1 .and. laneID == 1) partial(1) = interior
86     end if
87
88     end subroutine pi_gg
```

The first thing to notice is the use of the `grid_global` attribute on line 3, which is required when using cooperative groups to perform a synchronization across all threads launched by the kernel. The following line of code uses the cooperative_groups module, which provides the definitions of the grid_group derived type used to declare the variable gg on line 12 and the function this_grid() used for its initialization on line 20. The grid-stride loop can be written using the rank and size components of the grid_group derived type, as on line 23. After the grid-stride loop, the reduction within a warp and then within a block proceeds as before using the __shfl_xor() function, and one thread in each thread block writes its intermediate value to the global array partial on line 49. A synchronization across all threads in the kernel launch is performed on line 52 using the overloaded syncthreads() routine with the type(grid_global) variable gg as an argument, which ensures that all thread blocks have finished writing their intermediate results to the global array partial. After the grid-wide synchronization, the first thread block performs what was basically the final kernel in the two-kernel approach on lines 54–86. We need to make some changes since in the two-kernel approach, we required that the number of threads in the one thread block in the final kernel be both a power of two and the number of thread blocks used in the first kernel. However, the number of blocks launched in the grid_global kernel is determined from occupancy considerations, so we must modify the code to accommodate all possible values of gridDim%x. This can be seen in the block of code on lines 57–60. In the final kernel of the two-kernel approach, we could simply perform the assignment

```
p_s(threadIdx%x) = partial(threadIdx%x)
```

since the size of the partial array is equal to blockDim%x. In the grid_global kernel the partial array has gridDim%x values. We therefore use the block-stride loop on lines 58–60 with the initialization on line 57 to accumulate all values of the partial array amongst the blockDim%x threads of the first thread block. The reduction within each warp of the thread block happens on lines 63–66. Note that for cases where gridDim%x is smaller than blockDim%x, we have interior = 0, which is a neutral value for the reduction. We also pad the shared memory array with neutral values for when the number of warps in the thread block is less than the warpsize, which is effectively accomplished by the initialization on line 70. Note that the __shfl_xor() function uses the default width of the warpsize on line 79 rather than determines a custom width. If we were to use a custom width, we would still need to pad by neutral values up to a power of two, and it is more efficient to take the approach in the code than incur the overhead of using a custom width.

Note that when we synchronize between threads within a thread block, as on lines 38, 71, and 73, we call syncthreads() with the return value of the function this_thread_block(). This is not required as the default case, when syncthreads() is called with no argument, is a synchronization amongst threads in a thread block. We specify this argument for clarity since we are synchronizing across the grid and the thread block in this routine.

9.4 Accuracy of summation

The summation we used to find the number of points inside the circle used integer variables. Reductions involving floating-point variables are very common and important for a wide variety of numerical applications. When dealing with floating-point arithmetic, there are several numerical accuracy issues that can arise (rounding, cancellation of significant digits), and particular care should be taken in designing an algorithm that reduces these errors.

The standard way of summing a sequence of N numbers,

$$S = \sum_{i=1}^{N} x_i \, ,$$

is the use of the recursive formula (hence the term *recursive summation*):

$$
\begin{aligned}
S_0 &= 0, \\
S_i &= S_{i-1} + x_i, \quad i = 1, 2, \ldots, N, \\
S &= S_N.
\end{aligned}
$$

The accuracy and stability properties of the recursion have been extensively studied in the literature. Without going into too many details (an excellent in-depth error analysis is given by Higham (2002)), the main source of the error is the difference in magnitude between the running sum and the terms of the sequence. When summing two floating point numbers with big difference in magnitude, there is a loss of precision. In the extreme case the new term of the sequence added to the running sum could be completely lost. When both negative and positive operands are present, there is also the issue of subtractive cancellation.

How could we improve the accuracy of the sum?

- Minimize the intermediate sum by sorting the sequence. To keep the error small, we want the S_i term as small as possible, i.e., the smallest terms should be added first. This is very expensive, and it may be difficult or impossible to apply in general cases.
- Use an accumulator with higher precision. In double precision, there will be 53 bits to store the mantissa, and a loss of significant digits will be reduced or completely eliminated.
- Use multiple intermediate sums. The extreme case, *pairwise summation*, has also the nice property of exposing parallelism. This is the preferred solution on GPUs and the approach we used in the previous examples.
- Use a compensated sum, also known as *Kahan summation*. The basic idea is to have a correction term designed to reduce the rounding errors. It achieves better accuracy at the cost of increasing the arithmetic intensity by a factor of four, and it is still a serial algorithm. The algorithm is quite old (Kahan, 1965) and was written at a time when double precision was not supported on several architectures. Kahan summation is the most popular compensated summation technique, but there are several variations of this idea.

There are other algorithms (insertion, several variants of compensated sum); Higham (2002) is a good reference.

Let us explore sorting the sequence before doing the summation. To verify the effectiveness of sorting, we could sum a simple series, taking $N = 8192$ and $x(i) = 1/i$ or $x(i) = 1/i^2$. The elements in the two sequences are by construction sorted and with descending magnitude. We can do a forward sum (from $i = 1$ to N) and a backward sum (from $i = N$ to 1) and compare the accuracy to a sum where the accumulator is stored in double precision and produce Table 9.2.

As predicted by the error analysis, the sum where the smallest terms are added first, in this case the backward sequence from $i = N$ to 1, to minimize the running sum, returns the closest value to the reference sum.

Table 9.2 Sum of the series for $N = 8192$. For the single-precision results, the upper value is the sum, and the lower value is the error.

$x(i)$		Forward single precision	Backward single precision	Reference result
$1/i$	result	1.644725	1.644812	1.644812003408614
	error	8.6680685225104526E-005	1.5531721686556921E-008	
$1/i^2$	result	9.588196	9.588188	9.588190111622680
	error	5.6891585700213909E-006	1.9402359612286091E-006	

To examine the other algorithms, we are going to reuse an example from Barone et al. (2006), summing an array with 10 millions elements, all equal to 7.0. Clearly, in this case, sorting the array is not going to reduce the error. We are going to compare the sum computed by the intrinsic Fortran90 function sum(), the recursive sum with a single precision accumulator, the recursive sum with a double precision accumulator, the pairwise reduction, and the Kahan sum.

```
1   program sum_accuracy
2     implicit none
3     real, allocatable :: x(:)
4     real :: sum_intrinsic,sum_cpu, sum_kahan, sum_pairwise, &
5          comp, y, tmp
6     double precision :: sum_cpu_dp
7     integer :: i,inext,icurrent,  N=10000000
8
9     allocate (x(N))
10    x=7.
11
12    ! Summation using intrinsic
13    sum_intrinsic=sum(x)
14
15    ! Recursive summation
16    sum_cpu=0.
17    sum_cpu_dp=0.d0
18    do i=1,N
19       ! accumulator in single precision
20       sum_cpu=sum_cpu+x(i)
21       ! accumulator in double precision
22       sum_cpu_dp=sum_cpu_dp+x(i)
23    end do
24
25    ! Kahan summation
26    sum_kahan=0.
27    comp=0. ! running compensation to recover lost low-order bits
28
29    do i=1,N
30       y     = comp +x(i)
31       tmp   = sum_kahan + y      ! low-order bits may be lost
32       comp  = (sum_kahan-tmp)+y ! (sum-tmp) recover low-order bits
33       sum_kahan = tmp
34    end do
35    sum_kahan=sum_kahan +comp
```

```
36
37    ! Pairwise summation
38    icurrent=N
39    inext=ceiling(real(N)/2)
40    do while (inext >1)
41       do i=1,inext
42          if ( 2*i <= icurrent) x(i)=x(i)+x(i+inext)
43       end do
44       icurrent=inext
45       inext=ceiling(real(inext)/2)
46    end do
47    sum_pairwise=x(1)+x(2)
48
49    write(*, "('Summming ',i10, &
50        ' elements of magnitude ',f3.1)") N,7.
51    write(*, "('Sum with intrinsic function        =',f12.1, &
52        '  Error=', f12.1)")  &
53        sum_intrinsic, 7.*N-sum_intrinsic
54    write(*, "('Recursive sum with SP accumulator =',f12.1, &
55        '  Error=', f12.1)")  sum_cpu, 7.*N-sum_cpu
56    write(*, "('Recursive sum with DP accumulator =',f12.1, &
57        '  Error=', f12.1)")  sum_cpu_dp, 7.*N-sum_cpu_dp
58    write(*, "('Pairwise sum in SP                =',f12.1, &
59        '  Error=', f12.1)")  sum_pairwise, 7.*N-sum_pairwise
60    write(*, "('Compensated sum in SP             =',f12.1, &
61        '  Error=', f12.1)")  sum_kahan, 7.*N-sum_kahan
62
63    deallocate(x)
64 end program sum_accuracy
```

The output from compiling and running this simple Fortran code is

```
$ nvfortran -o accuracy_sum accuracy_sum.f90
$ ./accuracy_sum
Summming   10000000 elements of magnitude 7.0
Sum with intrinsic function       =   77603248.0   Error=   -7603248.0
Recursive sum with SP accumulator =   77603248.0   Error=   -7603248.0
Recursive sum with DP accumulator =   70000000.0   Error=         0.0
Pairwise sum in SP                =   70000000.0   Error=         0.0
Compensated sum in SP             =   70000000.0   Error=         0.0
```

As we can see from the output, both the intrinsic and recursive sums in single precision give us a wrong answer, overestimating the sum. The recursive sum with the double precision accumulator, the pairwise summation, and the Kahan summation are instead delivering the correct result. It should be mentioned that this is the ideal case for pairwise reduction, since all the arguments at each stage are equal.

If we increase the number of elements by a factor of two, then we will see that the two methods that were giving the incorrect result are still giving the wrong answer but are now underestimating the sum.

```
$ nvfortran -o accuracy_sum accuracy_sum.f90

$ ./accuracy_sum
Summming   20000000 elements of magnitude 7.0
```

```
Sum with intrinsic function        = 134217728.0   Error=   5782272.0
Recursive sum with SP accumulator = 134217728.0   Error=   5782272.0
Recursive sum with DP accumulator = 140000000.0   Error=        0.0
Pairwise sum in SP                 = 140000000.0   Error=        0.0
Compensated sum in SP              = 140000000.0   Error=        0.0
```

It is instructive to see how the error behaves when varying the range. Fig. 9.7 shows the sum computed with the recursive formula compared with the expected value and a plot of the error when the number of terms in the sequence vary over a wide range. We can observe two different regions in the error plot. The first part is where the main source of the error is coming from rounding (in this case, rounding up), causing an overestimation of the sum. The second part is where the main source of the error is due to the difference in magnitude that completely neglects the additional terms in the sum. The first value at which the sum is computed incorrectly is $N = 2396746$. This is easily computed since a single-precision IEEE floating-point number has 23 digits in the mantissa, plus an implicit leading digit, so the last number where there will be no loss of precision will be $2^{24}/7 = 2396745$.

The same behavior could be observed for sums in which the elements are all different but very small. Using double-precision representation for the floating-point numbers, the problem will still be present but appears when N in the order of 10^{16}.

Is there anything else we could learn from this example? Yes, there is another important aspect. Modern CPUs have vector instructions (SSE, SSE2, SSE3, SSE4, AVX) that enable the CPU to perform the same operation on multiple data (the exact number of concurrent operations will depend on the width of the vector hardware and the type of data used). After the debug phase, it is not unusual to enable aggressive optimizations with flags similar to -fast or -fastsse. If we recompile our simple example with the flag -fast, then we will see a similar behavior, but the errors will be smaller in magnitude.

```
$ nvfortran -fast  -o accuracy_sum_sse accuracy_sum.f90

$ ./accuracy_sum_sse
Summing   10000000 elements of magnitude 7.0
Sum with intrinsic function        = 70413008.0   Error=   413008.0
Recursive sum with SP accumulator = 70413008.0   Error=   413008.0
Recursive sum with DP accumulator = 70000000.0   Error=        0.0
Pairwise sum in SP                 = 70000000.0   Error=        0.0
Compensated sum in SP              = 70000000.0   Error=        0.0
```

With the -fast option, the compiler generates vector instructions and uses multiple accumulators. The multiple accumulators have a smaller magnitude of the single one, extending the range in which the sum is correct. To find out exactly what the compiler is doing, we had to inspect the assembler code and notice the use of HADDPS (Horizontal Add Packed Single-FP), which from two input vector registers {A0,A1,A2,A3} and {B0,B1,B2,B3} generates the output {A0+A1,A2+A3,B0+B1,B2+B3}.

We can also recompute the same sequence we used with the forward and backward summations to compare the errors of all the methods.

```
Summing      8192 elements of magnitude 1/(i)
Sum with intrinsic function = 0.9588196E+01  Error= 0.5689159E-05
Recursive SP forward sum    = 0.9588196E+01  Error= 0.5689159E-05
Recursive DP forward sum    = 0.9588190E+01  Error= 0.0000000E+00
```

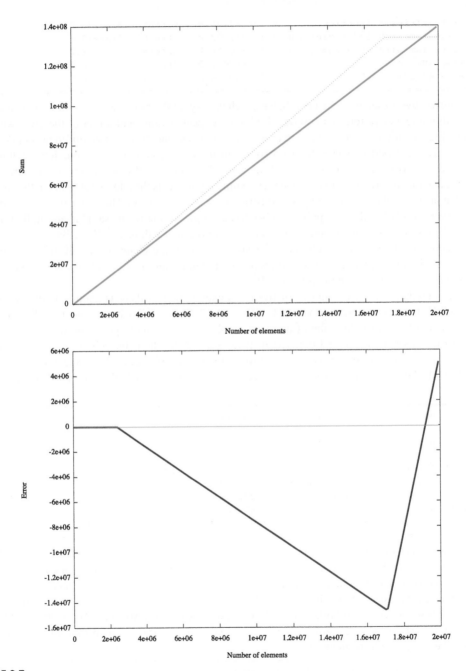

FIGURE 9.7

Top: Computed value for the recursive sum (dotted line) compared to exact result (solid line). Bottom: Difference between the two values.

```
Pairwise sum in SP         = 0.9588190E+01  Error=-0.3288733E-07
Compensated sum in SP      = 0.9588190E+01  Error=-0.3288733E-07

Summing      8192 elements of magnitude 1/(i*i)
Sum with intrinsic functio = 0.1644725E+01  Error=-0.8668069E-04
Recursive SP forward sum   = 0.1644725E+01  Error=-0.8668069E-04
Recursive DP forward sum   = 0.1644812E+01  Error= 0.0000000E+00
Pairwise sum in SP         = 0.1644812E+01  Error=-0.1347410E-06
Compensated sum in SP      = 0.1644812E+01  Error=-0.1553172E-07
```

This section reminds us that the effect of different algorithms and the proprieties of floating-point arithmetic could present us with unexpected results. When performing a sum on GPU, we are probably going to use something similar to a pairwise summation, which, as we have seen, has excellent accuracy. If we were going to compare the results with a naive implementation of the CPU, we could get quite different results. It is important to understand why this happens and which implementation gives a more precise result.

9.5 Option pricing

Now that we have all the basic components to perform a Monte Carlo simulation, let us increase the complexity of the problem: instead of computing the value of π, we will use the Monte Carlo method to value stock options. Without going into technical details (see Wilmott et al., 1995 and Higham, 2004), an option is a derivative financial instrument where the buyer gains the right (but not the obligation) to buy or sell an underlying stock. When the right is to buy, the option is called a *call*, and when the right is to sell, the option is called a *put*. The price at which the underlying asset may be traded is called the *exercise price* or *strike price*.

We will start with a simple European option, an option that can be exercised only at expiration. For this kind of option, there is an analytical solution, the Black–Scholes formula, that computes the value of the put and call. If we denote by *CND* the cumulative distribution function of the standard normal distribution and we define the Black–Scholes parameters d_1 and d_2 as

$$d_1 = \frac{\ln(S/E) + (r + \sigma^2/2)\tau}{\sigma\sqrt{\tau}},$$

$$d_2 = \frac{\ln(S/E) + (r - \sigma^2/2)\tau}{\sigma\sqrt{\tau}},$$

where

S is the asset price at time t,
E is the exercise (strike) price at time T,
σ is the volatility, a measure for the variation of price of the asset over time,
r is the risk-free annual interest rate,
τ is the time to expiration $(T - t)$.

The values for a call C and for a put P are

$$C(S,t) = CND(d_1)S - CND(d_2)Ee^{-r\tau},$$
$$P(S,t) = -CND(-d_1)S + CND(-d_2)Ee^{-r\tau}.$$

Now that we have a reference solution, we need to find a way of computing the same quantities using a Monte Carlo method. It can be shown (see Higham, 2004) that pricing the option is equivalent to find the expected value of the random variable

$$S(T) = S(t)\exp\left[(r - \sigma^2/2)\tau + \sigma\sqrt{\tau}Z\right],$$
$$V = e^{-rT}\Lambda\left(S(T)\right),$$

where Z is a normally distributed random number, and the pay-off function $\Lambda = \max(E - S_T, 0)$ for a European put or $\Lambda = \max(S_T - E, 0)$ for a European call. Once we compute the mean a and standard deviation b for a sequence of N samples, we can also compute a 95% *confidence interval*, a range in which there is a 95% probability of including the correct result,

$$\text{conf} = \left[a - \frac{1.96b}{\sqrt{N}}, a + \frac{1.96b}{\sqrt{N}}\right].$$

The structure of the code is going to be very similar to those we used to compute π. We will generate on the device a set of random numbers, this time with a normal distribution. For each random number, we will compute $S(T)$, the value of the stock at time T, apply the pay-off function Λ on this value, and discount the value at present time (the multiplication by the factor e^{-rT}). Once we have an array of values V, we will compute the mean and standard deviation to compute the expected value and the confidence interval. To compute the reference value, we need to evaluate the CND, which is not available in the standard set of functions provided by Fortran. This is done with Hasting's approximation, where the 5th-order polynomial is evaluated using Horner's rule. The code also accepts an additional argument on the command line to change the number of points used in the simulation. This is done using the `command_argument_count` function and `get_command_argument` subroutine, now standard in Fortran 2003. In this version, for the generation of the values of the call and put options at each point and for reductions, we still rely on CUF kernels. The first CUF kernel computes the values and means, and the second CUF kernel uses these values to compute the standard deviations. The timing is measured with CUDA events.

```
 1  module blackscholes_m
 2    use precision_m
 3  contains
 4
 5    real(fp_kind)  function CND( d )
 6      ! Cumulative Normal Distribution function
 7      ! using Hasting's formula
 8      implicit none
 9      real(fp_kind), parameter :: A1 =  0.31938153_fp_kind
10      real(fp_kind), parameter :: A2 = -0.356563782_fp_kind
11      real(fp_kind), parameter :: A3 =  1.781477937_fp_kind
12      real(fp_kind), parameter :: A4 = -1.821255978_fp_kind
```

```fortran
13       real(fp_kind), parameter :: A5 =  1.330274429_fp_kind
14       real(fp_kind) :: d, K, abs, exp, RSQRT2PI
15
16       K = 1.0_fp_kind/(1.0_fp_kind + 0.2316419_fp_kind * abs(d))
17       RSQRT2PI = 1._fp_kind/sqrt(8._fp_kind*atan(1._fp_kind))
18       CND = RSQRT2PI * exp( -0.5_fp_kind * d * d) *            &
19           (K * (A1 + K * (A2 + K * (A3 + K * (A4 + K * A5)))))
20       if( d .gt. 0._fp_kind ) CND = 1.0_fp_kind - CND
21       return
22     end function CND
23
24     subroutine blackscholes(callResult, putResult, &
25         S, E, R, sigma, T)
26       ! Black-Scholes formula for call and put
27       ! S = asset price at time t
28       ! E = exercise (strike) price
29       ! sigma = volatility
30       ! R = interest rate
31       ! T = time to expiration
32       implicit none
33       real(fp_kind) :: callResult, putResult
34       real(fp_kind) :: S, E, R, sigma, T
35       real(fp_kind) :: sqrtT, d1, d2, log, exp, expRT
36
37       if ( T > 0 ) then
38          sqrtT = sqrt(T)
39          d1 = (log(S/E)+(R+0.5_fp_kind*sigma*sigma)*T) &
40               /(sigma*sqrtT)
41          d2 = d1 -sigma*sqrtT
42          expRT = exp( -R * T)
43          callResult = ( S * CND(d1) - E * expRT * CND(d2))
44          putResult = callResult + E * expRT - S
45       else
46          callResult = max(S-E,0._fp_kind)
47          putResult  = max(E-S,0._fp_kind)
48       end if
49     end subroutine blackscholes
50   end module blackscholes_m
51
52   program  mc
53     use blackscholes_m
54     use curand
55     use cudafor
56     implicit none
57     real(fp_kind), allocatable, device :: deviceData(:), &
58         putValue(:),callValue(:)
59     real(fp_kind) :: S, E, R, sigma, T,Sfinal, &
60         call_price, put_price
61     real(fp_kind) ::  meanPut,meanCall, &
62         stddevPut, stddevCall, confidence
63     type(curandGenerator) :: gen
64     integer(kind=8) :: seed
```

```
65    integer :: i, n2, nargs, istat, N
66    type(cudaEvent) :: startEvent,stopEvent
67    real :: time
68    character*12 arg
69
70    istat=cudaEventCreate(startEvent)
71    istat=cudaEventCreate(stopEvent)
72
73    ! Number of samples
74    nargs=command_argument_count()
75    if ( nargs == 0 ) then
76       N = 1000000
77    else
78       call get_command_argument(1,arg)
79       read(arg,'(i)') N
80    endif
81
82    S      = 5._fp_kind;      E = 4._fp_kind
83    sigma  = 0.3_fp_kind;     R = 0.05_fp_kind
84    T      = 1._fp_kind
85
86    istat=cudaEventRecord(startEvent,0) !start timing
87
88    !Allocate arrays on GPU
89    allocate (deviceData(N),putValue(N),callValue(N))
90
91    if (fp_kind == singlePrecision) then
92       print *, " European option with random numbers"
93       print *, " in single precisionm using ",N," samples"
94    else
95       print *, " European option with random numbers"
96       print *, " in double precision using ",N," samples"
97    end if
98
99    ! Create pseudonumber generator
100   istat = curandCreateGenerator(gen, CURAND_RNG_PSEUDO_DEFAULT)
101
102   ! Set seed
103   seed=1234
104   istat= curandSetPseudoRandomGeneratorSeed( gen, seed)
105
106   ! Generate N floats/doubles on device w/ normal distribution
107   !istat= curandGenerateNormal(gen, deviceData, N, &
108   !      0._fp_kind, 1._fp_kind)
109   istat= curandGenerate(gen, deviceData, N, &
110        0._fp_kind, 1._fp_kind)
111
112   meanPut=0._fp_kind; meanCall=0._fp_kind
113   !$cuf kernel do <<<*,*>>>
114   do i=1,N
115      Sfinal= S*exp((R-0.5_fp_kind*sigma*sigma)*T &
116           +sigma*sqrt(T)*deviceData(i))
```

```
117        putValue(i) =exp (-R *T) * max (E-Sfinal,0._fp_kind)
118        callValue(i)=exp (-R *T) * max (Sfinal-E,0._fp_kind)
119        meanPut=meanPut+putValue(i)
120        meanCall=meanCall+callValue(i)
121     end do
122     meanPut=meanPut/N
123     meanCall=meanCall/N
124
125     stddevPut=0._fp_kind; stddevCall=0._fp_kind
126     !$cuf kernel do <<<*,*>>>
127     do i=1,N
128        stddevPut= stddevPut + (putValue(i)-meanPut) **2
129        stddevCall= stddevCall + (callValue(i)-meanCall) **2
130     end do
131     stddevPut=sqrt(stddevPut/(N-1) )
132     stddevCall=sqrt(stddevCall/(N-1) )
133
134     ! compute a reference solution using Black Scholes formula
135     call blackscholes(call_price,put_price,S,E,R,sigma,T)
136
137     print *, "Montecarlo  value of put option  =", meanPut
138     print *, "BlackScholes value of put option =", put_price
139     print *, "Confidence interval of put option  = [", &
140         meanPut -1.96*stddevPut/sqrt(real(N)),",",&
141         meanPut +1.96*stddevPut/sqrt(real(N)),"]"
142     print *, "Montecarlo value of call option  =", meanCall
143     print *, "BlackScholes value of call option=", call_price
144     print *, "Confidence interval of call option  = [", &
145         meanCall -1.96*stddevCall/sqrt(real(N)),",",&
146         meanCall +1.96*stddevCall/sqrt(real(N)),"]"
147
148     istat=cudaEventRecord(stopEvent,0)
149     istat=cudaEventSynchronize(stopEvent)
150     istat=cudaEventElapsedTime(time,startEvent,stopEvent)
151
152     print *,"Elapsed time (ms) :",time
153
154     deallocate (deviceData,putValue,callValue)
155
156     ! Destroy the generator
157     istat= curandDestroyGenerator(gen)
158
159 end program  mc
```

As we did for the code computing π, we will generate two versions, one using single precision and the other using double precision passing a preprocessor flag:

```
$ nvfortran -O3 -Minfo -o mc_european_single precision_m.F90 \
montecarlo_european_option.cuf -cudalib=curand

$ nvfortran -O3 -Minfo -DDOUBLE -o mc_european_double precision_m.F90 \
montecarlo_european_option.cuf -cudalib=curand
```

The output from the compilation confirms that the compiler was able to identify the reduction variables. Since we did not specify the execution configuration in the CUF directives, the choice is left to the compiler, and kernels are invoked with 128 threads:

```
128, CUDA kernel generated
    128, !$cuf kernel do <<< (*), (128) >>>
        Generating implicit reduction(+:meanput,meancall)
141, CUDA kernel generated
    141, !$cuf kernel do <<< (*), (128) >>>
        Generating implicit reduction(+:stddevput,stddevcall)
```

If we run the codes on a Quadro GV100 with no additional arguments, then it will use one million samples:

```
$ ./mc_european_single
  European option with random numbers in single precision
  using      1000000  samples
Montecarlo  value of put option  =   0.1276108
BlackScholes value of put option =   0.1280212
Confidence interval of put option = [ 0.1269989, 0.1282226]
Montecarlo value of call option  =   1.322458
BlackScholes value of call option=   1.323104
Confidence interval of call option = [ 1.319744, 1.325171]
Elapsed time (ms) :    11.57312

$ ./mc_european_double
  European option with random numbers in double precision
  using      1000000  samples
Montecarlo  value of put option  =   0.1280019167019663
BlackScholes value of put option =   0.1280215707263190
Confidence interval of put option  =
      [0.1273886989425720, 0.1286151344613607]
Montecarlo value of call option  =   1.322242692975767
BlackScholes value of call option=   1.323103872723463
Confidence interval of call option  =
      [1.319531953505466, 1.324953432446068]
Elapsed time (ms) :    11.79811
```

Notice that the run time for the single- and double-precision runs are very similar. To better understand the cause of this behavior, we could use nsys or nvprof. To replicate the output from nvprof, where both the kernels and the memcopies are in the same output, nsys requires a two-step approach: first, an nsys-rep file needs to be generated with nsys profile -o filename executable, and then a gpusum report could be generated with nsys stats --report gpusum filename:

```
$ nsys profile -o mc_european_sp ././mc_european_single
$ nsys stats --report gpusum mc_european_sp.nsys-rep
```

```
$ nvprof ./mc_european_single
 Time(%)      Time   Calls    Avg       Min       Max     Name
  62.30%   221.22us     1   221.22us   221.22us   221.22us  generate_seed
  13.55%   48.095us     1   48.095us   48.095us   48.095us  mc_142_gpu
  13.23%   46.976us     1   46.976us   46.976us   46.976us  mc_129_gpu
   9.14%   32.448us     1   32.448us   32.448us   32.448us  gen_sequenced
   1.07%   3.8080us     2   1.9040us   1.8560us   1.9520us  [memcpy DtoH]
   0.71%   2.5280us     2   1.2640us   1.1840us   1.3440us  [memcpy HtoD]

$ nvprof ./mc_european_double
 Time(%)      Time   Calls    Avg       Min       Max     Name
  55.60%   220.77us     1   220.77us   220.77us   220.77us  generate_seed
  16.80%   66.720us     1   66.720us   66.720us   66.720us  gen_sequenced
  13.06%   51.872us     1   51.872us   51.872us   51.872us  mc_129_gpu
  12.73%   50.527us     1   50.527us   50.527us   50.527us  mc_142_gpu
   1.21%   4.8000us     2   2.4000us   2.0160us   2.7840us  [memcpy DtoH]
   0.60%   2.3680us     2   1.1840us   1.1840us   1.1840us  [memcpy HtoD]
```

The profiler output clearly shows that a very large percentage of the time is spent in the random number generation function generate_seed_pseudo and this time is almost constant for the two cases (the seed generation is done using integer arithmetic, and it is independent). The seed generation could be sped up by adding a call to curandSetGeneratorOrdering() after the curandCreateGenerator() call or by choosing a different random number generator. Since the random number generation and all the computations are done directly on the GPU, the impact of the memcopies is minimal as we expected:

```
! Create pseudonumber generator
istat = curandCreateGenerator(gen, CURAND_RNG_PSEUDO_DEFAULT)
istat = curandSetGeneratorOrdering(gen, &
                            CURAND_ORDERING_PSEUDO_SEEDED)
```

If we increase the number of points to 100 million, we will see that now there is a clear difference in run time between the two cases, closer to the expected 2:1 ratio between single and double precision:

```
$ ./mc_european_single  100000000
  European option with random numbers
  in single precisionm using     100000000  samples
Montecarlo  value of put option  =    0.1279827
BlackScholes value of put option =    0.1280212
Confidence interval of put option  = [ 0.1279214, 0.1280440]
Montecarlo value of call option  =    1.323215
BlackScholes value of call option=    1.323104
Confidence interval of call option  = [ 1.322944, 1.323486]
Elapsed time (ms) :    18.53760

$ ./mc_european_double  100000000
  European option with random numbers
  in double precision using     100000000  samples
Montecarlo  value of put option  =    0.1280627958651803
BlackScholes value of put option =    0.1280215707263190
Confidence interval of put option  =
     [ 0.1280014892157413, 0.1281241025146192       ]
```

```
Montecarlo value of call option  =    1.322938547217486
BlackScholes value of call option=    1.323103872723463
Confidence interval of call option  =
    [ 1.322667148600870, 1.323209945834102]
Elapsed time (ms) :    31.06890
```

The real power of the Monte Carlo method shows when we consider more sophisticated options, for example, options that depend on the path of the stock during the contract period. Instead of going directly from time t to the expiration time T, like we did for the European option, we can set up a grid of points $t_j = j\Delta t$, with $0 \leq j \leq M$ and $\Delta t = T/M$ and compute the option value on each point:

$$S(t_{j+1}) = S(t_j)exp\left[(r - \sigma^2/2)\Delta t + \sigma\sqrt{\Delta t}Z_j\right].$$

Once we have the asset price on this underlying grid, we can compute min and max, test for barrier crossing, or integrals, depending on the payoff of the exotic option.

Finite difference method

In many fields of science and engineering, the governing system of equations takes the form of either ordinary or partial differential equations. One method of solving these equations is using finite differences, where the continuous analytical derivatives are approximated at each point on a discrete grid using values of neighboring points. In this chapter, we discuss how to optimize a particular nine-point one-dimensional scheme, although the method discussed can be applied to different finite difference approximations quite easily. A general discussion of finite difference methods and their properties can be found in Ferziger (1981) and Ferziger and Perić (2001). We also discuss how a 2D Laplace equation can be implemented in CUDA Fortran using a compact nine-point stencil.

10.1 Nine-point 1D finite difference stencil

Our first example uses a three-dimensional grid of size 128^3. For simplicity, we assume periodic boundary conditions and only consider first-order derivatives, although extending the code to calculate higher-order derivatives with other types of boundary conditions is straightforward.

The finite difference method uses a weighted summation of function values at neighboring points to approximate the derivative at a particular point. For a $(2N + 1)$-point stencil with uniform spacing Δx in the x-direction, a central finite difference scheme for the derivative in x can be written as

$$\frac{\partial f(x, y, z)}{\partial x} \approx \frac{1}{\Delta x} \sum_{i=-N}^{N} C_i f(x + i\Delta x, y, z)$$

and similarly for other directions. The coefficients C_i are typically generated from Taylor series expansions and can be chosen to obtain a scheme with desired characteristics such as accuracy, and in the context of partial differential equations, dispersion and dissipation. For explicit finite difference schemes such as the type above, larger stencils typically have a higher order of accuracy. For this study, we use a nine-point stencil that is eighth-order accurate. We also choose a symmetric stencil, which can be written as

$$\frac{\partial f_{i,j,k}}{\partial x} \approx a_x \left(f_{i+1,j,k} - f_{i-1,j,k} \right) + b_x \left(f_{i+2,j,k} - f_{i-2,j,k} \right) + c_x \left(f_{i+3,j,k} - f_{i-3,j,k} \right)$$
$$+ d_x \left(f_{i+4,j,k} - f_{i-4,j,k} \right),$$

where we specify the values of the function on the computational grid using the grid indices i, j, k rather than the physical coordinates x, y, z. Here the coefficients are $a_x = \frac{4}{5}\frac{1}{\Delta x}$, $b_x = -\frac{1}{5}\frac{1}{\Delta x}$, $c_x = \frac{4}{105}\frac{1}{\Delta x}$,

CUDA Fortran for Scientists and Engineers. https://doi.org/10.1016/B978-0-44-321977-1.00020-6
299

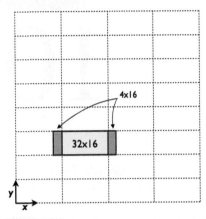
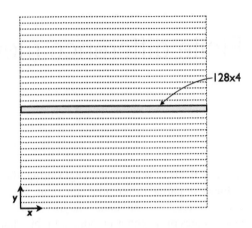

FIGURE 10.1

Possible tile configurations for the x-derivative calculation. On the left, there is a depiction of a tile needed for calculating the derivative at points in a 32×16 tiles. To calculate the derivative at points in this tile, data from two additional 4×16 sections must be loaded for each thread block. The data in these 4×16 sections are loaded twice, once by the thread block which calculates the derivative at that point and once by a neighboring thread block. As a result, one fourth of all of the data gets loaded twice. A better option is the 128×4 tile on the right, which for the 128^3 mesh loads each datum from global memory once.

and $d_x = -\frac{1}{280} \frac{1}{\Delta x}$, which is a typical eighth-order accurate scheme. For the derivative in the y- and z-directions, the index offsets in the equation are simply applied to indices j and k, and the coefficients are the same, except that Δy and Δz are used instead of Δx.

Because we calculate an approximation of the derivative at each point on the 128^3 periodic grid, the value of f at each point is used eight times, one time for each right-hand side term in the above expression. In designing a derivative kernel, we want to exploit this data reuse by fetching the values of f from global memory as few times as possible using shared memory.

10.1.1 Data reuse and shared memory

Each thread block can bring in a tile of data to shared memory, and then each thread in the block can access all elements of the shared memory tile as needed. How do we choose the best tile shape and size? Some experimentation is required, but characteristics of the finite-difference stencil and grid size provide some direction.

For coalesced global memory access, we want the tile size in the x-direction to be a multiple of 32. If the problem size allows, then it is more efficient to have the tile span the x-direction entirely. Doing so, we avoid the overlap of the tiles corresponding to half of the stencil size, as depicted on the left in Fig. 10.1. Here, to calculate the derivative in a 32×16 tile, the values of f not only from this tile but also from two additional 4×16 sections must be loaded by each thread block. Overall, the f values in the 4×16 sections get loaded twice, once by the thread block that calculates the derivative at that location and once by the neighboring thread block. As a result, 4×16 values out of 32×16, or a quarter of the values, get loaded from global memory twice.

A better choice of tile (and thread block), which calculates the derivative for the same number of points as above, is depicted on the right of Fig. 10.1. This tile avoids overlap altogether when calculating the x-derivative for our one-dimensional stencil on a grid of 128^3 since the tile contains all points in the direction of the derivative, as in the 128×4 tile shown. A minimal tile would have just one *pencil*, i.e., the one-dimensional array of all points in a direction. In our finite difference code, we parameterize the number of pencils to allow some experimentation.

10.1.2 The x-derivative kernel

The first kernel we discuss is the x-derivative kernel:

```
129   attributes(global) subroutine deriv_x(f, df)
130      implicit none
131
132      real(fp_kind), intent(in) :: f(mx,my,mz)
133      real(fp_kind), intent(out) :: df(mx,my,mz)
134
135      real(fp_kind), shared :: f_s(-3:mx+4,sPencils)
136
137      integer :: i,j,k,j_l
138
139      i = threadIdx%x
140      j = (blockIdx%x-1)*blockDim%y + threadIdx%y
141      ! j_l is local variant of j for accessing shared memory
142      j_l = threadIdx%y
143      k = blockIdx%y
144
145      f_s(i,j_l) = f(i,j,k)
146
147      call syncthreads()
148
149      ! fill in periodic images in shared memory array
150
151      if (i <= 4) then
152         f_s(i-4, j_l) = f_s(mx+i-5,j_l)
153         f_s(mx+i,j_l) = f_s(i+1,   j_l)
154      endif
155
156      call syncthreads()
157
158      df(i,j,k) = &
159            (ax_c *( f_s(i+1,j_l) - f_s(i-1,j_l) )   &
160            +bx_c *( f_s(i+2,j_l) - f_s(i-2,j_l) )   &
161            +cx_c *( f_s(i+3,j_l) - f_s(i-3,j_l) )   &
162            +dx_c *( f_s(i+4,j_l) - f_s(i-4,j_l) ))
163
164   end subroutine deriv_x
```

Here mx, my, and mz are the grid size parameters set to 128, and sPencils is 4, which is the number of pencils used to make the shared memory tile. (There are two pencil sizes used in this study; sPencils refers to a small number of pencils, and we discuss the use of a larger number of pencils later.) The indices i, j, and k correspond to the coordinates in the 128^3 mesh. The index i can also be used for the x-coordinate in the shared memory tile, whereas the index j_1 is the local coordinate in the y-direction for the shared memory tile. This kernel is launched with a block of 128 × sPencils threads, which calculates the derivatives on an $x \times y$ tile of 128 × sPencils.

The shared memory tile declared on line 135 has padding of four elements at each end of the first index to accommodate the periodic images needed to calculate the derivative at the endpoints of the x-direction. On line 145, data from global memory are read into the shared memory tile for f_s(1:mx,1:sPencils). These reads from global memory are perfectly coalesced. On lines 151–154, data are copied within shared memory to fill out the periodic images. Doing so allows the derivative to be calculated on lines 158–162 without any index checking. Note that here we assume that the endpoints in each direction are periodic images, so f(1,j,k)=f(mx,j,k), and similarly for the other directions. The threads that read the data from shared memory on lines 152 and 153 are not the same threads that write the data to shared memory on line 145, which is why the syncthreads() call on line 147 is required. Likewise, the synchronization barrier on line 156 is required since data from f_s(-3:0,j_1) and f_s(mx+1:mx+4,j_1) are accessed on lines 158–162 by threads other than those that wrote these values on lines 152 and 153.

10.1.2.1 *Performance of the x-derivative kernel*

Compiling this kernel for single precision data with the -gpu=ptxinfo option, we observe that this kernel requires only 16 registers and uses 2176 bytes of shared memory. At full occupancy, the number of registers per thread must be 32 or less (65,536 registers/2048 threads per multiprocessor). With a thread block size of 512 threads (128×4), at full occupancy, four thread blocks can concurrently reside on a multiprocessor, and the 2176 bytes of shared memory used per thread block times the maximum of four thread blocks per multiprocessor easily fit into the 48 KB of shared memory available in each multiprocessor. With such low resource utilization, we expect the kernel to run at full occupancy. These occupancy calculations assume that we have launched enough thread blocks to realize the occupancy, which is certainly our case as 128^2/sPencils or 4096 blocks are launched.

The host code launches this kernel multiple times in a loop and reports the average time of execution per kernel launch. The code also compares the result to the analytical solution at the grid points. On an A100 80GB GPU using single precision for this kernel, we have

```
Using shared memory tile of x-y: 128x4
                Thread block: 128x4x1
  RMS error:    1.7389872E-05
  MAX error:    7.0571899E-05
  Average time (ms):    1.2646399E-02
  Average Bandwidth (GB/s):    1326.640
```

We can use the technique discussed in Section 3.2 to get a feel for what is the limiting factor in this code. If we replace lines 158-162 above with

```
  df(i,j,k) = f_s(i,j_1)
```

then we have a memory-only version of the code, which obtains

```
x derivative mem with x-y tile: 128x4
  Average time (ms):    1.0188800E-02
```

Likewise, we can create a math-only version of the kernel:

```
attributes(global) subroutine derivative_math(f, df, val)
  implicit none

  real(fp_kind), intent(in) :: f(mx,my,mz)
  real(fp_kind), intent(out) :: df(mx,my,mz)
  integer, value :: val
  real(fp_kind) :: temp

  real(fp_kind), shared :: f_s(-3:mx+4,nPencils)

  integer :: i,j,k,j_l

  i = threadIdx%x
  j = (blockIdx%x-1)*blockDim%y + threadIdx%y
  ! j_l is local variant of j for accessing shared memory
  j_l = threadIdx%y
  k = blockIdx%y

  temp = &
      (ax_c *( f_s(i+1,j_l) - f_s(i-1,j_l) )    &
      +bx_c *( f_s(i+2,j_l) - f_s(i-2,j_l) )    &
      +cx_c *( f_s(i+3,j_l) - f_s(i-3,j_l) )    &
      +dx_c *( f_s(i+4,j_l) - f_s(i-4,j_l) ))

  if (val*temp == 1) df(i,j,k) = temp

end subroutine derivative_math
```

which obtains

```
Average time (ms):     7.6800003E-03
```

Given the above information, we know that the code is memory bound, as the memory- and math-only versions execute in approximately 80% and 61% of time the full kernel requires, respectively. The majority of the math operations are covered by memory requests, so we do have some overlap.

To try and improve performance, we need to reassess how we utilize memory. We load data from global memory only once into shared memory in a fully coalesced fashion, we have two syncthreads() calls required to safely access shared memory, and we write the output to global memory in a fully coalesced fashion. The coefficients ax_c, bx_c, cx_c, and dx_c used on lines 159–162 are in constant memory, which is cached on the chip. This is the optimal situation for constant memory, where each thread in a warp (and thread block) reads the same constant value. As operations with global and constant memories are fully optimized, we turn to see if we can do anything with the syncthreads() calls.

The derivative kernel has two calls to syncthreads(), one after data are read from global memory to shared memory and one after data are copied between shared memory locations. These barriers are needed when different threads write and then read the same shared memory values. Notice that it is possible to remove the first of these synchronization barriers by modifying the indexing to shared memory. For example, in the portion of the *x*-derivative code

```
145        f_s(i,j_l) = f(i,j,k)
146
147        call syncthreads()
148
149        ! fill in periodic images in shared memory array
150
151        if (i <= 4) then
152           f_s(i-4, j_l) = f_s(mx+i-5,j_l)
153           f_s(mx+i,j_l) = f_s(i+1,   j_l)
154        endif
```

we could remove this synchronization barrier on line 147 by replacing lines 151–154 with

```
if (i>mx-5 .and. i<mx) f_s(i-(mx-1),j_l) = f_s(i,j_l)
if (i>1    .and. i<6 ) f_s(i+(mx-1),j_l) = f_s(i,j_l)
```

Using this approach, the same thread that writes to a shared memory location on line 145 reads the data from shared memory in the above two lines of code. Although removing a synchronization barrier might seem like a sure performance win, when running the code, we obtain

```
Single syncthreads, using shared memory tile of x-y: 128x4
                                  Thread block: 128x4x1
  RMS error:      1.7389872E-05
  MAX error:      7.0571899E-05
  Average time (ms):     1.1878400E-02
  Average Bandwidth (GB/s):      1412.414
```

which is a slight improvement over the original code. In general, the additional index checks in the condition of an if statement can be slower than a syncthreads() call.

We can experiment with the tile parameters, in particular changing the value of sPencils. We observe an improvement going from an sPencils value of 4 to 2:

```
Using shared memory tile of x-y: 128x2
                     Thread block: 128x2x1
  RMS error:      1.7389872E-05
  MAX error:      7.0571899E-05
  Average time (ms):     1.2339200E-02
  Average Bandwidth (GB/s):      1359.668

Single syncthreads, using shared memory tile of x-y: 128x2
                                  Thread block: 128x2x1
  RMS error:      1.7389872E-05
  MAX error:      7.0571899E-05
  Average time (ms):     1.1468800E-02
  Average Bandwidth (GB/s):      1462.857
```

10.1.3 Derivatives in y and z

We can easily modify the x-derivative code to operate in the other directions. In the x-derivative, each thread block calculated the derivatives in an $x \times y$ tile of $128 \times$ sPencils. For the y-derivative, we can

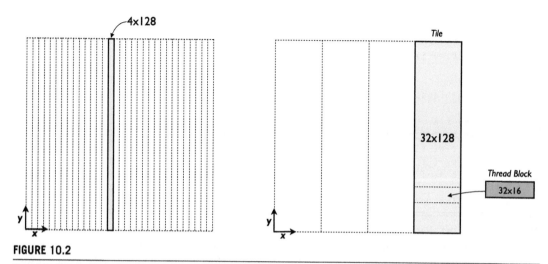

FIGURE 10.2

Possible tile configurations for the y-derivative calculation. Similarly to the x-derivative, where a 128×4 tile is used, we can use a 4×128 tile as depicted on the left. This approach loads each f value from global memory only once; however, the coalescing characteristics are poor. A better alternative is depicted on the right, where a tile with 32 points in x achieves perfect coalescing, and the tile having 128 points in y maintains the characteristic that f data get loaded only once. However, one problem with a 32×128 tile is that a one-to-one mapping of threads to elements cannot be used since 4096 threads exceed the limit of threads per block. This issue can be circumvented by using a thread block of 32×16 where each thread calculates the derivative at 8 points.

have a thread block calculate the derivative on a tile of sPencils $\times$ 128 in $x \times y$, as depicted on the left in Fig. 10.2. Likewise, for the z-derivative, a thread block can calculate the derivative in a $x \times z$ tile of sPencils $\times$ 128. The kernel below shows the y-derivative kernel using this approach.

```
255    attributes(global) subroutine deriv_y(f, df)
256       implicit none
257
258       real(fp_kind), intent(in)  :: f(mx,my,mz)
259       real(fp_kind), intent(out) :: df(mx,my,mz)
260
261       real(fp_kind), shared :: f_s(sPencils,-3:my+4)
262
263       integer :: i,i_l,j,k
264
265       i = (blockIdx%x-1)*blockDim%x + threadIdx%x
266       i_l = threadIdx%x
267       j = threadIdx%y
268       k = blockIdx%y
269
270       f_s(i_l,j) = f(i,j,k)
271
272       call syncthreads()
273
```

```
274     if (j <= 4) then
275         f_s(i_l,j-4) = f_s(i_l,my+j-5)
276         f_s(i_l,my+j) = f_s(i_l,j+1)
277     endif
278
279     call syncthreads()
280
281     df(i,j,k) = &
282         (ay_c *( f_s(i_l,j+1) - f_s(i_l,j-1) )   &
283         +by_c *( f_s(i_l,j+2) - f_s(i_l,j-2) )   &
284         +cy_c *( f_s(i_l,j+3) - f_s(i_l,j-3) )   &
285         +dy_c *( f_s(i_l,j+4) - f_s(i_l,j-4) ))
286
287   end subroutine deriv_y
```

By transposing the shared memory tile on line 261 in this manner we can maintain the property that each element from global memory is read in only once. The disadvantage of this approach is that with sPencils=4 points in x for these tiles, we no longer have perfect coalescing. The performance results bear this out:

```
Using shared memory tile of x-y: 4x128
                   Thread block: 4x128x1
RMS error:      1.7389550E-05
MAX error:      7.0571899E-05
Average time (ms):     2.1350401E-02
Average Bandwidth (GB/s):      785.8033
```

where we obtain roughly half the performance of the x-derivative kernel. In terms of accuracy, we obtain the same maximum error of the x-derivative but a different RMS error for essentially the same function. This difference is due to the order in which the accumulation is done on the host; simply, swapping the order of the loops in the host code error calculation would produce the same results.

One way to improve performance is to expand the tile to contain enough pencils to facilitate perfect coalescing. Such a tile is shown on the right in Fig. 10.2. Using such an approach would require a shared memory tile of $(128 + 8) \times 32$ elements or 17408 bytes in single precision, which is within the limit of 48 KB of static shared memory per multiprocessor. However, with a one-to-one mapping of threads to elements where the derivative is calculated, a thread block of 4096 threads would be required, beyond the limit of 1024 threads per thread block. The way to work around this limit is for each thread to calculate the derivative for multiple points, essentially using instruction-level parallelism. If we use a thread block of $32 \times 16 \times 1$ where each thread calculates the derivative at eight points, as opposed to a thread block of $4 \times 128 \times 1$ where each thread calculates the derivative at only one point, then we launch a kernel with the same number of threads per block but regain perfect coalescing. The following code accomplishes this:

```
292   attributes(global) subroutine deriv_y_1Pencils(f, df)
293     implicit none
294
295     real(fp_kind), intent(in) :: f(mx,my,mz)
296     real(fp_kind), intent(out) :: df(mx,my,mz)
297
```

```
298        real(fp_kind), shared :: f_s(lPencils,-3:my+4)
299
300        integer :: i,j,k,i_l
301
302        i_l = threadIdx%x
303        i = (blockIdx%x-1)*blockDim%x + threadIdx%x
304        k = blockIdx%y
305
306        do j = threadIdx%y, my, blockDim%y
307           f_s(i_l,j) = f(i,j,k)
308        enddo
309
310        call syncthreads()
311
312        j = threadIdx%y
313        if (j <= 4) then
314           f_s(i_l,j-4) = f_s(i_l,my+j-5)
315           f_s(i_l,my+j) = f_s(i_l,j+1)
316        endif
317
318        call syncthreads()
319
320        do j = threadIdx%y, my, blockDim%y
321           df(i,j,k) = &
322              (ay_c *( f_s(i_l,j+1) - f_s(i_l,j-1) )   &
323              +by_c *( f_s(i_l,j+2) - f_s(i_l,j-2) )   &
324              +cy_c *( f_s(i_l,j+3) - f_s(i_l,j-3) )   &
325              +dy_c *( f_s(i_l,j+4) - f_s(i_l,j-4) ))
326        enddo
327
328     end subroutine deriv_y_lPencils
```

where here lPencils is 32. Very little has changed from the previous kernel; the only difference is that the index j is used as a loop index on lines 306 and 320, rather than being calculated once, and is set to threadIdx%y on line 312 for copying periodic images. When compiling this code using -gpu=ptxinfo, we observe that each thread requires 23 registers, so register usage will not affect occupancy. However, with 17408 bytes of static shared memory used per thread block, a total of two thread blocks can reside on a multiprocessor at one time. These two thread blocks contain a total of 1024 threads, which results in an occupancy of 0.5, which should not be problematic since we are employing an eight-fold instruction-level parallelism. The results for this kernel are as follows:

```
Using shared memory tile of x-y: 32x128
                 Thread block: 32x16x1
  RMS error:    1.7389550E-05
  MAX error:    7.0571899E-05
  Average time (ms):    1.1878400E-02
  Average Bandwidth (GB/s):    1412.414
```

where we have recovered the performance of the x-derivative. Using a value of sPencil=2 shows an even wider disparity for these two approaches in the y-direction:

```
y derivatives

 Using shared memory tile of x-y: 2x128
                    Thread block: 2x128x1
  RMS error:.   1.7389550E-05
  MAX error:    7.0571899E-05
  Average time (ms):    3.6556803E-02
  Average Bandwidth (GB/s):    458.9355

 Using shared memory tile of x-y: 32x128
                    Thread block: 32x8x1
  RMS error:    1.7389550E-05
  MAX error:    7.0571899E-05
  Average time (ms):    1.0393600E-02
  Average Bandwidth (GB/s):    1614.187
```

where here each thread block has 256 threads, and the instruction-level parallelism in the latter case is 16-fold.

We might inquire as to whether using such a larger number of pencils in the shared memory tile will improve performance of the x-derivative code presented earlier. This ends up achieving basically the same performance:

```
 Using shared memory tile of x-y: 128x32
                    Thread block: 128x2x1
  RMS error:    1.7389872E-05
  MAX error:    7.0571899E-05
  Average time (ms):    1.1520000E-02
  Average Bandwidth (GB/s):    1456.356
```

10.1.4 Nonuniform grids

The previous discussion dealt with obtaining derivatives on grids that are uniform, i.e., grids where the spacings Δx, Δy, and Δz are constant and do not depend on the indices i, j, and k. There are, however, many situations where a nonuniform grid is desirable and even necessary. In the case of non-periodic boundaries, the function often has steep gradients in the boundary region, and we need to cluster grid points in such regions, as reducing the grid spacing throughout the entire domain would be prohibitive. In addition, when using a wide stencil in non-periodic cases, we need to use different schemes to calculate the derivatives at points near the boundary. Typically, a skewed stencil with lower accuracy at such points is used. Clustering of grid points near the boundary helps minimize the effect of the reduced accuracy in such regions.

A finite difference scheme for nonuniform grids can be implemented in several ways. One way is to start from the Taylor series used to determine the coefficients where the constant Δx of a uniform grid is replaced by the spatially dependent Δx_i in the nonuniform case. A second way, which is taken in this study, is to introduce a second (uniform) coordinate system and map the derivatives between the two systems. This method essentially boils down to applying the chain rule to the uniform-grid derivative we have already developed.

We discuss the development of the nonuniform finite-difference scheme for the x-derivative; application of this scheme to other directions is straightforward. If x is the physical domain where our grid points are distributed nonuniformly, and s is a computational domain where the grid spacing is uniform, then the derivative can be written as

$$\frac{df}{dx} = \frac{df}{ds}\frac{ds}{dx},$$

where the first derivative on the right-hand side is simply what has been calculated in the previous section. The remaining issue is choosing a nonuniform spacing and with it an expression for ds/dx. The two coordinate systems can be related by

$$dx = \xi(s)ds,$$

where ds is constant, and $\xi(s)$ is chosen to cluster points as desired. There are many documented choices for $\xi(s)$, but in our case, we choose

$$\xi(s) = C\left(1 - \alpha\sin^2(2\pi s)\right).$$

Recalling that s is between zero and one, this function clusters points around $s = 1/4$ and $s = 3/4$ for positive α. The constant C is chosen such that the endpoints in both coordinate systems coincide, namely the resultant expression for $x(s)$ has $x(1) = 1$. The degree of clustering is determined by the parameter α, and when $\alpha = 0$ (and $C = 1$), we recover uniform spacing. Substituting our expression for $\xi(s)$ into the differential form and integrating, we have

$$x = C\left[s - \alpha\left(\frac{s}{2} - \frac{\sin(4\pi s)}{8\pi}\right)\right] + D.$$

We want the endpoints of our two grids to coincide, i.e., for $x(s)$, we have $x(0) = 0$ and $x(1) = 1$. The first of these conditions is satisfied by $D = 0$, and the second by $C = 2/(2 - \alpha)$, and thus we have

$$x = \frac{2}{2 - \alpha}\left[s - \alpha\left(\frac{s}{2} - \frac{\sin(4\pi s)}{8\pi}\right)\right]$$

and

$$\frac{ds}{dx} = \frac{1 - \alpha/2}{1 - \alpha\sin^2(2\pi s)}.$$

The modifications to the CUDA Fortran derivative code required to accommodate a stretched grid are relatively easy. We simply turn the scalar coefficients ax_c, bx_c, cx_c, and dx_c along with their y and z counterparts, into arrays:

```
! stencil coefficients
! functions of index for streched grid
 real(fp_kind), constant :: &
    ax_c(mx), bx_c(mx), cx_c(mx), dx_c(mx), &
    ay_c(my), by_c(my), cy_c(my), dy_c(my), &
    az_c(mz), bz_c(mz), cz_c(mz), dz_c(mz)
```

and absorb ds/dx in these coefficients:

```
dsinv = real(mx-1)
do i = 1, mx
   s = (i-1.)/(mx-1.)
   x(i) = 2./(2.-alpha)*(s - alpha*(s/2. &
        - sin(2.*twoPi*s)/(4.*twoPi)))
   scale = (1.-alpha/2.)/(1.-alpha*(sin(twoPi*s))**2)

   ax(i) =  4./  5. * dsinv * scale
   bx(i) = -1./  5. * dsinv * scale
   cx(i) =  4./105. * dsinv * scale
   dx(i) = -1./280. * dsinv * scale
enddo
ax_c = ax; bx_c = bx; cx_c = cx; dx_c = dx
```

Once again, the y- and z-directions are modified similarly. These coefficients are calculated once as a preprocessing step, and therefore their calculation does not affect timing of the derivative kernel. However, the conversion of these variables from scalar to array does play a role in performance in how they are accessed. For example, in the x-derivative, these coefficient arrays are used as follows:

```
df(i,j,k) = &
     (ax_c(i) *( f_s(i+1,j_1) - f_s(i-1,j_1) )  &
     +bx_c(i) *( f_s(i+2,j_1) - f_s(i-2,j_1) )  &
     +cx_c(i) *( f_s(i+3,j_1) - f_s(i-3,j_1) )  &
     +dx_c(i) *( f_s(i+4,j_1) - f_s(i-4,j_1) ))
```

and likewise for the other directions. Making these changes and running the code result in the following performance:

| | Effective bandwidth (GB/s) | |
Routine	Uniform grid	Nonuniform grid
x derivative		
x-y tile: 128x2	1462	141
x-y tile: 128x32	1456	1063
y derivative		
x-y tile: 2x128	459	260
x-y tile: 32x128	1614	1394
z derivative		
x-z tile: 2x128	417	260
x-z tile: 32x128	1606	1388

where we have included the performance of the uniform grid for comparison. We see a modest performance degradation between nonuniform and uniform grids in the y- and z-directions when using the 32×128 shared memory tile, but all other cases show a considerable performance degradation for the nonuniform case, especially the x-derivative kernels. Once again, the only difference between the uniform and nonuniform derivative kernels is that the stencil coefficients are arrays rather than scalar values. Looking at the relevant y-derivative code

```
df(i,j,k) = &
    (ay_c(j) *( f_s(i_1,j+1) - f_s(i_1,j-1) )    &
    +by_c(j) *( f_s(i_1,j+2) - f_s(i_1,j-2) )    &
    +cy_c(j) *( f_s(i_1,j+3) - f_s(i_1,j-3) )    &
    +dy_c(j) *( f_s(i_1,j+4) - f_s(i_1,j-4) ))
```

and considering how a warp of threads accesses the coefficients, we can understand why this performs well in the 32×128 shared memory tile case. For a tile of 32×128, threads in a warp will have different values of i_1 but the same value of j when executing this statement. Each thread will take on several values of j as this statement is contained in a loop, but at any one time, all threads in a warp will have the same value of j. Therefore, from the perspective of a warp, the stencil coefficients ay_c(j), by_c(j), cy_c(j), and dy_c(j) are essentially scalar constants. Recall that constant memory is most efficient when all threads in a warp read the same value. When threads in a warp read different values from constant memory, the requests are serialized. This is the case where the smaller shared memory tile of 2×128 is used. A warp of 32 threads executing the code above will have sixteen different values of j and therefore read sixteen values of each coefficient. These requests are serialized, which is the reason why the performance in this case drops for the nonuniform case. A more drastic performance reduction is seen in the x derivative, where the 32 threads in a warp have different values of i, and a warp requests 32 contiguous values for each stencil coefficient. This access pattern for constant memory is largely responsible for the 90% degradation going from uniform to nonuniform grid.

The way to avoid the performance degradation observed above is simply to use device memory rather than constant memory for the stencil coefficients. We need only change the constant variable qualifier to device in the module declaration. Note that although reading contiguous array values is a poor access pattern for constant memory, it is an ideal access pattern for global or device memory since such a request is coalesced. Implementing the change from constant to global memory and rerunning the code, we can extend our table of results:

Routine	Effective bandwidth (GB/s)		
	Uniform grid	Nonuniform grid constant	Nonuniform grid device
x derivative			
x-y tile: 128x2	1462	141	1218
x-y tile: 128x32	1456	1063	1192
y derivative			
x-y tile: 2x128	459	260	455
x-y tile: 32x128	1614	1394	1218
z derivative			
x-z tile: 2x128	417	260	413
x-z tile: 32x128	1606	1388	1209

The conversion from constant to global memory for the stencil coefficients has greatly improved the x-derivative routines, as expected. For the y and z derivatives, using constant memory for the stencil coefficients is still preferable for the case with a 32×128 shared memory tile, as constant memory is optimally used.

10.2 2D Laplace equation

In this section, we solve the Laplace equation

$$\nabla^2 \phi = 0$$

in two dimensions using a compact nine-point two-dimensional stencil as described by Ferziger (1981). This iterative procedure calculates ϕ at iteration $n + 1$ from the values of ϕ from the previous iteration (n) at the eight neighboring points:

$$\phi_{i,j}^{n+1} = \frac{1}{5}(\phi_{i+1,j}^n + \phi_{i-1,j}^n + \phi_{i,j+1}^n + \phi_{i,j-1}^n) + \frac{1}{20}(\phi_{i+1,j+1}^n + \phi_{i+1,j-1}^n + \phi_{i-1,j+1}^n + \phi_{i-1,j-1}^n),$$

where i and j are the mesh coordinates in x and y. After the update is calculated at each point, we calculate the maximum difference or residual between iterations and base a stopping criterion on this maximum residual. We also stop the calculation if a set maximum number of iterations is performed.

We implement the above code in three ways: on the CPU, on the GPU using global memory, and on the GPU using shared memory. The CPU version of the code is

```
115   iter=0
116   do while ( maxResidual > tol .and. iter <= iterMax )
117      maxResidual = 0.0_fp_kind
118
119      do j=2,ny-1
120         do i=2,nx-1
121            aNew(i,j) = 0.2_fp_kind * &
122               (a(i,j-1)+a(i-1,j)+a(i+1,j)+a(i,j+1)) + &
123               0.05_fp_kind * &
124               (a(i-1,j-1)+a(i+1,j-1)+a(i-1,j+1)+a(i+1,j+1))
125
126            maxResidual = &
127               max(maxResidual, abs(aNew(i,j)-a(i,j)))
128         end do
129      end do
130
131      iter = iter + 1
132      if(mod(iter,reportInterval) == 0) &
133         print '(i8,3x,f10.6)', iter, maxResidual
134      a = aNew
135   end do
```

The do while loop on line 116 checks our stopping criteria for each iteration, and the doubly nested loop starting on line 119 calculates aNew, equivalent to ϕ^{n+1}, at each interior point. The maximum residual is updated within the nested loops on lines 126–127 if appropriate.

The kernel for the global memory method is

```
29   attributes(global) subroutine jacobiGlobal(a, aNew)
30      real(fp_kind), intent(in) :: a(nx,ny)
31      real(fp_kind) :: aNew(nx,ny)
32      integer :: i, j
33
```

```
34        i = (blockIdx%x-1)*blockDim%x + threadIdx%x
35        j = (blockIdx%y-1)*blockDim%y + threadIdx%y
36
37        if (i>1 .and. i<nx .and. j>1 .and. j<ny) then
38           aNew(i,j) = &
39                0.2_fp_kind * ( &
40                a(i-1,j) + a(i+1,j) + &
41                a(i,j-1) + a(i,j+1)) + &
42                0.05_fp_kind * (&
43                a(i-1,j-1) + a(i+1,j-1) + &
44                a(i-1,j+1) + a(i+1,j+1))
45        endif
46     end subroutine jacobiGlobal
```

Here global indices are calculated on lines 34 and 35, which are checked on line 37 to make sure the updated values are calculated only for interior points. This kernel is called from host code in the following code:

```
142   tBlock = dim3(BLOCK_X,BLOCK_Y,1)
143   grid = dim3(ceiling(real(nx)/tBlock%x), &
144        ceiling(real(ny)/tBlock%y), 1)
145
146   call initialize(a, aNew)
147
148   call cpu_time(start_time)
149
150   a_d = a
151   aNew_d = aNew
152
153   iter=0
154   do while ( maxResidual > tol .and. iter <= iterMax )
155      maxResidual = 0.0_fp_kind
156
157      call jacobiGlobal<<<grid, tBlock>>>(a_d, aNew_d)
158
159      !$cuf kernel do <<<*,*>>>
160      do j = 1, ny
161         do i = 1, nx
162            maxResidual = &
163                  max(maxResidual, abs(a_d(i,j)-aNew_d(i,j)))
164         enddo
165      enddo
166
167      iter = iter + 1
168      if(mod(iter,reportInterval) == 0) &
169           print '(i8,3x,f10.6)', iter, maxResidual
170      a_d = aNew_d
171   end do
172
173   a = aNew_d
174   call cpu_time(stop_time)
175   print '(a,f10.3,a)', '  Completed in ', &
```

```
176          stop_time-start_time, ' seconds'
```

In this code segment the Fortran intrinsic cpu_time is used to measure elapsed time for the overall procedure, including transfers between the host and device. After the jacobiGlobal kernel is called, a CUF kernel is used on lines 159–165 to calculate the maximum residual. The rest of the host code is similar to the CPU version, except that the elapsed time as measured by the host is printed out.

The shared memory kernel is

```
50    attributes(global) subroutine jacobiShared(a, aNew)
51      real(fp_kind), intent(in) :: a(nx,ny)
52      real(fp_kind) :: aNew(nx,ny)
53      real(fp_kind), shared :: t(0:BLOCK_X+1, 0:BLOCK_Y+1)
54      integer :: i, j, is, js
55
56      i = (blockIdx%x-1)*blockDim%x + threadIdx%x
57      j = (blockIdx%y-1)*blockDim%y + threadIdx%y
58      is = threadIdx%x
59      js = threadIdx%y
60
61      if (i > 1 .and. j > 1) &
62          t(is-1, js-1) = a(i-1, j-1)
63      if (i > 1 .and. j < ny .and. js >= BLOCK_Y-2) &
64          t(is-1, js+1) = a(i-1, j+1)
65      if (i < nx .and. j > 1 .and. is >= BLOCK_X-2) &
66          t(is+1,js-1) = a(i+1,j-1)
67      if (i < nx .and. j < ny .and. &
68          is >= BLOCK_X-2 .and. js >= BLOCK_Y-2) &
69          t(is+1,js+1) = a(i+1,j+1)
70
71      call syncthreads()
72
73      if (i > 1 .and. i < nx .and. j > 1 .and. j < ny) then
74        aNew(i,j) = 0.2_fp_kind * ( &
75              t(is,js-1) + t(is-1,js) + &
76              t(is+1,js) + t(is,js+1)) &
77              + 0.05_fp_kind * ( &
78              t(is-1,js-1) + t(is+1,js-1) + &
79              t(is-1,js+1) + t(is+1,js+1))
80      endif
81
82    end subroutine jacobiShared
```

where the shared memory tile t(0:BLOCK_X+1, 0:BLOCK_Y+1) is used to hold values from the previous iteration that are used to calculate updated values. Because the kernel is launched with BLOCK_X × BLOCK_Y threads per thread block, there are not enough threads to populate the shared memory tile in one read instruction. This kernel uses four instructions on lines 61–69 to populate the shared memory tile. Following the syncthreads() call, the calculation of the updated values is performed.

When we execute the code on an A100 80GB GPU, we obtain

```
$ ./laplace2D

Relaxation calculation on 8192 x 8192 mesh

CPU results

 Iteration    Max Residual
       10     0.023564
       20     0.011931
       30     0.008061
       40     0.006065
       50     0.004812
       60     0.004040
       70     0.003442
       80     0.003029
       90     0.002685
      100     0.002420

GPU global  results

 Iteration    Max Residual
       10     0.023564
       20     0.011931
       30     0.008061
       40     0.006065
       50     0.004812
       60     0.004040
       70     0.003442
       80     0.003029
       90     0.002685
      100     0.002420
 Completed in       0.334 seconds

GPU shared  results

 Iteration    Max Residual
       10     0.023564
       20     0.011931
       30     0.008061
       40     0.006065
       50     0.004812
       60     0.004040
       70     0.003442
       80     0.003029
       90     0.002685
      100     0.002420
 Completed in       0.307 seconds
```

The maximum residual for all cases at each printed iteration are the same, so the results are in agreement. The elapsed time for the global memory case does well, and the shared memory version is only slightly faster. In the previous edition of this book, we had a kernel that used the separate texture cache for read-only data such as the a(nx,ny) array. On current GPUs, the L1 and texture caches are unified, and we do not explicitly specify the use of the texture or read-only cache. If the compiler can detect that such data are read only, which is made explicitly clear with the intent(in) attribute on lines 30 and 51, then the compiler will issue a global memory load via the read-only cache. This can be confirmed by examining the PTX code via the -gpu=keep compiler option, which will contain lines like

```
ld.global.nc.f32        %f4, [%rd8+-65536];
```

where nc stands for non-coherent, or read-only. Essentially, the global memory version in this edition corresponds to the texture version in the previous edition, only with much less programming effort.

Applications of the fast Fourier transform

The Fourier transform is of fundamental importance in several fields, from image processing to computational physics, just to name a few. The discrete Fourier transform (DFT) is an approximation in which discrete samples of a function f in physical space can be transformed into the Fourier coefficients $\hat{f}$ via the relation

$$\hat{f}_k = \frac{1}{N} \sum_{j=0}^{N-1} e^{-\frac{2\pi \iota}{N} jk} f_j.$$

This formula can be rewritten as a matrix–vector product $\hat{f} = Wf$, where W is the so-called Fourier matrix with

$$(W_N)_{jk} = \frac{1}{N} e^{-\frac{2\pi \iota}{N} jk} = \frac{1}{N} \omega_N^{jk},$$

where ω_N is the primitive Nth root of unity. Instead of the expected arithmetic complexity of $O(N^2)$ operations typical for matrix–vector products, Cooley and Tukey (1965) introduced the fast Fourier transform (FFT) algorithm based on a divide-and-conquer approach, which results in an arithmetic complexity of $O(N \log_2 N)$ operations. In addition to this original FFT algorithm (also called the decimation-in-time algorithm), there are now several other commonly used FFT algorithms (e.g., decimation in frequency, Bluestein, prime factor). An extensive list of such algorithms can be found in Van Loan (1992).

11.1 CUFFT

Writing a high-performance FFT library is not an easy task. Fortunately, the CUFFT library contains a simple interface to FFTs that can transform arrays of any size, provided that enough device memory is available. If the array size can be expressed as $2^a \cdot 3^b \cdot 5^c \cdot 7^d$, then the CUFFT library executes highly optimized kernels.

The steps needed to call CUFFT are similar to those used by the FFTW library, a very well-known FFT library used on CPUs:

- *Create a plan.* This step performs all the allocations and initializations needed by the library. Depending on the dimensionality of the input data, there are different functions that accomplish this: cufftPlan1d, cufftPlan2d, and cufftPlan3d. In addition to these three functions, the function cufftPlanMany can be used to create a plan for performing multiple independent transforms whose

CUDA Fortran for Scientists and Engineers. https://doi.org/10.1016/B978-0-44-321977-1.00021-8

Table 11.1   Possible types of transforms: R (single-precision real data), C (single-precision complex data), D (double-precision real data), Z (double-precision complex data).

	Output	
	Real	Complex
Input Real	–	R2C/D2Z
Input Complex	C2R/Z2D	C2C/Z2Z

data are strided and/or offset in memory. For the 1D case, CUFFT can also transform multiple arrays at once by using a *batch* argument in `cufftPlan1d`.

- *Execute the plan.* Once a plan is created, a variety of routines can be called to compute the FFT of the input sequence. If the dimensions of the data do not change, then the routine can be called multiple times without creating a new plan. The function names are `cuffExecuteX2Y`, where X and Y represent the input and output data types as shown in Table 11.1. For complex-to-complex transforms, we will also need to supply the direction `CUFFT_FORWARD` for transforms from physical to Fourier space or `CUFFT_INVERSE` for transforms from Fourier to physical space. Real-to-complex transforms have an implicit direction (`CUFFT_FORWARD`) as do complex-to-real transforms (`CUFFT_INVERSE`). The latter case also assumes that the input data is Hermitian (to ensure that the inverse transform resulting in real values exists).
- *Destroy the plan.* This step releases the resources allocated when the plan is created. The function name is `cufftDestroy`.

The codes in this chapter use the `cufft` module, which contains the interfaces that allow CUDA Fortran to call the CUFFT library functions. One important remark is that the CUFFT library expects multidimensional data in row-major order, as is the default in C, not in column-major order as in FORTRAN. The Fortran `cufft` module follows this row-major order convention, so when dimensions are specified for multidimensional cases, they will need to be entered in reverse order. Therefore, for a Fortran array a(nx,ny), the plan configuration will be called with the dimension arguments as ny,nx. (In the first edition of this book a custom module was used, which followed the Fortran column-major convention.)

The CUFFT library is capable of doing transforms either *in-place*, where the same memory is used for both the input and output arrays so that the output array overwrites the input data, or *out-of-place*, where different memory is used for the input and output arrays. When doing transforms in place, we need to consider various memory requirements, which depend on the nature of the sequence (real or complex). A complex sequence of N points is transformed into a complex sequence of N points. If the input sequence is real, then starting from a sequence of N real numbers, we end up with a sequence of $N/2 + 1$ complex numbers. Due to the properties of the Fourier transform, the imaginary parts of the zero-wave number and of the highest-wave number $(N/2)$, also called the Nyquist wave number, are zero. As such, the content of the information is preserved (N real values are transformed to $N/2 - 1$ complex values plus two real values.) However, CUFFT explicitly stores these $N/2 + 1$ values. To do an in-place real-to-complex transform, the array needs to accommodate the largest case. A complex array of size $N/2 + 1$ has the same storage footprint as a real array of size $N + 2$.

Another important issue regarding FFTs is the normalization factor. With CUFFT, transforming an array back and forth between physical and Fourier spaces will give us the original data multiplied by the length of the transform:

$$IFFT(FFT(A)) = len(A) * A.$$

To get back our original data after a round trip through Fourier space, the data must be divided by the length of the array. There is also the possibility of adopting a data layout compatible with FFTW (a detailed description is available in the CUFFT manual available online at http://docs.nvidia.com), and the choice of the stream in which the library calls will execute using the cufftSetStream function. This is a very important optimization for several use cases as we will see later in the section illustrating convolutions.

Now that we have all the pieces in place, let us do a simple transform of a signal with period 2π,

$$f_j = \cos(2x_j) + \sin(3x_j),$$

defined on $x_j = (2\pi/N)j$, $j = 0, \ldots, N - 1$. Since the Fourier transform is defined as

$$\hat{f}_k = \frac{1}{N}\sum_{j=0}^{N-1} e^{-2\pi \imath \frac{jk}{N}} f_j = \frac{1}{N}\sum_{j=0}^{N-1} e^{-\imath k x_j} f_j \quad \text{for} \quad k = -\frac{N}{2}, -\frac{N}{2}+1, \ldots, \frac{N}{2}-1,$$

and remembering that by Euler's formula $e^{\imath x} = \cos x + \imath \sin x$, $\cos x = (e^{\imath x} + e^{-\imath x})/2$ and $\sin x = (e^{\imath x} - e^{-\imath x})/(2\imath)$, we are expecting to see two non-zero real coefficients of value 0.5 at $k = \pm 2$ (corresponding to the cosine term) and two non-zero imaginary coefficients with conjugate symmetry of value ∓ 0.5 at $k = \pm 3$ (corresponding to the sine term). Transforming a signal with known output is a good way to check the wave number layout of the library. Amplitudes for the positive wave numbers (from 0 to $N/2 - 1$) are returned in the positions 1 to $N/2$, whereas the amplitudes for the negative wave numbers (from -1 to $-N/2$) are returned in the reverse order in the positions $N/2 + 1, \ldots, N$. This is a typical arrangement for several FFT libraries. The code that performs this test is

```
1  program fft_test_c2c
2     use precision_m
3     use cufft
4     implicit none
5     integer, allocatable :: kx(:)
6     complex(fp_kind), allocatable :: cinput(:),coutput(:)
7     complex(fp_kind), allocatable, device :: cinput_d(:),coutput_d(:)
8
9     interface cufftExec
10        module procedure cufftExecC2C,cufftExecZ2Z
11     end interface cufftExec
12
13     integer :: i,n,plan,istat
14     real(fp_kind) :: pi=4._fp_kind*atan(1._fp_kind), h, theta
15
16     n=16
17     h=2._fp_kind*pi/real(n,fp_kind)
18
19     ! allocate arrays on the host
```

```
20    allocate(cinput(n),coutput(n),kx(n))
21
22    ! allocate arrays on the device
23    allocate(cinput_d(n),coutput_d(n))
24
25    ! initialize arrays on host
26    kx = [(i-1, i=1,n/2), (-n+i-1, i=n/2+1,n)]
27
28    do i=1,n
29        cinput(i)=(cos(2*real(i-1,fp_kind)*h)+sin(3*real(i-1,fp_kind)*h))
30    end do
31
32    ! copy arrays to device
33    cinput_d=cinput
34
35
36    ! initialize the plan for complex to complex transform
37    if (fp_kind == real32) istat = cufftPlan1D(plan,n,CUFFT_C2C,1)
38    if (fp_kind == real64) istat = cufftPlan1D(plan,n,CUFFT_Z2Z,1)
39
40    ! forward transform out of place
41    istat = cufftExec(plan,cinput_d,coutput_d,CUFFT_FORWARD)
42
43    ! copy results back to host
44    coutput=coutput_d
45
46    print *," Transform from complex array"
47    do i=1,n
48        write(*,'(i2,1x,2(f8.4),2x,i2,2(f8.4))') &
49             i,cinput(i),kx(i),coutput(i)/n
50    end do
51
52    ! release memory on the host and on the device
53    deallocate(cinput,coutput,kx,cinput_d,coutput_d)
54
55    ! destroy the plan
56    istat = cufftDestroy(plan)
57
58 end program fft_test_c2c
```

On line 9, there is a declaration of a generic interface that will map cufftExec() to either the single-precision cufftExecC2C() or double-precision cufftExecZ2Z() versions. Compiling and running the code, we can check that the frequencies are in the expected positions:

```
$ nvfortran -o fft_test_sp precision_m.F90 fft_test_c2c.cuf -cudalib=cufft
precision_m.F90:
fft_test_c2c.cuf:
$ nvfortran -DDOUBLE -o fft_test_dp precision_m.F90 fft_test_c2c.cuf \
-cudalib=cufft
precision_m.F90:
fft_test_c2c.cuf:
$ ./fft_test_sp
```

```
    Transform from complex array
  1    1.0000   0.0000    0  -0.0000   0.0000
  2    1.6310   0.0000    1   0.0000  -0.0000
  3    0.7071   0.0000    2   0.5000   0.0000
  4   -1.0898   0.0000    3   0.0000  -0.5000
  5   -2.0000   0.0000    4   0.0000   0.0000
  6   -1.0898   0.0000    5  -0.0000   0.0000
  7    0.7071   0.0000    6   0.0000   0.0000
  8    1.6310   0.0000    7   0.0000  -0.0000
  9    1.0000   0.0000   -8  -0.0000   0.0000
 10   -0.2168   0.0000   -7   0.0000  -0.0000
 11   -0.7071   0.0000   -6   0.0000   0.0000
 12   -0.3244   0.0000   -5  -0.0000  -0.0000
 13    0.0000   0.0000   -4   0.0000  -0.0000
 14   -0.3244   0.0000   -3   0.0000   0.5000
 15   -0.7071   0.0000   -2   0.5000  -0.0000
 16   -0.2168   0.0000   -1   0.0000   0.0000
```

The code that performs a real-to-complex transform "in place" is similar:

```
1   program fft_test_r2c
2     use cudafor
3     use precision_m
4     use cufft
5     implicit none
6     integer, allocatable :: kx(:)
7     real(fp_kind), allocatable :: rinput(:)
8     real(fp_kind), allocatable, device :: rinput_d(:)
9     complex(fp_kind), allocatable :: coutput(:)
10
11    integer :: i,n,istat,plan
12    real(fp_kind) :: twopi=8._fp_kind*atan(1._fp_kind),h
13
14    interface cufftExec
15       module procedure cufftExecR2C,cufftExecD2Z
16    end interface cufftExec
17
18    n=16
19    h=twopi/real(n,fp_kind)
20
21    ! allocate arrays on the host
22    allocate(rinput(n),coutput(n/2+1),kx(n/2+1))
23
24    ! allocate arrays on the device
25    allocate(rinput_d(n+2))
26
27    !initialize arrays on host
28    kx = [(i-1, i=1,n/2+1)]
29
30    do i=1,n
31       rinput(i)=(cos(2*real(i-1,fp_kind)*h)+ &
32            sin(3*real(i-1,fp_kind)*h))
33    end do
```

```
34
35     !copy arrays to device
36     rinput_d=rinput
37
38     ! Initialize the plan for real to complex transform
39     if (fp_kind == real32) istat=cufftPlan1D(plan,n,CUFFT_R2C,1)
40     if (fp_kind == real64) istat=cufftPlan1D(plan,n,CUFFT_D2Z,1)
41
42     ! Execute  Forward transform in place
43     istat=cufftExec(plan,rinput_d,rinput_d)
44
45     ! Copy results back to host
46     istat=cudaMemcpy(coutput,rinput_d,n/2+1,cudaMemcpyDeviceToHost)
47
48     print *," Transform from real array"
49     do i=1,n/2+1
50        write(*,'(i2,1x,i2,2(f8.4))') i,kx(i),coutput(i)/n
51     end do
52
53     !release memory on the host and on the  device
54     deallocate (rinput,coutput,kx,rinput_d)
55
56     ! Destroy the plans
57     istat=cufftDestroy(plan)
58
59  end program fft_test_r2c
```

The input array on the device is of dimension $N + 2$ to accommodate the extra elements in the output, since we are doing the transform in place. The input array on the host can be of dimension N, since there is no need to add extra space since the transform is done on the GPU. The first copy from host to device can be done with a simple assignment, even if there is a mismatch in the length of the array. The runtime will transfer N real elements from the host real array to the equivalent elements in the device array. Once the data is resident in device memory, a cufftExec call is invoked with the same input and output arrays. For the transfer of results back to the complex output array on the host, we cannot rely on the assignment since there is a type mismatch, and a call to cudaMemcpy() is needed with an explicit declaration of the direction. The size of the payload needs to be specified in elements of the source array, in this case the number of elements in rinput_d. The output will produce only half of the wave numbers, from 0 to $N/2$, and the other half can be obtained using Hermitian symmetry:

```
Transform from real array
 1  0   0.0000   0.0000
 2  1   0.0000   0.0000
 3  2   0.5000   0.0000
 4  3   0.0000  -0.5000
 5  4   0.0000   0.0000
 6  5   0.0000   0.0000
 7  6   0.0000   0.0000
 8  7   0.0000   0.0000
 9  8   0.0000   0.0000
```

For several applications, it is much easier to work in the Fourier space once the wave numbers are rearranged in a more natural layout, with the zero wave number at the center of the range. For example, MATLAB® provides functions called FFTSHIFT and IFFTSHIFT to achieve this. CUFFT is missing this capability, and we have to write our own. At first glance, we would think that the only way to achieve this is via a kernel that basically performs a copy while taking care of rearranging the wave numbers: part of the spectrum is shifted, and the other one is shifted and reversed. This would be a completely memory-bound kernel. There is another way to achieve this shift that takes advantage of the GPU's floating point performance. When N is an even number, if we multiply the input by a function

$$shift(i) = \exp[\iota \pi i] = (-1)^{(i+1)},$$

then the output of this modified input will give us a Fourier transform where the wave numbers are in natural order (Solomon and Brecon (2011)). When N is an odd number, the formula is more involved and requires a complex-valued expression. Each element of the original sequence needs to be multiplied by

$$shift(i) = \exp[\iota \pi (N - 1)/N * (i - 1)].$$

Since the multiplication is element-wise and the access pattern is quite simple, we can achieve optimal throughput. In multiple dimensions, we can compose the shifts. For example, a 2D sequence with even dimensions will have

$$shift(i, j) = shift(i) * shift(j) = (-1)^{(i+j+2)} = (-1)^{(i+j)}.$$

We will check this method by adding the following lines to the `fft_test_c2c` code before the FFT transform on line 40. After the data is in device memory, we call a CUF kernel to multiply each element by the proper factor for even or odd length:

```
if (mod(n,2).eq.0) then
   !$cuf kernel do <<<*,*>>>
   do i=1,n
     cinput_d(i)= cinput_d(i)*((-1._fp_kind)**(i+1))
   end do
 else
   !$cuf kernel do <<<*,*>>>
   do i=1,n
     theta=pi*(n-1)/n*(i-1)
     cinput_d(i)= cinput_d(i)*cmplx(cos(theta),sin(theta))
   end do
end if
```

We also add a constant N to the function, $f_j = \cos(2x_j) + \sin(3x_j) + N$, to better identify the zero wave number that will contain the average of the function and print the wave numbers in natural order, starting from $-N/2$.

```
Transform from complex array
1   17.0000   0.0000   -8   0.0000   0.0000
2   17.6310   0.0000   -7   0.0000   0.0000
3   16.7071   0.0000   -6   0.0000   0.0000
```

4	14.9102	0.0000	-5	0.0000	0.0000
5	14.0000	0.0000	-4	0.0000	0.0000
6	14.9102	0.0000	-3	0.0000	0.5000
7	16.7071	0.0000	-2	0.5000	0.0000
8	17.6310	0.0000	-1	0.0000	0.0000
9	17.0000	0.0000	0	16.0000	0.0000
10	15.7832	0.0000	1	0.0000	0.0000
11	15.2929	0.0000	2	0.5000	0.0000
12	15.6756	0.0000	3	0.0000	-0.5000
13	16.0000	0.0000	4	0.0000	0.0000
14	15.6756	0.0000	5	0.0000	0.0000
15	15.2929	0.0000	6	0.0000	0.0000
16	15.7832	0.0000	7	0.0000	0.0000

If we were to transform this shifted sequence back, we would need to multiply the output using a similar CUF kernel to remove the shift function. For sequences of even length, the inverse shift is identical to the forward shift $[\exp(\iota \pi i) = \exp(-\iota \pi i)]$, whereas when the length is odd, the inverse shift function is the complex conjugate.

11.2 Spectral derivatives

In Chapter 10, we have seen how finite differences could be used to compute approximate derivatives. There is another way of computing derivatives, known as spectral differentiation. Despite being more expensive from a computational point of view and less flexible with respect to the boundary conditions, spectral methods are in many cases preferred as they have superior accuracy and are commonly used in several computational physics fields, from computational fluid dynamics to optics.

An excellent explanation of the properties of spectral differentiation can be found in the books by Moin (2001) and Trefethen (2000). Here we limit the description and examples to periodic functions and linear examples, but spectral derivatives can be extended to non-periodic domains (using Chebyshev or Legendre polynomials) and non-linear cases (with particular attention to aliasing effects).

Once we have the Fourier coefficients $\hat{f}$, we can express the original function $f(x_j)$ as

$$f(x_j) = \sum_{k=-N/2}^{N/2-1} \hat{f}_k e^{\iota k x_j}.$$

The Fourier series for the derivative is

$$f'(x_j) = \sum_{k=-N/2}^{N/2-1} \iota k \hat{f}_k e^{\iota k x_j}.$$

Although the concept is quite simple, there are few important details to consider in the implementation of such a method (Trefethen, 2000). The algorithm to compute the first derivative of a periodic function from samples f_i is as follows:

- From f_i compute the Fourier coefficient $\hat{f}_i$ using an FFT.

- Multiply the Fourier coefficient $\hat{f}_i$ by $\imath k_x$. If N is even, then the coefficient of the derivative corresponding to $N/2+1$, the Nyquist frequency, needs to be multiplied by zero. (The imaginary part must be zero to generate a real function. The real part must be zero to preserve some symmetry properties of the derivative operator.) This step can also include the normalization factor.
- Transform back to the physical space using the inverse FFT to obtain f_i'.

The second derivative can be computed in a similar matter:

- From f_i compute the Fourier coefficient $\hat{f}_i$ using FFT.
- Multiply the Fourier coefficient $\hat{f}_i$ by $-k_x^2$. Since the multiplication factor is now real, there is no need for a special treatment of the Nyquist frequency. This step should also include the normalization factor.
- Transform back to the physical space using the inverse FFT to obtain f_i''.

Having discussed the procedure for calculating spectral derivatives, we compute the derivative of the function used in the previous section,

$$f_j = \cos(2x_j) + \sin(3x_j),$$

defined on $x_j = (2\pi/N)j$, $j = 0, \ldots, N-1$. The exact derivative is, of course,

$$f_j' = -2\sin(2x_j) + 3\cos(3x_j)$$

The code that performs this is

```
1   program fft_derivative
2     use precision_m
3     use cufft
4     implicit none
5     real(fp_kind), allocatable :: kx(:), derivative(:)
6     real(fp_kind), allocatable, device :: kx_d(:)
7
8     complex(fp_kind), allocatable :: cinput(:),coutput(:)
9     complex(fp_kind), allocatable, device :: cinput_d(:),coutput_d(:)
10
11    integer :: i,n,plan, istat
12    real(fp_kind) :: twopi=8._fp_kind*atan(1._fp_kind), h
13
14    interface cufftExec
15       module procedure cufftExecC2C, cufftExecZ2Z
16    end interface cufftExec
17
18    n=8
19    h=twopi/real(n,fp_kind)
20
21    ! allocate arrays on the host
22    allocate(cinput(n),coutput(n),derivative(n),kx(n))
23
24    ! allocate arrays on the device
25    allocate(cinput_d(n),coutput_d(n),kx_d(n))
```

```fortran
26
27     ! initialize arrays on host
28     kx = [((i-1),i=1,n/2), ((-n+i-1),i=n/2+1,n)]
29
30     ! Set the wave number for the Nyquist frequency to zero
31     kx(n/2+1) = 0._fp_kind
32
33     ! Copy the wave number vector to the device
34     kx_d = kx
35
36     do i=1,n
37        cinput(i) = (cos(2*real(i-1,fp_kind)*h) &
38              +sin(3*real(i-1,fp_kind)*h))
39        derivative(i) = (-2*sin(2*real(i-1,fp_kind)*h) &
40              +3*cos(3*real(i-1,fp_kind)*h))
41     end do
42
43     ! copy input to device
44     cinput_d = cinput
45
46     ! Initialize the plan for complex to complex transform
47     if (fp_kind == real32) istat=cufftPlan1D(plan,n,CUFFT_C2C,1)
48     if (fp_kind == real64) istat=cufftPlan1D(plan,n,CUFFT_Z2Z,1)
49
50     ! Forward transform out of place
51     istat = cufftExec(plan,cinput_d,output_d,CUFFT_FORWARD)
52
53     ! Compute the derivative in spectral space and normalize the FFT
54     !$cuf kernel do <<<*,*>>>
55     do i=1,n
56        output_d(i) = cmplx(0.,kx_d(i),fp_kind)*output_d(i)/n
57     end do
58
59     ! Inverse transform in place
60     istat = cufftExec(plan,output_d,output_d,CUFFT_INVERSE)
61
62     ! Copy results back to host
63     coutput = output_d
64
65     print *," First Derivative from complex array"
66     do i=1,n
67        write(*,'(i2,2(1x,f8.4),2x,e13.7)') i, real(coutput(i)), &
68              derivative(i), real(coutput(i))-derivative(i)
69     end do
70
71     !release memory on the host and on the device
72     deallocate(cinput,coutput,kx,derivative,cinput_d,output_d,kx_d)
73
74     ! Destroy the plan
75     istat = cufftDestroy(plan)
76
77  end program fft_derivative
```

After we compute the FFT, we multiply the data element-wise by `cmplx(0.,kx_d(i),fp_kind)` on the device using a CUF kernel, taking particular care to define the multiplication factor of the right precision using `fp_kind`. If we were to use `cmplx(0.,kx_d(i))`, we would lose double-precision accuracy in the final result. Finally, there is an additional in-place inverse transform to return to physical space. When we compile and run this code in both single and double precision and then compare the results to the analytic expression, we can verify that the result is correct to the round-off error. For double precision, we have

```
$ nvfortran -O2 -DDOUBLE -o spectral_dp precision_m.F90 \
    fft_derivative.cuf -cudalib=cufft
precision_m.F90:
fft_derivative.cuf:
$ ./spectral_dp
 First Derivative from complex array
  1    3.0000    3.0000   0.1332268E-14
  2   -4.1213   -4.1213   -.8881784E-15
  3   -0.0000   -0.0000   -.8927925E-16
  4    4.1213    4.1213   0.8881784E-15
  5   -3.0000   -3.0000   -.8881784E-15
  6    0.1213    0.1213   0.3108624E-14
  7    0.0000    0.0000   -.5882969E-15
  8   -0.1213   -0.1213   -.1665335E-14
```

whereas for single precision,

```
$ nvfortran -O2 -o spectral_sp precision_m.F90 \
    fft_derivative.cuf -cudalib=cufft
precision_m.F90:
fft_derivative.cuf:
$ ./spectral_sp
 First Derivative from complex array
  1    3.0000    3.0000   -.2384186E-06
  2   -4.1213   -4.1213   0.0000000E+00
  3   -0.0000    0.0000   -.2381143E-06
  4    4.1213    4.1213   0.0000000E+00
  5   -3.0000   -3.0000   0.0000000E+00
  6    0.1213    0.1213   -.5960464E-07
  7    0.0000   -0.0000   0.4447463E-06
  8   -0.1213   -0.1213   -.2086163E-05
```

11.3 Convolution

One of the most used properties of the FFT is that a convolution in the time domain can be expressed as the point-wise multiplication in the Fourier space:

$$conv(A, B) = IFFT[FFT(A) . * FFT(B)],$$

where .* denotes the element-wise multiplication. Another important operation, cross-correlation, can be implemented in a similar fashion by multiplying the conjugate transform of one array with the transform of the other:

$$crosscorr(A, B) = IFFT[conj(FFT(A)).*FFT(B)].$$

In this example, we are going to convolve two series, S1 and S2, of P 2D complex matrices of dimension (M, N), focusing on minimizing the overall execution time. Each series is represented as a 3D array of dimension (M, N, P).

A naive implementation would transfer S1 and S2 to the GPU, perform FFT(S1) and FFT(S2), multiply the two transformed series element-wise, and transform the result back to physical space. However, given the independence of the planes of data in S1 and S2, this is a situation where we can overlap data transfers and computation. Once plane n from S1, i.e., S1(:,:,n), and its corresponding plane S2(:,:,n) are in device memory, we can compute the correlation of these planes while transferring subsequent planes to the device. In addition, as soon as the convolution for slice n is complete, it can be transferred to host while overlapping the host-to-device transfer and another convolution computation. This approach is not only beneficial to overall execution time but also allows us to stage arrays on the GPU that do not fit in GPU memory. All that is required for optimal performance is enough planes resident in GPU memory to have effective overlap; four planes are usually sufficient. The convolution code that performs this overlap is

```
1   program fftOverlap
2     use cudafor
3     use precision_m
4     use cufft
5     use nvtx
6     implicit none
7
8     complex(fp_kind), allocatable,dimension(:,:,:) :: A,B,C
9   #ifndef MANAGED
10      attributes(pinned) :: A,B,C
11  #else
12      attributes(managed) :: A,B,C
13  #endif
14    complex(fp_kind), allocatable, dimension(:,:,:), device :: A_d,B_d
15    integer, parameter :: num_streams=4
16    integer :: nx, ny, nomega, ifr, i,j, stream_index, plan
17    integer :: clock_start,clock_end,clock_rate, istat
18    integer(kind=cuda_stream_kind) :: stream(num_streams)
19    real :: elapsed_time
20    real(fp_kind) :: scale
21
22    nx=512; ny=512;  nomega=196
23    scale = 1./real(nx*ny,fp_kind)
24
25    ! Initialize FFT plan
26    istat = cufftPlan2d(plan,ny,nx,CUFFT_C2C)
27
28    ! Create streams
29    do i = 1,num_streams
```

```
30      istat= cudaStreamCreate(stream(i))
31   end do
32
33   call SYSTEM_CLOCK(COUNT_RATE=clock_rate) ! Find the rate
34
35   ! Allocate arrays on CPU and GPU
36   allocate(A(nx,ny,nomega), B(nx,ny,nomega), C(nx,ny,nomega))
37   allocate(A_d(nx,ny,num_streams), B_d(nx,ny,num_streams))
38
39   ! Initialize arrays on CPU
40   A=cmplx(1.,1.,fp_kind); B=cmplx(1.,1.,fp_kind); C=cmplx(0.,0.,fp_kind)
41
42   ! Measure only the transfer time
43   istat=cudaDeviceSynchronize()
44
45   print *,"I/O only"
46   call SYSTEM_CLOCK(COUNT=clock_start) ! Start timing
47
48   call nvtxStartRange("I/O only")
49
50   do ifr=1,nomega
51      istat= cudaMemcpy(A_d(1,1,1),A(1,1,ifr),nx*ny)
52      istat= cudaMemcpy(B_d(1,1,1),B(1,1,ifr),nx*ny)
53      istat= cudaMemcpy(C(1,1,ifr),A_d(1,1,1),nx*ny)
54   end do
55
56   istat=cudaDeviceSynchronize()
57   call nvtxEndRange
58   call SYSTEM_CLOCK(COUNT=clock_end) ! End timing
59   elapsed_time=REAL(clock_end-clock_start)/REAL(clock_rate)
60   print *,"Elapsed time :",elapsed_time, &
61         "Sustained BW (GB/s):",3*sizeof(A)/elapsed_time/(1000**3)
62
63   ! Measure the transfer time H2D, FFT , IFFT and transfer time D2H
64
65   print '(/a)',"Single stream  loop"
66   istat=cudaDeviceSynchronize()
67   call SYSTEM_CLOCK(COUNT=clock_start) ! Start timing
68   call nvtxStartRange("Single Stream Loop")
69   stream_index = 1
70   istat=cufftSetStream(plan,stream(stream_index))
71   do ifr=1,nomega
72      istat= cudaMemcpy(A_d(1,1,stream_index),A(1,1,ifr),nx*ny)
73      istat= cudaMemcpy(B_d(1,1,stream_index),B(1,1,ifr),nx*ny)
74      istat=cufftExecC2C(plan ,A_d(1,1,stream_index),&
75            A_d(1,1,stream_index),CUFFT_FORWARD)
76      istat=cufftExecC2C(plan ,B_d(1,1,stream_index),&
77            B_d(1,1,stream_index),CUFFT_FORWARD)
78
79      ! Convolution and scaling of the  arrays
80      !$cuf kernel do(2) <<<*,(16,16),stream=stream(stream_index)>>>
81      do j=1,ny
```

```
82            do i=1,nx
83                B_d(i,j,stream_index)= A_d(i,j,stream_index)*&
84                    B_d(i,j,stream_index)*scale
85            end do
86        end do
87
88        istat=cufftExecC2C(plan ,B_d(1,1,stream_index),&
89            B_d(1,1,stream_index),CUFFT_INVERSE)
90        istat=cudaMemcpy( C(1,1,ifr),B_d(1,1,stream_index),nx*ny)
91    end do
92
93    istat=cudaDeviceSynchronize()
94    call nvtxEndRange
95    call SYSTEM_CLOCK(COUNT=clock_end) ! End timing
96    elapsed_time=REAL(clock_end-clock_start)/REAL(clock_rate)
97    print *,"Elapsed time :",elapsed_time
98
99    ! Overlap I/O and compute using multiple streams and async copies
100   print '(/a)',"Do loop with multiple streams"
101   call SYSTEM_CLOCK(COUNT=clock_start) ! Start timing
102
103   call nvtxStartRange("Multiple Streams Loop")
104   do ifr=1,nomega
105
106       ! assign a stream for the current plan
107       stream_index = mod(ifr,num_streams)+1
108
109       ! Set the stream used by CUFFT
110       istat=cufftSetStream(plan,stream(stream_index))
111
112       ! Send A to GPU
113
114       call nvtxStartRange("memcpy A",stream_index)
115       istat= cudaMemcpyAsync(A_d(1,1,stream_index),A(1,1,ifr),&
116                       nx*ny, stream(stream_index))
117       call nvtxEndRange
118       ! Execute forward FFTs on GPU
119       call nvtxStartRange("FFT A",stream_index)
120       istat=cufftExecC2C(plan ,A_d(1,1,stream_index),&
121           A_d(1,1,stream_index),CUFFT_FORWARD)
122       call nvtxEndRange
123
124       ! Send B to GPU
125       call nvtxStartRange("memcpy B",stream_index)
126       istat=cudaMemcpyAsync(B_d(1,1,stream_index), &
127           B(1,1,ifr),nx*ny, stream(stream_index))
128       call nvtxEndRange
129
130       ! Execute forward FFTs on GPU
131       call nvtxStartRange("FFT B",stream_index)
132       istat=cufftExecC2C(plan ,B_d(1,1,stream_index),&
133           B_d(1,1,stream_index),CUFFT_FORWARD)
```

```
134         call nvtxEndRange
135
136         ! Convolution and scaling of the  arrays
137         call nvtxStartRange("convolve ",stream_index)
138         !$cuf kernel do(2) <<<*,(16,16),stream=stream(stream_index)>>>
139         do j=1,ny
140            do i=1,nx
141               B_d(i,j,stream_index)= A_d(i,j,stream_index)* &
142                     B_d(i,j,stream_index)*scale
143            end do
144         end do
145
146         call nvtxEndRange
147         ! Execute inverse FFTs on GPU
148         call nvtxStartRange("IFFT ",stream_index)
149         istat=cufftExecC2C(plan ,B_d(1,1,stream_index), &
150               B_d(1,1,stream_index),CUFFT_INVERSE)
151
152         call nvtxEndRange
153         ! Copy results back
154         call nvtxStartRange("memcopy C ",stream_index)
155         istat=cudaMemcpyAsync( C(1,1,ifr),B_d(1,1,stream_index), &
156               nx*ny, stream=stream(stream_index))
157         call nvtxEndRange
158      end do
159
160      call nvtxEndRange
161      istat=cudaDeviceSynchronize()
162      call SYSTEM_CLOCK(COUNT=clock_end) ! Start timing
163      elapsed_time=REAL(clock_end-clock_start)/REAL(clock_rate)
164      print *,"Elapsed time :",elapsed_time
165
166      deallocate(A,B,C); deallocate(A_d,B_d)
167      istat= cufftDestroy(plan)
168
169  end program fftOverlap
```

The code has been instrumented with NVTX markers, and there are a few additional points that need to be highlighted. The first point is that since we are planning to use asynchronous data transfers, we need to use pinned memory for the host arrays. We also create an array of streams that corresponds to different planes of S1 and S2. We do all the transforms in place, so there is no need to allocate a third array on the GPU. On line 26, when the plan for the 2D FFT is created, the dimensions need to be transposed to accommodate the row-major ordering in CUFFT. The first do loop on lines 50–54 transfers A and B to the device and transfers C back to CPU memory, one plane at the time. The transfer is timed and will give us an indication on how fast we can go, once we optimize the data transfer. The second loop on lines 71–91 does the convolution one plane at the time. The convolution is performed using a CUF kernel. The difference in time between these loops will indicate how much time is spent in the computation. The final loop starting on line 104 is the optimized implementation. Each iteration selects a stream in round-robin fashion, sends a plane from S1 and S2 to the GPU memory using cudaMemcpyAsync, sets the stream for FFT functions using cufftSetStream, performs the convolution using CUF kernel (this time, we will need to specify the same stream of the other operations), transforms the result back to physical space, and sends it back to the CPU with another cudaMemcpyAsync call. All the work in one iteration is scheduled using the same stream. In theory, we should be able to achieve 2/3 of the I/O time (aside from the first two planes for S1 and S2 and the last one of the convolved matrix, the transfer back to CPU should be completely hidden) if the execution time is I/O limited, since we can hide all the computations. The optimized execution time can be written as max(2/3*I/O_time, compute_time) to accommodate the case in which the compute time is the dominant factor. We are going to use three different generations of GPUs: a V100 (Volta generation), a A100 (Ampere generation), and a H100 (Hopper generation). Aside from different computational performance and memory bandwidth, they also correspond to three different generations of PCI-e: gen3 (V100), gen4 (A100), and gen5 (H100). We are also going to run, on GH200, a Grace Hopper system in which the CPU (Grace, an ARM processor) is linked to the GPU (H100) via a very fast link called NVLink-C2C, which also delivers a CPU/GPU coherent memory model.

If we compile and run

```
$ nvfortran -O3 -Minfo -Mpreprocess -o exampleOverlapFFT   precision_m.F90 \
        exampleOverlapFFT_nvtx.cuf -cudalib=cufft,nvtx
```

we obtain the runtimes reported in the following table:

	V100	A100	H100	GH200
CPU to GPU	PCI-e Gen3	PCI-e Gen4	PCI-e Gen5	C2C
I/O only	1.010E-01 s	5.371E-02 s	2.769E-02 s	8.589E-03
Sustained bandwidth	12.2 GB/s	22.9 GB/s	44.5 GB/s	143.5 GB/s
Single stream loop	1.148E-01 s	6.289E-02 s	3.391E-02 s	2.976E-02
Loop with multiple streams	8.399E-02 s	4.064E-02 s	1.845E-02 s	1.272E-02

From the I/O only time we can compute the sustained bandwidth dividing the amount of data transferred ($3 \times 512 \times 512 \times 512 \times 8$ bytes for single-precision complex data) by the time. Various parameter choices and various hardware can move the limiting factor from I/O bandwidth to computation. On recent GPUs, this workload is limited by the transfer time. Clearly, a faster connection between the CPU and GPU (either via PCI-e or C2C) is a more relevant factor to decrease the runtime of this example.

We can use the nsys profiler to get better insight on the execution times and scheduling flow by running

```
$ nsys profile -t cuda,nvtx -o V100_overlapFFT   ./exampleOverlapFFT
```

A picture of the timeline is shown in Fig. 11.1. We could open the CUDA HW section in the nsys GUI to see all the NVTX markers and the work scheduled on different streams. One thing to notice is that in line 103, we insert a NVTX marker "Multiple Stream Loop", but there is no synchronization. In the lower portion of the figure, under "Threads", we can notice that the event is much shorter than the same ones under the "CUDA HW" section. The true execution time is the one from the "CUDA HW" section.

From the nsys report we could also print the GPU activity with

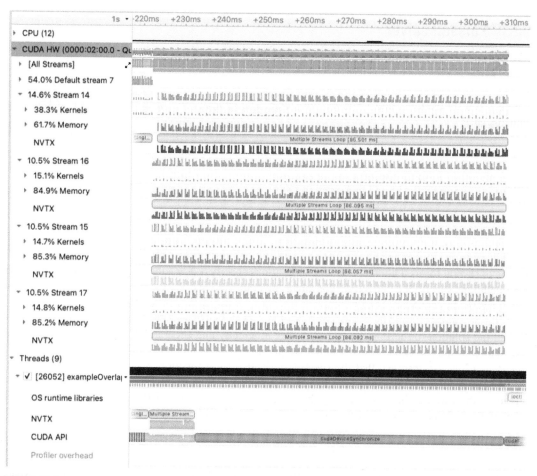

FIGURE 11.1

Nsys timeline.

```
$ nsys  stats --report cuda_gpu_sum V100_overlapFFT.nsys-rep
```

This report also confirms that most of the time is spent in moving data between CPU and GPU, making the bandwidth between the CPU and GPU the most important factor for this example:

Time (%)	Total Time (ns)	Instances	Avg (ns)	Med (ns)	Min (ns)	Max (ns)	StdDev (ns)	Category	Operation
59.7	217,424,544	1,179	184,414.4	170,464.0	1,184	256,544	22,218.3	MEMORY_OPER	[CUDA memcpy HtoD]
29.4	107,048,537	588	182,055.3	159,936.0	159,488	242,912	31,734.8	MEMORY_OPER	[CUDA memcpy DtoH]
5.7	20,632,893	1,176	17,545.0	13,376.0	11,744	38,208	5,596.0	CUDA_KERNEL	void regular_fft
3.7	13,591,874	1,176	11,557.7	8,528.5	7,392	30,176	4,112.9	CUDA_KERNEL	void vector_fft
1.1	3,859,960	196	19,693.7	19,552.0	9,536	29,984	3,435.9	CUDA_KERNEL	fftoverlap_136_gpu
0.4	1,607,391	196	8,201.0	8,224.0	7,456	8,704	197.5	CUDA_KERNEL	fftoverlap_82_gpu

11.4 Poisson solver

Many problems in computational physics require the solution of the Poisson equation

$$\nabla^2 u = \rho,$$

where ρ is a source term, and ∇^2 is the Laplacian. The general form of the Laplacian in d Cartesian dimensions is

$$\nabla^2 u = \sum_{i=1}^{d} \frac{\partial^2 u}{\partial x_i^2},$$

but here we focus on the two-dimensional problem

$$\frac{\partial^2 u}{\partial x^2} + \frac{\partial^2 u}{\partial y^2} = \rho.$$

In addition to satisfying the above equation, the solution must also satisfy boundary conditions, which can be of several forms. Dirichlet boundary conditions specify u along the boundary, Neumann boundary conditions specify the derivative of u along the boundary, and there can also be a mixture of these two types (Robin boundary conditions).

   If the domain shape and the boundary conditions are appropriate, then spectral methods can be used to find the solution to the Poisson equation very efficiently and accurately. This solution utilizes the calculation of the second derivative, which we presented for one-dimensional data in Section 11.2. In one dimension, we observed that the spectral derivative for a function f is calculated by taking the inverse Fourier transform of the product of the Fourier coefficient of the function $\hat{f}_{k_x}$ with the negative square of the wavenumber, $-k_x^2$. Taking the Fourier transform of our 2D Poisson equation, we obtain a set of algebraic equations for each pair of wavenumbers k_x, k_y:

$$-\left(k_x^2 + k_y^2\right) \hat{u}(k_x, k_y) = \hat{\rho}(k_x, k_y).$$

So after transforming the source term $\rho(x, y)$ in the physical space to $\hat{\rho}(k_x, k_y)$ in the Fourier space using a 2D FFT, we can obtain the Fourier coefficients $\hat{u}(k_x, k_y)$ by rearranging terms of the Poisson equation in the Fourier space:

$$\hat{u}(k_x, k_y) = -\frac{\hat{\rho}(k_x, k_y)}{(k_x^2 + k_y^2)}.$$

This solution is undefined at $k_x = k_y = 0$, corresponding to an unknown constant c to be specified. This is evident from the fact that if $u(x, y)$ is a solution to the Poisson equation, then so is $u(x, y) + c$. For problems with Dirichlet boundary conditions, the constant can be readily obtained. The final step to the solution is to transform $\hat{u}(k_x, k_y)$ back to the physical space using the inverse 2D FFT and apply the boundary conditions.

11.4.1 Vortex dynamics

We will illustrate the solution of the Poisson equation via spectral methods in the context of solving a 2D incompressible inviscid fluid flow in a periodic domain, using a vorticity-streamfunction formulation.

A streamfunction $\psi(x, y)$ in 2D is a scalar function from which the flow velocity components can be computed taking the partial derivatives $u = -\psi_y$ and $v = \psi_x$. The vorticity at any instant in time can be calculated from

$$\omega(x, y) = v_x - u_y = \psi_{xx} + \psi_{yy} = \nabla^2 \psi, \tag{11.1}$$

which is our Poisson equation. The flow evolution for this inviscid flow in a 2D domain is described by

$$\omega_t - \psi_y \omega_x + \psi_x \omega_y = 0. \tag{11.2}$$

As an initial condition, we choose an elliptical vortex positioned in the center of the domain by prescribing the streamfunction in the physical space:

```
101    ! Initial streamfunction  for elliptical vortex at the center of the domain
102    sigma=0.15_fp_kind
103    !$cuf kernel do(2)
104    do j=1,N
105       do i=1,N
106          psi(i,j)=-.25_fp_kind*exp(-(4._fp_kind*(x(i)-L/2)**2   &
107             + (y(j)-L/2)**2) &
108             /(2._fp_kind*sigma*sigma))
109       end do
110    end do
```

The initial vorticity field is computed from the streamfunction in Fourier space:

```
113    ! Initial vorticity= Nabla^2 psi
114
115    istat= FFT_exec_R2C(cufft_plan_r2c, psi, wh)
116    !$cuf kernel do(2)
117    do j=1,N
118       do i=1,Nh
119          lap = -(k_x2(i)**2+k_y2(j)**2)
120          if (i==1 .and. j==1) lap=1.0_fp_kind
121          wh(i,j) = wh(i,j)*lap*norm
122       end do
123    end do
```

Eq. (11.2) is solved in time using a 4th-order Runge–Kutta scheme. An artificial viscosity term, proportional to $\nabla^4 \omega$, is added to stabilize the solution. To advance the solution from t_n to $t_{n+1} = t_n + \Delta t$, the Runge–Kutta scheme will compute the following terms:

$$\frac{d\omega(t)}{dt} = F(\omega(t), t),$$
$$k_1 = F(\omega(t_n), t_n),$$
$$k_2 = F(\omega(t_n) + k_1 \Delta t/2, t_n + \Delta t/2),$$
$$k_3 = F(\omega(t_n) + k_2 \Delta t/2, t_n + \Delta t/2),$$
$$k_4 = F(\omega(t_n) + k_3 \Delta t, t_n + \Delta t),$$
$$\omega(t_{n+1}) = \omega(t_n) + \Delta t(k_1 + 2k_2 + 2k_3 + k_4)/6, \tag{11.3}$$

where $F = \psi_y \omega_x - \psi_x \omega_y - \nabla^4 \omega$, which is computed at each sub-step of the Runge–Kutta scheme. The term $F = \psi_y \omega_x - \psi_x \omega_y - \nabla^4 \omega$ is computed in the subroutine NLterm:

```
170    subroutine NLterm(nl,w0)
171       real(fp_kind),device:: nl(N,N),w0(N,N)
172       ! Vorticity in Fourier space
173       istat= FFT_exec_R2C(cufft_plan_r2c, w0, wh)
174       ! Compute non-linear terms
175
176       !$cuf kernel do(2)
177       do j=1,N
178          do i=1,Nh
179             lap=-(k_x2(i)**2+k_y2(j)**2)
180             if( i==1 .and. j==1) lap=real(1.,fp_kind)
181             v_x(i,j)= cmplx(0.,k_y(j),fp_kind)*wh(i,j)/lap*norm
182             v_y(i,j)= cmplx(0.,k_x(i),fp_kind)*wh(i,j)/lap*norm
183             w_x(i,j)= cmplx(0.,k_x(i),fp_kind)*wh(i,j)*norm
184             w_y(i,j)= cmplx(0.,k_y(j),fp_kind)*wh(i,j)*norm
185             psi_h(i,j)= wh(i,j)*(lap*lap)*norm
186          end do
187       end do
188
189       ! Non-linear term in physical space
190
191       istat=FFT_exec_C2R(cufft_plan_c2r, v_x,v_xr)
192       istat=FFT_exec_C2R(cufft_plan_c2r, v_y,v_yr)
193       istat=FFT_exec_C2R(cufft_plan_c2r, w_x,w_xr)
194       istat=FFT_exec_C2R(cufft_plan_c2r, w_y,w_yr)
195       istat=FFT_exec_C2R(cufft_plan_c2r, psi_h,psi)
196
197
198       !$cuf kernel do(2)
199       do j=1,N
200          do i=1,N
201             nl(i,j)=delta_t*(v_xr(i,j)*w_xr(i,j)&
202                   -v_yr(i,j)*w_yr(i,j)-hypervisc*psi(i,j))
203          end do
204       end do
205    end subroutine NLterm
```

Starting from the vorticity field ω^n at time step n, we compute its Fourier transform $\hat{\omega}^n$ on line 173. The streamfunction ψ^n is the solution of the Poisson equation (11.1), which relates the vorticity and streamfunction. In Fourier space, this is accomplished with a simple element-wise division by $-(k_x^2 + k_y^2)$. From $\hat{\omega}^n$ and $\hat{\psi}^n$ we can take the spectral derivatives to compute the terms ψ_y, ω_x, ψ_x, and ω_y, as performed in the CUF kernel on lines 181–184. In addition, the $\nabla^4 \hat{\omega}^n$ term is computed on line 185, which requires an element-wise multiplication in Fourier space by $(k_x^2 + k_y^2)^2$. Finally, the terms are transformed back to physical space on lines 191–195 to compute the non-linear terms in the loop on lines 198–202.

The computation of the four intermediate steps is carried out in the loop

```
142    w_old= w
143    do ns=1,nns
144       call NLterm(r(:,:,ns),w)
145       if (ns>1) call update(w,w_old,r(:,:,ns-1),alpha(ns))
146    end do
147    call NLterm(r(:,:,nns),w)
```

Once we have k_1 through k_4, the value of ω_{t_n+1} can be computed with Eq. (11.3):

```
149    !$cuf kernel do(2)
150    do j=1,n
151       do i=1,n
152          w(i,j)= w_old(i,j)+(r(i,j,1)+2._fp_kind*r(i,j,2) &
153                 + 2._fp_kind*r(i,j,3)+r(i,j,4))/6._fp_kind
154       end do
155    end do
```

As we have done several times in this book, we will compile for both single and double precision:

```
$ nvfortran -O3 -Mpreprocess ns2d.cuf -o ns2d -cudalib=cufft
$ nvfortran -DSINGLE -O3 -Mpreprocess ns2d.cuf -o ns2d_sp -cudalib=cufft
```

We use a default resolution $N = 256$, which can be overridden by an additional argument on the command line:

```
43    ! Standard resolution is 256, otherwise is read from command line
44    if(command_argument_count()==1) then
45       call get_command_argument(1,string)
46       read(string,*) N
47    else
48       N=256
49    end if
```

Table 11.2 Comparison of runtimes on different GPU generations.

	Precision	N	V100	A100	H100	GH200
Memory clock			850 MHz	1593 MHz	2619 MHz	2619 MHz
Memory bus width			4096 bit	5120 bit	5120 bit	6144 bit
Memory bandwidth			870 GB/s	1991 GB/s	3352 GB/s	4022 GB/s
Time per step (s)	Single	128	5.5E-4	4.7E-4	3.5E-4	3.4E-4
Time per step (s)	Single	256	5.3E-4	4.7E-4	3.4E-4	3.4E-4
Time per step (s)	Single	512	8.2E-4	6.0E-4	4.1E-4	4.1E-4
Time per step (s)	Double	128	6.0E-4	5.2E-4	3.6E-4	3.7E-4
Time per step (s)	Double	256	6.6E-4	5.4E-4	3.8E-4	3.7E-4
Time per step (s)	Double	512	1.2E-3	8.0E-4	5.1E-4	4.8E-4
Time per step (s)	Double	1024	3.5E-3	1.7E-3	1.0E-3	9.8E-4

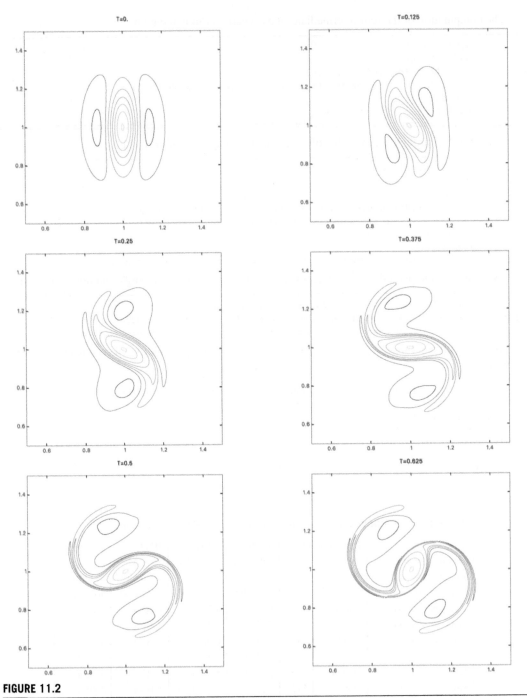

FIGURE 11.2

Time evolution of the vorticity field.

From the size of the mesh, the code will compute a suitable Δt to have a stable solution and the coefficient of the hyperviscosity. (To keep the code simple, there is no adaptive time step, and the single-precision simulation with a resolution of 1024 will diverge. This could be fixed with a more conservative time step or larger coefficient for hyperviscosity.)

This code is going to be memory-bound limited, since most of the operations are FFTs and combinations of scalar multiplication and vector addition (FFTs have a complexity of $O(N \log(N))$ and the SAXPY like operations complexity of $O(N)$). All the simulation data and working arrays are in GPU memory. The code will save snapshot of the vorticity field at specified interval, the only occasion when data is moved from the GPU to CPU memory, so transfer time and transfer speed should not play a relevant role. For the small problem sizes, the problem is too small to fill the GPU, as we can infer from the almost constant execution time between $N = 128$ and $N = 256$ as shown in Table 11.2. Fig. 11.2 shows the evolution of the vortex.

CHAPTER

Ray tracing

12

This case study on ray tracing is essentially a CUDA Fortran version of Peter Shirley's *Ray Tracing in One Weekend* book (Shirley, 2020a), which develops a simple ray-tracing application through a progressive set of examples without the use of any API. Shirley's series of books and associated code are readily available, online at http://raytracing.github.io, and are handy to have when going through this chapter although not necessary as all the topics and background needed to develop a ray-tracing code will be discussed. We go through the same examples in what follows, generating in fact the same images as in *Ray Tracing in One Weekend*, only done using Fortran. From the start we develop a single code base that can be compiled with Fortran or CUDA Fortran.

Although recent Fortran standards do support writing object-oriented code as is done with the C++ code in Peter Shirley's book, CUDA Fortran does not currently support many of the object-oriented features that Fortran does (e.g., classes, inheritance, and type-bound procedures). However, the code we develop will be object based (we will heavily use derived types in both host and device code).

12.1 Generating an image file

We first take care of how we are going to view the output from our ray-tracing codes. The image file format we use throughout this chapter is a plain text PPM file.

PPM file format

A simple example of the PPM file format is

```
P3
3 2
255
# The part above is the header
# "P3" identifies the file format (RGB colors in ASCII)
# "3 2" is the width and height of the image in pixels
# "255" is the maximum value for each color
# The part below is image data in RGB triplets
255   0   0   # red
  0 255   0   # green
  0   0 255   # blue
255 255   0   # yellow
0   255 255   # cyan
255 255 255   # white
```

CUDA Fortran for Scientists and Engineers. https://doi.org/10.1016/B978-0-44-321977-1.00022-X

where the comments below the three header lines clearly explain the format.

Implementation

Now let us look at a code that generates a PPM file, ppmExample.f90:

```
1    program main
2      !@cuf use cudafor
3      implicit none
4      integer, parameter :: nx = 400, ny = 200
5      integer :: i, j
6      type rgb
7         real :: v(3)
8      end type rgb
9      type(rgb) :: fb(nx, ny)
10     !@cuf type(rgb), device :: fb_d(nx, ny)
11
12     !@cuf associate (fb => fb_d)
13     !$cuf kernel do (2) <<<*,*>>>
14     do j = 1, ny
15        do i = 1, nx
16           fb(i,j)%v(1) = real(i)/nx
17           fb(i,j)%v(2) = real(j)/ny
18           fb(i,j)%v(3) = 0.2
19        end do
20     end do
21     !@cuf end associate
22
23     !@cuf fb = fb_d
24
25     ! ppm output
26
27     print "(a2)", 'P3'    ! indicates RGB colors in ASCII, must be flush left
28     print *, nx, ny        ! width and height of image
29     print *, 255           ! maximum value for each color
30
31     do j = ny, 1, -1
32        do i = 1, nx
33           print "(3(1x,i3))", int(255*fb(i,j)%v)
34        end do
35     end do
36
37   end program main
```

Ignoring the lines with the compiler directives (!@cuf and !$cuf) for the moment, this code is straightforward. We use an array of the derived type rgb defined on lines 6–8 to hold the red, green, and blue values of our image, which is 400×200 pixels as determined by the parameters nx and ny declared on line 4. The nested do loops on lines 14–20 assign RGB values to the components of the array, and lines 27–35 write the PPM format to the terminal. Compiling and running the file is done with

```
$ nvfortran -o ppmExampleHost ppmExample.f90
$ ./ppmExampleHost > ppmExample.ppm
```

FIGURE 12.1

Image generated from `ppmExample.f90`.

Compilation in this manner creates an executable that runs on the host and results in the output in Fig. 12.1.

The same source code can be compiled for execution on the GPU using CUDA Fortran, where the compiler directives !@cuf and !$cuf come into play. Any statement with the sentinel !@cuf is ignored when compiled for execution on the host, but the remainder of the line appears as a statement when compiled for execution on the GPU or device. Similarly, the directive !$cuf kernel do appears as a comment when the code is compiled for the host; however, when compiled for execution on the device, it indicates that the compiler should generate a kernel from the do loop(s) that follow. So when compiled for execution on the device, the statement on line 10 declares a version the RGB array that resides in GPU global memory, as indicated by the device attribute. The associate statement on line 12 associates the symbol fb with the device array fb_d, so that we can leave the contents of the nested do loop on lines 14–20 unaltered but still have the operations performed on the device. The statement on line 23 transfers the data from global memory on the GPU to the host. We can specify compilation for execution on the device with the -cuda compiler option:

```
$ nvfortran -o ppmExampleCUDA -cuda ppmExample.f90
$ ./ppmExampleCUDA > ppmExample.ppm
```

which generates the same image as the CPU version. For this simple case, there is no performance advantage to using the GPU; in fact, the data transfer from device to host is prohibitively expensive relative to the simple assignment performed on the device in the generated kernel. This example serves mostly as a simple demonstration of how to maintain a single source code that can be compiled for either host or device execution.

12.2 Vectors in CUDA Fortran

The second chapter in Peter Shirley's *Ray Tracing in One Weekend* (Shirley, 2020a) focuses on developing a C++ vector class used for position vectors and RGB colors. In Fortran, arrays are first-class objects, so the expression for the location of a three-dimensional point **p** on the ray defined by the ray origin **g** and direction **d**,

$$p(t) = t\mathbf{d} + \mathbf{g},$$

can be expressed in Fortran code simply as

```
1    real :: p(3), dir(3), origin(3), t
2    ...
3    p = t*dir+origin
```

As such, much of the benefit of developing a vector class in C++ is already baked into the language of Fortran.

There is however the issue of type safety in our ray-tracing code since we are dealing with two very different three-dimensional objects, position vectors and colors in RGB format. The approach taken here is to use a derived type for RGB color values and represent position vectors using intrinsic real arrays. Although the Fortran language does support object-oriented programming features such as classes, type-bound procedures, and inheritance, CUDA Fortran does not at this time. CUDA Fortran does support derived types and operator overloading, which we use in developing a module for the RGB type.

Implementation of the RGB module

Below is the specification section of the RGB module from the file rgb_m.F90:

```
1    module &
2    #ifdef _CUDA
3      rgbCUDA
4    #else
5      rgbHost
6    #endif
7
8      type rgb
9        real :: v(3)
10     end type rgb
11
12     interface assignment (=)
13        module procedure rgbEqR3 , r3EqRgb
14     end interface assignment (=)
15
16     interface operator(*)
17        module procedure rgbTimesR3 , r3TimesRgb , rgbTimesRgb , &
18             rgbTimesR , rTimesRgb
19     end interface operator(*)
20
21     interface operator(/)
22        module procedure rgbDivR3 , r3DivRgb , rgbDivRgb , rgbDivI
23     end interface operator(/)
24
25     interface operator(+)
26        module procedure rgbPlusR3 , r3PlusRgb , rgbPlusRgb
```

```
27    end interface operator(+)
28
29    interface operator(-)
30       module procedure rgbMinusR3, r3MinusRgb, rgbMinusRgb
31    end interface operator(-)
32
33  contains
```

To allow peaceful coexistence of the *.mod files compiled for host and CUDA execution, we name the module differently when compiled for the host and device, as indicated on lines 1–6. The rgb type itself is defined on lines 8–10, and interfaces used for operator and assignment overloading follow. A typical module procedure is

```
49    !@cuf attributes(device) &
50    function rgbTimesR3(rgbin, rin) result(res)
51      type(rgb), intent(in) :: rgbin
52      real(4), intent(in) :: rin(3)
53      real(4), intent(out) :: res(3)
54      res = rgbin%v * rin
55    end function rgbTimesR3
```

Note that these routines return arrays of real(4) rather than an instance of the rgb type, which can be (implicitly) converted to an rgb instance via the overloaded assignments when needed.

One last point to make before we leave the rgb module discussion is that in addition to creating different rgbHost.mod and rgbCUDA.mod files for the host and device, we also create separate object files rgb_m.host.o and rgb_m.CUDA.o.

12.3 **Rays, a simple camera, and background**

We have already introduced how we represent a ray in the previous section, where we used the expression

$$\mathbf{p}(t) = t\mathbf{d} + \mathbf{g}$$

to indicate a three-dimensional point $\mathbf{p}$ along a ray with origin $\mathbf{g}$ and in the direction $\mathbf{d}$, parameterized by the scalar t. In the code ray.F90, we define a ray derived type, which holds the three-dimensional coordinates of the origin and direction:

```
13    type ray
14       real :: origin(3)
15       real :: dir(3)
16    end type ray
17
18    interface ray
19       module procedure rayConstructor
20    end interface ray
```

We adopt the convention that the direction stored in the ray derived type be of unit length. Normalizing a vector to unit length can be done with the normalize() function:

```
24    !@cuf attributes(device) &
25    function normalize(a) result(res)
26      implicit none
27      real :: a(3), res(3)
28      res = a/sqrt(sum(a**2))
29    end function normalize
```

which is called from the ray constructor:

```
31    !@cuf attributes(device) &
32    function rayConstructor(origin, dir) result(r)
33      implicit none
34      !dir$ ignore_tkr (d) origin, (d) dir
35      real :: origin(3), dir(3)
36      type(ray) :: r
37      r%origin = origin
38      r%dir = normalize(dir)
39    end function rayConstructor
```

First ray-tracing code

With the ray derived type and its constructor created, we can now write our first ray-tracing code. Our approach is depicted in Fig. 12.2. We have a rectangular image represented by the frame in the plane $z = -1$ bounded by $-2 \le x \le 2$ and $-1 \le y \le 1$. For every pixel in the image, denoted by the pixel coordinates (u, v), we generate a ray that originates at the location of the eye or camera at $(0, 0, 0)$, passes through the pixel, and then intersects objects in the environment. The color recorded for the pixel is determined by what the ray intersects after passing through the pixel.

The code ray.F90 implements the approach described in Fig. 12.2. The specification section of the rayTracing module is

```
1    module rayTracing
2    #ifdef _CUDA
3      use rgbCUDA
4    #else
5      use rgbHost
6    #endif
7
8      real, parameter :: lowerLeftCorner(3) = [-2.0, -1.0, -1.0]
9      real, parameter :: horizontal(3) = [4.0, 0.0, 0.0]
10     real, parameter :: vertical(3) = [0.0, 2.0, 0.0]
11     real, parameter :: origin(3) = [0.0, 0.0, 0.0]
12
13     type ray
14        real :: origin(3)
15        real :: dir(3)
16     end type ray
17
18     interface ray
19        module procedure rayConstructor
20     end interface ray
```

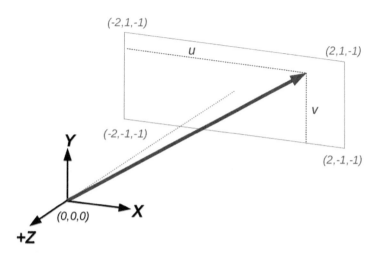

FIGURE 12.2

A ray intersecting an image. The ray originates at $(0, 0, 0)$, where the camera or eye is located, and intersects the image depicted by the rectangle on the plane $z = -1$. The image coordinates (u, v) are pixel coordinates relative to the lower left corner of the image. For every pixel in the image, a ray is generated that passes through the origin and the pixel. The pixel color is determined by what the ray intersects after passing through the image plane.

where in addition to the ray derived type and its constructor declaration, we have parameters for the image location (lowerLeftCorner) and size (horizontal and vertical) in physical coordinates, along with the location of the camera (origin). Besides the ray constructor and vector normalization functions that we have already described, the module subprogram section includes the function color(), which returns an RGB value for the input ray argument, and the render() subroutine, which generates the RGB values for the framebuffer or image. The render subroutine is

```
72    subroutine render(fb)
73       !@cuf use cudafor
74       implicit none
75       type(rgb) :: fb(:,:)
76       type(ray) :: r
77       real :: u, v
78       integer :: nx, ny, i, j
79
80       nx = size(fb,1)
81       ny = size(fb,2)
82
83 #ifdef _CUDA
84       block
85          type(rgb), device, allocatable :: fb_d(:,:)
86          type(dim3) :: tBlock, grid
87
88          allocate(fb_d(nx,ny))
89          tBlock = dim3(32,8,1)
```

```
90        grid = dim3((nx-1)/tBlock%x+1, (ny-1)/tBlock%y+1, 1)
91        call renderKernel <<<grid, tBlock>>>(fb_d, nx, ny)
92        fb = fb_d
93        deallocate(fb_d)
94     end block
95  #else
96     do j = 1, ny
97        do i = 1, nx
98           u = real(i)/nx
99           v = real(j)/ny
100          r = ray(origin, &
101               lowerLeftCorner + u*horizontal + v*vertical - origin)
102          fb(i,j) = color(r)
103       end do
104    end do
105 #endif
106    end subroutine render
```

and contains separate code blocks used for host and device execution. When compiled for the host, the code assigns a color to every pixel in the framebuffer in the nested loop on lines 96–104. It does this by calculating the (normalized) pixel coordinates (u, v) and using these values to determine the ray that passes through the pixel using the rayConstructor() function. It then invokes the color() function to get the RGB value corresponding to the ray. The color() function is

```
41  !@cuf attributes(device) &
42  function color(r) result(res)
43     implicit none
44     type(ray) :: r
45     type(rgb) :: res
46     real :: t
47     t = 0.5*(r%dir(2) + 1.0)
48     res = rgb((1.0-t)*[1.0, 1.0, 1.0] + t*[0.5, 0.7, 1.0])
49  end function color
```

which for the time being simply returns the color of the background or "sky", which is a simple gradient based on the vertical component of the ray.

When compiled for execution on the device, the block on lines 84–94 is executed, which launches the renderKernel() kernel:

```
51  #ifdef _CUDA
52     attributes(global) subroutine renderKernel(fb, nx, ny)
53        implicit none
54        type(rgb) :: fb(nx,ny)
55        integer, value :: nx, ny
56        type(ray) :: r
57        real :: dir(3)
58        real :: u, v
59        integer :: i, j
60        i = threadIdx%x + (blockIdx%x-1)*blockDim%x
61        j = threadIdx%y + (blockIdx%y-1)*blockDim%y
62        if (i <= nx .and. j <= ny) then
```

FIGURE 12.3

The image produced from `ray.F90`.

```
63        u = real(i)/nx
64        v = real(j)/ny
65        dir = lowerLeftCorner + u*horizontal + v*vertical - origin
66        r = ray(origin, dir)
67        fb(i,j) = color(r)
68     end if
69   end subroutine renderKernel
70 #endif
```

In the CUDA version, each thread is mapped to a pixel, so each thread calculates the color of one pixel, and all threads run in parallel. The pixel indices are calculated on lines 60 and 61, and if in bounds, the color is calculated on lines 63–67. Note that in comparison to lines 98–102 of the host version, the CUDA version stores the ray direction to a local variable `dir` on line 65 to avoid the compiler error of having to create a temporary array on the device when invoking the `rayConstructor()` function.

Compiling and running the code

```
$ make rayCUDA
nvfortran -c -o rgb_m.cuda.o -cuda   rgb_m.F90
nvfortran -o rayCUDA -cuda   ray.F90 rgb_m.cuda.o
ray.F90:
$ ./rayCUDA > ray.ppm
```

produce the image in Fig. 12.3.

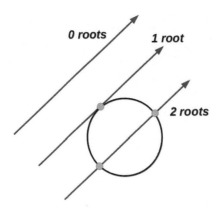

FIGURE 12.4

Depiction of how a ray can intersect the surface of a sphere, which corresponds to the number of roots in the quadratic equation.

12.4 Adding a sphere

Now let us add an object to our ray tracer. Spheres are good candidates, since calculating the point of intersection of a ray and the surface of a sphere is straightforward, as well as determining the sphere normal at the point of intersection.

Theory

The equation for points $\mathbf{p}$ on the surface of a sphere of radius R centered at $\mathbf{c}$ is

$$(\mathbf{p} - \mathbf{c}) \cdot (\mathbf{p} - \mathbf{c}) = R^2.$$

We want to determine if and where our ray intersects the sphere surface, so we substitute our parameterized ray equation

$$\mathbf{p}(t) = t\mathbf{d} + \mathbf{g}$$

into the equation for points on the sphere surface, which results in the following quadratic equation for t:

$$t^2|\mathbf{d}|^2 + 2t\mathbf{d} \cdot (\mathbf{g} - \mathbf{c}) + |\mathbf{g} - \mathbf{c}|^2 - R^2 = 0,$$

where the only unknown quantity is the parameter t. This quadratic equation has no roots for t if the discriminant is less than zero, indicating that the ray does not intersect the sphere, has one root if the discriminant is zero, corresponding to the case where the ray tangentially hits the sphere surface, or has two roots if the ray goes through the interior of the sphere with one entry and one exit point on the surface, as depicted in Fig. 12.4.

Implementation

In the code sphere.F90, we define the sphere derived type:

```
22      type sphere
23         real :: center(3), radius
24      end type sphere
```

and add the function hitSphere(), which tests whether the input ray and sphere intersect:

```
45      !@cuf attributes(device) &
46      function hitSphere(s, r) result(res)
47        implicit none
48        type(sphere) :: s
49        type(ray) :: r
50        real :: oc(3), a, b, c, disc
51        logical :: res
52        oc = r%origin - s%center
53        a = dot_product(r%dir, r%dir)
54        b = 2.0*dot_product(r%dir, oc)
55        c = dot_product(oc, oc) - s%radius**2
56        disc = b**2 - 4.0*a*c
57        res = (disc > 0.0)
58      end function hitSphere
```

We modify the color() function to color a ray red if it intersects the sphere; otherwise, it uses the background gradient as before:

```
60      !@cuf attributes(device) &
61      function color(r, s) result(res)
62        implicit none
63        type(ray) :: r
64        type(sphere) :: s
65        type(rgb) :: res
66        real :: t
67        if (hitSphere(s, r)) then
68           res = rgb([1.0, 0.0, 0.0])
69        else
70           t = 0.5*(r%dir(2) + 1.0)
71           res = rgb((1.0-t)*[1.0, 1.0, 1.0] + t*[0.5, 0.7, 1.0])
72        endif
73      end function color
```

In the main program, we declare and initialize a sphere (in host memory), which gets passed as an argument to the render() function:

```
139    program main
140      use rayTracing
141      implicit none
142      integer, parameter :: nx = 400, ny = 200
143      integer :: i, j
144      type(rgb) :: fb(nx,ny)
145      type(sphere) :: s
146
147      s = sphere([0.0, 0.0, -1], 0.5)
148
```

```
149    call render(fb, s)
150
151    ! ppm output
152
153    print "(a2)", 'P3'   ! indicates RGB colors in ASCII, must be flush left
154    print *, nx, ny       ! width and height of image
155    print *, 255          ! maximum value for each color
156    do j = ny, 1, -1
157       do i = 1, nx
158          print "(3(1x,i3))", int(255*fb(i,j)%v)
159       end do
160    end do
161
162 end program main
```

For CUDA Fortran compilation, we transfer the sphere to device memory and pass that as a kernel argument to renderKernel:

```
111       block
112          type(rgb), device, allocatable :: fb_d(:,:)
113          type(sphere), device :: s_d
114          type(dim3) :: tBlock, grid
115
116          allocate(fb_d(nx,ny))
117          s_d = s
118          tBlock = dim3(32,8,1)
119          grid = dim3((nx-1)/tBlock%x+1, (ny-1)/tBlock%y+1, 1)
120          call renderKernel<<<grid, tBlock>>>(fb_d, nx, ny, s_d)
121          fb = fb_d
122          deallocate(fb_d)
123       end block
```

Compiling and running the code generate the image in Fig. 12.5.

12.5 Surface normals and multiple objects

In the previous section, we focused on determining whether a ray intersects an object, specifically a sphere, and rendered the object simply by using a uniform color. In this section, we focus on how to shade the sphere based on the surface normal and modify the code to deal with multiple objects.

Surface normals

As depicted in Fig. 12.6, the surface normal at point **p** on the surface of a sphere is simply

$$\mathbf{n} = \frac{\mathbf{p} - \mathbf{c}}{R},$$

FIGURE 12.5

The image produced from sphere.F90.

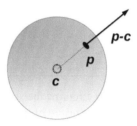

FIGURE 12.6

The surface normal at a point of the surface **p** of a sphere centered at **c** is in the direction of **p** − **c**.

where, once again, **c** and R are the center and radius of the sphere, respectively. One simple method to visualize the normal is to map each component of the normal from 0 to 1 and then map the x-, y-, and z-components to RGB values. This is done on lines 76–78 in the color() routine of normal.F90:

```
66   !@cuf attributes(device) &
67   function color(r, s) result(res)
68     implicit none
69     type(ray) :: r
70     type(sphere) :: s
71     type(rgb) :: res
72     real :: t, n(3)
73
74     t = hitSphere(s, r)
75     if (t > 0) then
76       n = r%dir*t + r%origin - s%center
77       n = normalize(n)
78       res = rgb(0.5*(n+1.0))
79     else
80       t = 0.5*(r%dir(2) + 1.0)
```

FIGURE 12.7

The image produced from `normal.F90`.

```
81          res = rgb((1.0-t)*[1.0, 1.0, 1.0] + t*[0.5, 0.7, 1.0])
82       endif
83    end function color
```

Note that in this code the routine `hitSphere()` returns the smallest root of the ray parameter t, representing the closest point of intersection from the origin of the ray, or -1 if there are no roots:

```
46    !@cuf attributes(device) &
47    function hitSphere(s, r) result(res)
48      implicit none
49      type(sphere) :: s
50      type(ray) :: r
51      real :: oc(3), a, b, c, disc
52      real :: res
53
54      oc = r%origin - s%center
55      a = dot_product(r%dir, r%dir)
56      b = 2.0*dot_product(r%dir, oc)
57      c = dot_product(oc, oc) - s%radius**2
58      disc = b**2 - 4.0*a*c
59      if (disc > 0.0) then
60          res = (-b -sqrt(disc))/(2.0*a)
61      else
62          res = -1.0
63      endif
64    end function hitSphere
```

We only consider positive values of t when determining if an intersection occurs, as indicated by the condition on line 75. These changes result in the image of Fig. 12.7.

Multiple objects

Now we will add the capability of rendering a scene with multiple objects. The approach taken by Shirley in his book was to define a base class `hitable` inherited by the `sphere` class. Since inheritance is not supported on the device in CUDA Fortran, we take a different approach.

While we could accommodate multiple spheres simply by making an array of the `sphere` type, we eventually will want to render scenes with different object types in our ray tracer. Therefore, in the `twoSpheres.F90`, we define an `environs` derived type:

```
26    type environs
27       integer :: nSpheres
28       type(sphere), &
29             !@cuf managed, &
30             allocatable :: spheres(:)
31    end type environs
```

which contains an allocatable array of spheres in addition to an integer holding the number of spheres in the array. In our main code the instance env of the `environs` type is created and initialized as follows:

```
216    type(environs) :: env
217    !@cuf attributes(managed) :: env
218
219    env%nSpheres = 2
220    call environsAlloc(env)
221
222    env%spheres(1) = sphere([0.0,  0.0,  -1.0], 0.5)
223    env%spheres(2) = sphere([0.0,  -100.5,  -1.0], 100.0)
224
225    call render(fb, env)
```

When compiled for CUDA Fortran, we declare the instance env with the managed attribute (line 217) to facilitate initialization on the host and use on the device without having to explicitly copy its contents from the host to device. When applied to an instance of a derived type, the managed attribute implicitly propagates down to all static members of the derived type. Therefore the nSpheres member of the env instance implicitly has the managed attribute. In contrast, allocatable members of a type must have the managed attribute specified explicitly in order to be a managed variable, as is done on line 29. Note that the managed attribute for the allocatable array is specified in the declaration statement on line 29 rather than on a separate `attributes(managed)` statement, as done on line 217 when declaring the env instance. Currently, `attributes(managed)` statements for members within a derived type are not supported.

Initialization of the env instance is done by specifying the number of spheres as on line 219, then calling the `environsAlloc()` routine

```
41    subroutine environsAlloc(env)
42       type(environs) :: env
43       !@cuf attributes(managed) :: env
44       allocate(env%spheres(env%nSpheres))
45    end subroutine environsAlloc
```

which allocates the spheres array. On lines 222 and 223 in the main code, we initialize the center and radius of each sphere. On line 225, we pass the env instance, along with the array for the resultant image, to the render() routine. The env variable gets passed down to the color routine.

Recall that in the previous version of the code, the color() routine called hitSphere() returned the ray parameter t where the ray intersected the sphere, if at all. The value of t was then used to calculate the sphere normal at the point of intersection with the sphere, and based on that, the routine returned the appropriate color. When dealing with multiple objects, the color routine is modified a bit:

```
128    !@cuf attributes(device) &
129    function color(r, env) result(res)
130      implicit none
131      type(ray) :: r
132      type(environs) :: env
133      type(rgb) :: res
134
135      type(hitRecord) :: rec
136      real :: t, n(3)
137
138      if (hitEnvirons(env, r, 0.0, huge(t), rec)) then
139          n = normalize(rec%normal)
140          res = rgb(0.5*(n+1.0))
141      else
142          t = 0.5*(r%dir(2) + 1.0)
143          res = rgb((1.0-t)*[1.0, 1.0, 1.0] + t*[0.5, 0.7, 1.0])
144      endif
145    end function color
```

Rather than calling hitSphere(), to see if the ray intersects a single sphere, the color() routine calls hitEnvirons() on line 138, which determines the closest intersection of the ray with any of the spheres. In addition to the environs and ray arguments, the hitEnvirons() routine passes the minimum and maximum allowable values of t for determining if a hit occurs, as well as a hitRecord variable that holds information about the hit:

```
33    type hitRecord
34        real :: t
35        real :: p(3)
36        real :: normal(3)
37    end type hitRecord
```

namely, the ray parameter t, the intersection point, and the surface normal at the point of intersection. The rec%normal component is subsequently used to determine the color.

The code for hitEnvirons() is

```
103    !@cuf attributes(device) &
104    function hitEnvirons(env, r, tmin, tmax, rec) result(res)
105      implicit none
106      type(environs) :: env
107      type(ray) :: r
108      real :: tmin, tmax
109      type(hitRecord) :: rec
110      logical :: res
```

```
111
112        type(hitRecord) :: recl
113        integer :: i
114        real :: closest
115
116        closest = tmax
117        res = .false.
118
119        do i = 1, env%nSpheres
120           if (hitSphere(env%spheres(i), r, tmin, closest, recl)) then
121              res = .true.
122              rec = recl
123              closest = recl%t
124           end if
125        end do
126     end function hitEnvirons
```

which loops over all the spheres, calling hitSphere() in each iteration on line 120. The arguments to this version of hitSphere() are similar to those of hitEnvirons(), where the fourth argument closest corresponds to the dummy argument tmax and is updated when a hit occurs, ensuring that the closest intersection with an object is returned from hitEnvirons() in the hitRecord argument. The code for this version of hitSpheres() is

```
66     !@cuf attributes(device) &
67     function hitSphere(s, r, tmin, tmax, rec) result(res)
68        implicit none
69        type(sphere) :: s
70        type(ray) :: r
71        real :: tmin, tmax
72        type(hitRecord) :: rec
73        logical :: res
74
75        real :: oc(3), a, b, c, disc, t
76
77        oc = r%origin - s%center
78        a = dot_product(r%dir, r%dir)
79        b = 2.0*dot_product(r%dir, oc)
80        c = dot_product(oc, oc) - s%radius**2
81        disc = b**2 - 4.0*a*c
82        if (disc >= 0.0) then
83           t = (-b -sqrt(disc))/(2.0*a)
84           if (t > tmin .and. t < tmax) then
85              rec%t = t
86              rec%p = r%dir*t + r%origin
87              rec%normal = (rec%p - s%center)/s%radius
88              res = .true.
89              return
90           end if
91           t = (-b +sqrt(disc))/(2.0*a)
92           if (t > tmin .and. t < tmax) then
93              rec%t = t
94              rec%p = r%dir*t + r%origin
```

FIGURE 12.8

The image produced from `twoSpheres.F90`.

```
 95              rec%normal = (rec%p - s%center)/s%radius
 96              res = .true.
 97              return
 98           end if
 99        end if
100        res = .false.
101     end function hitSphere
```

Note that this version of `hitSphere()` evaluates both roots of t if two roots exist because the first one may not be in `tmin-tmax` range.

Compiling and running the code produces the image in Fig. 12.8.

12.6 Antialiasing

The jagged edges of our spheres in the image of the previous section are fairly obvious. We might be tempted to address this issue by increasing the resolution of the image, but increasing the image resolution just makes the jagged edge more fine. Jagged edges do not appear in photos because the edge pixels are a blend of rays from both foreground and background. We can accomplish the same by tracing multiple rays per pixel and averaging over those rays.

The process of averaging over multiple rays per pixel is beneficial to more than just antialiasing. In the next section, we implement code for reflections from diffuse materials where the reflected ray is randomized. With just one ray per pixel, this type of randomization can create a grainy surface. Averaging over multiple rays per pixel alleviates that. This is especially true when we render scenes with limited lighting (as opposed to "daylight" background light that is currently implemented).

Implementation

The implementation of antialiasing is straightforward. An nRaysPerPixel parameter is defined in antialias.F90 at module scope:

```
8    ! anti-aliasing parameter
9    integer :: nRaysPerPixel
10   !@cuf attributes(managed) :: nRaysPerPixel
```

and is initialized in the main program:

```
273  ! antialiasing parameter
274  nRaysPerPixel = 100
```

In the render() subroutine for the host code, we have

```
231      do j = 1, ny
232         do i = 1, nx
233            c = [0.0, 0.0, 0.0]
234            do ir = 1, nRaysPerPixel
235               call random_number(rn)
236               u = (real(i-1) + rn(1))/nx
237               v = (real(j-1) + rn(2))/ny
238               r = ray(cam%origin, cam%lowerLeftCorner + &
239                       u*cam%horizontal + v*cam%vertical - cam%origin)
240               c = c + color(r, env)
241            end do
242            fb(i,j) = c/nRaysPerPixel
243         end do
244      end do
```

where on line 234, we have an additional do loop over the number of rays per pixel. Within the inner loop, we call the random_number() intrinsic to generate a pair of random numbers in the rn array on line 235, which are used to perturb the pixel coordinates u and v on lines 236 and 237. The ray is initialized on line 238, and the resulting color of that ray is accumulated in c on line 240. After the inner loop is complete, the pixel color is normalized and recorded to the image on line 242.

Completely unrelated to antialiasing, this version of the code has encapsulated the parameters for the camera into a derived type:

```
38   type camera
39      real :: lowerLeftCorner(3)
40      real :: horizontal(3)
41      real :: vertical(3)
42      real :: origin(3)
43   end type camera
```

which is initialized in the main program with

```
267  ! setup camera
268  cam%lowerLeftCorner = [-2.0, -1.0, -1.0]
269  cam%horizontal = [4.0, 0.0, 0.0]
270  cam%vertical = [0.0, 2.0, 0.0]
271  cam%origin = [0.0, 0.0, 0.0]
```

CUDA implementation

On the device, we modify the renderKernel() subroutine so that each device thread loops over the number of rays per pixel:

```
154    attributes(global) subroutine renderKernel(fb, nx, ny, env, cam)
155      use curand_device
156      implicit none
157      type(rgb) :: fb(nx,ny)
158      integer, value :: nx, ny
159      type(environs) :: env
160      type(camera) :: cam
161
162      type(ray) :: r
163      real :: dir(3)
164      real :: u, v
165      integer :: i, j
166
167      integer :: ir
168      type(rgb) :: c
169
170      type(curandStateXORWOW) :: h
171      integer(8) :: seed, seq, offset
172
173      i = threadIdx%x + (blockIdx%x-1)*blockDim%x
174      j = threadIdx%y + (blockIdx%y-1)*blockDim%y
175
176      if (i <= nx .and. j <= ny) then
177
178         ! initialize RNG
179         seed = nx*(j-1) + i + 4321
180         seq = 0
181         offset = 0
182         call curand_init(seed, seq, offset, h)
183
184         c = [0.0, 0.0, 0.0]
185         do ir = 1, nRaysPerPixel
186            u = (real(i-1)+curand_uniform(h))/nx
187            v = (real(j-1)+curand_uniform(h))/ny
188            dir = cam%lowerLeftCorner + &
189                  u*cam%horizontal + v*cam%vertical - cam%origin
190            r = ray(cam%origin, dir)
191            c = c + color(r, env)
192         end do
193         fb(i,j) = c/nRaysPerPixel
194      end if
195    end subroutine renderKernel
```

Random number generation is done on the device using the CURAND library via the curand_device module specified on line 155. Each thread initializes curand on line 182 and calls curand_uniform() on lines 186–187 within the loop over the rays per pixel. Because the seed variable is calculated on line 179 using thread indices, each device thread generates a different seed. The remainder of the loop is

FIGURE 12.9

The image produced from `antialias.F90` using 100 rays per pixel.

similar to the host code version, with the exception that the second argument to the `rayConstructor()` call on line 190 is precalculated on line 188 to avoid the temporary array creation error on the device.

Compilation of the code for CUDA is done with

```
$ make antialiasCUDA
nvfortran -c -o rgb_m.cuda.o -cuda  rgb_m.F90
nvfortran -o antialiasCUDA -cuda  -cudalib=curand antialias.F90 \
   rgb_m.cuda.o
antialias.F90:
```

where the CURAND library is specified. An image of the spheres in Fig. 12.8 with antialiasing is shown in Fig. 12.9.

12.7 Material types

Up to this point, we have not allowed any reflections from objects in our scene. We simply determine if a ray hits an object or not and record the color associated with the sphere (based on its normal vector at the point of contact) or background accordingly.

In this section, we now allow rays to reflect from objects. The general idea is to follow a ray and its reflections until it either hits a light source (our background gradient) or a maximum number of reflections is reached. How a ray interacts with an object depends on the type of material of the object. We will eventually have diffuse, metal, glass, even light emitting materials, but to begin, we focus on diffuse materials.

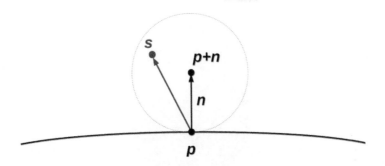

FIGURE 12.10

The reflection of a ray from a diffuse surface. The endpoint **s** of the reflected ray is a random point that lies within a unit radius sphere tangential to the point of intersection **p** on the diffuse surface. The sphere's center is **p + n**.

12.7.1 Diffuse materials

Light that reflects from diffuse objects has its direction randomized and its intensity attenuated by the surface properties. A way to randomize the reflected ray direction that approximates an ideal Lambertian surface is depicted in Fig. 12.10. The endpoint of the reflected ray is a random point in the unit-radius sphere tangential to the point of intersection.

The attenuation of the light ray is simply accumulated for each reflection off an object. In general the attenuation differs for each object and for each color component, which is why objects appear light or dark and why they have different colors. These aspects will be implemented in later sections; for now, we stick with gray objects of equal attenuation.

Implementation

Implementation of diffuse reflection in our ray tracer involves two components: extended use of random number generation and modifying the color routine to loop over reflections.

Random number generation

With the addition of randomizing the direction of reflection in our ray tracing code, we now use random number generation in multiple routines, the render() or renderKernel() routines, where random numbers are used to initialize the ray locations for antialiasing, and as we will see in the color() routine, to randomize the direction of the reflected ray. For the host code, this is not a problem as we simply call random numbers when needed. For CUDA, we need to do some bookkeeping. First, we need to store each thread's curandstateXORWOW instance at module scope, so random number calls can access them anywhere in our ray tracer:

```
1  module rayTracing
2  #ifdef _CUDA
3    use rgbCUDA
4    use curand_device
5  #else
6    use rgbHost
```

```
7   #endif
8
9     ! anti-aliasing parameter
10    integer :: nRaysPerPixel
11    !@cuf attributes(managed) :: nRaysPerPixel
12
13    !@cuf type(curandStateXORWOW), device, allocatable :: randState_d(:,:)
```

Here on line 13 the allocatable device array randState_d is declared. The use cudrand_device on line 4 is required for the definition of the curandStateXORWOW type. The array is allocated in the main code:

```
348   ! allocate RNG state array, initialization done in kernel
349   !@cuf allocate(randState_d(nx,ny))
```

and is initialized in the renderKernel() routine similarly to how curand_init() was called before, only using an element from randState_d() as the last argument:

```
249       ! initialize RNG
250       seed = nx*(j-1) + i + 4321
251       seq = 0
252       offset = 0
253       call curand_init(seed, seq, offset, randState_d(i,j))
```

To avoid making separate code modifications for host and CUDA versions every time a random number is called, we define a generic interface for random numbers whose specific routines are either host or CUDA versions depending on how the code is compiled:

```
48    interface randomNumber
49        module procedure :: rngScalar, rngArray
50    end interface randomNumber
51
52  contains
53
54  #ifdef _CUDA
55    attributes(device) function rngScalar() result(res)
56      implicit none
57      real :: res
58      integer :: i, j
59      type(curandStateXORWOW) :: h
60      i = (blockIdx%x-1)*blockDim%x + threadIdx%x
61      j = (blockIdx%y-1)*blockDim%y + threadIdx%y
62      h = randState_d(i,j)
63      res = curand_uniform(h)
64      randState_d(i,j) = h
65    end function rngScalar
66
67    attributes(device) function rngArray(n) result(res)
68      implicit none
69      integer, intent(in) :: n
70      real :: res(n)
71      integer :: i, j, k
```

```
72      type(curandStateXORWOW) :: h
73      i = (blockIdx%x-1)*blockDim%x + threadIdx%x
74      j = (blockIdx%y-1)*blockDim%y + threadIdx%y
75      h = randState_d(i,j)
76      do k = 1, n
77        res(k) = curand_uniform(h)
78      end do
79      randState_d(i,j) = h
80    end function rngArray
81  #else
82    function rngScalar() result(res)
83      real :: res
84      call random_number(res)
85    end function rngScalar
86
87    function rngArray(n) result(res)
88      integer, intent(in) :: n
89      real :: res(n)
90      call random_number(res)
91    end function rngArray
92  #endif
```

Note that we use the interface to accommodate scalar or array variants of random number generation as well.

Modifications to the color() routine

Aside from the changes to how random number generation is done, the other changes needed to implement diffuse reflection are in the color() routine:

```
191    !@cuf attributes(device) &
192    function color(r, env) result(res)
193      implicit none
194      integer, parameter :: maxDepth = 50
195      real, parameter :: shadowAcne = 0.001
196      type(ray) :: r
197      type(environs) :: env
198      type(rgb) :: res
199
200      type(ray) :: lray
201      type(hitRecord) :: rec
202      real :: t, n(3), dir(3), attenuation
203      integer :: depth
204
205      attenuation = 1.0
206      lray = r
207
208      res = [0.0, 0.0, 0.0]
209      do depth = 1, maxDepth
210        if (hitEnvirons(env, lray, shadowAcne, huge(t), rec)) then
211          n = normalize(rec%normal)
212          dir = n + randomPointInUnitSphere()
213          lray = ray(rec%p, dir)
```

```
214                attenuation = 0.5*attenuation
215            else
216                t = 0.5*(lray%dir(2) + 1.0)
217                res = rgb((1.0-t)*[1.0, 1.0, 1.0] + t*[0.5, 0.7, 1.0])
218                res = res * attenuation
219                exit
220            endif
221        end do
222    end function color
```

In Peter Shirley's book, multiple reflections were handled by making the color() routine recursive. With recursion not available in CUDA Fortran, we handle multiple reflections with the do loop from lines 209–221. For every iteration where an object is hit, a new direction is determined on line 212, a new ray is initialized with that direction on line 213, and the attenuation is updated on line 214. If an object is not hit on an iteration of the loop, then the background color is determined on lines 216–217 as before, only here it is modified by the attenuation from previous reflections on line 218, and then the thread exits.

The function randomPointInUnitSphere() called on line 212 of the color() routine uses a rejection method to determine random points in the unit sphere:

```
 94    !@cuf attributes(device) &
 95    function randomPointInUnitSphere() result(res)
 96      implicit none
 97      real :: res(3)
 98      do
 99         res = randomNumber(3)
100         res = 2*res - 1.0
101         if (sum(res**2) <= 1.0) exit
102      enddo
103    end function randomPointInUnitSphere
```

You may have noticed that on line 210 within the color() routine the hitEnvirons() routine is called with the shadowAcne parameter for the tmin dummy argument. A small positive value is used here to avoid the problem depicted in Fig. 12.11. Multiple reflections can arise due to numerical artifacts that result in additional (and erroneous) attenuation of a ray. By bounding tmin slightly away from zero such errors can be avoided. The output of diffuse.F90 with and without corrections for the shadow acne problem are shown in Fig. 12.12.

Before moving on to adding additional material types to our ray tracer, we should point out one minor change made when generating the PPM output file:

```
353    ! ppm output
354
355    print "(a2)", 'P3'    ! indicates RGB colors in ASCII, must be flush left
356    print *, nx, ny       ! width and height of image
357    print *, 255          ! maximum value for each color
358    do j = ny, 1, -1
359       do i = 1, nx
360          print "(3(1x,i3))", int(255*sqrt(fb(i,j)%v))
361       end do
362    end do
```

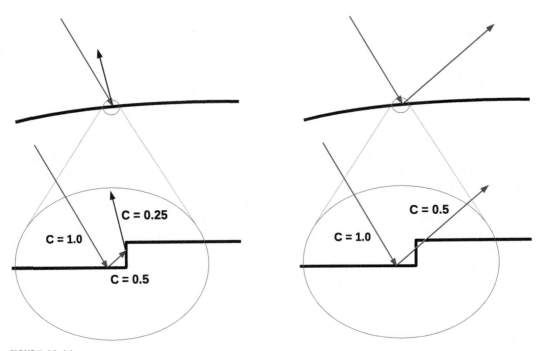

FIGURE 12.11

Depiction of the shadow acne problem. Due to finite precision, a smooth surface is represented by small steps, which can result in additional reflections (left). The change in direction is not important (these are randomized), but the additional reflection causes additional absorption by the material surface making the reflected ray is darker. The solution is depicted on the right, where reflections for small values of t are ignored. This is accomplished by using a small positive value for the `tmin` argument to `hitEnvirons()`.

On line 356, we take the square root of the RGB values. Most image viewers assume that the generated image has been "gamma corrected" in some fashion, and by taking the square root, we apply "gamma 2" correction.

12.7.2 Metal

Having implemented reflection from diffuse materials in the previous section, in this section, we add an additional material type, metal.

Theory

In contrast to diffuse materials, which scatter rays randomly, smooth metal objects act like mirrors where the normal component of an incident ray is inverted but the tangential components are preserved. The situation is depicted in Fig. 12.13. For an incident ray $\mathbf{v}$ and surface normal $\mathbf{n}$, the normal component of the reflected ray is

$$\mathbf{b} = -(\mathbf{v} \cdot \mathbf{n})\mathbf{n}.$$

FIGURE 12.12

Top: the image produced from `diffuse.F90`. Bottom: The image produced from `diffuse.F90` without correction for shadow acne (parameter `shadowAcne` set to zero).

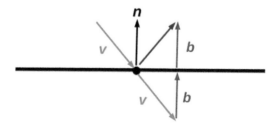

FIGURE 12.13

The reflected ray on a metal surface maintains the tangential components of the incident ray (**v**) but negates the normal component (**b**).

The tangential components of both the incident and reflected rays are

$$t = v - (v \cdot n)n,$$

and the reflected ray is the sum

$$r = b + t = v - 2(v \cdot n)n.$$

This is implemented in the reflect() routine in metal.F90:

```
162   !@cuf attributes(device) &
163   function reflect(rin, n) result(res)
164     implicit none
165     type(ray) :: rin
166     real :: n(3)
167     real :: res(3)
168     res = rin%dir - 2.0*dot_product(rin%dir,n)*n
169   end function reflect
```

Implementation

There are quite a few changes to the code to accommodate multiple material types. We break this down into two sections: the changes made in the specification section of the ray tracing module and changes to the main program and subroutines in the module. We start with the specification section.

Material derived types

In dealing with different materials, with different parameters, we could add components for all possible material parameters in our sphere derived type. However, this can result in much wasted memory in complex scenes with many objects, especially when we get around to implementing textures. Our approach to accommodating different materials is to define a different derived type for each material:

```
36   ! material types
37
38   enum, bind(c)
39       enumerator :: lambMat = 1, metalMat = 2
40   end enum
41
42   type lambertian
43       type(rgb) :: albedo
44   end type lambertian
45
46   type metal
47       type(rgb) :: albedo
48       real :: fuzz
49   end type metal
```

The lambertian (diffuse) material type contains an RGB instance albedo, which determines the proportion of light that is reflected from an incident ray for each color component. The metal material type contains a fuzz component as well an albedo component. The fuzz component allows us to have metal materials with a coarse or brushed finish.

If inheritance were available in CUDA Fortran, then we would have declared an abstract material class, which lambertian and metal would extend, and use dynamic typing to determine the specific type as needed. Since inheritance is not supported in CUDA Fortran, we use C pointers to instances of one of our material types, along with the enumerators on line 39 to keep track of the specific type, as is done in the sphere derived type:

```
53   type sphere
54       real :: center(3), radius
55       integer :: materialType
56       type(c_hostDevPtr) :: matPtr
57   end type sphere
```

The materialType member on line 55 of the sphere derived type is set to one of the material enumerators, and c_hostDevPtr is a macro that precompiles to the iso_c_binding type c_ptr for host code or the CUDA Fortran extension c_devptr for CUDA Fortran:

```
10   #ifdef _CUDA
11   #define c_hostDevPtr c_devptr
12   #define c_hostDevLoc c_devloc
13   #else
14   #define c_hostDevPtr c_ptr
15   #define c_hostDevLoc c_loc
16   #endif
```

In addition to specifying a material in the sphere derived type, we need to do the same in hitRecord:

```
66   type hitRecord
67       real :: t
68       real :: p(3)
69       real :: normal(3)
70       integer :: materialType
71       type(c_hostDevPtr) :: matPtr
72   end type hitRecord
```

These are all the changes made in the specification section in the ray-tracing module to accommodate multiple material types. We next discuss changes in the main code and module routines.

Initialization of spheres and material types

With the addition of a metal material, we extend our environment to include four spheres rather than two: two metal spheres are added to the previous two diffuse spheres. In the main code the initialization is done as follows:

```
415   type(lambertian)   :: lambArr(2)
416   !@cuf attributes(device) :: lambArr
417   type(metal) :: metalArr(2)
418   !@cuf attributes(device) :: metalArr
419   type(c_hostDevPtr) :: cPtr
420
421   ! setup environment
422   env%nSpheres = 4
```

```
423   call environsAlloc(env)
424
425   lambArr(1) = lambertian(rgb([0.8, 0.3, 0.3]))
426   cPtr = c_hostDevLoc(lambArr(1))
427   env%spheres(1) = sphere([0.0, 0.0, -1.0], 0.5, lambMat, cPtr)
428
429   lambArr(2) = lambertian(rgb([0.8, 0.8, 0.0]))
430   cPtr = c_hostDevLoc(lambArr(2))
431   env%spheres(2) = sphere([0.0, -100.5, -1.0], 100.0, lambMat, cPtr)
432
433   metalArr(1) = metal(rgb([0.8, 0.6, 0.2]), 1.0)
434   cPtr = c_hostDevLoc(metalArr(1))
435   env%spheres(3) = sphere([1.0, 0.0, -1.0], 0.5, metalMat, cPtr)
436
437   metalArr(2) = metal(rgb([0.8, 0.8, 0.8]), 0.3)
438   cPtr = c_hostDevLoc(metalArr(2))
439   env%spheres(4) = sphere([-1.0, 0.0, -1.0], 0.5, metalMat, cPtr)
```

We declare arrays to hold the material parameters for our two diffuse and two metal spheres on lines 415 and 417, respectively. We initialize each element of the material instances using the default constructors for that type. We then determine the address of that element using the c_hostDevLoc macro, which precompiles to either the iso_c_binding module's c_loc on the host or CUDA Fortran's c_devloc on the device. We then use this information, along with the sphere center and radius, to initialize each sphere.

Going down the call tree, the render() and renderKernel() routines remain unchanged. The next function to be modified is the color() function:

```
269   !@cuf attributes(device) &
270   function color(r, env) result(res)
271     implicit none
272     integer, parameter :: maxDepth = 50
273     real, parameter :: shadowAcne = 0.001
274     type(ray) :: r
275     type(environs) :: env
276     type(rgb) :: res
277
278     type(ray) :: lRay, scRay
279     type(hitRecord) :: rec
280     real :: t, n(3)
281     type(rgb) :: attenuation, scAtten
282     integer :: depth
283
284     attenuation = [1.0, 1.0, 1.0]
285     lRay = r
286
287     res = [0.0, 0.0, 0.0]
288     do depth = 1, maxDepth
289       if (hitEnvirons(env, lRay, shadowAcne, huge(t), rec)) then
290         if (scatter(lray, rec, scAtten, scRay)) then
291           attenuation = scAtten*attenuation
292           lRay = scRay
```

```
293            else
294                res = [0.0, 0.0, 0.0]
295                return
296            endif
297          else
298            t = 0.5*(lray%dir(2) + 1.0)
299            res = rgb((1.0-t)*[1.0, 1.0, 1.0] + t*[0.5, 0.7, 1.0])
300            res = res * attenuation
301            return
302          endif
303        end do
304      end function color
```

Here we introduce a call on line 290 to a new function scatter(), which given an incident ray (in the first argument), determines if and how that ray is scattered or absorbed (true or false return value). If the incident ray is scattered, then the attenuation and ray properties are updated. If the ray is absorbed, then we return the color black. Otherwise, the color() routine is the same as before.

The scatter() function and Cray pointers

The new scatter() function is responsible for determining how an incident ray is scattered by an object:

```
172    !@cuf attributes(device) &
173    function scatter(rin, rec, attenuation, rscattered) result(res)
174      implicit none
175      type(ray) :: rin
176      type(hitRecord) :: rec
177      type(rgb) :: attenuation
178      type(ray) :: rscattered
179      logical :: res
180
181      type(lambertian) :: lambPtr; pointer(lambCrayP, lambPtr)
182      type(metal) :: metalPtr;    pointer(metalCrayP, metalPtr)
183      real :: n(3), dir(3)
184
185      if (rec%materialType == lambMat) then
186        n = normalize(rec%normal)
187        dir = n + randomPointInUnitSphere()
188        rscattered = ray(rec%p, dir)
189        lambCrayP = transfer(rec%matPtr, lambCrayP)
190        attenuation = lambPtr%albedo
191        res = .true.
192      else if (rec%materialType == metalMat) then
193        n = normalize(rec%normal)
194        metalCrayP = transfer(rec%matPtr, metalCrayP)
195        dir = reflect(rin, n) + metalPtr%fuzz*randomPointInUnitSphere()
196        rscattered = ray(rec%p, dir)
197        attenuation = metalPtr%albedo
198        res = (dot_product(rscattered%dir, n) > 0)
199      end if
200
```

```
     end function scatter
```

Prior to calling `scatter()`, a hit has been recorded in the `hitRecord` argument, and its `materialType` component is used to branch to the appropriate treatment for that material. To access components of the specific material type, Cray pointers are used to transfer, or "cast" in C terminology, the C pointer to the correct type. For diffuse materials, we have declared the Cray pointer `lambCrayP` and the associated pointee `lambPtr`, which is used to dereference the pointer, on line 181. On line 189 the `transfer()` function is used to associate the pointer with `rec%matPtr`, whose `albedo` component is accessed through the pointee `lambPtr` on line 190. Access to the metal material's `albedo` and `fuzz` components is accomplished similarly in the next block of code. On line 195 the scattered direction is determined through the `reflect()` function call and modified by a term with the `fuzz` component. The value of `fuzz` is the amplitude of a random perturbation to the endpoint of the scattered ray. If the perturbation results in the ray's endpoint being below the surface of the object, then that ray is simply absorbed. This is the reason for using the dot product of the scattered direction and normal on line 198 in returning true or false from the scatter function.

Aside from the above changes, the only difference to the code is that the `hitSphere()` function must initialize the material parameters in the `hitRecord` instance when a hit is detected.

The image generated from the code with various values of `fuzz` is shown in Fig. 12.14.

12.7.3 Dielectrics

In this section, we add a third material type to the code, dielectrics.

Theory

When a light ray hits a dielectric, such as glass or water, part of the ray is reflected, and part of the ray is refracted or transmitted through the dielectric material. Because the speed of light is different in the dielectric, the transmitted ray changes direction according to Snell's law, as depicted in Fig. 12.15. Snell's law states that

$$n_i \sin(\theta_i) = n_t \sin(\theta_t),$$

where θ_i and θ_t are the angles between the incident and transmitted rays and the surface normal, and n_i and n_t are the indices of refraction for the incident and transmitted media.

Note that Snell's law applies to rays both entering and leaving a dielectric material. When a ray goes from a material with a larger index of refraction to a material with a smaller index of refraction, there is a range of incident angles to the interface where all of the ray is internally reflected, referred to as *total internal reflection*.

Aside from the case of total internal reflection, the relative amounts of reflected and transmitted light is dependent of the angle of incidence and can be approximated using Schlick's approximation (Schlick (1994)), where the specular reflection coefficient $R(\theta)$ is given by

$$R(\theta_i) = R_0 + (1 - R_0)(1 - \cos \theta_i)^5,$$

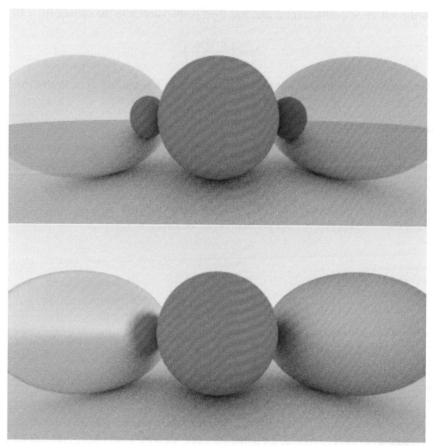

FIGURE 12.14

Image produced from `metal.F90`. The top image is created with the `fuzz` parameter of zero for both metal spheres. The bottom figure has `fuzz` values of 0.3 and 1.0 for the left and right spheres, respectively.

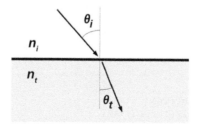

FIGURE 12.15

Depiction of how light is redirected when passing through an interface between two media with different indices of refraction. Snell's law states that $n_i \sin(\theta_i) = n_t \sin(\theta_t)$, where n_i and n_t are the indices of refraction for the incident and transmitted rays.

where R_0 is the reflection coefficient for incident light perpendicular to the surface ($\theta_i = 0$),

$$R_0 = \left(\frac{n_i - n_t}{n_i + n_t} \right)^2 .$$

Note that for our ideal dielectric, all light is either reflected or transmitted, none is absorbed.

Implementation

The first order of business is to add a dielectric material derived type, whose sole component is the index of refraction:

```
35    ! material types
36
37    enum, bind(c)
38        enumerator :: lambMat = 1, metalMat = 2, dielMat = 3
39    end enum
40
41    type lambertian
42        type(rgb) :: albedo
43    end type lambertian
44
45    type metal
46        type(rgb) :: albedo
47        real :: fuzz
48    end type metal
49
50    type dielectric
51        real :: refractiveIndex
52    end type dielectric
```

Just as we created a reflect() routine for metal surfaces, we have a refract() routine for dielectrics:

```
174    !@cuf attributes(device) &
175    function refract(rin, n, niOverNt, refDir) result(res)
176        implicit none
177        type(ray) :: rin          ! incident ray
178        real :: n(3)              ! unit surface normal
179        real :: niOverNt          ! incident/transmitted refractive index ratio
180        real :: refDir(3)         ! direction of refracted ray
181        logical :: res            ! refracted (.true.) or reflected (.false.)
182
183        real :: rproj, cosT2
184
185        rproj = dot_product(rin%dir,n)
186        cosT2 = 1.0 - niOverNt**2*(1-rproj**2)
187        if (cosT2 > 0.0) then
188            refDir = niOverNt*(rin%dir - rproj*n) - sqrt(cosT2)*n
189            res = .true.
190        else
191            res = .false.
192        end if
```

```
193   end function refract
```

The refract() function implements Snell's law of refraction and returns true if some of an incident ray is refracted or false if there is total internal reflection. If some of the incident ray is refracted, then the direction of the refracted ray is returned in refDir.

Rather than generating both reflected and refracted rays when an incident ray hits a dielectric material interface (and there is no total internal reflection), we take a probabilistic approach and either reflect or refract the incident ray. This approach is implemented in the scatter() function by the block added for dielectrics:

```
229       else if (rec%materialType == dielMat) then
230
231           attenuation = [1.0, 1.0, 1.0]
232           block
233               real :: niOverNt, cosine, rn, reflectProb
234
235               dielCrayP = transfer(rec%matPtr, dielCrayP)
236               ! determine if inside or outside dielectric
237               if (dot_product(rin%dir, rec%normal) > 0.0) then
238                   ! incident ray in dielectric
239                   n = -rec%normal
240                   niOverNt = dielPtr%refractiveIndex
241                   cosine = niOverNt * &
242                        dot_product(rin%dir, rec%normal)/sqrt(sum(rin%dir**2))
243               else
244                   ! incident ray outside dielectric
245                   n = rec%normal
246                   niOverNt = 1.0/dielPtr%refractiveIndex
247                   cosine = - dot_product(rin%dir, rec%normal)/sqrt(sum(rin%dir**2))
248               end if
249
250               ! determine if scattered ray is refracted or reflected
251               if (refract(rin, n, niOverNt, dir)) then
252                   reflectProb = schlick(cosine, dielPtr%refractiveIndex)
253               else
254                   reflectProb = 1.0
255               end if
256
257               rn = randomnumber()
258               if (rn < reflectProb) then
259                   dir = reflect(rin, rec%normal)
260                   rscattered = ray(rec%p, dir)
261               else
262                   rscattered = ray(rec%p, dir)
263               end if
264               res = .true.
265           end block
266
267       endif
```

The code on lines 235–248 calculates the ratio of index of refractions and the cosine factor for the Schlick approximation based on whether the incident ray is inside or outside the dielectric material. The refract() routine is then called on line 251 to determine whether part of the incident ray is refracted, and if so, then the direction of the refracted ray is returned in dir. The probability that the incident ray should be reflected is then calculated by calling the schlick() routine on line 252, or in the case of total internal reflection, it is set to 1.0 on line 254. A random number is generated on line 257 and compared with the probability of reflection on line 258, where either the reflected or refracted ray is returned. The schlick() routine is

```
271    ! Schlick approximation
272    !@cuf attributes(device) &
273    function schlick(cosine, refractiveIndex) result(res)
274      implicit none
275      real :: cosine, refractiveIndex
276      real :: res
277      res = ((1-refractiveIndex)/(1+refractiveIndex))**2
278      res = res + (1.0-res)*(1-cosine)**5
279    end function schlick
```

In the main program, we initialize our spheres with

```
493    type(lambertian) :: lambArr(2)
494    !@cuf attributes(device) :: lambArr
495    type(metal) :: metalArr(1)
496    !@cuf attributes(device) :: metalArr
497    type(dielectric) :: dielArr(1)
498    !@cuf attributes(device) :: dielArr
499    type(c_hostDevPtr) :: cPtr
500
501    ! setup environment
502    env%nSpheres = 5
503    call environsAlloc(env)
504
505    lambArr(1) = lambertian(rgb([0.1, 0.2, 0.5]))
506    cPtr = c_hostDevLoc(lambArr(1))
507    env%spheres(1) = sphere([0.0, 0.0, -1.0], 0.5, lambMat, cPtr)
508
509    lambArr(2)= lambertian(rgb([0.8, 0.8, 0.0]))
510    cPtr = c_hostDevLoc(lambArr(2))
511    env%spheres(2) = sphere([0.0, -100.5, -1.0], 100.0, lambMat, cPtr)
512
513    metalArr(1) = metal(rgb([0.8, 0.6, 0.2]), 0.0)
514    cPtr = c_hostDevLoc(metalArr(1))
515    env%spheres(3) = sphere([1.0, 0.0, -1.0], 0.5, metalMat, cPtr)
516
517    dielArr(1) = dielectric(1.5)
518    cPtr = c_hostDevLoc(dielArr(1))
519    env%spheres(4) = sphere([-1.0, 0.0, -1.0], 0.5, dielMat, cPtr)
520    env%spheres(5) = sphere([-1.0, 0.0, -1.0], -0.45, dielMat, cPtr)
```

Note that we have modified our fourth sphere to be a dielectric material and added a fifth dielectric sphere with negative radius. Using the latter results in the surface normal pointing inward, so we are in

FIGURE 12.16

The image produced from `dielectric.F90`.

effect creating a glass shell by using two spheres with the same center but radii of 0.5 and −0.45. The image produced from this code is shown in Fig. 12.16.

12.8 **Positionable camera**

Up to this point, we have not changed our viewing perspective. We could change the viewing perspective simply by initializing the fields in our camera instance (lowerLeftCorner, horizontal, vertical, and origin) differently, but we take this time to make positioning the camera a bit more user friendly. We take the approach depicted in Fig. 12.17. We specify two points lookFrom and lookAt with the plane of the image perpendicular to those points. We also specify a vector indicating up, vup. From these three parameters we can determine the image coordinate system ($\mathbf{u}$, $\mathbf{v}$, $\mathbf{w}$) as follows:

$$\mathbf{w} = \frac{\mathbf{L}_{from} - \mathbf{L}_{at}}{|\mathbf{L}_{from} - \mathbf{L}_{at}|},$$

$$\mathbf{u} = \frac{\mathbf{v}_{up} \times \mathbf{w}}{|\mathbf{v}_{up} \times \mathbf{w}|},$$

$$\mathbf{v} = \mathbf{w} \times \mathbf{u}.$$

We determine the size of the image by a vertical field of view parameter vfov and an aspect ratio aspect, used to get a horizontal field of view.

In the code, we leave our camera derived type alone but initialize a camera instance with the cameraConstructor() function:

```
178   function cameraConstructor(lookFrom, lookAt, vup, vfov, aspect) result(cam)
179     implicit none
180     real :: lookFrom(3), lookAt(3), vup(3), vfov, aspect
```

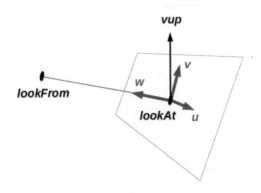

FIGURE 12.17

Depiction of the coordinate systems with a positionable camera.

```
181      type(camera) :: cam
182
183      real :: u(3), v(3), w(3), theta, halfHeight, halfWidth, pi
184
185      w = (lookFrom - lookAt)/sqrt(sum((lookFrom-lookAt)**2))
186      u = cross(vup, w)/sqrt(sum(cross(vup, w)**2))
187      v = cross(w, u)
188
189      pi = 4.0*atan(1.0)
190      theta = vfov*pi/180.0
191      halfHeight = tan(theta/2.0)
192      halfWidth = halfHeight*aspect
193
194      cam%origin = lookFrom
195      cam%lowerLeftCorner = cam%origin - halfWidth*u - halfHeight*v - w
196      cam%horizontal = 2.0*halfWidth*u
197      cam%vertical = 2.0*halfHeight*v
198    end function cameraConstructor
```

which makes use of the cross-product routine:

```
134    function cross(a, b) result(c)
135      implicit none
136      real :: a(3), b(3), c(3)
137      c(1) = a(2)*b(3) - a(3)*b(2)
138      c(2) = a(3)*b(1) - a(1)*b(3)
139      c(3) = a(1)*b(2) - a(2)*b(1)
140    end function cross
```

Initializing the camera in the main program with

```
558    ! setup camera
559    cam = camera(lookFrom = [-2.0,2.0,1.0], &
560         lookAt = [0.0,0.0,-1.0], &
561         vup = [0.0, 1.0, 0.0], vfov = 20.0, aspect = real(nx)/ny)
```

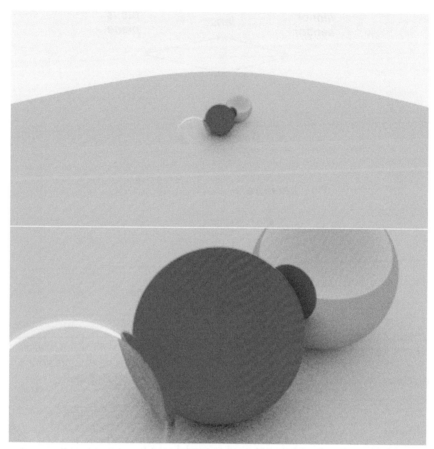

FIGURE 12.18

The image produced from `camera.F90` with a vertical field of view of 90° (top) and 20° (bottom).

results in the bottom image in Fig. 12.18. We can zoom out simply by changing the `vfov` parameter, as was done to produce the top image in Fig. 12.18.

12.9 Defocus blur

Real cameras need to have an aperture to gather enough light to create an image. The larger the aperture, the more the light gathered, but the more the image is out of focus. A lens is used to bring objects at a particular distance, the focal length, into focus. In our virtual camera, we effectively have a perfect sensor and do not need an aperture. We only introduce an aperture and lens when we want to introduce a depth of field, or *defocus blur*.

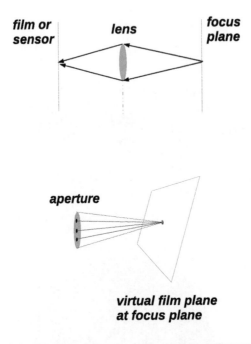

FIGURE 12.19

A real camera with a lens within a finite aperture will focus light from objects at the focal distance on the film plane (top). We model this by having rays originate from random locations within a disc representing the aperture. These rays will be in focus at a virtual film plane located at the focal distance.

Implementation

To add defocus blur to our code, we do not need to model rays traveling through the lens and onto a sensor. We can start rays from the surface of the lens and send them toward a virtual film plane located at the focal length, as depicted in Fig. 12.19. Since we use multiple rays per pixel for antialiasing, we do not have to generate any new rays to implement defocus blur; we simply need to modify the origin of the existing rays.

We modify our camera derived type to include a lensRadius parameter, which specifies the aperture size, as well as the image coordinate system u, v, and w:

```
77    type camera
78        real :: lowerLeftCorner(3)
79        real :: horizontal(3)
80        real :: vertical(3)
81        real :: origin(3)
82        real :: u(3), v(3), w(3)
83        real :: lensRadius
84    end type camera
```

Storing the image coordinate system in the camera type is needed when we randomly displace points on the (infinitely thin) lens surface, which is parallel to the image plane. The random perturbation on the lens surface is done using the randomPointInUnitDisk() function:

```
155    !@cuf attributes(device) &
156    function randomPointInUnitDisk() result(res)
157      implicit none
158      real :: res(2)
159      do
160         res = randomNumber(2)
161         res = 2*res - 1.0
162         if (sum(res**2) <= 1.0) exit
163      enddo
164    end function randomPointInUnitDisk
```

which is simply a two-dimensional version of our randomPointInUnitSphere() function.

We add two optional arguments to our cameraconstructor() function, the aperture and distToFocus:

```
191    function cameraConstructor(lookFrom, lookAt, vup, vfov, aspect, &
192             aperture, distToFocus) result(cam)
193      implicit none
194      real :: lookFrom(3), lookAt(3), vup(3), vfov, aspect
195      real, optional :: aperture, distToFocus
196      type(camera) :: cam
197
198      real :: u(3), v(3), w(3), theta, halfHeight, halfWidth, pi
199      real :: focalLength
200
201      w = (lookFrom - lookAt)/sqrt(sum((lookFrom-lookAt)**2))
202      u = cross(vup, w)/sqrt(sum(cross(vup, w)**2))
203      v = cross(w, u)
204
205      pi = 4.0*atan(1.0)
206      theta = vfov*pi/180.0
207      halfHeight = tan(theta/2.0)
208      halfWidth = halfHeight*aspect
209
210      if (present(distToFocus)) then
211         focalLength = distToFocus
212      else
213         focalLength = 1.0
214      end if
215
216      cam%origin = lookFrom
217      cam%lowerLeftCorner = cam%origin &
218           - focalLength*(halfWidth*u + halfHeight*v + w)
219      cam%horizontal = 2.0*halfWidth*u*focalLength
220      cam%vertical = 2.0*halfHeight*v*focalLength
221      cam%u = u
222      cam%v = v
223      cam%w = w
```

```
224        if (present(aperture)) then
225            cam%lensRadius = aperture/2
226        else
227            cam%lensRadius = 0.0
228        end if
229
230    end function cameraConstructor
```

If these optional arguments are not present, then the focalLength is set to one, and the lensRadius is set to zero, and we recover the previous code with no defocus blur (i.e., having a camera with a perfect sensor).

In the renderKernel() routine, we apply defocus blur on lines 489–492, where we randomly perturb the ray origin by an amount proportional to the lensRadius:

```
489            ! defocus blur origin
490            rd = randomPointInUnitDisk()
491            origin = cam%origin + &
492                cam%lensRadius*rd(1)*cam%u + cam%lensRadius*rd(2)*cam%v
```

The cam%u and cam%v vectors are used here to place the perturbation in the plane of the lens. A similar modification is made to the render() function on lines 546–549:

```
546            ! defocus blur offset
547            rd = randomPointInUnitDisk()
548            origin = cam%origin + &
549                cam%lensRadius*rd(1)*cam%u + cam%lensRadius*rd(2)*cam%v
```

Note that if lensRadius is zero, then no perturbation occurs, and we have a perfect sensor.

The changes above are the only modifications to the ray-tracing module needed to implement defocus blur. To test the these changes out, we modify the main program to call camera() with

```
603    ! setup camera
604    cam = camera( &
605        lookFrom = [3.0,3.0,2.0], &
606        lookAt = [0.0,0.0,-1.0], &
607        vup = [0.0, 1.0, 0.0], &
608        vfov = 20.0, &
609        aspect = real(nx)/ny, &
610        aperture = 2.0, &
611        distToFocus = sqrt(sum( ([3.0,3.0,2.0]-[0.0,0.0,-1.0])**2 )))
```

which produces the image in Fig. 12.20.

12.10 **Where next?**

At this point in Peter Shirley's book, the ray-tracing code is put to work rendering a complex scene consisting of hundreds of spheres, which was used as the cover of his book. We generate the same image. Nothing in our ray tracing module changes, only the initialization of the scene in host code:

FIGURE 12.20

The image produced from defocusBlur.F90.

```
569   program main
570     use rayTracing
571     implicit none
572     integer, parameter :: nx = 1200, ny = 800
573     integer, parameter :: maxNSpheres = 501
574     integer :: i, j
575     type(rgb) :: fb(nx,ny)
576     type(environs) :: env
577     !@cuf attributes(managed) :: env
578     type(camera) :: cam
579     !@cuf attributes(managed) :: cam
580
581     real :: chooseMat, center(3)
582     integer :: ia, ib
583
584     type(lambertian) :: lambArr(maxNSpheres)
585     !@cuf attributes(device) :: lambArr
586     type(metal) :: metalArr(maxNSpheres)
587     !@cuf attributes(device) :: metalArr
588     type(dielectric) :: dielArr(maxNSpheres)
589     !@cuf attributes(device) :: dielArr
590     type(c_hostDevPtr) :: cPtr
591     integer :: iLamb, iMetal, iDiel
592
593     ! setup environment
594     env%nSpheres = maxNSpheres
595     call environsAlloc(env)
596
597     lambArr(1) = lambertian(rgb([0.5, 0.5, 0.5]))
```

```
598     cPtr = c_hostDevLoc(lambArr(1))
599     env%spheres(1) = sphere([0.0, -1000.0, 0.0], 1000.0, lambMat, cPtr)
600
601     dielArr(1) = dielectric(1.5)
602     cPtr = c_hostDevLoc(dielArr(1))
603     env%spheres(2) = sphere([0.0, 1.0, 0.0], 1.0, dielMat, cPtr)
604
605     lambArr(2) = lambertian(rgb([0.4, 0.2, 0.1]))
606     cPtr = c_hostDevLoc(lambArr(2))
607     env%spheres(3) = sphere([-4.0, 1.0, 0.0], 1.0, lambMat, cPtr)
608
609     metalArr(1) = metal(rgb([0.7, 0.6, 0.5]), 0.0)
610     cPtr = c_hostDevLoc(metalArr(1))
611     env%spheres(4) = sphere([4.0, 1.0, 0.0], 1.0, metalMat, cPtr)
612
613     iLamb = 2
614     iMetal = 1
615     iDiel = 1
616     i = 4
617
618     do ia = -11, 10
619        do ib = -11, 10
620            chooseMat = rngHost()
621            center = [ia+0.9*rngHost(), 0.2, ib+0.9*rngHost()]
622            if ( sqrt(sum((center-[4.0, 0.2, 0.0])**2)) > 0.9 ) then
623                if (chooseMat < 0.8) then ! diffuse
624                    i = i+1
625                    iLamb = iLamb+1
626                    lambArr(iLamb) = lambertian(rgb([ &
627                        rngHost()*rngHost(), &
628                        rngHost()*rngHost(), &
629                        rngHost()*rngHost()]))
630                    cPtr = c_hostDevLoc(lambArr(iLamb))
631                    env%spheres(i) = sphere(center, 0.2, lambMat, cPtr)
632                else if (chooseMat < 0.95) then !metal
633                    i = i+1
634                    iMetal = iMetal+1
635                    metalArr(iMetal) = metal(rgb([ &
636                        0.5*(1.0+rngHost()), &
637                        0.5*(1.0+rngHost()), &
638                        0.5*(1.0+rngHost())]), 0.0)
639                    cPtr = c_hostDevLoc(metalArr(iMetal))
640                    env%spheres(i) = sphere(center, 0.2, metalMat, cPtr)
641                else ! dielectric
642                    i = i+1
643                    iDiel = iDiel+1
644                    dielArr(iDiel) = dielectric(1.5)
645                    cPtr = c_hostDevLoc(dielArr(iDiel))
646                    env%spheres(i) = sphere(center, 0.2, dielMat, cPtr)
647                end if
648            end if
649        end do
```

```
650   end do
651
652   ! even though 501 were allocated, not all iterations in the above
653   ! resulted in adding a sphere, so update number of spheres
654   env%nSpheres = i
655
656   ! setup camera
657   cam = camera( &
658        lookFrom = [13.0,2.0,3.0], &
659        lookAt = [0.0,0.0,0.0], &
660        vup = [0.0, 1.0, 0.0], &
661        vfov = 20.0, &
662        aspect = real(nx)/ny, &
663        aperture = 0.1, &
664        distToFocus = 10.0)
665
666   ! antialiasing parameter
667   nRaysPerPixel = 100
668
669   ! allocate RNG state array, initialization done in kernel
670   !@cuf allocate(randState_d(nx,ny))
671
672   call render(fb, env, cam)
673
674   ! ppm output
675
676   print "(a2)", 'P3'    ! indicates RGB colors in ASCII, must be flush left
677   print *, nx, ny       ! width and height of image
678   print *, 255          ! maximum value for each color
679   do j = ny, 1, -1
680      do i = 1, nx
681         print "(3(1x,i3))", int(255*sqrt(fb(i,j)%v))
682      end do
683   end do
684
685 end program main
```

The scene consists of three large spheres, one lambertian, one metal, and one dielectric, and hundreds of smaller spheres with random placement and random material types. Note that random numbers here are generated by calling the specific routine rngHost() directly since the scene is initialized on the host, regardless of whether the ray tracing is done on the host or on the GPU.

Although the code can be compiled and run on either the CPU or GPU, be warned that execution of the host can take a considerable amount of time; on a desktop machine, generating the image takes about a half an hour when compiled for CPU execution. Note that there has been no attempt to optimize the code for the CPU, so this is not a statement on CPU performance, only a warning that in case you are wondering whether the code has hung, give it some time to complete. The image you get should look something like that in Fig. 12.21.

This concludes the topics covered in Peter Shirley's *Ray Tracing in One Weekend* book (Shirley, 2020a), but there are two other books in the series. In the remaining sections, we cover a few additional

FIGURE 12.21

The image produced from `cover.F90`.

topics, some of which are covered in the Peter Shirley's second book of the series *Ray Tracing: The Next Week* (Shirley, 2020b).

12.11 Triangles

Up to this point the environments we have visualized have consisted entirely of spheres. To make things more general, we add triangles to the type of objects we can add to the environment.

Theory

We need a method to determine if, and where, a ray intersects a triangle. We use the approach developed by Möller and Trumbore (1997), which expresses a point in a triangle in terms of its barycentric coordinates. A point in a triangle can be expressed as a linear combination of the triangle's vertices:

$$\mathbf{p} = w\mathbf{v}_1 + u\mathbf{v}_2 + v\mathbf{v}_3,$$

where the coefficients or barycentric coordinates are non-negative and satisfy $w + u + v = 1$. Defining the edge vectors $\mathbf{e}_1 = \mathbf{v}_2 - \mathbf{v}_1$ and $\mathbf{e}_2 = \mathbf{v}_3 - \mathbf{v}_1$ and substituting $w = 1 - u - v$, we have

$$\mathbf{p} = \mathbf{v}_1 + u\mathbf{e}_1 + v\mathbf{e}_2.$$

Recall the parameterized equation for a ray is

$$\mathbf{p}(t) = t\mathbf{d} + \mathbf{g}.$$

Setting these expressions equal and rearranging terms, we have

$$\begin{bmatrix} | & | & | \\ -\mathbf{d} & \mathbf{e}_1 & \mathbf{e}_2 \\ | & | & | \end{bmatrix} \begin{bmatrix} t \\ u \\ v \end{bmatrix} = \begin{bmatrix} | \\ \mathbf{b} \\ | \end{bmatrix},$$

where $\mathbf{b} = \mathbf{g} - \mathbf{v}_1$. This system of equations can be solved using Cramer's rule:

$$\begin{bmatrix} t \\ u \\ v \end{bmatrix} = \frac{1}{|-\mathbf{d}, \mathbf{e}_1, \mathbf{e}_2|} \begin{bmatrix} |\mathbf{b}, \mathbf{e}_1, \mathbf{e}_2| \\ |-\mathbf{d}, \mathbf{b}, \mathbf{e}_2| \\ |-\mathbf{d}, \mathbf{e}_1, \mathbf{b}| \end{bmatrix}.$$

The determinant $|-\mathbf{d}, \mathbf{e}_1, \mathbf{e}_2|$ can be written as the triple product $\mathbf{d} \cdot (\mathbf{e}_2 \times \mathbf{e}_1)$, and if it is equal to zero, then the ray lies parallel to the plane of the triangle, and therefore no intersection occurs. For cases where the ray does intersect the plane of the triangle, the point of intersection will lie in the triangle if the conditions $0 \leq u \leq 1$, $0 \leq v \leq 1$, and $u + v \leq 1$ are met.

Expressing the determinants as triple products, using the invariance properties under a circular shift of the three operands, and swapping the positions of the operators, we have

$$\begin{bmatrix} t \\ u \\ v \end{bmatrix} = \frac{1}{(\mathbf{d} \times \mathbf{e}_2) \cdot \mathbf{e}_1} \begin{bmatrix} (\mathbf{b} \times \mathbf{e}_1) \cdot \mathbf{e}_2 \\ (\mathbf{d} \times \mathbf{e}_2) \cdot \mathbf{b} \\ (\mathbf{b} \times \mathbf{e}_1) \cdot \mathbf{d} \end{bmatrix},$$

where only two cross products are required, $\mathbf{c}_1 = \mathbf{b} \times \mathbf{e}_1$ and $\mathbf{c}_2 = \mathbf{d} \times \mathbf{e}_2$. Substituting these expressions, we get

$$\begin{bmatrix} t \\ u \\ v \end{bmatrix} = \frac{1}{\mathbf{c}_2 \cdot \mathbf{e}_1} \begin{bmatrix} \mathbf{c}_1 \cdot \mathbf{e}_2 \\ \mathbf{c}_2 \cdot \mathbf{b} \\ \mathbf{c}_1 \cdot \mathbf{d} \end{bmatrix}.$$

Implementation

Having sorted out the math for ray–triangle intersection, we can now turn to adding triangles to the code. We accommodate different objects similarly to what we did for different materials. In the specification section of the rayTracing module in triangle.F90, we declare the triangle derived type:

```
54    ! objects
55
56    enum, bind(c)
57       enumerator :: sphereShape = 1, triShape = 2
```

```
58    end enum
59
60    type object
61       integer :: shapeType
62       type(c_hostDevPtr) :: objPtr
63    end type object
64
65    type sphere
66       real :: center(3), radius
67       integer :: materialType
68       type(c_hostDevPtr) :: matPtr
69    end type sphere
70
71    type triangle
72       real :: v1(3), v2(3), v3(3)
73       integer :: materialType
74       type(c_hostDevPtr) :: matPtr
75       logical :: cull
76    end type triangle
```

which consists of the three vertices, material type, material pointer, and the logical cull. The cull member determines if the triangle is one-sided (cull=.true.) or two-sided. Triangles used to construct, for example, a pyramid will have only a single visible side, in which case cull=.true.. For such cases, the order of the three vertices in the triangle is important as the right-hand rule is used to determine the outward normal. We also declare a generic object type called object on lines 60–63, which consists of a shapeType parameter and an object pointer. We add allocatable arrays of both objects and triangles to our environs type:

```
78    type environs
79       integer :: nObjects
80       type(object), &
81          !@cuf managed, &
82          allocatable :: objects(:)
83       integer :: nSpheres
84       type(sphere), &
85          !@cuf managed, &
86          allocatable :: spheres(:)
87       integer :: nTriangles
88       type(triangle), &
89          !@cuf managed, &
90          allocatable :: triangles(:)
91    end type environs
```

This concludes the changes made to the specification section of the module for implementing triangles in our ray tracer. At this point, you may be wondering why we have an object type at all. We could simply have arrays of sphere and triangle types in the environs type and search both of these arrays for the closest hit. That is a valid approach and would work well for the types of scenes we have used for demonstration. However, to render complex scenes efficiently, we want to eventually implement bounding volume hierarchies where we store objects in a tree based on their physical location. Having a single array of generic object types facilitates such a reordering.

In terms of the routines added to the ray tracing module, we add a `hitTriangle()` routine:

```
376   !@cuf attributes(device) &
377   function hitTriangle(tri, r, tmin, tmax, rec) result(res)
378     implicit none
379     type(triangle) :: tri
380     type(ray) :: r
381     real :: tmin, tmax
382     type(hitRecord) :: rec
383     logical :: res
384     real, parameter :: epsilon = 0.00001
385
386     real :: e1(3), e2(3) ! edges of triange
387     real :: b(3)          ! RHS
388     real :: c1(3), c2(3) ! cross product temp vectors
389     real :: D, Dinv       ! determinant and its inverse
390     real :: t, u, v       ! distance along ray and barycentric coordinates
391
392     res = .false.
393
394     ! two edges of triangle
395     e1 = tri%v2 - tri%v1
396     e2 = tri%v3 - tri%v1
397
398     ! calculate determinant of A=[-r%dir, e1, e2]
399     c2 = cross(r%dir, e2)
400     D = dot_product(c2, e1)
401     if (tri%cull) then
402        if (D < epsilon) return
403     else
404        if (D < epsilon .and. D > -epsilon) return
405     end if
406     Dinv = 1.0/D
407
408     ! b of Ax=b
409     b = r%origin - tri%v1
410
411     ! u barycentric coordinate
412     u = dot_product(c2, b)*Dinv
413     if (u<0.0 .or. u>1.0) return
414
415     ! v barycentric coordinate
416     c1 = cross(b, e1)
417     v = dot_product(c1, r%dir)*Dinv
418     if (v<0.0 .or. u+v>1.0) return
419
420     ! calculate t
421     t = dot_product(c1, e2)*Dinv
422
423     if (t > tmin .and. t < tmax) then
424        res = .true.
425        rec%p = t*r%dir + r%origin
426        c1 = cross(e1, e2)
```

```
427        rec%normal = normalize(c1)
428        if (D < 0.0) rec%normal = -rec%normal
429        rec%materialType = tri%materialType
430        rec%matPtr = tri%matPtr
431      end if
432    end function hitTriangle
```

where we implement the algorithm specified above in the *Theory* section. Note that for culled triangles, we only need consider positive values of the determinant (line 402), whereas for two-sided triangles, the determinant must simply be bounded away from zero (line 404). Because we use the cross() function on the device when compiled with CUDA Fortran, as well as on the host for use in cameraConstructor(), we declare the routine with attributes(host,device):

```
160    !@cuf attributes(host,device) &
161    function cross(a, b) result(c)
162      implicit none
163      real :: a(3), b(3), c(3)
164      c(1) = a(2)*b(3) - a(3)*b(2)
165      c(2) = a(3)*b(1) - a(1)*b(3)
166      c(3) = a(1)*b(2) - a(2)*b(1)
167    end function cross
```

The hitTriangle() routine is called from the hitEnvirons() routine:

```
475    !@cuf attributes(device) &
476    function hitEnvirons(env, r, tmin, tmax, rec) result(res)
477      implicit none
478      type(environs) :: env
479      type(ray) :: r
480      real :: tmin, tmax
481      type(hitRecord) :: rec
482      logical :: res
483
484      type(hitRecord) :: recl
485      integer :: i
486      real :: closest
487
488      type(sphere) :: spherePtr; pointer(sphereCrayP, spherePtr)
489      type(triangle) :: triPtr; pointer(triCrayP, triPtr)
490
491      closest = tmax
492      res = .false.
493
494      do i = 1, env%nObjects
495        if (env%objects(i)%shapeType == sphereShape) then
496          sphereCrayP = transfer(env%objects(i)%objPtr, sphereCrayP)
497          if (hitSphere(spherePtr, r, tmin, closest, recl)) then
498            res = .true.
499            rec = recl
500            closest = recl%t
501          end if
502        else if (env%objects(i)%shapeType == triShape) then
```

```
503                triCrayP = transfer(env%objects(i)%objPtr, triCrayP)
504                if (hitTriangle(triPtr, r, tmin, closest, rec1)) then
505                    res = .true.
506                    rec = rec1
507                    closest = rec1%t
508                end if
509            end if
510        end do
511    end function hitEnvirons
```

which is modified to loop over the array of object types, casting each element to either a sphere or triangle using Cray pointers before calling the hitSphere() or hitTriangle() routines, respectively.

The last change we make to the ray tracing module in this section is to the environsAllocate() routine:

```
192    subroutine environsAlloc(env)
193        type(environs) :: env
194        !@cuf attributes(managed) :: env
195        env%nObjects = env%nSpheres + env%nTriangles
196        allocate(env%spheres(env%nSpheres))
197        allocate(env%triangles(env%nTriangles))
198        allocate(env%objects(env%nObjects))
199    end subroutine environsAlloc
```

Note that the nSpheres and nTriangles components must be initialized before calling the routine.

In the main program, we add a single triangle to the 5-sphere scene:

```
681    ! setup environment
682    env%nSpheres = 5
683    env%nTriangles = 1
684    call environsAlloc(env)
685
686    lambArr(1) = lambertian(rgb([0.1, 0.2, 0.5]))
687    cPtr = c_hostDevLoc(lambArr(1))
688    env%spheres(1) = sphere([0.0, 0.0, -1.0], 0.5, lambMat, cPtr)
689
690    lambArr(2) = lambertian(rgb([0.8, 0.8, 0.0]))
691    cPtr = c_hostDevLoc(lambArr(2))
692    env%spheres(2) = sphere([0.0, -100.5, -1.0], 100.0, lambMat, cPtr)
693
694    metalArr(1) = metal(rgb([0.8, 0.6, 0.2]), 0.0)
695    cPtr = c_hostDevLoc(metalArr(1))
696    env%spheres(3) = sphere([1.0, 0.0, -1.0], 0.5, metalMat, cPtr)
697
698    dielArr(1) = dielectric(1.5)
699    cPtr = c_hostDevLoc(dielArr(1))
700    env%spheres(4) = sphere([-1.0, 0.0, -1.0], 0.5, dielMat, cPtr)
701    env%spheres(5) = sphere([-1.0, 0.0, -1.0], -0.45, dielMat, cPtr)
702
703    metalArr(2) = metal(rgb([0.7, 0.7, 0.7]), 0.0)
704    cPtr = c_hostDevLoc(metalArr(2))
```

FIGURE 12.22

The image produced from `triangle.F90`.

```
705    env%triangles(1) = triangle( &
706       [ -3.0, 0.0, -3.0], &
707       [ 3.0, 0.0, -3.0], &
708       [ 0.0, 3.0, -3.0], &
709       metalMat, cPtr, .false.)
710
711    ! take care of object pointers to spheres/triangles
712
713    do i = 1, env%nSpheres
714       env%objects(i)%shapeType = sphereShape
715       cPtr = c_hostDevLoc(env%spheres(i))
716       env%objects(i)%objPtr = cPtr
717    end do
718    do i = 1, env%nTriangles
719       env%objects(env%nSpheres+i)%shapeType = triShape
720       cPtr = c_hostDevLoc(env%triangles(i))
721       env%objects(env%nSpheres+i)%objPtr = cPtr
722    end do
```

which generates the image in Fig. 12.22.

Before we leave the subject of triangles, we should mention some changes that can be made to improve performance in scenes that use triangles heavily. Having each triangle store a cull member is useful for experimenting with the effects of culling, which is why the approach is taken here, but with many triangles it can be inefficient. To get around this, we can cull all triangles, and for a two-sided triangle define an additional triangle with two of the vertices swapped (hence the normal is reflected). This allows us to have different materials on the different sides of the two-sided triangles as well. Another approach is to define two triangle "shapes", oneSidedTriangle and twoSidedTriangle, with separate hit functions. Storing all three vertices in the triangle derived type is also wasteful, as typically a vertex is shared amongst many triangles. Defining an array of vertices and storing pointers to the three vertices in the triangle derived type is a more efficient approach. However, in this chapter, we use only a few triangles in a scene, e.g., to define lights in the next section, so the approach used in the code above is adequate.

12.12 Lights

Up to this point, we have lit our image with our background gradient, or "sky" if you want to think of it that way. We trace a ray as it interacts with objects in our environment, keeping track of the attenuation from each object. We follow the ray until it either reaches the maximum number of reflections/refractions, in which case we assign the color black to the ray, or it hits the background, where we assign a color from the background gradient that gets modified by the accumulated attenuation. Because attenuation is a commutative process, this is the same as starting a ray at the background and tracing it to the camera (except that by starting a ray at the camera and choosing the direction we know that it will intersect the image.)

We can add light sources other than the background to our scene by introducing a different material type. This material type will differ from the previous materials in that it can have color values above 1.0 to allow greater illumination after multiple interactions with other objects and in that there are no reflections or refractions from objects of this new type, just as there are no reflections or refractions from our background.

Implementation

We begin with adding a `light` material type to our collection:

```
35    ! material types
36
37    enum, bind(c)
38        enumerator :: lambMat = 1, metalMat = 2, dielMat = 3, lightMat = 4
39    end enum
40
41    type lambertian
42        type(rgb) :: albedo
43    end type lambertian
44
45    type metal
46        type(rgb) :: albedo
47        real :: fuzz
48    end type metal
49
50    type dielectric
51        real :: refractiveIndex
52    end type dielectric
53
54    type light
55        type(rgb) :: albedo
56    end type light
```

The `light` material type has the same contents as our `lambertian` type, but objects with the `light` material type will have a different return type from the `scatter()` routine.

Because we add lighted objects to our scene, we want to be able to change the background gradient easily without having to modify the contents of the color routine. We do this by changing the environs type of the lights.F90 code:

```
82    type environs
83       integer :: nObjects
84       type(object), &
85          !@cuf managed, &
86          allocatable :: objects(:)
87       integer :: nSpheres
88       type(sphere), &
89          !@cuf managed, &
90          allocatable :: spheres(:)
91       integer :: nTriangles
92       type(triangle), &
93          !@cuf managed, &
94          allocatable :: triangles(:)
95       type(rgb) :: zenith, nadir
96    end type environs
```

where on line 95, we have added the zenith and nadir components, which are used to make the background gradient.

In the rest of the rayTracing module, we only change two routines, scatter() and color(). In the scatter() routine, we add a block for the light material type:

```
367       else if (rec%materialType == lightMat) then
368
369          lightCrayP = transfer(rec%matPtr, lightCrayP)
370          attenuation = lightPtr%albedo
371          res = .false.
372
373       endif
```

where we set the attenuation and set the return value res to false. In the color() routine the main loop becomes

```
544       do depth = 1, maxDepth
545          if (hitEnvirons(env, lRay, shadowAcne, huge(t), rec)) then
546             if (scatter(lray, rec, scAtten, scRay)) then
547                attenuation = scAtten * attenuation
548                lRay = scRay
549             else if (rec%materialType == lightMat) then
550                res = scAtten * attenuation
551                return
552             else
553                res = [0.0, 0.0, 0.0]
554                return
555             endif
556          else
557             t = 0.5*(lray%dir(2) + 1.0)
558             res = rgb((1.0-t)*env%nadir%v + t*env%zenith%v)
559             res = res * attenuation
```

```
560          return
561       endif
562    end do
```

If the call to scatter() on line 546 returns false and the condition on line 549 is true (the object is a light), then the attenuation is updated, and the thread returns from the routine.

Our main program is updated in several ways. When initializing the environment, we specify the zenith and nadir components:

```
697    ! setup environment
698    env%nSpheres = 5
699    env%nTriangles = 2
700    call environsAlloc(env)
701    env%zenith = rgb([0.0, 0.0, 0.0])
702    env%nadir = rgb([0.0, 0.0, 0.0])
```

In this case, we turn off any background illuminations, and the only light in our scene comes from a square light composed of two triangles:

```
722    lightArr(1) = light(rgb([5.0, 5.0, 5.0]))
723    cPtr = c_hostDevLoc(lightArr(1))
724    env%triangles(1) = triangle( &
725         [ -1.0, 1.5, 1.0], &
726         [  1.0, 1.5, 0.0], &
727         [  1.0, 1.5, 1.0], &
728         lightMat, cPtr, .false.)
729    env%triangles(2) = triangle( &
730         [ -1.0, 1.5, 1.0], &
731         [ -1.0, 1.5, 0.0], &
732         [  1.0, 1.5, 0.0], &
733         lightMat, cPtr, .false.)
```

Recall that we allow values of albedo components greater than 1.0 to increase illumination of our scene, which in this case we set to 5.0. Although values larger that one are advantageous for rays with many reflections, we must also take care that values written to the PPM output file are clamped to valid values, which is done on line 771:

```
764    ! ppm output
765
766    print "(a2)", 'P3'     ! indicates RGB colors in ASCII, must be flush left
767    print *, nx, ny         ! width and height of image
768    print *, 255            ! maximum value for each color
769    do j = ny, 1, -1
770       do i = 1, nx
771          where (fb(i,j)%v > 1.0) fb(i,j)%v = 1.0
772          where (fb(i,j)%v < 0.0) fb(i,j)%v = 0.0
773          print "(3(1x,i3))", int(255*sqrt(fb(i,j)%v))
774       end do
775    end do
```

One consequence of turning off the background illumination is that the resulting image can become very dark and grainy. To some extent, we have taken care of the "dark" aspect by allowing albedo values

FIGURE 12.23

Image produced from `lights.F90`. The top image is created with 100 rays per pixel, and the bottom figure with 10,000 rays per pixel.

of light material to be greater than 1.0, but this does not address the graininess issue. The graininess is due to rays terminating at either a very bright light or a pitch black background. When you have diffuse surfaces where the direction of reflection is randomized, then to some extent, the graininess is built in. Our only recourse here is to increase the number of rays per pixel to smooth out the random distribution. The effect of this approach can be seen in the resulting images of Fig. 12.23, which use 100 and 10,000 rays per pixel.

12.13 Textures

Up to this point, every object in the images we have rendered has uniform material properties. In this section, we break this restriction and implement textured surfaces. This topic was discussed in Chapter 3 of Peter Shirley's second book *Ray Tracing: The Next Week* (Shirley, 2020b).

Theory

There are many types of textures, ranging from mapping an image to a surface to complex procedural textures. We implement a solid texture, where we define a function of the spatial coordinates and assign different material types and/or parameters based on the value of the function at the point where the ray hits the object. For example, we can define a two-dimensional checkerboard texture by using different material properties based on the sign of the function

$$f(x, z) = \sin(ax) \sin(az),$$

where a is a parameter that determines the size of squares in the checker pattern.

Implementation

We implement textures as new material types. Our checkerboard texture material type is

```
59   type checkerTexture
60       integer :: oddMatType, evenMatType
61       type(c_hostDevPtr) :: oddMatPtr, evenMatPtr
62       real :: scale
63   end type checkerTexture
```

which consists of two pointers to the constituent material types and parameters that indicate the type of material and the scale of the pattern.

Along with introducing this new material type, we introduce a new categorization of material types and change the scatter() routine accordingly. The first category of material types consists of the base material types, which are the types previously implemented (lambertian, metal, dielectric, and light), and the second category consists of the composite material types, such as our checkerboard texture. Previously, for all of the base material types, we handled the scattering of rays by different blocks in the scatter() routine. We now turn these blocks of code into separate scatter functions; for instance, scattering of rays that hit diffuse objects are now done with the scatterLambertian() function:

```
302   !@cuf attributes(device) &
303   function scatterLambertian(rin, rec, attenuation, rscattered) result(res)
304     implicit none
305     type(ray) :: rin
306     type(hitRecord) :: rec
307     type(rgb) :: attenuation
308     type(ray) :: rscattered
309     logical :: res
310
311     real :: n(3), dir(3)
312     type(lambertian) :: lambPtr; pointer(lambCrayP, lambPtr)
313
314     n = normalize(rec%normal)
315     dir = n + randomPointInUnitSphere()
316     rscattered = ray(rec%p, dir)
317     lambCrayP = transfer(rec%matPtr, lambCrayP)
318     attenuation = lambPtr%albedo
```

```
319        res = .true.
320      end function scatterLambertian
```

and similarly we introduce scatterMetal(), scatterDielectric(), and scatterLight() functions. We have not changed how scattering is done for any of the types, just how it is packaged. The main scatter() function now is

```
404    !@cuf attributes(device) &
405    function scatter(rin, rec, attenuation, rscattered) result(res)
406      implicit none
407      type(ray) :: rin
408      type(hitRecord) :: rec
409      type(rgb) :: attenuation
410      type(ray) :: rscattered
411      logical :: res
412
413      real :: n(3), dir(3)
414      type(hitRecord) :: lrec
415      integer :: matType
416
417      ! make local copy of hit record which can be modified
418      ! for textured materials
419
420      lrec = rec
421
422      ! for textured materials find the base material
423      ! at point p and store to lrec
424
425      if (rec%materialType == checkerMat) then
426         block
427           type(checkerTexture) :: checkPtr; pointer(checkCrayP, checkPtr)
428           real :: t
429           type(c_hostDevPtr) :: matPtr
430
431           checkCrayP = transfer(lrec%matPtr, checkCrayP)
432           t = sin(checkPtr%scale*lrec%p(1))*sin(checkPtr%scale*lrec%p(3))
433           if (t > 0) then
434              lrec%materialType = checkPtr%oddMatType
435              lrec%matPtr = checkPtr%oddMatPtr
436           else
437              lrec%materialType = checkPtr%evenMatType
438              lrec%matPtr = checkPtr%evenMatPtr
439           end if
440         end block
441      end if
442
443      ! process the (base) material
444
445      if (lrec%materialType == lambMat) then
446         res = scatterLambertian(rin, lrec, attenuation, rscattered)
447      else if (lrec%materialType == metalMat) then
448         res = scatterMetal(rin, lrec, attenuation, rscattered)
```

FIGURE 12.24

Image produced from `texture.F90`.

```
449    else if (lrec%materialType == dielMat) then
450       res = scatterDielectric(rin, lrec, attenuation, rscattered)
451    else if (lrec%materialType == lightMat) then
452       res = scatterLight(rin, lrec, attenuation, rscattered)
453    endif
454
455  end function scatter
```

We first handle our composite material on lines 425–441. Our function used to determine the checkerboard pattern is on line 432. Based on the sign of its value at the hit point `lrec%p`, we assign one of the two base material types stored in the composite type. In the following block of code on lines 445–453, we process the base material by calling the specific scatter routines we just wrote. Note that for this block of code, the distinction of whether the material type of the object is a composite material or base material is lost, we just deal with the particular material at that point.

Other composite materials can be added similarly: we just define a new composite material type, add code that determines the base material type at the hit point in the `scatter()` routine, and then call the specific scatter routine for that base type. Note that if recursive routines were available on the device, then we could have handled this differently and would not need to distinguish between base and composite material types, but with the restriction of no recursive routines in our ray tracing module, the above method is a good approach.

In the main program, we initialize our large sphere with the checkerboard type:

```
792  ! for checkered "earth" define the odd and even materials
793  lambArr(2) = lambertian(rgb([0.4, 0.4, 0.0]))
794  lambArr(3) = lambertian(rgb([0.8, 0.8, 0.8]))
795  cOddPtr = c_hostDevLoc(lambArr(2))
796  cEvenPtr = c_hostDevLoc(lambArr(3))
797  checkTex(1) = checkerTexture(lambMat, lambMat, &
798      cOddPtr, cEvenPtr, 5.0)
```

```
799   cPtr = c_hostDevLoc(checkTex(1))
800   env%spheres(2) = sphere([0.0, -100.5, -1.0], 100.0, checkerMat, cPtr)
```

which produces the image in Fig. 12.24.

Appendices

System and environment management

A.1 Environment variables

There are a variety of environment variables that can control certain aspects of CUDA Fortran compilation and execution.

A.1.1 General

CUDA_LAUNCH_BLOCKING, when set to 1, forces execution of kernels to be synchronous, that is, after launching, a kernel control will return to the CPU only after the kernel has completed. This provides an efficient way to check whether host-device synchronization errors are responsible for unexpected behavior. By default launch blocking is off.

CUDA_VISIBLE_DEVICES can be used to make certain devices invisible on the system and to change the enumeration of devices. A comma-separated list of integers is assigned to this variable, which contains the visible devices and their enumeration as seen from the subsequent execution of CUDA Fortran programs. Recall that device enumeration begins with 0. (We can use the deviceQuery code presented earlier or the utility nvaccelinfo to obtain the default enumeration of devices.)

CUDA_DEVICE_ORDER can have values FASTEST_FIRST and PCI_BUS_ID. The default is FASTEST_FIRST, which causes CUDA to enumerate the devices from fasted to slowest. PCI_BUS_ID enumerates devices in ascending order of the PCI bus ID.

CUDA_MANAGED_FORCE_DEVICE_ALLOC can be zero or one. When set to 1, it forces the driver to place all managed allocations in device memory. The default is 0.

CUDA_MODULE_LOADING introduced in CUDA 11.7 can have values EAGER and LAZY. As of CUDA 12.2, the default is LAZY and results in kernels and host modules being loaded only when utilized, which can greatly reduce memory usage.

CUDA_MPS_CLIENT_PRIORITY can have values of 0 (normal) or 1 (below normal), which is used to prioritize application execution on systems where CUDA Multi-Process Service (MPS) is used.

A.1.2 Just-in-time compilation

CUDA_CACHE_DISABLE, when set to 1, disables caching, meaning that no binary code is added to or retrieved from the cache

CUDA_CACHE_MAXSIZE specifies the size of the compute cache in bytes. Default values are platform dependent. Binary codes that exceed this limit are not cached, and older binary codes are evicted from the cache as needed.

```
+---------------------------------------------------------------------------+
| NVIDIA-SMI 545.23.06         Driver Version: 545.23.06   CUDA Version: 12.3 |
|-----------------------------------------+----------------------+----------------------+
| GPU  Name            Persistence-M | Bus-Id        Disp.A | Volatile Uncorr. ECC |
| Fan  Temp    Perf    Pwr:Usage/Cap |          Memory-Usage | GPU-Util  Compute M. |
|                                     |                       |               MIG M. |
|=====================================+=======================+======================|
|   0  NVIDIA A100 80GB PCIe     On  | 00000000:4B:00.0 Off |                    0 |
| N/A  29C    P0      42W / 300W  |     4MiB / 81920MiB |      0%      Default |
|                                     |                       |             Disabled |
+-------------------------------------+-----------------------+----------------------+
|   1  NVIDIA A100 80GB PCIe     On  | 00000000:98:00.0 Off |                    0 |
| N/A  31C    P0      44W / 300W  |     4MiB / 81920MiB |      0%      Default |
|                                     |                       |             Disabled |
+-------------------------------------+-----------------------+----------------------+
|   2  NVIDIA A100 80GB PCIe     On  | 00000000:B1:00.0 Off |                    0 |
| N/A  33C    P0      43W / 300W  |     4MiB / 81920MiB |      0%      Default |
|                                     |                       |             Disabled |
+-------------------------------------+-----------------------+----------------------+

+---------------------------------------------------------------------------+
| Processes:                                                                |
|  GPU   GI   CI       PID   Type   Process name                GPU Memory |
|        ID   ID                                                    Usage  |
|===========================================================================|
|  No running processes found                                               |
+---------------------------------------------------------------------------+
```

FIGURE A.1

Default output of nvidia-smi on a system with three A100 GPUs.

CUDA_CACHE_PATH controls the location of the compute cache. By default the cache is located at ~/.nv/ComputeCache on Linux and %APPDATA%\NVIDIA\ComputeCache in Windows.

CUDA_FORCE_PTX_JIT, when set to 1, forces the driver to ignore all embedded binary code in an application and to just-in-time compile embedded PTX code. This option is useful for testing if an application has embedded PTX code and if the embedded code works. If this environment variable is set to 1 and a kernel does not have embedded PTX code, then it will fail to load.

CUDA_DISABLE_PTX_JIT, when set to 1, disables the just-in-time compilation of embedded PTX code. If this environment variable is set to 1 and a kernel does not have embedded binary code of a compatible architecture, and the JIT cache either does not contain compiled code for the kernel or has been disabled with CUDA_CACHE_DISABLE, then the kernel will fail to load. This environment variable can be used to validate that an application has the compatible SASS code generated for each kernel.

A.2 nvidia-smi – System Management Interface

Additional control of devices on a system is available through the System Management Interface utility, nvidia-smi, which is bundled with the NVIDIA driver on all Linux platforms. The man pages for nvidia-smi contain an extensive list of options. In this section, we demonstrate some of the more common uses of the utility.

Without any options, nvidia-smi lists some basic information on all attached NVIDIA GPUs, as can be seen in Fig. A.1. A simple list of devices on the system can be obtained from the output of nvidia-smi -L:

```
$ nvidia-smi -L
GPU 0: NVIDIA A100 80GB PCIe (UUID: GPU-xxxxxx)
GPU 1: NVIDIA A100 80GB PCIe (UUID: GPU-xxxxxx)
GPU 2: NVIDIA A100 80GB PCIe (UUID: GPU-xxxxxx)
```

A.2.1 Enabling and disabling ECC

There are several ways we can determine whether ECC is enabled of disabled on a device. The field ECCEnabled of the cudaDeviceProp derived type can be used to query the ECC status of the current device, and the utility nvaccelinfo also displays whether ECC is enabled or disabled for all attached devices.

From nvidia-smi we can obtain more detailed information about ECC and enable or disable ECC. Querying the ECC status for a device using nvidia-smi is done as follows:

```
$ nvidia-smi -i 0 -q -d ECC

==============NVSMI LOG==============

Timestamp                             : Mon Dec 11 10:52:33 2023
Driver Version                        : 545.23.06
CUDA Version                          : 12.3

Attached GPUs                         : 3
GPU 00000000:4B:00.0
    ECC Mode
        Current                       : Enabled
        Pending                       : Enabled
    ECC Errors
        Volatile
            SRAM Correctable          : 0
            SRAM Uncorrectable        : 0
            DRAM Correctable          : 0
            DRAM Uncorrectable        : 0
        Aggregate
            SRAM Correctable          : 0
            SRAM Uncorrectable        : 0
            DRAM Correctable          : 0
            DRAM Uncorrectable        : 0
```

where device 0 is specified by the -i 0 option, and the ECC output is specified by the -d ECC option. Most of the output from this command lists the errors for the different memory types. Volatile error counters track the number of errors since the last driver load, whereas aggregate errors persist indefinitely. Single-bit errors are correctable, and double-bit errors are uncorrectable.

The ECC mode near the top of this output displays both the current and pending fields. The pending ECC mode will become the current ECC mode upon reboot or reset. The ECC mode can be disabled as follows (assuming root privileges):

```
$ nvidia-smi -i 0 -e 0
Disabled ECC support for GPU 00000000:4B:00.0
All done.
Reboot required.
```

At this point the ECC mode status printed by `nvidia-smi -i 0 -q -d ECC` is

```
    ECC Mode
        Current                    : Enabled
        Pending                    : Disabled
```

For the pending change to take effect, a reboot of the machine is required, after which the ECC mode status is

```
    ECC Mode
        Current                    : Disabled
        Pending                    : Disabled
```

We emphasize that for devices with HBM memory, there is no performance penalty when ECC is enabled.

A.2.2 Compute mode

The compute mode determines if multiple host processes or threads can use the same GPU. The three compute modes, from least to most restrictive, are:

default: 0   In this mode, multiple host threads can use the same device;
exclusive process: 3   In this mode, only a single context can be created by a single process system-wide, and this context can be current to all threads of that process;
prohibited: 2   In this mode, no contexts can be created on the device.

As with the ECC status, the compute mode can be determined using the `cudaDeviceProp` derived type via the `computeMode` field and by the `nvaccelinfo` utility. Using `nvidia-smi`, we can query the compute mode as follows:

```
$ nvidia-smi -q -i 0 -d COMPUTE

==============NVSMI LOG===============

Timestamp                           : Mon Dec 11 10:57:14 2023
Driver Version                      : 530.30.02
CUDA Version                        : 12.1

Attached GPUs                       : 1
GPU 00000000:01:00.0
    Compute Mode                    : Default
```

which indicates that device 0 is in the default compute mode. The compute mode can be changed (assuming root privileges) by using the -c option:

```
$ sudo nvidia-smi -i 0 -c 3
Set compute mode to EXCLUSIVE_PROCESS for GPU 00000000:01:00.0.
All done.
```

The effect of changing the compute mode is immediate:

```
$ nvidia-smi -q -i 0 -d COMPUTE

==============NVSMI LOG==============

Timestamp                         : Mon Dec 11 10:58:57 2023
Driver Version                    : 530.30.02
CUDA Version                      : 12.1

Attached GPUs                     : 1
GPU 00000000:01:00.0
    Compute Mode                  : Exclusive_Process
```

Upon reboot or reset of the device, the compute mode will reset to the default compute mode.

A.2.3 Persistence mode

When persistence mode is enabled on a GPU, the driver remains initialized even when there are no active clients, and as a result, the driver latency is minimized when running CUDA applications. On systems running the X Window System, this is not an issue, as the X Window client is always active, but on headless systems where X is not running, it is important to avoid driver reinitialization when launching CUDA applications by enabling persistence mode.

Persistence mode is disabled by default and reverts to disabled when the device is reset or the system is rebooted. We can determine whether the persistence mode is enabled or not from the general query output of nvidia-smi:

```
$ nvidia-smi -q -i 0

==============NVSMI LOG==============

Timestamp                         : Mon Dec 11 11:01:57 2023
Driver Version                    : 530.30.02
CUDA Version                      : 12.1

Attached GPUs                     : 1
GPU 00000000:01:00.0
    Product Name                  : NVIDIA GeForce RTX 2060
    Product Brand                 : GeForce
    Product Architecture          : Turing
    Display Mode                  : Enabled
    Display Active                : Disabled
    Persistence Mode              : Disabled
    ...
```

The persistence mode can be enabled (assuming root privileges) using the -pm option to nvidia-smi as follows:

```
$ sudo nvidia-smi -i 0 -pm 1
Enabled persistence mode for GPU 00000000:01:00.0.
All done.
```

There is a way to enable the persistence mode at boot time via a system daemon; we refer to the NVIDIA driver documentation.

A.2.4 Topology

Topological information about the system, including how the GPUs are connected with each other and to CPUs, is provided by the nvidia-smi topo command. All available options are described by the help information via nvidia-smi topo -h. In this section, we touch on only a few.

The communication matrix for the system can be printed with nvidia-smi topo -m. An example of the output is

```
$ nvidia-smi topo -m
          GPU0      GPU1      GPU2      GPU3      CPU Affinity      NUMA Affinity
GPU0      X         PHB       SYS       SYS       0-9,20-29         0
GPU1      PHB       X         SYS       SYS       0-9,20-29         0
GPU2      SYS       SYS       X         PHB       10-19,30-39       1
GPU3      SYS       SYS       PHB       X         10-19,30-39       1

Legend:

  X     = Self
  SYS   = Connection traversing PCIe as well as the SMP interconnect
          between NUMA nodes (e.g., QPI/UPI)
  NODE  = Connection traversing PCIe as well as the interconnect
          between PCIe Host Bridges within a NUMA node
  PHB   = Connection traversing PCIe as well as a PCIe Host Bridge
          (typically the CPU)
  PXB   = Connection traversing multiple PCIe bridges
          (without traversing the PCIe Host Bridge)
  PIX   = Connection traversing at most a single PCIe bridge
  NV#   = Connection traversing a bonded set of # NVLinks
```

on a four-GPU system utilizing PCI interconnects. A legend for the symbols in the connectivity matrix is printed along with the matrix. On a DGX Station, a system with 4 V100 GPUs connected by NVLink, we will see a similar output (omitting the legend for brevity):

```
$ nvidia-smi topo -m
          GPU0      GPU1      GPU2      GPU3      CPU Affinity      NUMA Affinity
GPU0      X         NV1       NV1       NV2       0-39              N/A
GPU1      NV1       X         NV2       NV1       0-39              N/A
GPU2      NV1       NV2       X         NV1       0-39              N/A
GPU3      NV2       NV1       NV1       X         0-39              N/A
```

From this output we see that the GPUs are connected via NVLink.

The P2P status of the system can be displayed with nvidia-smi topo -p2p cap, where cap is the specified capability, which can be one of r (P2P read), w (P2P write), n (NVLink), a (atomics), and p (prop). P2P status for the system above is

```
$ nvidia-smi topo -p2p r
          GPU0      GPU1      GPU2      GPU3
  GPU0    X         OK        TNS       TNS
  GPU1    OK        X         TNS       TNS
  GPU2    TNS       TNS       X         OK
  GPU3    TNS       TNS       OK        X

Legend:

  X     = Self
  OK    = Status Ok
  CNS   = Chipset not supported
  GNS   = GPU not supported
  TNS   = Topology not supported
  NS    = Not supported
  U     = Unknown
```

where P2P communication is available between the pairs of GPU0/GPU1 and GPU2/GPU3. Running the same command on the DGX Station (once again omitting the legend for brevity) shows how all the GPUs are capable of P2P communication with each other:

```
$ nvidia-smi topo -p2p r
          GPU0      GPU1      GPU2      GPU3
  GPU0    X         OK        OK        OK
  GPU1    OK        X         OK        OK
  GPU2    OK        OK        X         OK
  GPU3    OK        OK        OK        X
```

References

Barone, L., Marinari, E., Organtini, G., Ricci-Tersenghi, F., 2006. Programmazione Scientifica. Linguaggio C, algoritmi e modelli nella scienza. Pearson.

Cooley, J., Tukey, J., 1965. An algorithm for the machine calculation of complex Fourier series. Mathematics of Computation 19 (90), 297–301.

Ferziger, J.H., 1981. Numerical Methods for Engineering Application. Wiley, New York.

Ferziger, J.H., Perić, M., 2001. Computational Methods for Fluid Dynamics, 3rd, rev. ed. Springer, Berlin.

Gropp, W., Lusk, E., Skjellum, A., 1999. Using MPI: Portable Parallel Programming with the Message-Passing Interface. MIT Press, Cambridge, MA.

Harris, M., Sengupta, S., Owens, J.D., 2007. Parallel prefix sum (scan) with CUDA. In: Nguyen, Hubert (Ed.), GPU Gems 3. Addison Wesley, pp. 851–876.

Higham, D., 2004. An Introduction to Financial Option Valuation: Mathematics, Stochastics and Computation. Cambridge University Press.

Higham, N., 2002. Accuracy and Stability of Numerical Algorithms. SIAM: Society for Industrial and Applied Mathematics.

Kahan, W., 1965. Further remarks on reducing truncation errors. Communications of the ACM 8 (1), 40.

Metcalf, M., Reid, J., Cohen, M., 2011. Modern Fortran Explained. Oxford University Press, Oxford, UK.

Möller, T., Trumbore, B., 1997. Fast, minimum storage ray-triangle intersection. Journal of Graphics Tools 2, 21–28.

Moin, P., 2001. Fundamentals of Engineering Numerical Analysis. Cambridge University Press.

Schlick, C., 1994. An inexpensive BRDF model for physically-based rendering. Computer Graphics Forum 13 (3), 233–246.

Shirley, Peter, 2020a. Ray Tracing in One Weekend. http://raytracing.github.io/v3.

Shirley, Peter, 2020b. Ray Tracing the Next Week. http://raytracing.github.io/v3.

Snir, M., Otto, S.W., Huss-Lederman, S., Walker, D.W., Dongarra, J., 1996. MPI – The Complete Reference. MIT Press, Cambridge, MA.

Solomon, C., Brecon, T., 2011. Fundamentals of Digital Image Processing: A Practical Approach with Examples. Wiley, New York.

Trefethen, L., 2000. Spectral Methods in MATLAB. SIAM: Society for Industrial and Applied Mathematics.

Van Loan, C.F., 1992. Computational Frameworks for the Fast Fourier Transform. SIAM: Society for Industrial and Applied Mathematics.

Wilmott, P., Howison, S., Dewynne, J., 1995. The Mathematics of Financial Derivatives: A Student Introduction. Cambridge University Press.

Index

Printed and bound by CPI Group (UK) Ltd, Croydon, CR0 4YY

12/09/2024

01033924-0005